MOVIE ACTING,
THE FILM READER

WITHDRAWN
D0208863

Movie Acting, The Film Reader explores one of the most central aspects of cinema: film acting. Combining recent scholarship with classic essays, *Movie Acting* examines key issues such as: What constitutes film acting? How is film acting different from stage acting? How is acting different in different genres? Providing detailed analyses of specific actors such as Lillian Gish, Marlon Brando and Sidney Poitier, and covering acting styles such as silent film pantomime, The Method, and performance in avant-garde film, the essays in *Movie Acting* are grouped into four sections, each with a section introduction by Pamela Robertson Wojcik.

Sections include:

- *Ontology of the film actor*—on the nature of film acting
- *The creation of the film actor*—on the early history and construction of film acting as a profession and an aesthetic
- *Style and technique*—case studies of acting styles in specific films and genres
- *Character and type*—on types, typecasting and character actors

Contributors Rudolf Arnheim, Cynthia Baron, Donald Bogle, Ben Brewster, Stanley Cavell, Andrew Higson, Lea Jacobs, Henry Jenkins, Siegfried Kracauer, Charles Musser, James Naremore, Roberta Pearson, John O. Thompson, David Thomson, Virginia Wright Wexman, Patricia White, Pamela Robertson Wojcik.

Pamela Robertson Wojcik is Associate Professor of Film, TV and Theatre at the University of Notre Dame. She is the author of *Guilty Pleasures: Feminist Camp from Mae West to Madonna* (1996) and co-editor with Arthur Knight of *Soundtrack Available: Essays on Film and Popular Music* (2002).

IN FOCUS

In Focus: Routledge Film Readers
Series Editors: Steven Cohan (Syracuse University) and Ina Rae Hark (University of South Carolina)

The *In Focus* series of readers is a comprehensive resource for students on film and cinema studies courses. The series explores the innovations of film sudies while highlighting the vital connection of debates to other academic fields and to studies of other media. The readers bring together key articles on a major topic in film studies, from marketing to Hollywood comedy, identifying the central issues, exploring how and why scholars have approached it in specific ways, and tracing continuities of thought among scholars. Each reader opens with an introductory essay setting the debates in their academic context, explaining the topic's historical and theoretical importance, and surveying and critiquing its development in film studies.

Exhibition, The Film Reader
Edited by Ina Rae Hark

Experimental Cinema, The Film Reader
Edited by Wheeler Winston Dixon and Gwendolyn Audrey Foster

Hollywood Comedians, The Film Reader
Edited by Frank Krutnik

Hollywood Musicals, The Film Reader
Edited by Steven Cohan

Horror, The Film Reader
Edited by Mark Jancovich

Movie Acting, The Film Reader
Edited by Pamela Robertson Wojcik

Movie Music, The Film Reader
Edited by Kay Dickinson

Stars, The Film Reader
Edited by Marcia Landy and Lucy Fischer

Forthcoming titles:

Color, The Film Reader
Edited by Angela Dalle Vacche and Brian Price

Marketing, The Film Reader
Edited by Justin Wyatt

Reception, The Film Reader
Edited by Barbara Klinger

Queer Cinema, The Film Reader
Edited by Harry Benshoff and Sean Griffin

MOVIE ACTING, THE FILM READER

Edited by
Pamela Robertson Wojcik

Routledge
Taylor & Francis Group
NEW YORK AND LONDON

First published 2004
by Routledge
29 West 35th Street, New York, NY 10001

Simultaneously published in the UK
by Routledge
11 New Fetter Lane, London EC4P 4EE

Routledge is an imprint of the Taylor & Francis Group

Selection and editorial material © 2004 Pamela Robertson Wojcik
Individual chapters © contributors

Designed and typeset in Novarese and Scala Sans
by Keystroke, Jacaranda Lodge, Wolverhampton
Printed and bound in Great Britain
by MPG Books Ltd, Bodmin, Cornwall

All rights reserved. No part of this book may be reprinted or reproduced or utilized in any form or by any electronic, mechanical, or other means, now known or hereafter invented, including photocopying and recording, or in any information storage or retrieval system, without permission in writing from the publishers.

Library of Congress Cataloging in Publication Data
A catalog record for this book has been requested

British Library Cataloguing in Publication Data
A catalogue record for this book is available from the British Library

ISBN 0–415–31024–5 (hbk)
ISBN 0–415–31025–3 (pbk)

Contents

PART FOUR: CHARACTER AND TYPE 165

Acknowledgments

This book would not have been possible without the help of my student assistant, Aggie Noble, series editors Steven Cohan and Ina Rae Hark, and the generosity of the publishers and authors represented here. In addition, the University of Notre Dame Institute for Scholarship in the Liberal Arts provided much-needed financial support for permission fees.

I gratefully acknowledge reprint permissions given by the following copyright holders and authors.

1 Siegfried Kracauer, "Remarks on the Actor" from *Theory of Film: The Redemption of Physical Reality* (New York: Oxford University Press, 1960), 93–101. Reprinted by permission of Oxford University Press.

2 Stanley Cavell, "Audience, Actor, and Star" and "Types; Cycles as Genres" from *The World Viewed: Reflections on the Ontology of Film* (Cambridge, MA: Harvard University Press, 1979), 25–37. © 1971, 1974, 1979 by Stanley Cavell. Reprinted by permission of the publisher.

3 John O. Thompson, "Screen Acting and the Commutation Test" from *Screen* 19.2 (1978), 55–69.

4 Charles Musser, "The Changing Status of the Actor" from *Before Hollywood: Turn-of-the-Century American Film* (New York: Hudson Hills Press in Association with the American Federation of Arts, 1987), 57–62. By permission of Charles Musser.

5 Roberta Pearson, "The Histrionic and Verisimilar Codes in the Biograph Films" from *Eloquent Gestures: The Transformation of Performance Style in the Griffith Biograph Films* (Berkeley: University of California Press, 1992), 38–52. Reprinted by permission of the publisher.

6 Ben Brewster and Lea Jacobs, "Pictorial Styles and Film Acting" from *Theatre to Cinema: Stage Pictorialism and the Early Feature Film* (Oxford: Oxford University Press, 1997), 99–110. Reprinted by permission of Oxford University Press.

7 Cynthia Baron, "Crafting Film Performances: Acting in the Hollywood Studio Era" from the anthology *Screen Acting*, edited by Alan Lovell and Peter Krämer (New York: Routledge, 1999), 31–45.

8 James Naremore, "Lillian Gish in *True Heart Susie* (1919)" from *Acting in the Cinema* (Berkeley: University of California Press, 1988), 99–113. Reprinted by permission of the publisher.

9 Henry Jenkins, "'A High-Class Job of Carpentry': Toward a Typography of Early Sound

Comedy" from *What Made Pistachio Nuts? Early Sound Comedy and the Vaudeville Aesthetic* (New York: Columbia University Press, 1992), 127–152. Reprinted by permission of the publisher.

10 Virginia Wright Wexman, "Masculinity in Crisis: Method Acting in Hollywood" from *Creating the Couple: Love, Marriage and Hollywood Performance* (Princeton: Princeton University Press, 1997), 160–179. Reprinted by permission of Princeton University Press.

11 Andrew Higson, "Film Acting and Independent Cinema" from *Screen* 27.3 (1986): 110–132.

12 Pamela Robertson Wojcik, "Typecasting," from *Criticism* 45, no. 2 (Spring 2003).

13 Donald Bogle, "The 1950s: Black Stars" from *Toms, Coons, Mulattoes, Mummies and Bucks: An Interpretive History of Blacks in American Films* (New York: Continuum, 2001), 159–183. © 1973, 1989, 1994, 2001 by Donald Bogle. Reprinted by permission of The Continuum International Publishing Group.

14 Rudolf Arnheim, "In Praise of Character Actors" from *Film Essays and Criticism*, translated by Brenda Benthein (Madison: University of Wisconsin Press, 1997), 52–54. Reprinted by permission of The University of Wisconsin Press.

15 David Thomson, "The Lives of Supporting Players" from *Film Comment* (Nov/Dec 1989), 32–34. Reprinted by permission of the author.

16 Patricia White, "Supporting Character: The Queer Career of Agnes Moorehead" from *Out in Culture: Gay, Lesbian and Queer Essays on Popular Culture*, edited by Corey Creekmur and Alexander Doty (Durham: Duke University Press, 1995), 91–114. © 1995 by Duke University Press. Reprinted by permission of publisher.

Movie Acting,

The Film Reader

General Introduction

There is much popular discourse about stars and film roles—in film reviews, fan magazines, gossip, entertainment news programs, fashion magazines, biographies, autobiographies, and more. But despite the attention to actors, there is little popular discussion of *acting* in movies. Beyond stating that a particular performance is good or bad, most popular writing, including reviews and criticism, does not describe in any detail the specifics of what an actor does on screen in terms of physical or vocal technique, training, or theory of acting.

Until recently, acting has also been largely neglected in scholarly writing on film. While the actor is central to the majority of films made, and certainly to those feature films taught in undergraduate and graduate courses and enjoyed by the general public, academic film studies have tended to disregard discussions of film acting. This neglect can be seen in David Bordwell and Kristin Thompson's *Film Art: An Introduction*—the bible of most introductory film courses taught in the US—which devotes a chapter each to film editing, cinematography, and sound, but only mentions acting in passing as an aspect of mise-en-scène, and then treats it largely as an issue of blocking, or moving the actor from one camera set-up to the next. Likewise, other introductory texts, such as Pam Cook and Mieke Bernink's *The Cinema Book* or Robert Kolker's *Film, Form, and Culture*, only touch on acting briefly, electing in the former to discuss on-screen performance solely in terms of the extratextual star text, or circulation of the star's image, and, in the latter to reductively state that "A performance is created *by* the film's structure, its mise-en-scène, and editing . . . film acting is part of the continuity style" (Kolker 2002, 78).

This neglect of acting can be attributed to several different causes. In part, acting has probably been marginalized within film studies precisely because of its seeming dominance within popular discourse on the movies. In addition, the tendency in popular discourse toward evaluative criticism in film reviews or internet discussions goes against the ethos of academic film criticism, which typically eschews qualitative judgments of films in favor of ideological or formalist critique.

In addition, film acting can seem transparent and resistant to description or analysis. First, it can be very difficult to describe acting—to characterize what an actor does with his or her hands, voice, or smile. Though most of us feel we know a good performance from a bad, few of us can articulate exactly what an actor does to create a performance; we are either convinced by it or not. Second, because much film acting—at least in Hollywood—tends to favor "invisible" naturalistic styles, and because Hollywood acting generally occurs within the star system, film acting is often perceived as not being acting at all. As Leo Braudy writes, "[S]tage acting is still popularly considered to be superior to film acting. An actor who does a good job disappears into his role, while the bad (read 'film') actor is only playing himself" (Braudy 1999, 423). Thus, since performance and persona are seen as inseparable, descriptions of acting in film tend to be descriptions of an actor's persona across a body of work, or an analysis of type, rather than close descriptions of individual performances.

Moreover, within film studies there has been a bias against the more theatrical elements of film and a tendency to focus on the distinctively cinematographic. On the one hand, despite the fact that film acting differs markedly from acting in theater—precisely because of its dependence on specifically cinematic techniques of editing, framing, etc.—acting has been lumped together with other "theatrical" aspects of the mise-en-scène, such as sets, costumes, make-up, and lighting. Paradoxically, on the other hand, film acting has been seen as merely an effect of cinematic technique. In other words, while the actor is viewed as part of the mise-en-scène, and linked to theatrical components, his or her performance is viewed as an effect of framing, sound, and, in particular, editing—a composite created during post-production. These contradictory views contribute to the perception that film acting isn't really acting.

Acting in early film theory

These views of film acting as simultaneously "invisible," an aspect of mise-en-scène, and largely an effect of editing have their roots in early film theory. Initially, as Charles Musser points out, when films were first made, there was not yet a category of the film actor. Early cinema has been famously described by Tom Gunning as a "cinema of attractions" linked to novelties, amusements, and modes of display and spectacle, rather than narrative. Early film included actors from theater and vaudeville, entertainers from the circus, boxers, dancers, and non-actors caught in actualities or put on screen for staged events (Musser 1987; Musser 1990, 3; Gunning 1990). Rather than acting, their activity on film was understood as a form of modeling, or posing (DeCordova 1990, 34ff.). Even as film narrative developed and the category of the film actor and then the star came into being, theorists felt a strong need to distinguish the categories of stage acting and film acting.

For instance, in his 1916 *The Film: A Psychological Study*, Hugo Münsterberg distinguishes between film and theater by citing film's ability to transcend the limitations of real time and space, and thus create forms that mirror internal mental processes rather than objective reality: "[T]he photoplay tells us the human story by overcoming the forms of the outer world, namely space, time and causality, and by adjusting the events to the forms of the inner world, namely attention, memory, imagination, and emotion" (Münsterberg 1970, 74). For Münsterberg, much of the appeal of cinema rests in its ability to manipulate objective reality through framing and editing techniques such as flashbacks, which function like memory, or crosscutting, which allows for a division of interest, or the close-up, which focuses attention. With respect to film acting, Münsterberg claims both that the photoplay is "further away from physical reality" than the stage drama and that the film actor "stands nearer to life" than the stage actor (Münsterberg 1970, 75–76). This seeming inconsistency depends upon two claims about film acting. On the one hand, Münsterberg emphasizes that film distances us from the body of the actor through photography and editing; and thus flattens reality and "sacrifices . . . the space values of the real theater" (Münsterberg 1970, 77). On the other hand, he suggests that, due to techniques like close-ups, film acting can be less external than stage acting—the actor employs smaller gestures—and thus more naturalistic and transparent.

Though writing after the advent of sound, in his *Theory of the Film*, Béla Balàzs evinces a preference for silent cinema over sound film because he views silent cinema as being at a further remove from mere recorded reality than sound film. Similar to Münsterberg, he celebrates early film's difference from theater and views film's ability to show details in close-up as allowing a greater range of expression. As a result, he privileges small facial expressions and "mute expression" as the essence of film acting:

> The film first made possible what, for lack of better description, I call the "polyphonic" play of features. By it I mean the appearance on the same face of contradictory expressions . . . In the silent film, facial expression, isolated from its surroundings, seemed to penetrate to a strange new dimension of the soul. It revealed to us a new world—the world of microphysiognomy which could not otherwise be seen with the naked eye or in everyday life . . . The silent film has here brought an attempt to present a drama of the spirit closer to realization than any stage play has ever been able to do.
>
> (Balàzs 1952, 64–65, 73)

Balàzs attributes much of the power of film acting to the close-up, and seems at times to suggest that the close-up enables access to some unmediated truth: "However disciplined and practically hypocritical a face may be, in the enlarging close-up we see even that it is concealing something, that it is looking a lie" (Balàzs 1952, 62). While the "lie" of a close-up requires an extremely subtle performance—an actor conveying two or more emotions simultaneously—Balàzs' description of the "polyphonic play of features" relegates much of the power of this performance to framing and editing techniques that show the "secret language of dumb things" (Balàzs 1952, 47).

In a different vein, Walter Benjamin also highlights the difference between film acting and stage acting in his famous essay, "The Work of Art in the Age of Mechanical Reproduction." Benjamin emphasizes the fragmentary nature of film acting as opposed to stage acting insofar as the performance is "composed of many separate performances," filmed out of sequence, filmed from varying angles, and selectively edited, so that the film "need not respect the performance as an integral whole." In addition, Benjamin furthers Münsterberg's claim about the film actor's lack of presence as a defining characteristic. He argues that because the film actor's performance is mechanically reproduced—and not presented live and in person—both the actor and the audience relate differently to the performance. The film actor cannot adjust his performance to the audience; it exists without him as an inorganic mechanically reproduced record of multiple fragmentary performances, and is neither changeable nor interactive. Thus, the audience can subject the film actor's performance to "tests" from a critical distance rather than be absorbed by the "aura" of the actor or the character he portrays. And, most importantly for later Marxist and psychoanalytic theories of identification, Benjamin states, "the audience's identification with the actor is really an identification with the camera" (Benjamin 1969, 230, 228). In other words, without the live presence of an actor, film viewers identify with the eye of the camera that records the performance rather than the performance itself.

Each of these early theorists perceive film acting as different in kind from stage acting, and suggest that film acting is inseparable from film editing and framing. Münsterberg and Balàzs view the effects of close-ups and other cinematic techniques as providing greater access to character interiority, and allowing more subtle gestures than stage acting. By extension, they suggest that performances on film allow for greater possibilities for identification. By contrast, Benjamin suggests that the destruction of the aura in mechanical reproduction allows the viewer a more distracted and potentially critical view. In each case, it is the film's technique of showing the actor that influences the style of acting, and cinematic technique—whether framing, editing or, more broadly, mechanical reproduction—that seems to determine the effects of the performance. In these accounts, the role of the film actor is not easily distinguished from that of other props, or "dumb things" Balàzs describes. Indeed, summing up this view in 1933, Rudolf Arnheim bluntly described the actor as a "stage prop chosen for its characteristics and . . . inserted at the proper place" (Arnheim 1933, 176).

Of course, the strongest proponents of this view of film actors as "props" can be found in Soviet film theory. Going beyond theorists who view cinematic effect as producing a different kind of effect from stage acting, Soviet directors actively promote a re-conceptualization of acting for film. Sergei Eisenstein, for instance, states:

> The Moscow Art Theatre is my deadly enemy. It is the exact antithesis of all I am trying to do. They string their emotions together to give a continuous illusion of reality. I take photographs of reality and then cut them up so as to produce emotions.
>
> (Wollen 1969, 65)

Against naturalistic, Stanislavskian stage techniques, Soviet directors view proper cinematic acting as reliant on the Kuleshov effect and *typage*. The Kuleshov effect proffers the principle that, in the absence of an establishing shot, a viewer will infer a spatial relation between discrete shots. In other words, when presented with a series of shots, viewers assume or construct a relationship of space, time and/or narrative among them. The principle is based on the so-called Kuleshov experiment in which the Soviet theorist Lev Kuleshov took a single shot of an actor's "inexpressive" off-screen glance and intercut it with various objects—a plate of soup, a child playing, a coffin. According to Kuleshov, depending upon which shot was linked to the actor's face, viewers read wildly different emotions into his "inexpressive" glance (Kuleshov 1974, 200).[1] The Kuleshov effect clearly emphasizes the Soviet reliance on montage and implicitly denies the actor's power over his performance.

The theory of *typage* advocated by Kuleshov, Eisenstein, and Pudovkin eliminates the need for the trained actor altogether. Arguing that "real things in real surroundings constitute cinematographic material," Kuleshov states that "imitating, pretending, playing are unprofitable, since this comes out poorly on screen" (Kuleshov 1974, 56, 63). For example, he relates, "If you need a tall, stout man, but your actor is thin, and you pad your thin actor with cushions, and the like . . . the results on screen will be obviously false, theatrical, a prop, a game." Therefore, he claims:

> Because film needs real material and not a pretense of reality—owing to this, it is not theater actors but "types" who should act in film—that is people who, in themselves, as they were born, constitute some kind of interest for cinematic treatment. That is, a person with an exterior of character, with a definite, brightly expressive appearance could be such a cinematic "type."
>
> (Kuleshov 1974, 6364)

Typage favors non-actors and "real" people over trained actors, and assumes that meaning and expression will be created contextually through juxtaposition of a physical type with other montage elements.[2] In fact, under the rules of *typage* the filmed non-actor may not even know what roles he plays. For instance, according to a famous Eisenstein anecdote, when he cast non-actors in *Ten Days*, "Everyone wanted to play the Bolsheviks and no one wanted to play the Mensheviks . . . [so] we gave the actors the text of an inflammatory speech and they spoke it with great fervor. After this we added titles that said the exact opposite" (Eisenstein 1988, 198). The theory of *typage*, then, reduces acting to a specialized form of typecasting combined with editing and intertitles.[3]

The disappearance of the actor in formalist and *Screen* theory

While early film theory aims to describe or proscribe the essence of film acting, and distinguish it from stage acting, later film theories largely disregard the role of the actor altogether. In 1970s *auteur* theory, for instance, emphasis is placed on the director's world-view and acting is for the most part dismissed. In one of the most striking statements of the actor's irrelevance for the *auteur* theory, Peter Wollen refers to the actor's contribution, along with that of the producer and cameraman, as so much "noise":

> This concept of "noise" needs further elaboration. It is often said that a film is the result of a multiplicity of factors, the sum total of a number of different contributions. The contribution of the director—the "directorial factor," as it were—is only one of these, though perhaps the one which carries the most weight. I do not need to emphasize that this view is quite the contrary of the *auteur* theory and has nothing in common with it at all. What the *auteur* theory does is to take a group of films—the work of one director—and analyze their structure. Everything irrelevant to this, everything non-pertinent, is considered logically secondary, contingent, to be discarded.
>
> (Wollen 1969, 104)

Certainly, some *auteurists* might acknowledge the contribution of certain actors to a director's overall style or world-view—such as the role played by the ensemble of actors in Preston Sturges films or the distinction between Sturges's use of Joel McCrea and Eddie Bracken.[4] But Wollen's characterization of acting as "irrelevant," "secondary," "contingent," and "to be discarded" in *auteur* theory seems true to the tendency of most *auteurists* to ignore the collaborative role of actors in favor of asserting the director's shaping vision.

Genre theory, similarly, neglects acting. Rather than a focus on individual authors, such as directors or actors, or even individual films, genre theory examines broad trends among groups of films. As Rick Altman points out, on a textual level, these trends might be semantic, involving iconography, mise-en-scène, or, character types; or syntactic, involving the organization of semantic elements in plot structures, ideology, or other deeper structures (Altman 1999). Certainly, modes of performance differ sufficiently among melodrama, the Western, comedy, *film noir*, and the musical to enable genre theorists to characterize acting style as a defining feature of genre; yet, for the most part, genre theorists have attended more to visual style, narrative structure, thematic opposition, and historical context than on performance. As a result, differences in performance style have been conflated with differences among character types (contrasting the Western hero and the *film noir* hero, for instance) or structural elements (allowing that musicals require musical performance, whereas melodrama would by definition not include a musical number).[5] The work that has been done on acting and genre has tended to focus on a few stars in certain genres, such as slapstick comedy, creating what Henry Jenkins and Kristine Brunovska Karnick refer to as a "cult of personality" around stars like Chaplin or Keaton, rather than provide an analysis of the acting conventions of a particular genre more generally (Jenkins and Karnick 1995, 149).[6] There are exceptions, of course, but much work remains to be done on acting and genre.

As film theory shifted increasingly toward semiotic and then psychoanalytic models in what has come to be called *Screen* theory (named after the crucial journal site where much of the discussion took place), discussion of acting was subsumed into discussions of identification and the actor's role was again largely conceived as an effect of framing and editing. Work by Christian Metz, Jean Louis Baudry, and others built on Benjamin's claim that the viewer identifies with the camera as a mode of primary identification and only cited the actor as a feature of secondary identification, in his role as a character with whom the audience could identify. But psychoanalytic theory views identification as less an effect of performance, or even the particulars of a role, than of point-of-view shots, which create a relay for the viewer's gaze within the film. Metz, for instance, claims that the spectator might identify with the character or even the actor, as an *other*, but, due to the imaginary status of the cinema, ultimately "the spectator *identifies with himself*, with himself as a pure act of perception (as wakefulness, alertness): as the condition of possibility of the perceived and hence as a kind of transcendental subject."[7] With its emphasis on suture, and the viewer's identification with the camera, *Screen* theory treats the filmed human form as a textual place marker, a figure through whose eyes the viewer might situate himself or whose off-screen gaze conjures a lack, an empty space or absent person, to be fulfilled through editing.

Laura Mulvey's famous intervention in the psychoanalytic debate around identification in "Visual Pleasure and Narrative Cinema" served to remind us to take into account the gender of filmed bodies as sites of spectacle, narrative agency, and point-of-view shots (Mulvey 1974). But Mulvey's interest in film performance was still focused on a character's role in the narrative (active vs. passive) or moments of heightened performance, and especially musical numbers that would emphasize the female character's to-be-looked-at-ness. Still, despite the fact that she did not discuss acting explicitly, Mulvey's contribution is not to be overlooked: her analysis of the gender politics of performance and spectatorship underpin much contemporary work on acting and stardom.

The actor rediscovered

Since the 1970s, a few trends in film theory and criticism have challenged the precepts of *Screen* theory and opened the door to considerations of film acting. One of these has been the development of star studies within the broader rubric of cultural studies. Associated initially with the Birmingham Centre for Contemporary Cultural Studies, which was formed in 1964 as an intellectual center and a site of postgraduate research, cultural studies developed into a wide-ranging school of thought that was especially influential in Britain and America in the 1980s and 1990s. Cultural studies, as practiced at the Centre, was very influenced by British Marxist and socialist theory, especially the work of Raymond Williams, Richard Hoggart, and E.P. Thompson, all of whom viewed popular culture as an important and worthy object of study, particularly as a site of working-class struggle. Cultural studies views culture and popular culture not as something distinct but as part of everyday life, and including areas not previously considered culture like shopping, going to bars, and dating. In this, cultural studies is influenced by the semiotic strain of *Screen* theory, which views all aspects of life as sign systems, but rather than an emphasis on the text, cultural studies directs its interest in decoding signs and languages more strongly at the ways in which people use culture, how ideology functions, and how people resist ideology. Cultural studies tends, therefore, to address issues of reception and pleasure, and especially pleasure understood as resistant practice. Where *Screen* theory tended to ignore history or context, cultural studies embeds its analysis of cinema in cultural and historical contexts, to better understand cinema's ideological function, negotiations, and contradictions.

Richard Dyer's influential book *Stars* emerged out of the cultural studies framework and established the theoretical principles that have guided most studies of film stars to date. Dyer considers both the "sociological" and semiotic components of film stars, their status as social phenomenon, considered both at the levels of production and consumption, and their status as image and sign. Dyer defines the star's image as a "structured polysemy, that is, the finite multiplicity of meanings and affects they embody and the attempt to structure them so that some meanings and affects are foregrounded and others are masked or displaced" (Dyer 1979, 3). His consideration of this "structured polysemy" attends not only to studio publicity and other deliberate attempts to produce the star image, but also to the extratextual circulation of the star image in fan magazines, photographs, scandal, gossip, and other modes of consumption and reception. While largely interested in the actor as icon or sign, Dyer includes performance as an aspect of how we read stars as signs, and offers some concrete descriptive parameters for analyzing acting on film. In addition, he considers the potential role of the actor as *auteur*, in cases where the star can be seen as the primary shaping vision behind a work; and suggests that star image and performance style need to be taken into account in any theory of authorship, insofar as texts tend to be constructed around the star's image and fashioned by the star's performance.

Since the publication of Dyer's book, film studies and cultural studies have developed a deep and impressive body of work on the film star. However, star studies have not been inclined to deal extensively with acting *per se*. Star studies—including my own work in *Guilty Pleasures: Feminist Camp from Mae West to Madonna*—are apt to focus on a star's extratextual circulation, fandom, type, and ideological meaning without necessarily attending in any exact and descriptive way to what the actor does on screen to produce him or herself as a type, and without situating the actor in larger acting traditions. Most star studies will make some attempt at analyzing performance traits of an individual stars; but rather than analyze individual performances in terms of acting style, these analyses tend to extract particular mannerisms or gestures that are repeated across a body of films as a feature of the star's persona.

Rather than conventional theories of acting, most star studies have been influenced by performance studies as an interdisciplinary area of study. Performance studies developed in specific contrast to theater studies and more traditional discussions of acting; and tends, therefore, to discuss performance through anthropological and other theoretical models linked to everyday performance and ritual rather than offer concrete discussions of film acting or its theatrical predecessors.[8] The notion of performance allows us to widen our conception of film acting to include not only traditional schools of acting, such as Stanislavskian or Method-based styles, but also modes of performance from other media, such as radio, vaudeville, circus, or drag shows. Performance includes cultural codes of body language as well as unique gestures and mannerisms attributed to the individual actor's idiolect, or personal employment of body language and other sign systems. Thus, for instance, my analysis of Mae West does not include any discussion of conventional theories of acting, but does include discussion of West's borrowings from vaudeville, burlesque, female impersonation, and African-American musical styles, as well as descriptions of the subtle and utterly idiosyncratic gestures and intonations that make up the camp and ironic West idiolect.[9]

In addition to cultural studies and performance studies, another key turn in film theory that has generated new work on film acting has been a new historicism in film studies. At the height of *Screen* theory, there had been a sharp ideological divide between those practicing film theory and history, but a new generation of scholars emerged, concurrent with the rise of cultural studies, who brought history to bear on theory, and, likewise, brought theoretical perspectives to historical investigation. This new generation of scholars, including Tom Gunning, Miriam Hansen, Andrè Gaudreault, Thomas Elsaesser, and Charles Musser, were well versed in *Screen* theory, but, like contemporary scholars associated with cultural studies, they questioned the elision of history in semiotic and psychoanalytic theory and the concomitant construction of a theoretical spectator, who was seen to be passively dominated by a hypnotic and all-powerful cinematic apparatus. Like cultural studies, the new theoretically informed historicism seeks to place film in its cultural and historical context, but where cultural studies tends to investigate contemporary practices and pleasures as sites of resistance, these historians look to earlier moments, including not only silent cinema but also earlier theorists like those associated with the Frankfurt School, to provide possible models of resistance and alternative practices.

This new historicism in film studies challenges developmental models of film history that reduce cinematic history to a series of "firsts" in an evolutionary march toward classical style. Scholars examine early cinema's aesthetics, modes of production, exhibition, and reception as offering alternatives, or roads not taken, rather than be viewed as "primitive" failures or bumps along the road. In terms of acting, these newer histories aim to get past taken-for-granted ideas about silent cinema being dominated by "stilted" or theatrical acting that had to be overcome to achieve classical invisibility; and try instead to understand the technological and institutional reasons for the different style, and its aesthetic appeal. Offering particularly deep analysis of acting in the silent era, historicist approaches to acting—represented in this volume by the work of Charles Musser, Roberta Pearson, Lea Jacobs, and Ben Brewster—provide models for further scrutiny of different historical periods and national styles.

Issues and topics in acting

The combined influences of cultural studies, performance studies, and historicism in film theory have led to renewed interest in film acting, and there has in recent years been an increasing number of publications on film acting, including many books and essays represented here. While there has been increasing attention to acting and other aspects of performance, there is not yet a clearly defined field of study. First, although there is a great deal of work on acting, much of it occurs under various sub-fields of film studies, such as star studies, queer theory, race and ethnicity studies, histories of silent film, performance studies, and interdisciplinary studies of the relationship between theater and film, as well as more conventional theories of acting. These various sub-fields are not always pitched to the same audiences and are not always read in conjunction with each other. Thus, taking examples from this anthology, a reader interested in D.W. Griffith or the history of silent cinema may read Roberta Pearson's book *Eloquent Gestures: The Transformation of Performance Style in the Griffith Biograph Films*, but may not be aware of Patricia White's insightful comments on character acting in her book *UnInvited: Classical Hollywood Cinema and Lesbian Representability*; and a reader interested in theories of acting may look at James Naremore's *Acting in the Cinema* but may not consider Donald Bogle's work on African-American stereotypes in *Toms, Coons, Mulattoes, Mammies, and Bucks: An Interpretive History of Blacks in American Films* to be relevant for a discussion of acting.

In addition, and related to the dispersal of ideas described above, studies of film acting have not themselves been theorized in the way that, for example, genre studies have. While discussions of acting inevitably invoke various theories of acting, such as the principles of Stanislavski or Delsarte, scholars of acting do not typically reflect upon their own practice to ask "What constitutes the field of study of acting?" or "What do we talk about when we talk about acting?" Just as genre theory has benefited from reflecting upon its own practice, to clarify what constitutes genre and genre theory, studies of acting would benefit from a consideration of the field of study, not least to help underscore how wide-ranging our conception of acting might be.

In sorting a field of study, one could approach the topic from many angles. We could, for instance, consider which topics and issues in acting stem from other more clearly defined fields of study, such as genre, authorship, stardom, and history. Alternately, we could attempt to categorize the work already done on acting to determine what issues and topics have arisen. But it seems to me that in order to capture the variety and distinctness of acting as a field of study, it is necessary to consider the questions that have not yet been asked as well as those that have, and not to limit those questions to areas of study with which we are already familiar. In what follows, I have attempted to tentatively raise questions that seem to me to be key to understanding acting. I have grouped these into five large issues: *ontological questions, stylistic questions, questions of authorship, historical questions*, and *ideological questions*. Some of these questions overlap with other areas of study, some have been covered in previous film writing, and some may suggest areas of study for future scholarship. There is some repetition among categories and there are likely to be gaps and omissions.

1 *Ontological questions*. This cluster of questions relates to many of the questions raised by early film theory and includes additional questions about the status and meaning of film acting today. Broadly, under this rubric, we could ask, "What constitutes film acting?" How is film acting different from stage acting? To what degree is film acting a function of what an actor does with his voice, face and body and to what degree is it technologically determined? What are the specifically cinematic components of acting? How do editing, framing, and sound effect or produce film performance? What exceeds the cinematic? To what degree does an actor's technique or idiolect shape the film experience? When and how can aspects of persona and performance outweigh the function of close-ups and other cinematic techniques? To what degree do extratextual factors affect film performance? Is film acting inseparable from conceptions of stardom and type?
2 *Stylistic questions*. This category aims to consider specific modes of acting in films rather than ontological questions about the meaning of acting. Questions here all fall under the larger question of "What are the differences among acting styles?" What, for instance, constitutes realism? How have concepts of realism been altered by historically changing tastes? How does

pantomime differ from melodramatic gesture? How do we appreciate the difference between Stanislavskian realism and Method-based realism when looking externally at performances? What non-realist modes have been employed in film? What are the differences in performance style for various genres? Is there a particular mode of acting employed for *film noir* vs. the Western? Should we consider the requirements of special effects in action sequences as part of an acting style? Can musical performance or martial arts be considered acting? What differences are there in performance style among different national traditions? Is there a different style of acting in Bollywood vs. Hollywood or France vs. Japan? How do we categorize an actor's individual idiolect? What differences are there in the style of acting employed by character actors vs. stars? Do actors in ensemble pieces act differently than actors in more hierarchical films? How does film acting change when film styles change? For instance, is 1970s acting different from acting in the 1950s or 1990s?

3 *Questions of authorship*. This category builds on *auteurist* approaches as well as star studies to ask, "Who is responsible for a film performance?" To what degree does a star function as author? If films are star vehicles, who is driving the car? To what degree do ensembles, such as those associated with Preston Sturges, John Cassavetes, or Paul Thomas Anderson, function as authors? To what degree do directors shape performances? To what degree should cameramen, editors, sound designers, or lighting technicians be said to create a performance? How important is casting and the role of the casting director? How did the shift from the studio system to producer package deals affect film performance? What effect do extratextual materials, such as gossip or scandal, have on our understanding of a film performance? To what degree is a film text modified by extra-cinematic practices of fandom such as imitation, copying, and consumption (Stacey 1994)?

4 *Historical questions*. This very broad category would include questions about various historical contexts through which acting is produced and received. Looking at various histories, such as histories of technology, institutional histories, labor history, art history, world history, and more, we would ask, "How have historical changes altered film acting?" In thinking about technology, for example, we might ask how changing technologies, such as digital imaging, have affected film acting (even eliminating the need for it in *The Hulk* or the role of the Gollum in *Lord of the Rings: The Two Towers*). How did acting alter in its transition from live theater to silent cinema, and from silent cinema to sound film? How does ADR (automatic dialogue replacement) affect performance? Alternately, we could consider how institutional shifts in the industry have altered performance. How, for example, have actor contracts changed since the demise of the classical studio system? What are the effects of globalization on film performance? What are the influences of different national traditions on each other in multinational productions? Has there been a loss of national cultural specificity in performance with the globalization of film stars from Hong Kong or Australia? Or, in terms of art history, we might ask how film acting has been influenced by postmodern aesthetics. Was there such a thing as Pop acting? Is there a modernist performance style?

5 *Ideological questions*. Though ideological questions lurk in all these categories, here the emphasis is primarily on the ideological effects of film acting. Under this category, we would ask, "What does film acting mean?" What is the value of film acting? What values do we attach to acting and actors? How does film acting reflect or alter our ideas about human identity? How do actors and acting reflect or modify our perception of love and other human relationships? Should the demographics of film casts reflect the demographics of society? How have filmic representations of race, sexuality and gender shaped our understanding of

persons and politics in the real world? How do stars reflect, contradict or negotiate dominant ideologies? Do alternative reception practices, such as camp or cult fandom, constitute resistance to the dominant ideology? Are different acting styles, or different conceptions of realism, produced by ideological shifts in the culture?

As these questions—which are by no means exhaustive—suggest, the possible field of study for film acting is enormous. Some of these questions may seem to exceed the boundaries of what is conventionally considered film acting. My point in raising such wide-ranging questions is that, as long as we are talking about films made with human bodies and/or voices, film acting is central to most questions we would ask about film. At a minimum, we should recognize that film acting touches upon numerous areas of inquiry and provides a means of exploring areas such as technological change, genre, and institutional history, from a new perspective.

Contents of the book

The essays collected here respond in various ways to many, though not all, of these questions. Some essays are influenced by cultural studies, performance studies, and historicism. Others represent relatively rare discussions of acting in formalist, ontological, or popular discussions of film. The first section of the book, "Ontology of the Film Actor," includes essays that take up the question, "What constitutes film acting?" In different ways, these essays address the ways and degree to which film acting differs from stage acting; how film acting is shaped by cinematic techniques such as framing, editing, and sound; the meaning and function of type; and the role of the star as constitutive of certain kinds of filmmaking and of our understanding of film texts. The next section, "The Creation of the Film Actor," takes an historical approach to the question of what constitutes an actor. The essays here offer detailed analysis of the construction of film acting as a profession and mode of performance from the silent era into the classical studio era; and include institutional and aesthetic history. The section on "Style and Technique" examines four distinct styles of performance—the work of silent star Lillian Gish in the film melodramas of D. W. Griffith; generic modes of performance in early sound comedy; Method acting in 1950s cinema, especially Marlon Brando's role in *On the Waterfront*; and non-realist performance modes in independent cinema. The final section, "Character and Type," emphasizes the ways in which acting both reflects and is constitutive of ideas about identity, and offers historical and textual investigations of type and typecasting not only in the work of stars, including African-American stars, but also in the work of character actors.

This book does not include essays by key theorists of acting such as Kuleshov, Pudovkin, Brecht, Stanislavski, or Strasberg. This deficiency, in part, reflects a deliberate choice on my part to include essays that offer theoretically and historically informed descriptions of actual film performances and practices, rather than proscriptive ideals. In addition, I decided not to include them because I felt that these essays are already relatively well known and have been published in numerous other places. And, furthermore, many of these theories and ideas are discussed in some detail throughout the book in individual essays.

Readers may be disappointed to discover that the essays here do not, for the most part, deal with acting styles in countries other than America. This bias is an unintended product of editorial choices that, to a degree, reflect the partiality of published scholarly work on acting. Ideally, this narrow focus allows one to consider changing conceptions of acting in the American context.

Of course, in neglecting other national traditions, such as Japanese or Indian cinema, the book misses out on investigating different approaches to film and cross-cultural comparisons of acting styles and theories. Similarly, the essays here predominately apply to film acting from the silent era through the classical period and do not address the ways in which film acting has changed in post-classical and postmodern cinema. And, other than one essay on African-American stars, the essays here do not address issues of race, ethnicity, multiculturalism, or colonialism. It is my hope that this collection inspires future work on acting in these and other areas.

These gaps aside, this collection offers wide-ranging, perceptive, and informative essays on film acting. Offering varied approaches and a broad mixture of subjects, they provide a fascinating glimpse of how far-reaching and varied discussions of film acting can be. Taken together, they offer students and others interested in film acting an overview of key issues and topics in the history of film acting, as well as nicely detailed analyses of specific actors, roles, styles, and practices. As all of these essays demonstrate, film acting is no longer a topic to be neglected.

Pamela Robertson Wojcik
June, 2003

Notes

1 There is some dispute as to whether the Kuleshov experiment actually took place. At a minimum, Pudovkin, who worked together with Kuleshov on it, disagrees about the content of the shots. The original footage does not exist and there is no evidence that it was shown to a naïve audience. See Holland 1989 and Kepley 1986.
2 While Soviet theorists argued for a particular style of acting suited to one conception of realism, much Hollywood lore about acting unwittingly adopts a similar view of the actor's role. In the perhaps apocryphal tale of Spencer Tracy's advice to a young actor—"Just say your lines and don't bump into the furniture"—or in accounts of actors being told to make a gesture or walk in a certain direction without being told why, one can hear traces of Soviet theory and the idea that what constitutes acting on screen in as much an effect of cinematic technique and post-production as it is what the actor himself does.
3 For more on *typage* and typecasting, see my essay "Typecasting" in this volume.
4 For an *auteurist* analysis of romantic comedy that takes into account the unique contributions of individual actors and performances as well as the guiding vision of the director, see Harvey 1987.
5 On the exclusion of performance from the field of genre study, see DeCordova 1995.
6 Karnick and Jenkins's anthology does include a sub-section on performance, and includes chapters not only on stars such as Mae West and Buster Keaton, but also on early slapstick. Jenkins's book, *What Made Pistachio Nuts? Early Sound Comedy and the Vaudeville Aesthetic* also provides an important contribution to the study of genre and performance, and portions are reprinted in this volume.
7 See Metz 1977, 49; Jean Louis Baudry, "Ideological Effects of the Basic Cinematic Apparatus" and "The Apparatus: Metapsychological Approaches to the Impression of Reality in Cinema" in Baudry and Cohen 1999, 345–355 and 760–777. See also the following essays on suture in

Braudy and Cohen 1999, 118–164: Daniel Dayan, "The Tutor Code of Classical Cinema," William Rothman "Against 'The System of the Suture,'" Kaja Silverman "On Suture," and Nick Browne, "The Spectator-in-the-Text: The Rhetoric of *Stagecoach*." The concept of suture emphasizes that the viewer is situated in a film and made to forget the cuts and negations that are inherent to film through continuity editing, and especially through shot-reverse shots and point-of-view shots.

8 Key originary texts for performance studies include Goffman 1959 and Turner 1988.

9 Other studies of West that address these issues include Curry 1996, Hamilton 1995, and Leider 2000.

PART ONE

ONTOLOGY OF THE FILM ACTOR

Introduction

Almost as soon as cinema began, and certainly as soon as staged or fictional events were filmed, critics and theorists began to question the ontological status of film acting. Initially, film acting had to be differentiated from stage acting. As I discussed in the General Introduction, early film theorists grappled with the status of film acting not just from within the context of silent cinema but continuing into the sound era, when the nature of film acting, now supplemented with dialogue, altered again. Interestingly, however, as sound became dominant and film acting would seem to have stabilized, theorists in the classical sound era and beyond have still sought to appraise the elemental qualities of film acting. The essays in this section each attempt to define fundamental features of film acting, approaching the subject from three distinct viewpoints.

Siegfried Kracauer's "Remarks on the Actor" is excerpted from his broad *Theory of Film: The Redemption of Physical Reality*, which was first published in 1960 but was written over roughly a twenty-year period in both Marseilles and the United States, after Kracauer fled Germany. In his *Theory of Film*, Kracauer argues that, as an extension of photography, the essence of cinema lies in its ability to record and reveal reality. In particular, as Miriam Hansen points out, he views cinema as both an expression of and medium for modernity, especially in its ability to stage encounters with contingency and chance (Hansen 1997). Kracauer's views on acting thus engage questions of realism and material aesthetics, unlike Münsterberg and Balàzs, each of whom privilege film's ability to distort rather than record reality.

Kracauer argues that the stage actor and the film actor differ in two key ways: first, in terms of the "qualities they must posses to meet the demands of their media," and, second, in terms of "the functions they must assume" in their respective media. Under the rubric of "qualities," Kracauer claims that the film actor differs from the stage actor in his "emphasis on being," by which he means that the film actor must act as if he is not acting, but just exists as his character. Also, in line with his emphasis on the element of contingency and chance in realism, Kracauer argues that film actors, unlike their theater counterparts, should appear casual, "fortuitous," and on the "fringe of indeterminacy," rather than seeming deliberate or purposeful. Additionally, Kracauer suggests, in terms similar to the Soviets, that unlike the stage actor, who can resort to more extreme costume and make-up, the film actor will be dependent upon his physique, and his "real" appearance will be symptomatic of his character.

As for "function," Kracauer argues that theatrical plays revolve around character almost exclusively, whereas films are not exclusively human, but place the actor in the context of other props, landscapes, and images, so that he stands as an "object among objects." Nonetheless, while seeming to reproduce earlier arguments about the actor as mere effect of editing, Kracauer attributes different functions to different kinds of actors. He links the use of non-actors in film to the recording function of cinema, and suggests that they lend a documentary touch to narrative films. Rather than functioning as individuals, the non-actor represents a whole group of people, such as a class or segment of society. While both the star and the non-actor function as types defined by their physical appearance, Kracauer claims that the star stands out as an individual, not a member of a large category of people. He contrasts both types with the professional actor who requires training in order to sustain characterization, and can disappear into a role.

Stanley Cavell's comments on acting in the two brief excerpts here touch upon similar themes but diverge from Kracauer in a few key ways. Approaching the subject of acting from a literary philosophical background, Cavell, like Kracauer, links his discussion of types to his ideas about the necessities of the film medium. Like Kracauer, Cavell claims that humans are not "ontologically favored" in photographs and thus we always view the actor in relation to a world of objects. In addition, Cavell emphasizes projection as an essential difference between stage and screen that assures the absence of both the performer and the audience. Cavell admits that someone is present in a film, if only via a photographic relay. But, whereas the character dominates the stage performance, and allows the spectator to be absorbed into the role, the actor in film "takes the role onto himself" and dominates the film. Thus, Cavell suggests that all screen actors create types. Rather than merely importing types from other art forms, such as melodrama or folklore, Cavell says that film created new types, combinations of types, and/or modifications of types. Whereas Kracauer differentiates between the non-actor and the star as type, Cavell differentiates between stereotypes, which would be linked to large categories of people, and the actor as individual type: "For what makes someone a type is not his similarity with other members of that type but his striking separateness from other people." The screen actor, then, including character actors as well as stars, represents actor, character, and individual at once.

Like Kracauer and Cavell, John O. Thompson considers features of screen acting related to type. But rather than compare stage and screen, Thompson applies the semiotic technique of commutation to the analysis of screen acting in order to denaturalize the assumed fit between actor and role that both Kracauer and Cavell describe, and to open a potential space for ideological critique. Commutation in linguistics makes a substitution between words or phonemes to determine whether the substitution at the level of signifier makes a correlative change in the signified. In applying this to actors—substituting Shirley Temple for Judy Garland in *The Wizard of Oz*, for instance, or switching the roles of Jimmy Stewart and John Wayne in *The Man Who Shot Liberty Valance*—Thompson aims to consider not merely *if* a difference results, but *which* difference. He considers film performance as a bundle of distinctive features, each potentially distinguishing, that include the particularities of individual performances, such as a character's smile or gait, as well as the actor's physical type and general persona. Thompson acknowledges a hierarchy in film among stars, character actors, extras, chorus girls, and stuntmen—a pecking order reflected in how commutable the individual person is in a role—but, with his emphasis on aspects of performance, he opens up ways of talking about the lower orders of actors and even non-actors, as well as stars.

Since the publication of these essays, the ontological status of film acting has undergone further changes. Future theorists may wish to consider whether and how changing technologies have again altered the nature of film acting; or the difference between film and television acting; or the ways in which stage acting has become more cinematic as theater has progressively adopted more multimedia technologies; and how actors from stage and screen—both film and TV—become less distinguishable from one another as they increasingly cross over from one medium to the other.

Remarks on the Actor

1

SIEGFRIED KRACAUER

The film actor occupies a unique position at the junction of staged and unstaged life. That he differs considerably from the stage actor was already recognized in the primitive days when Réjane and Sarah Bernhardt played theater before the camera; the camera let them down pitilessly. What was wrong with their acting, the very acting which all theatergoers raved about?

Stage actor and screen actor differ from each other in two ways. The first difference concerns the qualities they must possess to meet the demands of their media. The second difference bears on the functions they must assume in theatrical plays and film narratives respectively.

Qualities

How can the stage actor's contribution to his role be defined in terms of the cinema? To be sure, like the film actor, he must draw on his nature in the widest sense of the word to render the character he is supposed to represent; and since his projective powers are rarely unlimited, a measure of type-casting is indispensable for the stage also. But here the similarities end. Due to the conditions of the theater, the stage actor is not in a position directly to convey to the audience the many, often imperceptible details that make up the physical side of his impersonation; these details cannot cross the unbridgeable distance between stage and spectator. The physical existence of the stage performer is incommunicable. Hence the necessity for the stage actor to evoke in the audience a mental image of his character. This he achieves by means of the theatrical devices at his disposal—a fitting make-up, appropriate gestures and voice inflections, etc.

Significantly, when film critics compare the screen actor with the stage actor they usually speak of the latter's exaggerations, overstatements, amplifications.[1] In fact, his mask is as "unnatural" as his behavior, for otherwise he would not be able to create the illusion of naturalness. Instead of drawing a true-to-life portrait which would be ineffective on the stage, he works with suggestions calculated to make the spectators believe that they are in the presence of his character. Under the impact of these suggestions they visualize what is actually not given them. Of course, the play itself supports the actor's conjurer efforts. The situations in which he appears and the verbal references to his motives and fears and desires help the audience to complement his own definitions so that the image he projects gains in scope and depth. Thus he may attain a magic semblance of life. Yet life itself, this flow of subtle modes of being, eludes the stage. Is it even aspired to in genuine theater?

Emphasis on being

Leonard Lyons reports the following studio incident in his newspaper column: Fredric March, the well-known screen and stage actor, was making a movie scene and the director interrupted him. "Sorry, I did it again," the star apologized. "I keep forgetting—this is a movie and I mustn't act."[2]

If this is not the whole truth about film acting it is at least an essential part of it. Whenever old films are shown at the New York Museum of Modern Art, the spectators invariably feel exhilarated over expressions and poses which strike them as being theatrical. Their laughter indicates that they expect film characters to behave in a natural way. Audience sensibilities have long since been conditioned to the motion picture camera's preference for nature in the raw. And since the regular use of close-ups invites the spectator to look for minute changes of a character's appearance and bearing, the actor is all the more obliged to relinquish those "unnatural" surplus movements and stylizations he would need on the stage to externalize his impersonation. "The slightest exaggeration of gesture and manner of speaking," says René Clair, "is captured by the merciless mechanism and amplified by the projection of the film."[3] What the actor tries to impart—the physical existence of a character—is overwhelmingly present on the screen. The camera really isolates a fleeting glance, an inadvertent shrug of the shoulder. This accounts for Hitchcock's insistence on "negative acting, the ability to express words by doing nothing."[4] "I mustn't act," as Fredric March put it. To be more precise, the film actor must act as if he did not act at all but were a real-life person caught in the act by the camera. He must seem to *be* his character.[5] He is in a sense a photographer's model.

Casualness

This implies something infinitely subtle. Any genuinely photographic portrait tends to sustain the impression of unstaged reality; and much as it concentrates on the typical features of a face, these features still affect us as being elicited from spontaneous self-revelations. There is, and should be, something fragmentary and fortuitous about photographic portraits. Accordingly, the film actor must seem to be his character in such a way that all his expressions, gestures, and poses point beyond themselves to the diffuse contexts out of which they arise. They must breathe a certain casualness marking them as fragments of an inexhaustible texture.

Many a great film maker has been aware that this texture reaches into the deep layers of the mind. René Clair observes that with screen actors spontaneity counts all the more, since they have to atomize their role in the process of acting;[6] and Pudovkin says that, when working with them, he "looked for those small details and shades of expression which . . . reflect the inner psychology of man."[7] Both value projections of the unconscious. What they want to get at, Hanns Sachs, a film-minded disciple of Freud's, spells out in psychoanalytical terms: he requests the film actor to advance the narrative by embodying "such psychic events as are before or beyond speech . . . above all those . . . unnoticed ineptitudes of behavior described by Freud as symptomatic actions."[8]

The film actor's performance, then, is true to the medium only if it does not assume the airs of a self-sufficient achievement but impresses us as an incident—one of many possible incidents—of his character's unstaged material existence. Only then is the life he renders truly cinematic. When movie critics sometimes blame an actor for overacting his part, they do not necessarily mean that he acts theatrically; rather, they wish to express the feeling that his acting is, somehow, too purposeful, that it lacks that fringe of indeterminacy or indefiniteness which is characteristic of photography.

Physique

For this reason the film actor is less independent of his physique than the stage actor, whose face never fills the whole field of vision. The camera not only bares theatrical make-up but reveals the delicate interplay between physical and psychological traits, outer movements and inner changes. Since most of these correspondences materialize unconsciously, it is very difficult for the actor to stage them to the satisfaction of an audience which, being in a position to check all pertinent visual data, is wary of anything that interferes with a character's naturalness. Eisenstein's 1939 claim that film actors should exert "self-control . . . to the millimeter of movement"[9] sounds chimerical; it testifies to his ever-increasing and rather uncinematic concern for art in the traditional sense, art which completely consumes the given raw material. Possessed with formative aspirations, he forgot that even the most arduous "self-control" cannot produce the effect of involuntary reflex actions. Hence the common recourse to actors whose physical appearance, as it presents itself on the screen, fits into the plot—whereby it is understood that their appearance is in a measure symptomatic of their nature, their whole way of being. "I choose actors exclusively for their physique," declares Rossellini.[10] His dictum makes it quite clear that, because of their indebtedness to photography, film productions depend much more than theatrical productions on casting according to physical aspects.

Functions

From the viewpoint of cinema the functions of the stage actor are determined by the fact that the theater exhausts itself in representing inter-human relations. The action of the stage play flows through its characters; what they are saying and doing makes up the content of the play—in fact, it is the play itself. Stage characters are the carriers of all the meanings a theatrical plot involves. This is confirmed by the world about them: even realistic settings must be adjusted to stage conditions and, hence, are limited in their illusionary power. It may be doubted whether they are intended at all to evoke reality as something imbued with meanings of its own. As a rule, the theater acknowledges the need for stylization.*

* In his *Stage to Screen*, Vardac submits that the realistic excesses of the nineteenth-century theater anticipated the cinema. To the extent that the theater then tried to defy stage conditions, he argues, it was already pregnant with the new, still unborn medium.

Realistic or not, stage settings are primarily designed to bear out the characters and their interplay; the idea behind them is not to achieve full authenticity—unattainable anyway on the stage—but to echo and enhance the human entanglements conveyed to us by acting and dialogue. Stage imagery serves as a foil for stage acting. Man is indeed the absolute measure of this universe, which hinges on him. And he is its smallest unit. Each character represents an insoluble entity on the stage; you cannot watch his face or his hands without relating them to his whole appearance, physically and psychologically.

Object among objects

The cinema in this sense is not exclusively human. Its subject matter is the infinite flux of visible phenomena—those ever-changing patterns of physical existence whose flow may include human manifestations but need not climax in them.

In consequence, the film actor is not necessarily the hub of the narrative, the carrier of all its meanings. Cinematic action is always likely to pass through regions which, should they contain human beings at all, yet involve them only in an accessory, unspecified way. Many a film summons the weird presence of furniture in an abandoned apartment; when you then see or hear someone enter, it is for a transient moment the sensation of human interference in general that strikes you most. In such cases the actor represents the species rather than a well-defined individual. Nor is the whole of his being any longer sacrosanct. Parts of his body may fuse with parts of his environment into a significant configuration which suddenly stands out among the passing images of physical life. Who would not remember shots picturing an ensemble of neon lights, lingering shadows, and some human face?

This decomposition of the actor's wholeness corresponds to the piecemeal manner in which he supplies the elements from which eventually his role is built. "The film actor," says Pudovkin, "is deprived of a consciousness of the uninterrupted development of the action in his work. The organic connection between the consecutive parts of his work, as a result of which the distinct whole image is created, is not for him. The whole image of the actor is only to be conceived as a future appearance on the screen, subsequent to the editing of the director."[11]

"I mustn't act"—Fredric March is right in a sense he himself may not have envisaged. Screen actors are raw material;[12] and they are often made to appear within contexts discounting them as personalities, as actors. Whenever they are utilized this way, utter restraint is their main virtue. Objects among objects, they must not even exhibit their nature but, as Barjavel remarks, "remain, as much as possible, below the natural."[13]

Types

The non-actor

Considering the significance of the screen character's unstaged nature and his function as raw material, it is understandable that many film makers have felt tempted to rely on non-actors for their narrative. Flaherty calls children and animals the finest of all film material because of their spontaneous actions.[14] And Epstein says: "No set, no costume can have the aspect, the cast of truth. No professional faking can produce the admirable technical gestures of a topman or a fisherman. A smile of kindness, a cry of rage are as difficult to imitate as a rainbow in the sky or the turbulent ocean."[15] Eager for genuine smiles and cries, G. W. Pabst created them artificially when shooting a carousal of anti-Bolshevist soldiery for his silent film, *The Love of Jeanne Ney*: he herded together a hundred-odd Russian ex-officers, provided them with vodka and women, and then photographed the ensuing orgy.[16]

There are periods in which non-actors seem to be the last word of a national cinema. The Russians cultivated them in their revolutionary era, and so did the Italians after their escape from Fascist domination. Tracing the origins of Italian neorealism to the immediate postwar period, Chiaromonte observes: "Movie directors lived in the streets and on the roads then, like everybody else. They saw what everybody else saw. They had no studios and big installations with which to fake what they had seen, and they had little money. Hence they had to improvise, using real streets for their exteriors, and real people in the way of stars."[17] When history is made in the streets, the streets tend to move onto the screen.* For all their differences in ideology and technique, *Potemkin* and *Paisan* have this "street" quality in common; they feature environmental situations rather than private affairs, episodes involving society at large rather than stories centering upon an individual conflict. In other words, they show a tendency toward documentary.

Practically all story films availing themselves of non-actors follow this pattern. Without exception they have a documentary touch. Think of such story films as *The Quiet One*, *Los Olvidados*, or the De Sica films, *The Bicycle Thief* and *Umberto D.*: in all of them the emphasis is on the world about us; their protagonists are not so much particular individuals as types representative of whole groups of people. These narratives serve to dramatize social conditions in general. The preference for real people on the screen and the documentary approach seem to be closely interrelated.

The reason is this: it is precisely the task of portraying wide areas of actual reality, social or otherwise, which calls for "typage"—the recourse to people who are part and parcel of that reality and can be considered typical of it. As Rotha puts it: "'Typage' . . . represents the least artificial organisation of reality."[18] It is not accidental that film directors devoted to the rendering of larger segments of actual life are inclined to condemn the professional actor for "faking." Like Epstein, who turns against "professional faking," Rossellini is said to believe that actors "fake emotions."[19] This predilection for non-actors goes hand in hand with a vital interest in social patterns rather than individual destinies. Buñuel's *Los Olvidados* highlights the incredible callousness of despondent juveniles; the great De Sica films focus on the plight of the unemployed and the misery of old age insufficiently provided for. Non-actors are chosen because of their authentic looks and behavior. Their major virtue is to figure in a narrative which explores the reality they help constitute but does not culminate in their lives themselves.

* A notable exception was the German cinema after World War I: it shunned outer reality, withdrawing into a shell. See Kracauer, *From Caligari to Hitler*, pp. 58–60.

The Hollywood star

In institutionalizing stars, Hollywood has found a way of tapping natural attractiveness as if it were oil. Aside from economic expediency, though, the star system may well cater to inner needs common to many people in this country. This system provides variegated models of conduct, thus helping, however obliquely, pattern human relationships in a culture not yet old enough to have peopled its firmament with stars that offer comfort or threaten the trespasser—stars not to be mistaken for Hollywood's.

The typical Hollywood star resembles the non-actor in that he acts out a standing character identical with his own or at least developed from it, frequently with the aid of make-up and publicity experts. As with any real-life figure on the screen, his presence in a film points beyond the film. He affects the audience not just because of his fitness for this or that role but for being, or seeming to be, a particular kind of person—a person who exists independently of any part he enacts in a universe outside the cinema which the audience believes to be reality or wishfully substitutes for it. The Hollywood star imposes the screen image of his physique, the real or a stylized one, and all that this physique implies and connotes on every role he creates. And he uses his acting talent, if any, exclusively to feature the individual he is or appears to be, no matter for the rest whether his self-portrayal exhausts itself in a few stereotyped characteristics or brings out various potentialities of his underlying nature. The late Humphrey Bogart invariably drew on Humphrey Bogart whether he impersonated a sailor, a private "eye," or a night club owner.

But why is any one chosen for stardom while others are not? Evidently, something about the gait of the star, the form of his face, his manner of reacting and speaking, ingratiates itself so deeply with the masses of moviegoers that they want to see him again and again, often for a considerable stretch of time. It is logical that the roles of a star should be made to order. The spell he casts over the audience cannot be explained unless one assumes that his screen appearance satisfies widespread desires of the moment—desires connected, somehow, with the patterns of living he represents or suggests.

The professional actor

Discussing the uses of professional actors and non-actors, Mr. Bernard Miles, himself an English actor, declares that the latter prove satisfactory only in documentary films. In them, says he, "non-actors achieve all, or at any rate most, that the very best professional actors could achieve in the same circumstances. But this is only because most of these pictures avoid the implications of human action, or, where they do present it, present it in such a fragmentary way as never to put to the test the training and natural qualities which differentiate an actor from a non-actor." Documentary, he concludes, "has never faced up to the problem of sustained characterization."[20]

Be this as it may, the majority of feature films does raise this problem. And challenged to help solve it, the non-actor is likely to forfeit his naturalness. He becomes paralyzed before the camera, as Rossellini observes;[21] and the task of restoring him to his true nature is often impossible to fulfill. There are exceptions, of course. In both his *Bicycle Thief* and *Umberto D.*, Vittorio De Sica—of whom they say in Italy that he "could lure even a sack of potatoes into acting"[22]—succeeds in making people who never acted before portray coherent human beings. Old Umberto D., a rounded-out character with a wide range of emotions and reactions, is all the more memorable since his whole past seems to come alive in his intensely touching presence. But one should keep in mind that the Italians are blessed with mimetic gifts and have a knack of expressive gestures. Incidentally, while producing *The Men*, a film about paraplegic veterans, director Fred Zinnemann found that people who have undergone a powerful emotional experience are particularly fit to re-enact themselves.[23]

As a rule, however, sustained characterization calls for professional actors. Indeed many stars are. Paradoxically enough, the over-strained non-actor tends to behave like a bad actor, whereas an actor who capitalizes on his given being may manage to appear as a candid non-actor, thus achieving a second state of innocence. He is both the player and the instrument; and the quality of this instrument—his natural self as it has grown in real life—counts as much as his talent in playing it. Think of Raimu. Aware that the screen actor depends upon the non-actor in him, a discerning film critic once said of James Cagney that he "can coax or shove a director until a scene from a dreamy script becomes a scene from life as Cagney remembered it."[24]

Only few actors are able to metamorphose their own nature, including those incidental fluctuations which are the essence of cinematic life. Here Paul Muni comes to mind—not to forget Lon Chaney and Walter Huston. When watching Charles Laughton or Werner Krauss in different roles, one gets the feeling that they even change their height along with their parts. Instead of appearing as they are on the screen, such protean actors actually disappear in screen characters who seem to have no common denominator.

Notes

1 See, for instance, Lindgren, *The Art of the Film*, pp. 156–7; Barbaro, "Le cinéma sans acteurs," in *Le Rôle intellectuel du cinéma*, p. 227; Barjavel, *Cinéma total* . . . , p. 81.
2 Quoted by Lyons, "The Lyons Den," *New York Post*, June 5, 1950.
3 Clair, *Réflexion faite*, p. 187.
4 "Film Crasher Hitchcock," *Cue*, May 19, 1951.
5 Cf. Barjavel, op. cit. pp. 84–5.
6 Clair, op. cit. p. 187.
7 Quoted by Rotha, *Documentary Film*, p. 143, from Pudovkin, "Acting—The Cinema *v.* the Theatre," *The Criterion*, vol. VIII, no. 1.
8 Sachs, "Film Psychology," *Close Up*, Nov. 1928, vol. III, no. 5:9.
9 Eisenstein, *Film Form*, p. 192.
10 Rossellini, "Dix ans de cinéma (I)," *Cahiers du cinéma*, Aug.–Sept. 1955, vol. IX, no. 50:9. See also Balàzs, *Der sichtbare Mensch*, pp. 55–6.
11 Pudovkin, *Film Technique and Film Acting*, part I, p. 109.
12 Cf. Cooke, *Douglas Fairbanks*, p. 6.
13 Barjavel, *Cinéma total* . . ., p. 81.
14 Cited by Rotha, *Documentary Film*, p. 149. See also Rotha, *The Film Till Now*, p. 363.
15 Quoted by Marie Epstein, "Biographical Notes," in Bachmann, ed., *Jean Epstein*, 1897–1953; *Cinemages*, no. 2:8.
16 See Kracauer, *From Caligari to Hitler*, p. 175.
17 Chiaromonte, "Rome Letter: Italian Movies," *Partisan Review*, June 1944, vol. XVI, no. 6:628.
18 Rotha, *Documentary Film*, p. 148. See also Nicholl, *Film and Theatre*, p. 172.

19 Reynolds, *Leave It to the People*, p. 147.
20 Miles, "Are Actors Necessary?" *Documentary News Letter*, April 1941, vol. 2, no. 4:71.
21 Rossellini, "Dix ans de cinéma (I)," *Cahiers du cinéma*, Aug.–Sept. 1955, vol. IX, no. 50:9.
22 Chiaromonte, op. cit. p. 623.
23 Zinnemann, "On Using Non-Actors in Pictures," *The New York Times*, Jan. 8, 1950.
24 Ferguson, "Life Goes to the Pictures," *films*, Spring 1940, vol. 1, no. 2:22.

References

Bachmann, Gideon, ed. *Jean Epstein, 1897–1953*. Special issue of *Cineimages* 2 (1955).

Balàzs, Bela. *Der sichtbare Mensch; oder, Die Kultur des Films*. Wien, Leipzig: Deutsch-österreichischer Verlag, 1924.

Barbaro, Umberto. "Le cinema sans auteurs." In *Le Rôle intellectuel du cinema*, 225–234. Paris: Institut de Coopération Intellectuelle, Société des nations, 1937.

Benjamin, Walter. "Ueber einige Motive bei Baudelaire." *Zeitschrift fuer Sozialforschung* VIII. 1 (1939): 50–91.

Chiaromonte, Nicola. "A Note on the Movies." *Instead* 4 (1948).

Clair, René. *Rèflexion faite: Notes pour servir à l'histoire de l'art cinématographique de 1920 à 1950*. Paris, 1951.

Cohen-Séat, Gilbert. *Essai sur les principles d'une philosophie du cinema I. Introduction générale: Notions fondamentales et vocabulaire de filmologie*. Paris, 1946.

Cooke, Alistair. *Douglas Fairbanks: The Making of a Screen Character*. New York: Museum of Modern Art, 1940.

Eisenstein, Sergei M. *Film Form: Essays in Film Theory*. Edited and translated by Jay Leyda. New York: Harcourt Brace and Co., 1949.

Epstein, Jean. *Le Cinématographe vu de l'Etna*. Paris, 1926.

Kracauer, Siegfried. *From Caligari to Hitler*. Princeton: Princeton University Press, 1947.

—— "Silent Film Comedy." *Sight and Sound* 21.1 (Aug.–Sept. 1951): 261–263.

Laffay, Albert. "Les grand thèmes de l'écran." *La Revue du cinema* II.12 (April 1948): 3–19.

Léger, Fernand. "A propos du cinema." In *Intelligence du cinematographe*, edited by Marcel L'Herbier, 337–340. Paris, 1946.

Lindgren, Ernest. *The Art of the Film: An Introduction to Film Appreciation*. London: George Allen & Unwin, 1948.

Pudovkin, V.I. *Film Technique and Film Acting*. Translated by Ivor Montagu. New York: Grove Press, 1949.

Reynolds, Quentin. *Leave it to the People*. New York: Random House, 1948.

Rotha, Paul. *Documentary Film*. London: Spring Books, 1952.

—— *The Film Till Now*. With an additional section, "The Film Since Then," by Richard Griffith. London: Spring Books, 1967.

Scheffauer, Herman G. "The Vivifying of Space." In *Introduction to the Art of Movies*, edited by Lewis Jacobs, 76–85. New York: Noonday Press, 1960.

Sève, Lucien. "Cinéma et méthode." *Revue internationale de filmologie* 1.1 (Jul.–Aug. 1947): 42–46; 1.2 (Sept.–Oct. 1947): 171–174; and 1.3 and 1.4 (Oct. 1947): 351–355.

Stern, Seymour. "D.W. Griffith and the Movies." *The American Mercury*, LXVIII.303 (March 1949): 308–319.

Tyler, Parker. "The Film Sense and the Painting Sense." *Art Digest* (15 Feb. 1954): 10–12, 27–28.

Vardac, A. Nicholas. *Stage to Screen: Theatrical Method from Garrick to Griffith*. Cambridge, MA: Harvard University Press, 1949.

Reflections on the Ontology of Film

2

STANLEY CAVELL

Audience, actor, and star

The depth of the automatism of photography is to be read not alone in its mechanical production of an image of reality, but in its mechanical defeat of our presence to that reality. The audience in a theater can be defined as those to whom the actors are present while they are not present to the actors.[1] But movies allow the audience to be mechanically absent. The fact that I am invisible and inaudible to the actors, and fixed in position, no longer needs accounting for; it is not part of a convention I have to comply with; the proceedings do not have to make good the fact that I do nothing in the face of tragedy, or that I laugh at the follies of others. In viewing a movie my helplessness is mechanically assured: I am present not at something happening, which I must confirm, but at something that has happened, which I absorb (like a memory). In this, movies resemble novels, a fact mirrored in the sound of narration itself, whose tense is the past.

It might be said: "But surely there is the obvious difference between a movie house and a theater that is not recorded by what has so far been said and that outweighs all this fiddle of differences. The obvious difference is that in a theater we are in the presence of an actor, in a movie house we are not. You have said that in both places the actor is in our presence and in neither are we in his, the difference lying in the mode of our absence. But there is also the plain fact that in a theater a real man is *there*, and in a movie no real man is there. That is obviously essential to the differences between our responses to a play and to a film." What that means must not be denied; but the fact remains to be understood. Bazin meets it head on by simply denying that "the screen is incapable of putting us 'in the presence of' the actor"; it, so to speak, relays his presence to us, as by mirrors.[2] Bazin's idea here really fits the facts of live television, in which the thing we are presented with is happening simultaneously with its presentation. But in live television, what is present to us while it is happening is not the world, but an event standing out from the world. Its point is not to reveal, but to cover (as with a gun), to keep something on view.

It is an incontestable fact that in a motion picture no live human being is up there. But a human *something* is, and something unlike anything else we know. We can stick to our plain description of that human something as "in our presence while we are not in his" (present *at* him, because looking at him, but not present *to* him) and still account for the difference between his live presence and his photographed presence to us. We need to consider what is present or, rather, since the topic is the human being, *who* is present.

One's first impulse may be to say that in a play the character is present, whereas in a film the actor is. That sounds phony or false: one wants to say that both are present in both. But there is more to it, ontologically more. Here I think of a fine passage of Panofsky's:

> Othello or Nora are definite, substantial figures created by the playwright. They can be played well or badly, and they can be "interpreted" in one way or another; but they most definitely exist, no matter who plays them or even whether they are played at all. The character in a film, however, lives and dies with the actor. It is not the entity "Othello" interpreted by Robeson or the entity "Nora" interpreted by Duse, it is the entity "Greta Garbo" incarnate in a figure called Anna Christie or the entity "Robert Montgomery" incarnate in a murderer who, for all we know or care to know, may forever remain anonymous but will never cease to haunt our memories.[3]

If the character lives and dies with the actor, that ought to mean that the actor lives and dies with the character. I think that is correct, but it needs clarification. Let us develop it slightly.

For the stage, an actor works himself into a role; for the screen, a performer takes the role onto himself. The stage actor explores his potentialities and the possibilities of his role simultaneously; in performance these meet at a point in spiritual space—the better the performance, the deeper the point. In this respect, a role in a play is like a position in a game, say, third base: various people can play it, but the great third baseman is a man who has accepted and trained his skills and instincts most perfectly and matches them most intimately with his discoveries of the possibilities and necessities of third base. The screen performer explores his role like an attic and takes stock of his physical and temperamental endowment; he lends his being to the role and accepts only what fits; the rest is nonexistent. On the stage there are two beings, and the being of the character assaults the being of the actor; the actor survives only by yielding. A screen performance requires not so much training as planning. Of course, both the actor and the performer require, or can make use of, experience. The actor's role is his subject for study, and there is no end to it. But the screen performer is essentially not an actor at all: he *is* the subject of study, and a study not his own. (That is what the content of a photograph is—its subject.) On a screen the study is projected; on a stage the actor is the projector. An exemplary stage performance is one which, for a time, most fully creates a character. After Paul Scofield's performance in *King Lear*, we know who King Lear is, we have seen him in flesh. An exemplary screen performance is one in which, at a time, a star is born. After *The Maltese Falcon* we know a new star, only distantly a person. "Bogart" *means* "the figure created in a given set of films." His presence in those films is who he is, not merely in the sense in which a photograph of an event is that event; but in the sense that if those films did not exist, Bogart would not exist, the name "Bogart" would not mean what it does. The figure it names is not only in our presence, we are in his, in the only sense we could ever be. That is all the "presence" he has.

But it is complicated. A full development of all this would require us to place such facts as these: Humphrey Bogart was a man, and he appeared in movies both before and after the ones that created "Bogart." Some of them did not create a new star (say, the stable groom in *Dark Victory*), some of them defined stars—anyway meteors—that may be incompatible with Bogart (e.g., Duke Mantee and Fred C. Dobbs) but that are related to that figure and may enter into our later experience of it. And Humphrey Bogart was both an accomplished actor and a vivid subject for a camera. Some people are, just as some people are both good pitchers and good hitters; but there are so few that it is surprising that the word "actor" keeps on being used in place of the more beautiful and more accurate word "star"; the stars are only to gaze at, after the fact, and their actions divine our projects. Finally, we must note the sense in which the creation of a (screen) performer is also the creation of a character—not the kind of character an author creates, but the kind that certain real people are: a type.

Types; cycles as genres

Around this point our attention turns from the physical medium of cinema in general to the specific forms or genres the medium has taken in the course of its history.

Both Panofsky and Bazin begin at the beginning, noting and approving that early movies adapt popular or folk arts and themes and performers and characters: farce, melodrama, circus, music hall, romance, etc. And both are gratifyingly contemptuous of intellectuals who could not come to terms with those facts of life. (Such intellectuals are the alter egos of the film promoters they so heartily despise. Roxy once advertised a movie as "Art, in every sense of the word"; his better half declaims, "This is not art, in any sense of the word.") Our question is, why did such forms and themes and characters lend themselves to film? Bazin, in what I have read of him, is silent on the subject, except to express gratitude to film for revivifying these ancient forms, and to justify in general the legitimacy of adaptation from one art to another. Arnold Hauser, if I understand him, suggests wrong answers, in a passage that includes the remark "Only a young art can be popular,"[4] a remark that not only is in itself baffling (did Verdi and Dickens and Chaplin and Frank Loesser work in young arts?) but suggests that it was only natural for the movies to pick up the forms they did. It *was* natural—anyway it happened fast enough—but not because movies were destined to popularity (they were at first no more popular than other forms of entertainment). In any case, popular arts are likely to pick up the forms and themes of high art for their material—popular theater naturally *burlesques*. And it means next to nothing to say that movies are young, because we do not know what the normal life span of an art is supposed to be, nor what would count as a unit of measure. Panofsky raises the question of the appropriateness of these original forms, but his answer is misleading.

> The legitimate paths of evolution [for the film] were opened, not by running away from the folk art character of the primitive film but by developing it within the limits of its own possibilities. Those primordial archetypes of film productions on the folk art level—success or retribution, sentiment, sensation, pornography, and crude humor—could blossom forth into genuine history, tragedy and romance, crime and adventure, and comedy, as soon as it was realized that they could be transfigured—not by an artificial injection of literary values but by the exploitation of the unique and specific possibilities of the new medium.[5]

The instinct here is sound, but the region is full of traps. What are "the unique and specific possibilities of the new medium"? Panofsky defines them as dynamization of space and spatialization of time—that is, in a movie things move, and you can be moved instantaneously from anywhere to anywhere, and you can witness successively events happening at the same time. He speaks of these properties as "self-evident to the point of triviality" and, because of that, "easily forgotten or neglected." One hardly disputes this, or its importance. But we still do not understand what makes these properties "the possibilities of the medium." I am not now asking how one would know that these are *the* unique and specific possibilities (though I will soon get back to that); I am asking what it means to call them possibilities at all.

Why, for example, didn't the medium begin and remain in the condition of home movies, one shot just physically tacked on to another, cut and edited simply according to subject? (Newsreels essentially did, and they are nevertheless valuable, enough so to have justified the invention of moving pictures.) The answer seems obvious: narrative movies emerged because someone "saw the possibilities" of the medium—cutting and editing and taking shots at different distances from the subject. But again, these are mere actualities of film mechanics: every home movie and newsreel contains them. We could say: To make them "possibilities of the medium" is to realize what will give them *significance*—for example, the narrative and physical rhythms of melodrama, farce, American comedy of the 1930s. It is not as if film-makers saw these possibilities and then looked for something to apply them to. It is truer to say that someone with the wish to make a movie saw that certain established forms would give point to certain properties of film.

This perhaps sounds like quibbling, but what it means is that the aesthetic possibilities of a medium are not givens. You can no more tell what will give significance to the unique and specific aesthetic possibilities of projecting photographic images by thinking about them or seeing some, than you can tell what will give significance to the possibilities of paint by thinking about paint or by looking some over. You have to think about painting, and paintings; you have to think about motion pictures. What does this "thinking about them" consist in? Whatever the useful criticism of an art consists in. (Painters before Jackson Pollock had dripped paint, even deliberately. Pollock made dripping into a medium of painting.) I feel like saying: The first successful movies—i.e., the first moving pictures accepted as motion pictures—were not applications of a medium that was defined by given possibilities, but the *creation of a medium* by their giving significance to specific possibilities. Only the art itself can discover its possibilities, and the discovery of a new possibility is the discovery of a new medium. A medium is something through which or by means of which something specific gets done or said in particular ways. It provides, one might say, particular ways to get through to someone, to make sense; in art, they are forms, like forms of speech. To discover ways of making sense is always a matter of the relation of an artist to his art, each discovering the other.

Panofsky uncharacteristically skips a step when he describes the early silent films as an "unknown language . . . forced upon a public not yet capable of reading it."[6] His notion is (with good reason, writing when he did) of a few industrialists forcing their productions upon an addicted multitude. But from the beginning the language was not "unknown"; it was known to its creators, those who found themselves speaking it; and in the beginning there was no "public" in question; there were just some curious people. There soon was a public, but that just proves how easy the thing was to know. If we are to say that there was an "unknown" something, it was less like a language than like a fact—in particular, the fact that something is intelligible. So while it may be true, as Panofsky says, that "for a Saxon peasant of around 800 it was not easy to understand the meaning of a picture showing a man as he pours water over the head of another man," this has nothing special to do with the problems of a moviegoer. The meaning of that act of pouring in certain communities is still not easy to understand; it was and is impossible to understand for anyone to whom the practice of baptism is unknown. Why did Panofsky suppose that comparable understanding is essential, or uniquely important, to the reading of movies? Apparently he needed an explanation for the persistence in movies of "fixed iconography"—"the well-remembered types of the Vamp and the Straight Girl . . . the Family Man, and the Villain," characters whose conduct was "predetermined accordingly"—an explanation for the persistence of an obviously primitive or folkloristic element in a rapidly developing medium. For he goes on, otherwise inexplicably, to say that "devices like these became gradually less necessary as the public grew accustomed to interpret the action by itself and were virtually abolished by the invention of the talking film." In fact such devices persist as long as there are still Westerns and gangster films and comedies and musicals and romances. *Which* specific iconography the Villain is given will alter with the times, but that his iconography remains specific (i.e., operates according to a "fixed attitude and attribute" principle)[7] seems undeniable: if Jack Palance in *Shane* is not a Villain, no honest home was ever in danger. Films have changed, but that is not because we don't need such explanations any longer; it is because we can't *accept* them.

These facts are accounted for by the actualities of the film medium itself: types are exactly what carry the forms movies have relied upon. These media created new types, or combinations and ironic reversals of types; but there they were, and stayed. Does this mean that movies can never create individuals, only types? What it means is that this is the movies' way of creating individuals: they create *individualities*. For what makes someone a type is not his similarity with other members of that type but his striking separateness from other people.

Until recently, types of black human beings were not created in film: black people were stereotypes—mammies, shiftless servants, loyal retainers, entertainers. We were not given, and were not in a position to be given, individualities that projected particular *ways* of inhabiting a social role; we recognized only the role. Occasionally the humanity behind the role would manifest itself and the result was a revelation not of a human individuality, but of an entire realm of humanity becoming visible. When in *Gone With the Wind* Vivien Leigh, having counted on Butterfly McQueen's professed knowledge of midwifery, and finding her as ignorant as herself, slaps her in rage and terror, the moment can stun us with a question: What was the white girl assuming about blackness when she believed the casual claim of a black girl, younger and duller and more ignorant than herself, to know all about the mysteries of childbirth? The assumption, though apparently complimentary, is dehumanizing—with such creatures knowledge of the body comes from nowhere, and in general they are to be trusted absolutely or not at all, like lions in a cage, with whom you either do or do not know how to deal. After the slap, we are left with two young girls equally frightened in a humanly desperate situation, one limited by a distraction which expects and forgets that it is to be bullied, the other by an energetic resourcefulness which knows only how to bully. At the end of Michael Curtiz' *Breaking Point*, as the wounded John Garfield is carried from his boat to the dock, awaited by his wife and children and, just outside the circle, by the other woman in his life (Patricia Neal), the camera pulls away, holding on the still waiting child of his black partner, who only the unconscious Garfield knows has been killed. The poignance of the silent and unnoticed black child overwhelms the yarn we had been shown. Is he supposed to symbolize the fact of general human isolation and abandonment? Or the fact that every action has consequences for innocent bystanders? Or that children are the real sufferers from the entangled efforts of adults to straighten out their lives? The effect here is to rebuke Garfield for attaching so much importance to the loss of his arm, and generally to blot out attention to individual suffering by invoking a massive social evil about which this film has nothing to say.

The general difference between a film type and a stage type is that the individuality captured on film naturally takes precedence over the social role in which that individuality gets expressed. Because on film social role appears arbitrary or incidental, movies have an inherent tendency toward the democratic, or anyway the idea of human equality. (But because of film's equally natural attraction to crowds, it has opposite tendencies toward the fascistic or populistic.) This depends upon recognizing film types as inhabited by figures we have met or may well meet in other circumstances. The recognized recurrence of film performers will become a central idea as we proceed. At the moment I am emphasizing only that in the case of black performers there was until recently no other place for them to recur in, except just the role within which we have already met them. For example, we would not have expected to see them as parents or siblings. I cannot at the moment remember a black person in a film making an ordinary purchase—say of a newspaper, or a ticket to a movie or for a train, let alone writing a check. (*Pinky* and *A Raisin in the Sun* prove the rule: in the former, the making of a purchase is a climactic scene in the film; in the latter, it provides the whole subject and structure.)

One recalls the lists of stars of every magnitude who have provided the movie camera with human subjects—individuals capable of filling its need for individualities, whose individualities in turn, whose inflections of demeanor and disposition were given full play in its projection. They provided, and still provide, staples for impersonators: one gesture or syllable of mood, two strides, or a passing mannerism was enough to single them out from all other creatures. They realized the myth of singularity—that we can still be found, behind our disguises of bravado and cowardice, by someone, perhaps a god, capable of defeating our self-defeats. This was always more important than their distinction by beauty. Their singularity made them more like us—anyway, made their difference from us less a matter of metaphysics, to which we must accede, than a matter of responsibility, to which we must bend. But then that made them even more glamorous. That they should be able to stand upon their singularity! If one did that, one might be found, and called out, too soon, or at an inconvenient moment.

What was wrong with type-casting in films was not that it displaced some other, better principle of casting, but that factors irrelevant to film-making often influenced the particular figures chosen. Similarly, the familiar historical fact that there are movie cycles, taken by certain movie theorists as in itself a mark of unscrupulous commercialism, is a possibility internal to the medium; one could even say, it is the best emblem of the fact that a medium had been created. For a cycle is a genre (prison movies, Civil War movies, horror movies, etc.); and a genre is a medium.

As Hollywood developed, the original types ramified into individualities as various and subtle, as far-reaching in their capacities to inflect mood and release fantasy, as any set of characters who inhabited the great theaters of our world. We do not know them by such names as Pulcinella, Crispin, Harlequin, Pantaloon, the Doctor, the Captain, Columbine; we call them the Public Enemy, the Priest, James Cagney, Pat O'Brien, the Confederate Spy, the Army Scout, Randolph Scott, Gary Cooper, Gable, Paul Muni, the Reporter, the Sergeant, the Sheriff, the Deputy, the D.A., the Quack, the Shyster, the Other Woman, the Fallen Woman, the Moll, the Dance Hall Hostess. Hollywood was the theater in which they appeared, because the films of Hollywood constituted a world, with recurrent faces more familiar to me than the faces of the neighbors of all the places I have lived.

The great movie comedians—Chaplin, Keaton, W. C. Fields—form a set of types that could not have been adapted from any other medium. Its creation depended upon two conditions of the film medium mentioned earlier. These conditions seem to be necessities, not merely possibilities, so I will say that two necessities of the medium were discovered or expanded in the creation of these types. First, movie performers cannot project, but are projected. Second, photographs are of the world, in which human beings are not ontologically favored over the rest of nature, in which objects are not props but natural allies (or enemies) of the human character. The first necessity—projected visibility—permits the sublime comprehensibility of Chaplin's natural choreography; the second—ontological equality—permits his Proustian or Jamesian relationships with Murphy beds and flights of stairs and with vases on runners on tables on rollers: the heroism of momentary survival, Nietzsche's man as a tightrope across an abyss. These necessities permit not merely the locales of Keaton's extrications, but the philosophical mood of his countenance and the Olympic resourcefulness of his body; permit him to be perhaps the only constantly beautiful and continuously hilarious man ever seen, as though the ugliness in laughter should be redeemed. They permit Fields to mutter and suffer and curse obsessively, but heard and seen only by us; because his attributes are those of the gentleman (confident swagger and elegant manners, gloves, cane, outer heartiness), he can manifest continuously, with the remorselessness of nature, the psychic brutalities of bourgeois civilization.

Notes

1 This idea is developed to some extent in my essays on *Endgame* and *King Lear* in *Must We Mean What We Say?* (New York: Scribner's, 1969).
2 André Bazin, *What is Cinema?*, trans. Hugh Gray (Berkeley: University of California Press, 1967), 97.
3 Erwin Panofsky, "Style and Medium in the Moving Pictures," repr. in Daniel Talbot, ed., *Film* (New York: Simon and Schuster, 1959), 28.
4 Arnold Hauser, "The Film Age," repr. in Talbot, *Film*, 74.
5 Panofsky, "Style and Medium in the Moving Pictures," 18.
6 Ibid. 24.
7 Ibid. 25.

Screen Acting and the Commutation Test

3

JOHN O. THOMPSON

I

At the moment, only those who oppose the semiotic study of the cinema seem to want to talk about screen acting. Since a good deal of the meaning of the fiction film is borne by its actors and their performances, this amounts to leaving an important territory in the hands of the enemy (to put it over-belligerently). And some of the standard doctrines and endlessly rediscovered 'truths' about actor and role, screen vs stage and so on may be inhibiting not only critical but also creative practice in the cinema. Yet it is understandable why this gap in the semiotic programme remains. Performances seem ineffable, and thinking about them induces reverie rather than analysis.

In this essay I want to propose the controlled extension of one semiotic technique as a way of rehabilitating one mode of reverie. The technique is called the *commutation test* in European structural linguistics. I hope it will be plain that I do not believe that importing the technique will suddenly make our discourse about acting 'scientific': any advantage it brings will be more modest. However, I do think we need to start prompting a more methodical and reflexive discourse in this whole area, and here the *test* may help.

II

To begin with, here is a quotation from a recent essay by David Thomson which exemplifies, very flexibly and intelligently, the reverie approach to screen acting. The point the quotation first makes is a familiar one. Brecht, summing up a conversation with Adorno in his diary in 1942, asserted that 'the theatre's first advantage over the film is . . . in the division between play and performance', and continued 'the mechanical reproduction gives everything the character of a result: unfree and inalterable'.[1] Thomson says the same thing, and then – but hesitantly, as if the exercise he proposes is somehow methodologically indefensible – manoeuvres around this apparent blockage at the heart of the cinema's 'nature':

> Stage parts are like concertos – they are supple, lofty and impersonal enough to take on all corners. But parts in films live only briefly: like virginity, once taken, they are not there

> to be inhabited again. Before shooting, all manner of choices may perplex the film-makers and keep the part blurred: Kim Novak's part(s) in *Vertigo* were designed for Vera Miles; Shirley Temple was first choice to play Dorothy in *The Wizard of Oz* – imagine how 'Over the Rainbow' might have been cosy and wistful instead of the epitome of heartbreaking dreams. . . . Once a film is made no one else can play the part. . . . the text in movies is the appearance.
>
> All credit then to Andrew Sarris . . . for indicating the waste in arguing over Vivien Leigh or Merle Oberon in Wyler's *Wuthering Heights*. And yet . . . the critic can usefully learn things about film through such speculations. . . . If *Vertigo* had had Vera Miles then the girl might have been as near to breakdown as the wife in *The Wrong Man*, and not the numb pawn of the plot that makes Novak pathetic and touching. . . . Or – think how sentimental *Kane* might be if Spencer Tracy had been the tycoon. That is useful if only to show how little conventional feeling the film has.[2]

What I am struck by is an analogy between 'such speculations' and an 'operative concept . . . already found in Trubetzkoy, but . . . established under its present name by Hjelmslev and Udall, at the Fifth Congress of Phonetics in 1936'.[3] The name given was *commutation*, a word with unfortunate penal implications in English but originally synonymous with 'substitution'.[4] Roland Barthes discusses the commutation test in *Elements of Semiology*, but in a very compressed manner:

> The commutation test consists of artificially introducing a change in the plane of expression (signifiers) and in observing whether this change brings about a correlative modification on the plane of contents (signifieds). . . . if the commutation of two signifiers produces a commutation of the signifieds one is assured of having got hold, in the fragment of syntagm submitted to the test, of a syntagmatic unit: the first sign has been cut off from the mass.[5]

Giulio Lepschy puts it even more briefly:

> By the *commutation test* we can check whether an exchange of elements on one plane entails a corresponding exchange on the other plane: if so we have two different elements; otherwise we have two variants of the same element.[6]

What do these formulations mean? Some differences in language make a difference semantically; others don't, though they are perceptible and may bear information about the speaker's region, social class, sex, and so forth; still others are imperceptible save by means of sophisticated measuring instruments. The difference between *p* and *b* is of the first sort (*path* and *bath* are different words), while that between a higher *a* as pronounced in the north of England and the lower *a* of the south is of the second sort (*bath* is the same word with either *a*). The commutation test strictly speaking simply involves trying out a sound change and observing whether a meaning change is produced or not. *Which* meaning change may be irrelevant, because of the arbitrary, unmotivated linkage in language between sound and meaning.[7] Thus, at the phonological level, there is no regularity in the shift of meaning produced by a given substitution: *path* is not to *bath* in any relation such that *pushed* and *bushed* are in the same relation. But at the morphological level – the level of minimal *meaning* units

– some such alternations show significant regularities: e.g. *ride:rode*; *stride:strode*. This takes us into an area in which Saussure was prepared to speak of the linguistic sign's *relative motivation*.[8] How does this compare with what Thomson is doing? He is proposing the substitution in thought of one actor for another, in order to observe not merely *if* a difference in meaning results but *which* difference results. And he is doing so in a context in which we naturally feel that motivation of the sign is important: our sense of whether X is 'right for the part'[9] depends upon canons of suitability governing the signifier(actor) – signified(role) link which we generally assume to be non-arbitrary. One useful effect of thinking about commutation with the phonological analogy in mind is that it encourages us to query these assumptions about suitability, which turn out to be suffused with ideology and to shift with history. But there is no reason to believe that somehow with analysis all motivation should be shown to be illusory (reduction of cinema to language): ideology is not illusion.

III

It might seem that testing for whether substituting one actor for another makes any difference to a film's meaning would be pointless: 'Of course it must!' But this is not so. The stuntman, for instance, or the nude-scene stand-in both supply presences to the screen which have to seem indistinguishable from those of the actor or actress who is being stood in for: here much trouble is taken to ensure that the actual substitution of one body for another makes no difference to the text. Extras may generally be commuted with little if any change of meaning resulting. It's interesting to find that Equity's agreement with Thames Television explicitly defines an extra as 'a performer who is not required to give individual characterisations'[10] – that is, a performer who need not, indeed should not, *distinguish* himself or herself. It is not surprising that one un-distinguished figure can be indistinguishably replaced by another. What constraints there are on meaning-preserving replacements seem to operate on the level of the crowd (or a more abstract unit such as the set of passers-by through the whole film): we would notice if *everyone* on the streets happened to be female, or to be bald, and so forth. There is an intermediate range of quite minor characters where the situation is blurred, but since the more films one has seen the more subtle individuations one picks up in the minor roles, it might be safest to treat them as functioning distinctively for the 'ideal viewer'. But occasionally indistinguishability is sought deliberately for the sake of the narrative. In Hitchcock's *Strangers on a Train* the promiscuity and vulgar funlovingness of Guy's wife Miriam is in part established by having her taken to the amusement park by *two* bland young men – who remain indistinguishable from one another over repeated viewings.

IV

Commutation is a device which is designed to allow us consciously to grasp units which were previously invisible, submerged in the smooth operation of the sign system in question. This is why it can work introspectively: one *asks oneself* if a change in the signifier would make a difference, and the answer can surprise one. To reject such devices as unnecessary is to claim that one possesses already both a competence in the language in question and a working theory of that competence. Where phonology is concerned, the latter claim is unlikely to be justified, because we devote so little attention ordinarily to observing minutely the sounds of our speech. But if all that the commutation of actors reveals is that Cary Grant is not Gary Cooper, it certainly isn't worth the trouble: our existing grasp of that gross difference is adequate enough already. If commutation is to justify itself in screen acting analysis, it must reveal something more delicate and less obvious. Why shouldn't we think of a screen performance as composed of 'finer' elements, *features* in the linguistic sense?

> Each of the segments in a word can be described as being the sum of a number of components or features. Thus the consonant *m* at the beginning of the word *man* can be said to have the feature of being voiced, the feature of being made at the bilabial place of articulation, the feature of being a nasal, and so on.[11]

The obvious answer is that John Wayne is more complex than a phoneme: whereas a phoneme can be characterized exhaustively in terms of a restricted number of features (Jakobson and Halle manage with twelve),[12] such an analysis is out of the question for the actor's rich and shifting screen presence. But if we move from phonological features to semantic features, the suggestion may not seem so wild. While no one could claim that we are even near to a generally acceptable account of natural language semantics, it can at least be said that:

> most current semantic theories, and many traditional ones too, analyze meaning into 'smaller' component meanings, and assign to a lexical item a semantic representation consisting of a complex of semantically primitive elements.[13]

Here a typical feature would be not ±*voiced* or ±*nasal* but ±*abstract* or ±*animate* or ±*male*. How far decomposition into semantic features can be taken is currently a highly controversial question[14] but it seems undeniable that componential analysis captures many necessary generalizations about the meaning relations between a word and the rest of the lexicon.

V

Let us see how far the notion of a film performance as a bundle of distinctive features can take us. Each feature functions as a potential distinguisher both within the film itself and in the indefinitely-extending space established by viewers' familiarity with cinema in general. For instance John Wayne's features contrast not only with James Stewart's in the films they both appear in but with Jean-Paul Belmondo's, even if the two actors have never in fact been textually juxtaposed. Texts leave some features and feature-contrasts wholly unthematized and others only implicitly thematized in order to concentrate explicitly on comparatively few. Unthematized features could be altered or redistributed without any change in the meaning of the film resulting. Members of a chain-gang or a chorus-line are distinguished from one another, like the rest of us, by the colour of their eyes; but switching eye-colours around would generally make no difference to the text. Perhaps most feature-contrasts are only lightly or implicitly thematized: switching features turns out when one thinks about it to make some difference – perhaps a great deal: a woman in the chain-gang? – but the film operates in such a way as not to encourage one to think about this. Here the commutation test has a useful de-naturalizing function. The canons of verisimilitude, plausibility, referentiality and so on that are operating suddenly become visible: *of course* there aren't co-ed chain gangs, the athletic hero can't be a dwarf, the Western hero can't have a Liverpool accent. In every film certain contrasts become highly thematized, presenting themselves as 'what the film is about'. Two or more characters are set up as rivals, as alternative love- or hate-objects (for other characters or the audience or both), as debaters, as couples, etc. *The Good, the Bad and the Ugly*; Wayne and Stewart in *The Man Who Shot Liberty Valance*; Bogart and Bacall *passim*; Ava Gardner and Grace Kelly in *Mogambo*; the cousins in *Les Cousins*: here and everywhere in the cinema the audience is explicitly called upon to compare and contrast.

So far we have been talking about features as they pertain to actors as 'nouns', but there is no reason in principle not to extend the programme to the analysis of characters' actions (to the enacted equivalents of 'verb' or 'adjective' predicates) and to the manner in which the actions are performed ('adverbial' features). For critical and pedagogical purposes it is sometimes helpful to restrict oneself to, or at least to set out from, contrasts explicitly thematized in a particular film; this guarantees the pertinence of the features scrutinized and keeps the set of possibilities to be commuted finite. Since, for example, we have no satisfactory finite list of types of smile (although we can assign smiles to categories fairly precisely – thin-lipped, crazy, timid, etc.), running through smile-types at random can seem pointless. But the contrast between the smiles of Ava Gardner and Grace Kelly in *Mogambo* is part of the system of that film. Imagining switching the smiles around, so that the young, inexperienced blonde has the sensual, shrewd, good-humoured smile while the older, experienced brunette has the repressed, seldom-used smile, teaches us a good deal about the system of assumptions about types of women which Ford is working within here.[15] Yet it would be wrong always to limit commutation to contrasts embodied in the text. Commuting smiles in *Mogambo* with smile-types wholly foreign to the film (a crazy smile or a cruel smile, say) might or might not be unprofitable depending on the investigation in hand. Such a commutation might be pertinent to an examination of the bounds of decorum within which women in a film like *Mogambo* must keep if the overall good-humour of the action is to be sustained and the audience remain unthreatened. When the feature in question is part of a clearly limited paradigmatic set, we need worry even less about applying commutation independently of the film's own thematized contrasts. Perhaps the most obvious example of such a set is the male–female opposition: commutation here almost always has dramatic effects which get us to the heart of 'ordinary sexism' very quickly.

VI

Does one test by commuting whole actors or just features? This will depend. Commuting actors may be wasteful and lead to blurry intuitions: if it is already clear which feature is pertinent, manipulating it on its own may be indicated. And what presents itself as a whole-actor commutation may really be a single-feature commutation in disguise. Take the following sharp comment by Marjorie Bilbow, reviewing *Looking for Mr. Goodbar*:

> A woman seeking the release of sex without love will still attract moral judgements when films about men doing exactly the same thing are taken for granted. In fact, it makes a salutary mental exercise to transpose the lead characters in *Mr. Goodbar* and Truffaut's

> *The Man Who Loved Women*, which is primarily a light comedy. Both die sudden and violent deaths at the end; which of the two would you then say is being punished for sinning?[16]

Clearly Marjorie Bilbow is not actually proposing that we check the differences between Diane Keaton and Charles Denner (or between the roles they play) feature by feature as we transpose them. The relevant feature – gender – is already obvious. The use of speaking of the whole roles here is that it points up that not only sexual behaviour but ultimate fate stays constant under transposition; what varies as gender varies is the moral evaluation of that fate. Thus the *unexpected* 'unit' that the commutation isolates lies on the plane of the film's ethical signifieds. In general, whole-actor commutation is useful when it is not yet clear which feature(s) will turn out to be pertinently differential, or how one feature aligns itself with others to effect a single thematized contrast. One feature of Diane Keaton as Teresa in *Mr. Goodbar* is her hair colour; but how this operates as a signifier in the film comes into focus less when we commute just hair colours – can she be a red-head? – than when we commute Keaton with Tuesday Weld as the blonde older sister, whose dyed-blondeness goes with *only-apparent* innocence in her father's eyes but with *real* dumbness, contrasting with Teresa's educatedness, sincerity, guilt in her father's eyes.

VII

The sort of 'units' that commuting actors isolates – features or traits – are themselves clearly not unanalysable primitives: a tempting but very ambitious programme would be to aim at a decomposition of physiognomies, smiles, gaits, and similar behaviours into distinctive features specified in physiological terms in the same way that phonological features are specified in terms of the mechanisms of the mouth, throat and tongue. Someone with a penchant for rigour might claim that characterizations such as 'nervous smile' or 'crazy smile' are hopelessly imprecise and impressionistic ('tight-lipped smile' being closer to a satisfactory description). However, there are good reasons for not taking the rigourist too seriously, though students of the cinema probably should pay more attention to recent advances in the study of non-verbal communication than we usually do.[17] One trouble with the rigourist's programme is that for many inquiries it would be diversionary: the level of codedness one is interested in is more 'macro', more capable of being related to economic, political and ideological structures. But there is also a problem in principle about the search for primitive elements of behaviour: we have no guarantee that concepts such as 'suave, sophisticated manners', 'crazy smile', 'dizziness' (as in 'dizzy blonde') group together behaviours which are physiologically unitary. That is, there are almost certainly a number of muscularly distinct smiles which in this culture we would group together as 'crazy', and this would be even more true of what 'sophistication' or 'ruggedness' collect; yet it is at the level of these cultural groupings that we need to operate. Too 'micro' an analysis can destroy the object we are concerned with.

Commutation does respond to one element in the rigourist's reproach, in that its effect is to keep before our attention how problematic the terms we use to characterize differences among performances are. There seem to be differences without terms to capture them,[18] and terms which bundle together an indefinite range of differences. (But in this respect our discourse about performance is like our discourse about everything else: it is how natural language operates.) This allows for considerable mobility over time in the conceptualizing of performances and their details: to recapture the terms that would have been used to characterize features of a silent film performance, for instance, often requires a considerable effort of historical imagination.

VIII

Analysing an advertisement for Chanel No. 5 perfume consisting of a close-up of Catherine Deneuve, a picture of a bottle of the perfume, the brand-name in large letters at the bottom of the page and 'Catherine Deneuve for Chanel' in small letters just above this, Judith Williamson sees Chanel as using 'what Catherine Deneuve's face *means to us*' already to establish 'what Chanel No. 5 is trying to mean to us, too':

> It is only because Catherine Deneuve has an 'image', a significance in one sign system, that she can be used to create a new system of significance relating to perfumes. If she were not a film star and famous for her chic type of French beauty, if she did not *mean* something to us, the link made between her face and the perfume would be meaningless. So it is not her face as such, but its position in a system of signs where it signifies flawless French beauty, which makes it useful as a piece of linguistic currency to sell Chanel.[19]

Meaning in a sign system depends on difference; Williamson chooses as a differing woman-sign a model who appears in the ad campaign for Fabergé's *Babe* perfume:

> Catherine Deneuve has significance only in that she is not, for example, Margaux Hemingway. . . . The significance of [the latter's] novelty, youth and 'Tomboy' style, which has value only *in relation* to the more typically 'feminine' style usually connected with modelling, is carried over to the perfume: which is thus signified as new and 'fresh', in relation to other established perfumes. There would be no significance at all in the fact that Margaux Hemingway is wearing a karate outfit and has her hair tied back to look almost like a man's, were it not that *other* perfume ads show women wearing pretty dresses and with elaborately styled hair.[20]

I think Williamson's discussion may overstate the ultimate reducibility to difference of this whole realm of signification, but this is not to say that difference is not immensely important. I want to use Deneuve as an example of the operation of 'the formal relations of pre-existing systems of differences', because the systems are not only what 'advertisements appropriate'[21] but are in the cinema important determinants of *casting*.

Williamson's argument is that we have a much more secure grasp of the difference between Deneuve and Hemingway than have, or could ever have ('perfumes *can* have no particular significance')[22] – with respect to the product; so that transferring the former difference to the latter realm has a persuasive, because cognitive, effect.[23] The question is, in what sense do those firm Deneuve–Hemingway differences exist before one makes that specific comparison? It arises for me with special force in this particular case because it was possible for me fully to follow Williamson's discussion although I knew nothing whatsoever of Margaux Hemingway before reading it. In effect, Williamson has performed a Deneuve–Hemingway commutation, and my prior ignorance of one element in the commutation has not prevented it from 'working'. How can this be? Actually, the significances which Williamson ascribes to Deneuve – '*famous* for her *chic* type of *French* beauty . . . *flawless*' – are not in an uncomplicatedly differential relationship to those of the Hemingway 'image'. Logically enough, but also as if to compensate for Deneuve's +*fame*, Hemingway has +*novelty* whereas Deneuve has –*novelty* (the link between her and Chanel has been maintained for an unusually long time). But one would hardly assign –*chic* to Hemingway (although the *type* of chic shifts); her –*French* trait is not unequivocal ('Margaux' vs 'Margo',[24] and perhaps a whiff of 'American-in-Paris'-ness left over from another Hemingway); and while someone engaged in karate seems unlikely to maintain 'flawless beauty', one clearly could not speak of a 'flawed beauty'. The underlying contrast seems to involve something like ±*mobility*: Hemingway can retain her sort of beauty in motion, whereas one cannot imagine the Chanel Denueve being able to move much without her beauty becoming flawed.

What seems to happen is that such individual images as Deneuve's or Hemingway's find or make their place(s) within a network of differences already provided for *by the language*; it is within language that the contrast 'feminine'/'Tomboy' is kept 'in place', and this is a necessary condition for that contrast's embodiment both in the real and in image-deployment within specialized discourses like advertising. At this level, the same contrast ±*feminine* could be embodied by an indefinite number of different figures. But conversely each individual figure is a composite of an indefinite number of determinations, and while only a subset of these will be highlighted by any given commutation, it will still put into play contrasts involving more than a single feature. This means that a contrast on ±*mobility* will always involve more than *just* that once the specific feature-bundle 'Margaux Hemingway' is chosen to embody one pole, even when the other pole is left general ('other perfume ads show women wearing pretty dresses and with elaborately styled hair'); and it will become even richer once the specific feature-bundle 'Catherine Denueve' is installed at the other pole. This detailed richness is what could not have existed before I knew about Margaux Hemingway, and each new bit of data I acquire about the image enriches the contrast further. But the concepts to illustrate which Williamson posed the contrast of the two images are not dependent upon this richness: many models and actresses could have been chosen who would have embodied any one feature contrast just as well.

The main difference between choosing a model for an advertisement and casting for a film is that the requirements of narrative structure in film, however constraining on their own level, put the features of the actor into play more actively than advertisements do. If there is a single image of Deneuve at work in the Chanel ads and in her films, it is presented and developed more unpredictably where narrative brings out its potential ambiguities.

When Burt Reynolds asked Robert Aldrich to direct him in *Hustle*, Aldrich said:

> 'I'll do this picture on one condition: that you help me get Miss Chanel.' Because the woman's part had been written for an American, and I didn't think it worked that way. I think our middle-class mores just don't make it credible that a policeman can have a love relationship with a prostitute. Because of some strange quirk in our backgrounds, the mass audience doesn't believe it. It's perfectly all right as long as she's not American. So Burt accepted this as a condition, and we put up our money and went to Paris, and waited on the great lady for a week, and she agreed to do the picture.[25]

Here the role in the script included the feature +*American*, and the director modified this to –*American* on credibility grounds. Whether or not Aldrich's unacceptability intuition about the cluster +*American* +*prostitute* +*loved by policeman* was idiosyncratic[26] (the casting of Deneuve seems to me to be splendid, but I wouldn't have thought credibility was its strong point), certainly underdetermines the choice of Deneuve from the very large set of un-American actresses. The associative leap to 'Miss Chanel' shows that more of the 'Deneuve' feature-bundle was involved, and the tone of the remark about 'waiting on the great lady'[27] might suggest that part of this might be a certain wish to flaw the 'unflawed', to exploit the possibilities of the Miss-Chanel-as-prostitute twist. But there must be something about the bundle which facilitates this twist anyway, since any specification of Deneuve's image in terms of film roles would have to take Buñuel's *Belle du Jour* as a central text. While it and *Hustle* draw on the features that make Deneuve an appropriate signifier for Chanel, both films in different ways put these features at the service of narratives which draw out their darker implications – in *Belle du Jour* the – *mobility* feature is used to connote both frigidity and corpselikeness; in *Hustle* the 'flawlessness' is made to begin to crack around the edges.

A Catherine Deneuve ad and a Catherine Deneuve film clearly both operate as closed texts to a greater or lesser degree (both *Belle du Jour* and *Hustle* being more open than many, as it happens, whereas a more conventional film such as Terence Young's *Mayerling* might even exceed Chanel ads in closure): but the mechanisms by which they achieve their closure are different, and are themselves made visible by the commutation we achieve by holding Deneuve constant while changing the textual practices which serve as the context of her presentation. The ever-open possibility of doing this leaves the Chanel advertisements open to a certain subversion. So does the way that the Deneuve image is built up from appearances of which some are so narratively charged: Chanel cannot prevent us from thinking of the parts Deneuve has played for Buñuel and Aldrich, with their unwanted, unsettling features.

IX

There is room for a great deal of detailed research on the history of casting. The breathless run-through of casts once contemplated for well-known films given in a recent article by Linda Rosencrantz[28] illustrates the sort of material which could be of great use in determining which star images were contemplatable for which roles at a given time. It would be good to have accounts of actual casting practice detailed enough to serve as a control on the intuitions commutation affords us about possible and impossible matchings of actor to role. Clearly, casting is subject to powerful ideological constraints. A given role must be filled by someone who possesses or can assume the features felt necessary to sustain it, and both the determination of the features in the script and the organization of their textualisation in the course of filming will be governed by ideological assumptions about what is 'natural' and 'goes without saying'.

In Don Siegel's *The Shootist*, John Wayne plays an aging gunfighter dying of cancer and James Stewart plays the doctor who diagnoses the disease. I have never met anyone who could imagine the casting reversed, yet it's hard to see why. Most people, after some thought, say that they can imagine Stewart in the Wayne role (it helps to think back to Stewart's unmannered performances in Anthony Mann Westerns). What seems 'ungrammatical' is Wayne as a doctor. But what is it that we think we know about doctors that makes Wayne's bundle of traits incompatible with his being one? An adjective which sometimes gets used to describe Wayne is 'rugged': this is not incompatible with delicacy, as any reviewing of *Rio Bravo* reminds us, but it does seem incompatible with the sort of *indoor* and *studied* (the product of study) delicacy of movement that a doctor, especially a surgeon, is felt to need. Of course the frontier doctor in Westerns isn't exactly a Dr. Kildare, but his lack of polish is generally presented as a *decline*, however good-natured, from an earlier level of competence reached 'back East'. The frontier doctor can thus deviate in the direction of a certain ruggedness (often on account of Drink), but he generally retains such unrugged features as – *tall* and – *athletic*. A counter-example in terms of these specific features, Victor Mature's Doc Holiday in Ford's *My Darling Clementine*, is tall and athletic but consumptive, alcoholic and bookish; commuting Wayne with Mature here would be unthinkable.

This would seem to suggest, that, outside the specific generic context of the Hospital drama, the medical profession is somehow not seen as *macho* enough to sustain a central position within the Hollywood narrative. (Think how impossible it is that *The Shootist* be *about* James Stewart.) Yet this is puzzling, because the medical profession clearly does not lack prestige in America. Why should the role of gunman be worth so much more narratively? This is the sort of question that the facts revealed by commutation force us to ask. They are not easily dealt with by any 'reflection' or 'inverted reflection' model of ideology in fiction – whether what is thought to be reflected is the real or the producing culture's ideal.

X

I want to conclude briefly by returning to Brecht's 'fundamental reproach', which was that because in the cinema the role and the performer are one, there is no possibility of introducing the sorts of gap between them that promotes reflection. There is a problem here, but it does not seem to be insuperable if we are prepared to take as our unit of experience of the cinema, not just the text itself as subject to/contributor to a larger system of possibilities and impossibilities which is like, and to a large extent depends upon, our language. This involves recognizing that like language the sign systems of the cinema are never texually embodied all at once: to restrict analysis to the 'text itself', to rule out counter-factual statements on methodological grounds, would be a surrender to dogmatic empiricism.

A limited gap is opened between actor and role, I think, by the star system itself, with its encouragement to the viewer to see a single figure on the screen as both role and star. What is needed to exploit that gap and open it wider is an awareness, which teaching can promote, of the dependence of both role-meaning and star-meaning upon a network of differences correlated with one another in seemingly naturalized, hence suspect, ways. My practical claim for the commutation test is that it promotes in the viewer the right sort of suspicion.

Notes

1 Ben Brewster, 'The fundamental reproach (Brecht)', *Cine-tracts*, no. 2, Summer 1977, pp. 44–53.
2 David Thomson, 'The look on an actor's face', *Sight and Sound*, vol. 46, no. 4, Autumn 1977, pp. 240–44.

3 Roland Barthes, *Elements of Semiology*, London, 1967, p. 65.

4 This is the Oxford English Dictionary's third sense for the word. The first usage it records in this sense is, as so often when concepts which will turn out to be useful to a science of signs are concerned, theological. Hooker in 1597 wrote of 'a kind of mutuall commutation . . . whereby those concrete names God, and Man, when we speake of Christ doe take interchangeably one anothers roome'. The legal sense arises naturally enough: commutation is 'the substitution of a lesser punishment for a greater'.

5 Barthes, op. cit.

6 Giulio C. Lepschy, *A Survey of Structural Linguistics*, London, 1970, p. 72.

7 Barthes, op. cit., p. 66, quotes a machine-translation expert to just this effect: '"The difference between the significations [is] of use, the significations themselves being without importance" (Belevitch).'

8 See Ferdinand de Saussure, *Course in General Linguistics*, London, 1974, pp. 131–34.

9 Note that, if 'the text in movies is the appearance' and the 'result' is really 'unfree and inalterable' absolutely – i.e. if for Thomson the medium intrinsically forces actor and role to coalesce utterly for the spectator – it is hard to see how our question of 'rightness for the part' could even be raised.

10 Quoted in Manuel Alvarado and Edward Buscombe, *Hazell: The Making of a TV Series*, London, 1978, p. 20.

11 Peter Ladefoged, *A Course in Phonetics*, New York, 1975, p. 235.

12 See Roman Jakobson and Morris Halle, *Fundamentals of Language*, The Hague, 1971, or Ladefoged, op. cit., pp. 240–49.

13 Janet Dean Fodor, *Semantics: Theories of Meaning in Generative Grammar*, Hassocks, 1977, p. 144.

14 See Fodor, pp. 143–214 for an up-to-date and detailed account of recent argument in the field.

15 The system in question is clearly rather widespread; exactly the same distribution of smile-types, correlated in the same way to hair-colour, turns up in Rohmer's *Ma Nuit Chez Maud*.

16 *Screen International*, no. 129, 11 March 1978, p. 30.

17 An especially heroic research project in this area is that of Ekman and Friesen, who are endeavouring to specify a Facial Action code by isolating minimal units of muscular activity in the face: '. . . we spent the better part of a year with a mirror, anatomy texts, and cameras. We learned to fire separately the muscles in our own faces.' So far the minimum units isolated number about forty-five, and the researchers have performed and photographed 'between four and five thousand facial combinations' of these units. 'If we wish to learn all the facial actions which signal emotion and those that do not . . . such a method . . . is needed.' See Paul Ekman and Wallace V. Friesen, 'Measuring facial movement', *Environmental Psychology and Nonverbal Behaviour*, no. 1, Fall 1976, pp. 56–75.

18 Cf. Eugene A. Nida, *Componential Analysis of Meaning*, The Hague, 1975, p. 19: 'It would be a mistake to think that one can always describe easily the relations between related meanings. For some sets of meanings there may be no readily available terms with which one can talk about the differences. This is true, for example, of colors. We readily recognise that the colors *violet*, *blue*, *green*, *yellow*, *red*, etc., differ from one another, but we do not have the kind of metalanguage with which we can easily speak about the differences. One could employ technical terminology based on the wavelengths of different colors, but this does not represent the manner in which we normally conceive of color differences.' It would take us too far afield to go into the matter here, but it should be mentioned that both

Wittgenstein and Lacan deny that there could be a true metalanguage for describing human action.

19 *Decoding Advertisements: Ideology and Meaning in Advertising*, London, 1978, p. 25.

20 Ibid., p. 26.

21 Ibid., p. 27.

22 Ibid., p. 25. Smells may be meaningless but they are certainly evocative. For a very interesting discussion of why evocativeness may be raised by the fact that 'there is no semantic field of smells', see Dan Sperber, *Rethinking Symbolism*, Cambridge, 1975, pp. 115–19.

23 '. . . this seems like the reverse of "totemism", where *things* are used to differentiate groups of people . . .', Williamson, op. cit., p. 27.

24 An interesting problem: is there anything 'French' about the image of Catherine Deneuve if her name is taken away? (What happens if the Chanel ad remains just as it is save for the substitution of, say, 'Shirley Saunders for Chanel'?)

25 Stuart Byron (interviewing Robert Aldrich) '"I can't get Jimmy Carter to see my movie!"', *Film Comment*, no. 13, March–April 1977, p. 52.

26 In *The Choirboys* the cluster reappears, but its 'unacceptability' now inscribed within the text itself in the form of the violence of 'bad' sado-masochistic relationship leading to the policeman's shame and suicide.

27 The phrase helps clarify a second Deneuve Chanel ad reproduced by Williamson, op. cit., p. 28, in which a head-and-shoulders photograph of Deneuve with Chanel bottles bears the text 'It's one of the pleasures of being a woman'. The image might be puzzling because Deneuve is unsmiling, stern-looking, not obviously enjoying any 'pleasure' – save, perhaps, that of being 'the great lady'.

28 'The role that got away', *Film Comment*, no. 14, Jan.–Feb. 1978, pp. 42–48.

PART TWO

THE CREATION OF THE FILM ACTOR

Introduction

Early cinema's link to novelty and attractions, rather than narrative or theater, meant that not only actors from vaudeville and theater, but also non-actors caught in actualities, dancers, athletes, models, and other entertainers were put on screen. In the earliest days of cinema, an exhibitor might show one film consisting of documentary footage of a train passing by or a city street, followed by a film of a beautiful barely clad woman dancing, followed by a muscleman modeling his physique, then a stage actor "performing" a monologue in costume. In these early films, it was not only the case that the human subjects were not "ontologically favored" by the camera in relation to other objects, but also that various human subjects were of equal status. Actors and non-actors were on equal footing and neither was recognizably acting, at least not according to the understanding of acting developed in theater. Rather than acting *per se*, the actors who did participate in films were likely to be objects of display, like their non-acting counterparts. Their work on film was viewed as modeling or posing, not acting.

Instead of an organic outgrowth of stage acting, the film actor was virtually an original creation and film acting a novel profession. Whereas the essays in the last section attempted to define the ontological characteristics of the film actor as opposed to the stage actor, the essays in this section examine the transition from stage to screen historically, looking at institutional requirements, labor issues, and aesthetic transformations in light of changing technologies.

Charles Musser's essay traces the changing status of the film actor from film's beginnings to 1915. He details how film acting went from being an anonymous, casual, and intermittent profession—often assumed part-time by stage actors who were embarrassed to be associated with the new low form—to become a full-time profession that rivaled stage acting as a source of recognition, financial reward, and artistic satisfaction. Musser explains how deeply imbricated institutional issues, labor issues, and aesthetic issues were in the creation of the film actor. As film companies increased their rate of production to meet the demands of nickelodeons for story films, they hired permanent stock companies of actors. The regular rotation of actors meant that audiences began to recognize individual players, creating the conditions for a developing star system. Eventually the star system not only altered the structure of the industry, in terms of salary and publicity, but also effected changes in the mode of representation, such as the use of close-ups to focus attention on audience favorites. The rise of the feature film brought artistic respectability to the motion picture and enabled high-profile crossovers from the theater to present their work to the mass market, helping to legitimate the cinema at the same time it provided the actors with new artistic challenges.

Roberta Pearson also focuses on early cinema, and particularly the transitional period between 1908 and 1913 when film's narrative techniques were reformulated. Her essay analyzes how actors in the films of D. W. Griffith gradually shifted from a "histrionic" mode of performance derived from nineteenth-century theater to a "verisimilar" style that approximated contemporary perceptions of realistic behavior. "Histrionic" acting adopted conventionalized gestures to externalize emotion and substitute for language. Rather than a simple or static style, however, "histrionic" performance could include a range of gestures, from very small to very broad, or, as Pearson says, "checked" to "unchecked." The "verisimilar" code dropped more conventionalized codes of gesture from the histrionic style in favor of more individualized gestures. It included greater use of props, smaller gestures, and more attention to the face and eyes. Arguing against a strict model of evolution, Pearson argues that the histrionic and verisimilar existed alongside one another until about 1912 when the verisimilar code largely displaced the histrionic, though the histrionic was still used for moments of great emotional intensity.

Ben Brewster and Lea Jacobs also examine the convergence of "realistic" styles and what they call "pictorial" styles in film acting during the transitional period from 1908 to 1912. But they argue that posing, a feature of Pearson's "histrionic" code, should not be theoretically opposed to realism or viewed as a precursor to realism. Instead, Brewster and Jacobs suggest that theatrical styles of posing are modified to accommodate film technique. For instance, they argue that the lack of sound, the relatively small size of the actor's image—due to the great figure/camera distance and small exhibition screen—and compressed duration of a one-reel narrative may have led stage actors to adopt a *more* emphatic use of gesture in film than they would have employed on stage. Ultimately, by 1912, new editing techniques begin to interfere with the actor's performance and displaced some of the traditional functions associated with acting, such as directing the viewer's attention within a space, underscoring dramatic situations or regulating the pace of a scene. According to Brewster and Jacobs, it is not the case that editing *permitted* a verisimilar style, but the pace of a highly edited film virtually *required* it.

While the creation of the film actor and a film acting aesthetic may seem to have been fully developed by the time the classical style was established, Cynthia Baron's essay suggests that the creation of the film actor was an ongoing process and that acting professionals were still responding to new challenges in studio productions of the 1930s and 1940s. First, Baron describes how the transition to sound transformed production practices. As sound created an increasing demand for actors trained on stage, sound cinema ironically created competition with theater and led to the decline of stage productions, thus depleting acting labor resources and forcing film studios to develop other ways of training talent. No longer able to rely on a steady stream of stage actors, studios adopted their own increasingly systematic methods for training actors. Then, film performances were the result of an increased division of labor as dialogue coaches, dialogue directors, drama coaches, and drama schools became an integral, but hidden, part of the production process. Interestingly, with augmented focus on actor training, stage acting and screen acting were no longer viewed as fundamentally different. Acting professionals found ways to integrate techniques developed in silent cinema with techniques and principles of stage acting. In particular, film acting teachers and coaches advocated strategies derived from, or closely resembling, the Moscow Art Theatre and Stanislavki's system.

The Changing Status of the Actor

4

CHARLES MUSSER

> The Kalem Girl is charming,
> And fair as the flowers in May.
> Her eyes are the sweetest upon the screen:
> They have stolen my heart away[1]

The year 1915 was one of accomplishment and triumph for the still young film industry. D. W. Griffith's *The Birth of A Nation* was released and quickly hailed as cinema's first masterwork. Poet Vachel Lindsay published *The Art of the Moving Picture*, comparing the movie house to an art gallery, while Harvard philosopher Hugo Münsterberg wrote *The Photoplay: A Psychological Study*, contending that cinema was a major art form of the twentieth century. In less than twenty years, film practice had undergone an astounding series of transformations which made this new recognition possible. The changing role and status of the film actor was one aspect of these transformations.[2]

When projected moving pictures were a novelty, in 1896, an exhibitor's program might follow one scene of Annabelle Moore dancing against a black background with another view of a wave crashing against the shore. These subjects were of equal status: only in later years would the subject of such "scenics" become the background for the actor's performance. Until at least 1904, production personnel, nonprofessionals, and stage actors took turns performing for the camera. J. Stuart Blackton and Albert Smith alternated working behind and in front of the camera—with Blackton playing the tramp in *Burglar on the Roof* (Vitagraph, 1898) and Smith acting as magician in *The Vanishing Lady* (Vitagraph, 1898). The woman-on-the-street whose dress is lifted by air from a subway grate in *What Happened on Twenty-Third Street* (Edison, 1901) is on a par with the skilled performer in *Trapeze Disrobing Act* (Edison, 1901).

With the rise of story films in 1903–04, actors became a more important part of film production. *Rube and Mandy at Coney Island* (Edison, 1903) is a transitional film in this regard. In many scenes, Coney Island served as a backdrop for the performers' comic business, but in others the scenic impulse was still dominant. By the time of *The Suburbanite* (Biograph, 1904), the comic characters had assumed a more central position in the mise-en-scène. As a result, the actor's skills were increasingly called upon to create a rudimentary character. Although motion picture acting thus began to emerge as a more unified practice, the motion picture actor as such did not as yet exist. Theatrical personnel usually worked with production companies only for brief periods of time. Stage actor Will Rising was "in hard luck" when he appeared as the judge in *The Kleptomaniac* (Edison, 1905).[3] When the Edison Company made *Daniel Boone* (1906), producer Edwin S. Porter and stage manager Wallace McCutcheon hired many of their actors from a theatrical troupe presenting the Wild West show *Pioneer Days* at the New York Hippodrome. Porter and McCutcheon had to adapt their schedule to the actors' principal commitment—the show. To complete their cast, the two collaborators also had a casting call for this one film. In this way, film companies treated each film as an individual project and hired actors on a per film basis. Film acting was part-time, occasional work: a way for stage actors to supplement their income. It also was a form of anonymous employment in most circumstances. A film company rarely revealed the names of its cast: high-toned projects were among the few exceptions.

The casual, intermittent relationship between actors and film companies, prevalent before 1907, proved impractical as these companies increased their rate of production to meet the nickelodeon theaters' insatiable demands for one-reel story films. Efficient production required producers to create permanent stock companies of actors. Film acting soon became salaried employment, requiring a full-time commitment. Actress Gene Gauntier, who had enjoyed some prominence in repertory theater, agonized over her decision to stay with the Kalem Company on a long-term basis.[4] When it came down to making a final choice, players were often persuaded by the steady income received from film work. By 1908, there was a growing group of people who had become professional moving picture actors.

The decision to enter the film industry on a permanent basis was a particularly complicated one for actors conscious of the cinema's low status. Prestigious newspapers such as the *Chicago Tribune* asserted that films shown in nickelodeons encouraged wickedness and "not a single thing connected with them had influence for good."[5] In addition, film acting was considered less artistically demanding than stage performance. David Belasco saw cinema as a pale imitation of the theater, a form of entertainment that would soon lose its popularity. With moving pictures "the audience would always be wholly wanting the indescribable bond of sympathy which existed between the actor and his audience."[6] Action, not acting, was considered the keynote of motion pictures, and cinema apparently required neither the character psychology nor the actor's personality that stage performers brought to their work.

Even as critics were dismissing the film actor's profession, changes in film practice were actively reshaping the actor's role. Fiction films were heavily indebted (both directly and indirectly) to other narrative forms such as the novel, short story, and dramatic work. Story construction assumed a clear hierarchy of characters. For example, *Foul Play* (Vitagraph, 1906) focuses on three primary characters: a man who is framed for a crime, the man's wife, and the villain. The film also includes several secondary characters, such as the bank owner, as well as a cast of bit players. Upon such a hierarchy, the motion picture "star system" was to be constructed. Star systems in related practices such as theater and vaudeville, a cultural preoccupation with authorship, and the audience's desire for realistic yet larger-than-life heroes were just some of the added factors that made this development "logical" and even "natural."

From 1907 through 1909, an implicit contradiction existed between the film narratives with their hierarchy of characters and the methods of production which treated every actor the same way—at least all were paid the same amount. Actors were either regular members of a stock company or day players. Yet the stock company system meant that some actors appeared weekly in a studio's offerings. Regular moviegoers soon recognized leading players and nicknamed them "The Vitagraph Girl" (Florence Turner), "The Kalem Girl" (Gene Gauntier), or "The Biograph Girl" (first Florence Lawrence, later Marion Leonard and Mary Pickford).

Changes in representation techniques enhanced those very qualities that were said to be the mark of a successful stage performance. Biograph director D. W. Griffith, in particular, introduced a more restrained, realistic acting style which developed the psychology of his characters. As he and other directors moved their cameras closer to the performers, the actors' personalities came through with increasing strength. By early 1910, one prominent critic asserted that

> a competent actor or actress has practically the same chance of coming to the front on the motion picture stage as he or she has on the ordinary stage. That is what they are doing. So it comes about that the personalities of these good people are of growing interest to the public.[7]

Increasingly the spectator was experiencing not only a character and his/her psychology, but the personality of the actor who created that character as well. One need only contrast Lou Delaney's performances in *Foul Play* (Vitagraph, 1906) and *A Tin-Type Romance* (Vitagraph, 1910) to see the changes wrought in the intervening years.

Production companies, trade papers, and exhibitors were flooded with questions about audience favorites—not only their names, but their marital status. During late 1909, when the Edison Company found itself at a commercial disadvantage with films that were not very popular, the company sought to exploit this interest by featuring its principal players in promotional materials.[8] Such practices were not only designed to popularize company performers, but, by emphasizing the actors' experience with prestigious theatrical companies, they increased the prestige of moving pictures in general and Edison subjects in particular. A few months later, Kalem made another breakthrough: they offered exhibitors a lobby display with the names and pictures of its players. Despite the success of this innovation, *Moving Picture World* cautioned, "While the pictures have attained a distinct prominence in the theatrical field and are now regarded as a standard attraction, the people playing the parts in them are very sensitive about having their identity become known. . . . They have an undisguised impression that the step from regular productions to the scenes before the camera is a backwards one."[9]

Leading actors were increasingly treated as stars, at least on a rudimentary level. Competitive bidding for the services of leading players began in December 1909, when Carl Laemmle hired away Biograph Girl Florence Lawrence for his Independent Moving Picture Company (IMP) and announced that she would be known as the IMP girl. That March, St. Louis newspapers suddenly reported the death of Miss Lawrence. Her many admirers were distraught, and Laemmle, who was almost certainly responsible for this misinformation, capitalized on the publicity with a special tour for his very much alive star.[10] The Vitagraph Company responded to this competitive move by holding "A Vitagraph Night for the Vitagraph Girl" in Brooklyn, New York. The patrons in the jammed theater sang choruses of the popular song "The Vitagraph Girl" and demanded an encore so they could sing it again.[11] Such reactions gave the emerging stars new confidence. When Kalem Girl Gene Gauntier was asked if she had given up the stage, she responded,

> Why I haven't given it up. There is just as much art in moving picture acting, and more scope for individuality—and certainly fewer who can do it well, besides a greater field. Who knows what will be the status of the motion picture actor in ten years? It is on the flood while the theatrical situation, to put it mildly, is uncertain.[12]

Her faith was to be quickly confirmed.

When Florence Lawrence left Biograph for IMP, Mary Pickford soon took her place. A reviewer commented on "the pleasing kittenish playfulness of the little lady that played ingenue parts" at Biograph and predicted that "she has a future if she doesn't permit her head to get swelled."[13] When Lawrence left IMP for the Lubin Company late in 1910, Laemmle lured Pickford away from Biograph by offering a salary of $175 a week. Laemmle, who understood the commercial possibilities of star power better than most of his contemporaries, did not try to promote her as the next IMP girl, but as Mary Pickford. More than a leading player, she was a star in her own right. Many of her IMP films, such as *The Dream* (1911), were star vehicles. The story's principal function was to foreground Pickford's personality, as the actress became the dominant element of the film. In a marketing ploy, Laemmle, after firmly establishing that Pickford was at IMP, stopped associating her with any specific films in his advertisements. Film exchanges were forced to purchase all the IMP films if they were to get all the Pickford films.

Between 1908 and 1911, only truly dedicated spectators or "fanatics," followed the careers of leading players. Even for this group, information was hard to gather. In February 1911, however, the *New York Telegraph* added a motion picture section to its Sunday editions, featuring portraits of leading players from all the companies. Vitagraph's J. Stuart Blackton also started the monthly *Motion Picture Story Magazine* which presented film narratives re-written as short stories and published photographs and brief biographies of the stars. Both publications were designed for spectators rather than for members of the industry.

Increasingly exhibitors were urged to "play up the personality of the player." To aid their efforts, the Edison Company began to advertise the names of leading actors for each of its films—this by July 1911.[14] The projection of slides as a primitive trailer or coming attraction was one approach: "Run a slide that you've a Vitagraph coming with Miss Turner, and then flash Miss Turner's slide. It is more than doubly effective."[15] Soon the business of promotion was too important to leave to the exhibitor who might—or might not—provide his patrons with the desired information. By mid-1912 several companies were using head titles to credit the leading actors. Edison, still struggling with its relatively unpopular films, went even further and introduced each player with a title caption when he or she first appeared on screen.[16] Short subjects, such as *Ancient Temples of Egypt* (Kalem, 1912), which showed the Kalem stock company visiting the Egyptian ruins, were ways to show actors "behind the scenes" and arouse even greater interest in their private lives as well as on-screen performances. Such innovations in promotion enabled the casual moviegoer to identify the players on the screen.

Biograph, in contrast to virtually all the other companies, refused to divulge even the names of its leading performers. This prompted one angry fan to write,

> How do you feel when, attending a play on the legitimate stage, the stupid usher forgets to give you a programme? Rather uncomfortable, eh? You feel like giving Mr. Usher a good, swift kick. At present the Biograph Company is playing the role of the stupid

> usher—ruining their otherwise good photoplays by the stupid narrow-minded policy of "reticence" that they foolishly adhere to.[17]

Film companies faced a terrible dilemma over the best ways to exploit their key actors. On one hand, "the manufacturer cannot be blamed for wanting to preserve the incognito of player and producer, for the instinct of self-preservation is a natural law and the 'star' system invariably creates abuses" such as salary demands. On the other, "the manufacturer can only avail himself of the advantage derived from the exploitation of personality since the situation has run away from him."[18] While Biograph argued that the company, not the individual players, was the guarantee of quality, its director, Griffith, assured the company's continued favor by turning one actor after another into a popular player. These "anonymous stars" were a contradiction in terms, and the Biograph Company lost many players, tired of anonymity, to its competitors. This was a luxury none of its rivals could afford. Biograph was a classic case of uneven development: advances in one area (Griffith's directorial innovations) allowed the company to be unresponsive in others (promotion).

As the star system emerged, it altered the structure of the industry. By 1911–12, a name player was often the most important commercial element, and salaries reflected this shift. They were said to run from $35 to $75 a week for regular players but up to $400 and $500 in the case of stars.[19] Elite actors justified their cost. When the Majestic Company appeared in late 1911, its success was assured because Mary Pickford was joining the organization—leaving behind Laemmle whose $175 a week must have begun to seem paltry. By the second half of 1912, stars were using their enhanced status to start their own production companies. Gene Gauntier and director Sidney Olcott left Kalem to form the Gene Gauntier Feature Players Company, while Helen Gardner left Vitagraph for a similar purpose. These "authors" of leading roles used their position to claim authorship of the overall film.[20]

The emergence of the star system also had an impact on the mode of representation. Close-ups and other compositional strategies, which were largely absent in films of 1908–09, were developed by directors who were not only interested in telling a clear, logical story but in focusing attention on their popular performers. Griffith's *The Old Actor* (Biograph, 1912) is an interesting deviation from this dominant approach. Mary Pickford, who had rejoined Biograph, was the film's obvious star personality, but she was made to play a supporting role. Moreover, when Griffith uses a closer view, he moves in on the old actor, not Pickford. The director isolates a particular moment when the central character, played by W. Christie Miller (himself an old actor), reads Shakespeare.[21] Role and reality converge.

Within a few years, the film industry had produced and pushed to new extremes a star system similar to that in other cultural practices, notably the theater. This, however, did not mean the acceptance of cinema as an art form by "the better classes of the community." When interviewing the newspaper editors who were not only members of these elite classes but helped to shape their opinion, *Moving Picture World* found that "the present status of the motion picture came in for much hostile criticism," although the opinion makers felt "the pictures will do greater and better things in the future."[22] As Clayton Hamilton then observed as he reflected on cinema's cultural status, "the domain of criticism is co-extensive with the domain of art."[23] Until prominent newspapers reviewed films as cultural works instead of citing them as disturbing examples of low culture, the cinema could not be considered a serious art form. Late in 1911, the *New York Tribune* was still complaining about the film industry's excessive depiction of elopements; it was not until late 1915 or early 1916 that leading members of the New York press—the *Herald*, *Tribune*, *World*, and *Times*—finally offered this kind of attention to select films.

One of the developments crucial to film's elevation in status was the appearance of the feature film. It "raised the moving picture to a plane on which it has won the admiration and loyalty of millions of new followers."[24] Many of these early subjects came from Europe. When the Italian-made *Dante's Inferno* was released in the United States during 1911 in five reels (approximately an hour and a half), it was shown at legitimate theaters with ticket prices as high as seventy-five cents.[25] One particularly important group of films starred Sarah Bernhardt: *Camille* (over two reels, Franco American Film Company, advertised in the United States in February 1912), *Queen Elizabeth* (3 reels, Famous Players Film Company, July 1912) and *La Tosca* (Universal Features, October 1912). Adolph Zukor, theatrical producer Daniel Frohman, and Edwin Porter acquired the American rights to *Queen Elizabeth* and with it convinced James O'Neill, James Hackett, and other theater stars to appear in feature-length adaptations of successful plays. As Zukor explained, "When they learned the elaborate manner in which we are going to stage their productions, their attitude changed. They saw that it would be to their advantage, that it would arouse popular interest not only in their productions but in their personalities as well."[26] Unlike the many American players who had defected to the motion picture industry in previous years, these actors were immensely successful in the theater, catering to the cultural tastes of the "better classes." Their acceptance of cinema, even as a means to record their stage performances for posterity, was an important step that was noted in the press. *Prisoner of Zenda* (Famous Players Film Company, 1913) with James Hackett was even reviewed favorably in New York newspapers. As the *World* observed, "The exhibition was unexpectedly successful for it sustained the interest and suspense of the audience to the end."[27]

When asked about the attitude of the most successful stars toward moving pictures, Daniel Frohman responded, "Most of them are trying to figure out how they can become photoplayers with the most possible grace and with the least possible loss of dignity. But they will soon come to it."[28] The formation of the Jesse L. Lasky Feature Film Motion Picture Company in December 1913 offered such an opportunity for many players. Its first film, *The Squaw Man* (February 1914) was based on a well-known stage play, starred the renowned stage actor Dustin Farnum, and was heartily praised in the press. Four months later Lasky acquired the motion picture rights to Belasco's past and future theatrical productions including *The Girl of the Golden West*.[29] The original stage actors were supposed to re-create their roles whenever possible. While this did not always happen, the Lasky company gained access to actors associated with Belasco. In the case of Cecil B. DeMille's film adaptation, *The Girl of the Golden West* (January 1915), the performances were declared to equal those in the original play. After seeing the film, Belasco praised it and another adaptation as "decidedly artistic successes" and acknowledged that the medium could achieve a realism that eluded him on the stage. The "merciless eye" of the camera could be more demanding than the stage in settings and even—although this went unstated—for actors.[30]

Even before *The Birth of A Nation* was released in February 1915, Frohman articulated an increasingly common position. He claimed that theatrical stars making the transition to film "can degrade their art by appearing in silly and inconsequential subjects, but they can assist themselves as well as their art of the theatre by appearing in dignified dramatic productions."[31] Because moving pictures had a much larger audience base, actors could use the cinema to increase the size of their following. Frohman was also implying that the ideal actor was someone who could move back and forth between theater and moving pictures. As 1915 began, film not only rivaled theater as a source of recognition and financial reward, but, it was felt, offered actors a different kind of artistic challenge.

Notes

1 *New York Dramatic Mirror* (5 June 1912), p. 26.
2 Aspects of the star system have been described by other film historians, including Richard Dyer, *Stars* (London: British Film Institute, 1979); and Janet Staiger, "Seeing Stars," *Velvet Light Trap* (Summer 1983), pp. 10–14.
3 Richard Outcault to Edwin S. Porter, 3 or 4 March 1904, Porter Affidavit, Edison National Historic Site, Edison, New Jersey.
4 Gene Gauntier, "Blazing the Trail," unpublished manuscript, Museum of Modern Art.
5 *Chicago Tribune*, 10 April 1907 (reprinted in *Moving Picture World* [20 April 1907], p. 101).
6 "Films and the Drama," *Film Index* (5 September 1908), p. 4.
7 "On the Screen," *Moving Picture World* (3 February 1910), p. 167.
8 *Edison Kinetogram* (1 October 1909), p. 13; and ibid. (15 October 1909), p. 13.
9 "Photographs of Moving Picture Actors. A New Method of Lobby Advertising," *Moving Picture World* (15 January 1910), p. 50.
10 "The IMP Leading Lady," *Moving Picture World* (2 April 1910), p. 517.
11 "A Vitagraph Night for the Vitagraph Girl," *Film Index* (23 April 1910), p. 3.
12 "The Kalem Girl," *Film Index* (7 May 1910), p. 3.
13 *New York Dramatic Mirror* (16 April 1910), p. 18.
14 *Moving Picture World* (15 July 1911), p. 58.
15 "Advertising for Exhibitors," *Moving Picture World* (18 October 1911), p. 195.
16 *New York Dramatic Mirror* (29 May 1912), p. 24.
17 *New York Dramatic Mirror* (18 October 1911), p. 28.
18 "Credit Where Credit is Due," *Moving Picture World* (14 October 1911), p. 107.
19 *Motion Picture Story Magazine* (August 1911), p. 144.
20 Michel Foucault, "What is an Author?" in *Language, Counter-memory and Practice* ed. Donald F. Bouchard (Ithaca Cornell Press, 1977); and Robert Arnold, Nicholas P. Humy, and Ana M. Lopez, "Rereading Adaptation: A Farewell to Arms," *Iris* 1, no. 1 (1983), pp. 101–13.
21 Miller was the second oldest actor in the film business in 1913: *Moving Picture World* (12 April 1913), p. 152.
22 *Moving Picture World* (9 December 1911), p. 792.
23 Clay Hamilton in *The Bookman*, quoted in "Sign of the Harvest," *Moving Picture World* (5 August 1911), pp. 272–73.
24 "Achievements of 1911," *Moving Picture World* (13 January 1912), p. 106.
25 *Moving Picture World* (26 August 1911), p. 530.
26 "Achievements of 1911," *Moving Picture World* (13 January 1912), p. 106.
27 "Complete Play in Movies," *New York World* (19 February 1913), p. 7.
28 *Moving Picture World* (26 October 1912), p. 335.

29 "Lasky Gets Belasco Plays," *Moving Picture World* (6 June 1914), p. 1412.
30 "Pictures and Stage Totally Different," *New York Telegraph* (10 January 1915), p. 1D.
31 "Film Work Great for Actors," interview with Daniel Frohman, *New York Telegraph* (1 January 1915), p. 5.

The Histrionic and Verisimilar Codes in the Biograph Films

5

ROBERTA PEARSON

The histrionic code

Film scholars may increasingly supplement textual analysis with knowledge of how a particular text both relates to other texts and functions in the larger culture, but close formalist analysis still remains an important methodology in cinema studies and other disciplines. Even Tony Bennett and Janet Woollacott, who believe that the text is "an inconceivable object," nonetheless do not suggest that "texts have no determinate properties—such as a definite order of narrative progression—which may be analyzed objectively."[1] In this chapter [. . .] I shall focus on these "determinate properties." [. . .]

It may help to begin by formulating some general principles about the actors' use of the histrionic code at various points in the early Biographs. Most shots in these films fall into one of five categories:

1 the tableau;
2 everyday activity;
3 conversations;
4 heightened emotions and action scenes with more than one performer; and
5 gestural soliloquies in which an actor emotes while alone in the frame.[2]

As a rule, the performances in these categories tend to range from the checked to the unchecked histrionic code.

1 *Modified tableau*. Although the Biographs borrowed the tableau from the stage melodrama, they somewhat modified its usage. In the theatre, performers used the tableau to convey intense emotions in nonverbal form, freezing in place with arms fully extended outward, downward, or upward at an act's climax. A contemporary print depicting the second act of *East Lynne* shows the actors in the act-ending tableau: In the center a man sits in a chair, hands clasping head in an agony of despair. A young girl kneels at his feet, her right hand reaching up in supplication. To the left, an elderly gentleman has both hands raised high above his head in an appeal-to-heaven posture. To the right, a stern woman points at the girl with her left hand, while her right hand is held perpendicular to her body, the finger pointing to the door in one of the most parodied of all histrionic gestures.[3]

Obviously, the Biographs retained the goal of expressing strong emotion in nonverbal fashion but somewhat modified the technique. The actors eschewed fully extended gestures and kept their arms close to their bodies, expressing emotional intensity through a comparative lack of movement rather than absolute stillness. The only motionless tableau in the Biographs occurs in *A Corner in Wheat* (1909) at the moment when the poor line up to buy the overpriced bread and become perfectly motionless, contrasting with the frenzied activity of the Wheat King's party.

Usually, the actors make small gestures that contrast markedly with the more common broad gestures of the histrionic code and thus convey the impression of relative motionlessness. In the last shot of *A Drunkard's Reformation*, Arthur Johnson and Linda Arvidson sit in front of the fire with their little girl. The child sits on the floor before her father's chair, the mother sits on the arm of the chair. Arvidson has her arm around Johnson, and they hold hands. With his free hand, Johnson gestures to the girl, as if to credit her with his reformation.

2 *Everyday activity*. In scenes of everyday activity characters are shown going about their normal routine prior to the introduction of narrative disequilibrium. They might be shown at work, like the farmers plowing their fields in the opening shot of *A Corner in Wheat*, or at home, like the happy family at the beginning of *The Lonely Villa* (1909). In these shots, gesture helps to establish a character and that character's relation to other characters. The characters often handle props, such as books, or the tools of their trade, that prevent fully extended outward movements.[4] Gestures tend to be close to the body, fairly slow, unstressed, and not held for any significant time.

In the first shot of *Lady Helen's Escapade* (1909), Florence Lawrence portrays a bored, wealthy woman. She sits in a chair beside a table on which her arm rests, her hand dangling loosely over the front. When a maid offers food, she rejects it with a languid wave of the hand. Then she heaves a sigh, shoulders visibly moving, and yawns. All her gestures are slow, and with the exception of the wave, her arms and hands stay close to her body.

3 *Conversation*. In the Biographs, conversations among characters involve a great many gestures of a type we might call, to use a semantic term, "diectic" or "anaphoric"—the gestural equivalent of verbal "shifters," personal pronouns and words indicating place, such as *here* and *there*.[5] In the films, these meanings are expressed by inward movements, indicating I or *here*, and outward movements, indicating *you*, *there*, or similar ideas. In *A Convict's Sacrifice* (1909), the released convict, James Kirkwood, talks to a laborer, Henry Walthall, who is eating his lunch. Kirkwood points to the food and to himself and Walthall hands him the dinner pail. Then Walthall asks his boss to hire Kirkwood, pointing at himself and then the convict, as if to vouch for his behavior.

Conversational gestures usually fall somewhere between the contained stillness of the tableau and the frantic extended movement of the gestural soliloquy. In *The Voice of the Violin* (1909), Arthur Johnson proposes to Marion Leonard. He declares himself with both hands on his chest, then extends his arms one on either side of the woman. No, she says, with her hand on her chest, then points to him, then puts her hand back on her chest. We can see the gradual modifications in the histrionic code by looking at another marriage proposal, from a film released the following year: In *A Summer Idyl* (1910), Walthall proposes to a society woman (Stephanie Longfellow), who rejects him. He leans closer to her, his hand on his chest, then extends his other hand to her palm up. Then he takes her hand in both of his. She says no, and he pleads with right hand extended to her, left hand on his chest, the fingers relaxed. All his motions are slow and graceful, and his arms are never fully extended outward like Johnson's.

Because Walthall stresses his gestures less than Johnson, the performance does not connote the same degree of theatricality. This becomes clear in comparing the way each actor places his hands on his chest. Johnson uses both hands with the palms flattened, to modern eyes parodying a lover declaring himself, as the pose absolutely reeks of theatricality. Walthall places one hand lightly on his chest, the palm slightly raised and fingers slightly cupped. Though Walthall employs a conventional gesture, the lack of emphasis reduces the deliberate self-consciousness of the histrionic code.

4 *Heightened emotions and action scenes*. Categories 4 and 5 most closely resemble the stereotyped ideas of "melodramatic" acting, as performers tend to resort more to the unchecked histrionic code. The arms are fully extended upward, outward, or downward, the gestures are often more heavily stressed and quickly performed than in everyday activities or conversation, and poses are held longer. In *A Test of Friendship* (1909), Arthur Johnson receives the news that he has been ruined (financially, not morally, this latter being a woman's prerogative). His hands clutch his head and then come down, fingers spread, as his arms are held straight out to his sides. He bows his head, and his hands drop to his sides. He then looks up and clenches his fists.

In *The Call of the Wild* (1908), we see two performers enacting heightened emotions. A woman (Florence Lawrence) rejects the proposal of a "civilized Indian" (he wears a suit and attends parties). The veneer of civilization immediately vanishing, the rejected suitor (Charles Inslee) leads an Indian band on the warpath, captures his beloved, and proceeds to work his will upon her. He kisses her, and she falls to her knees, arms outstretched. Her left hand points to her chest and then to heaven, while her right hand points to him. He points to his Indian followers, as if to say, "I am one of them." She points to heaven again, her arm straight up and fully extended. Finally seeing the light, he raises both arms, sinks to his knees, lowers his head on his arms. She then points off screen right, as if to say, "Come back with me." Here we see a mixture of the diectic gesture and the unchecked histrionic code.

5 *Gestural soliloquies*. In the gestural soliloquy, the quality of the gesture remains the same as with heightened emotions, but the quantity increases. In the previous category, no single performer enacts an elaborate series of gestures because the other actors collaborate in creating an emotional effect or in telling the story. Gestural soliloquies often occur at emotional high points in which the characters undergo emotional catharsis. The characters in this situation often have only one point to make: "I am angry," "I am grief-stricken," or "I am desperate," and employ a series of gestures (sometimes repeating the same gesture), all of which express the same state of mind. While narratively redundant, the cumulative effect of the gestures is to increase the emotional impact, in keeping with the heightened emotional states characteristic of the melodramatic form. Though this repetition runs counter to injunctions against "the useless multiplication of gesture," each gesture remains distinctly separate, preserving the digital nature of the histrionic code.

[. . .]

The gestural soliloquy was also used to trace a character's thought processes, though the verisimilar code would better suit this function. In this case, rather than simply heightening emotional effect, the soliloquies serve to advance the narrative. In *A Burglar's Mistake* (1909), a husband (Harry Solter) contemplates suicide. As he holds the gun, he sees a toy that his young child has left in his office. He gestures to the door with his free hand, his arm extended behind him. Then he makes a fist in the air and brings his arm sharply down and up in a semi-circle as he decides on a course of action. Note, however, that the performer's gestures might be incomprehensible without the presence of the toy, showing precisely how difficult it is to discuss performance in isolation from other signifying practices.

The verisimilar code

Describing the operation of the verisimilar code in the Biographs presents a more daunting task than describing the histrionic. Because the verisimilar code was intended to mimic reality and create individual characterizations, one cannot turn to mechanical formulations and prescriptions such as are found in the histrionic-code instruction manuals. Nor can one evolve general categories, illustrating each with examples, as with the histrionic code. But the discussion of the theatrical verisimilar code in the previous chapter, in conjunction with the recent work of film scholars, can point to the key characteristics of the verisimilar code in the Biograph films. As we have seen from looking at the verisimilar code in the theatre, byplay and props formed an important part of this performance style. In addition, as Gunning, Thompson, and Staiger have all asserted, use of the face and eyes constituted an extremely important component of the new style of acting in the cinema, which makes sense given the differences between the two media.[6]

The New York Hat (1912) seems a particularly appropriate starting point for the discussion of the verisimilar code, because . . . [it] contributed to Griffith's reputation among film scholars as the originator of "subtle, restrained" acting. It also features Mary Pickford, one of the "Griffith actresses" whom posterity has judged to excel at the new style, and Lionel Barrymore, a Broadway-trained actor in one of his first film roles. Both Barrymore and Pickford have scenes in which the characters' thoughts are revealed through a combination of gesture, expressions, glances, and props, so that we can begin our discussion with a look at two sequences that combine all the key components of the verisimilar code.[7]

Just before her death, Pickford's mother writes a letter requesting that her minister, Barrymore, buy her daughter an occasional gift. Barrymore buys Pickford the fancy New York hat of the title. The town gossips immediately begin to circulate slanderous rumors, and Pickford's harsh father tears up the hat. All ends happily as the misunderstanding is cleared up, and Barrymore and Pickford seem destined for a rosy future.

In the second shot of the film, Barrymore opens the mother's letter and the packet of money that accompanies it. As he reads the letter, his mouth opens in surprise. He picks up the money with a thoughtful expression and looks straight out, almost at the camera, while holding the money. He looks at the letter again and laughs. Placing his hand flat on the desk, he mouths "I'll do it." He nods his head "yes" and looks at the letter again while smiling.

In a four-shot scene, Pickford examines her old hat, decides it won't do, and asks her father for a new one. In the first shot, the standard three-quarter shot of 1912, the father sits at his desk on the left and Pickford stands on the right side of the frame, her right hand at her side and her head slightly tilted as she looks up at a mirror on the wall next to her and straightens her jacket. In a cut to a medium shot, Pickford takes a hat off the wall and brushes off the top with a sad expression. She puts the hat on, examines her reflection, and glances in the direction of her father. An intertitle states, "Daddy, can I have a new hat?" In three-quarter shot again, Pickford stands with one hand out to her father and the other touching her hat, but he gestures her away. In another cut to medium shot, Pickford takes a pair of gloves from a hook near a mirror, and straightens the mirror. She arranges the gloves in her left hand, smiles, and looks in the mirror. Looking doubtful, she takes the hat off, hangs it up, and shakes her head. Again she looks in the mirror, looks at the gloves, smiles and smooths her hair with her hand. Even without the intertitle, Pickford's performance clearly establishes her character's decision to ask for the hat and her shifting emotions, as she first tries to make do with the old hat and then decides to do the best she can without it.

Although the various elements of the code all work together to externalize mental processes, as in the above example, one can better understand the actual operation of the verisimilar code by isolating, insofar as possible, each component. We start by examining several examples of byplay, the small, realistic touches the actors called "bits of business," which are the performance equivalents of Barthes's realistic effect.[8]

The God Within (1912), with Henry Walthall, Lionel Barrymore, Blanche Sweet, and Claire McDowell, recounts the intertwined fates of two couples. Barrymore seduces Sweet and leaves her pregnant, while Walthall's wife, McDowell, announces to her husband that she too is expecting a child. McDowell dies in childbirth, Sweet's baby is born dead, Sweet acts as a wet nurse to the motherless child, and all turns out well as Walthall and Sweet form a family at the end. The acting of the principals is verisimilarly coded, and all four employ bits of business in their interchanges with other characters.

Near the start of the film, Barrymore comes to tell Sweet that he is leaving town. She sits alone, waiting for him, and when she hears his knock, wipes away her tears, clasps her hands in her lap, and smiles. As they talk, she stands close to him, her hand stroking his lapel, and then leans closer to whisper that she is pregnant. Barrymore rubs the back of his neck in perplexity and then gestures to the door with his thumb. As McDowell tells Walthall that she is pregnant her actions are similar to Sweet's. She takes his sleeve, fingers his collar, puts a hand on his shoulder, and whispers in his ear. When the doctor proposes to Walthall that he take Sweet into his home, Walthall scratches the back of his neck as he thinks. At the film's end, Barrymore comes to Walthall's cabin and proposes to Sweet. Walthall returns home and also proposes to her. Sweet picks Walthall, signaling her decision by taking his hand. The two men converse over the seated woman, and, as they talk, Sweet tilts her head so that her cheek touches her and Walthall's linked hands, the small gesture registering her character's fulfillment and happiness.

These kinds of small gestures can be combined to create the verisimilar equivalent of the gestural soliloquy, in which characters express intense emotions. But while the intent is the same, the nature of the gestures is vastly different. In *The Lesser Evil* (1911), Blanche Sweet is trapped in a boat's cabin, with only the captain standing between her and a crew of would-be rapists. She stands at the cabin door, hands around the bolt, looking upward and perfectly still except for the slight movement of her hands on the bolt. She then reloads the captain's gun, opens the door to hand him the weapon, then rebolts the door. She leans against the door, her right hand on the bolt and left hand to her face.

The impact of this scene admittedly depends on her expression as well as her gestures, but Biograph actors were fully capable of fulfilling Strindberg's wish that important scenes be acted with the back to the audience. To return to *The God Within*, Walthall has a gestural soliloquy at his wife's deathbed. His hat in his hand, he looks down at his wife and baby while he raises his hat to his mouth as if to stifle a sob. He turns his back to the camera, showing only about one-quarter of his face in profile, bows his head, and raises his hand to his eyes.

After a moment, he turns slightly back, wipes his eyes, looks down again, and kneels at the bedside. He rests his head on his upraised hand while his fingers pull at his hair. Until he kneels, we do not get a good view of his face, and his grief is indicated by posture and hand movements alone.

The byplay in *The God Within* externalizes thoughts and emotions and delineates character. But "bits of business" could also directly establish character type or create psychological complexity. In *The Broken Cross* (1911), the residents of a boarding house include a gum-chewing, slovenly servant girl and a hip-swinging, eye-batting manicurist. In *The God Within*, Barrymore reveals his character's bravado and untrustworthiness by hooking his thumbs in his waistcoat pockets. [. . .]

Byplay also entailed the use of props. [. . .] In a scene from *The Inner Circle* (1912) the use of props augments the fully developed gestural byplay of the verisimilar code. An intertitle, "The Lonely Widower and his child," precedes the film's first shot. A little girl sits in a chair in a tenement room, and her father (Adolphe Lestina) enters. He walks slowly, head bowed, and carries a flower. He looks at the child, smiles slightly, sniffs the flower and turns to look at a picture on a table behind him. His hand barely raised from the table, he extends his bent index finger toward the picture, then rests his hand on the table. The father turns to his child and offers her the flower, but she is sleeping. He straightens, looks at the picture, places the flower in front of it, rests his hands on the table, and looks up, before waking and hugging the child.

In this shot the gestures and props develop the portrait of the Lonely Widower announced by the intertitle, but Lestina communicates his sorrow for his dead wife with an upward glance, and his pity for his orphaned child by looking from the picture to her. This brings us to the second important element of the verisimilar code, the use of the eyes and the face. As in Lestina's case, the direction of the look often suffices to convey a character's thoughts (given the narrative context, that is). In [an] example from *Friends* [1912], Walthall returns from the gold fields unaware that Barrymore has preempted his place in Pickford's affections. As he and Pickford embrace; he looks over her shoulder to see the picture of Barrymore she has left out. A dawning realization crosses his face, but the mere fact of his seeing the photo indicates that the character's suspicions have been aroused. [. . .]

As the trade press would have said, "You can really see the actors think!" Occasionally, the later Biographs devote entire shots to a character's thoughts, with the actors reflecting on the previous action and moving very little if at all. In *Friends*, after Pickford receives a visit from Barrymore she lets him out and remains motionless, her hand on the doorknob and her eyes moving from side to side. In a similar scene in *The Lesser Evil*, Blanche Sweet has just gotten a proposal from her longtime beau. She pauses at the front door of her house, with her hands at her sides and her head down. She looks up slightly, smiles, then goes into the house. Nor is it only women mooning over their sweethearts who pause in reflection. In *Friends*, the doctor tells Walthall to wait outside while he goes inside to deliver the baby. Walthall stands for a moment with his hand on the doorknob, motionless except for his eyes moving from side to side as he contemplates his wife's fate.

[. . .]

[M]any of the "thinking" and "reflection" shots cannot and should not be separated from the editing patterns of which they are a part, nor, for that matter, from the entire narrative context. This is particularly the case with the reaction shot that reveals mental processes precisely through the accumulation of shots. With the 1911 films, the three-shot–point-of-view pattern began to be standardized, as several films feature sequences in which characters look through windows and then react to what they see, the reaction shot sometimes in closer scale than the rest of the film (*The Chief's Daughter*, *Enoch Arden*, *His Mother's Scarf*, *The Two Sides*).

The code shift

By 1912 most performers, under most circumstances, in most Biographs employed the verisimilar code, some being more adept at it than others. Using the word *adept* comes perilously close to making a value judgment about good and bad acting. What does *adept* mean in this context? Those performers skilled in the new style used smaller gestures, gave them less emphasis, and melded them into a continuous flow. The less skilled retained elements of the histrionic code: while they might not use conventional gestures, their movements tended to be larger, more emphasized, and more discrete. Skilled performers also used more byplay and bits of business to construct their characters. Those performers whom subsequent generations have valorized as good (i.e., Blanche Sweet, Bobby Harron, Henry Walthall, Lillian Gish, Mary Pickford, Mae Marsh) are the ones who mastered the verisimilar code, so that it is possible in this instance to identify the components of "good acting" or at least specify what most people probably mean by "good acting" in the Biographs.

By 1912, however, the histrionic code had not entirely vanished. Actors still represented conversation with diectic gestures and the occasional conventional gesture.[9] In *The Black Sheep* (1912) a father warns off his daughter's suitor (Charles West). The father gestures with his thumb over his shoulder in his daughter's direction, raises his hand like a police officer halting traffic, and shakes his head. In *The New York Hat*, the village gossips tell Pickford's father (Charles Mailes) about the minister's purchase of the hat. Their leader (Claire McDowell) takes his arm, points offscreen, and touches her hat. The father points to his chest, then his head, looks severe, clenches his fists, nods, and says thank you.

The histrionic code persisted not only in conversations but also during emotional high points. In *The New York Hat*, the father comes upon his daughter wearing the new hat. He spreads his arms wide with fists clenched, as he asks where she got it. When she answers, he runs his hands across the top of his head and yells at her, raising his clenched fists in the air. In *The Lesser Evil*, Sweet's fiancé (Edwin August) sees Sweet being kidnapped. He raises his hands high above his head, staggers back, and waves his arms.

Perhaps it was only actors less skilled at the verisimilar code who resorted to the histrionic at times of great emotion? This does not seem to be the case. Even such a master of the verisimilar code as Henry Walthall, capable, as we have seen, of portraying intense grief with his back to the camera, uses histrionic gestures. In *The God Within*, when the doctor wishes him to take his baby to Sweet, Walthall makes the standard gesture of rejection, his hand near his head, arm bent at the elbow and then brought downward and out in a thrusting-away movement. Is editing perhaps the explanatory factor? To some extent, certainly, but the histrionic code can appear in a reaction shot. In *The Inner Circle*, Lestina looks through a window, seeing his daughter in the house under which he has just planted a bomb. He staggers back, arms wide, clenching his fists.

Just as the histrionic code lasts into 1912, we can find traces of the verisimilar as early as 1908. In *One Touch of Nature* Florence Lawrence's child has died. She sits quietly staring ahead until she picks up the child's doll and gently strokes its head, the use of the prop seeming to inhibit histrionic gestures.

The presence of the two codes in films made during the same year, and, sometimes even in the same film, prevents simply declaring that the verisimilar code replaced the histrionic on a precise date in a certain film. While one can identify 1910 and 1911 as the crucial transitional years, during which the codes mingle more frequently than previously or subsequently, we cannot reduce the matter to a question of chronology, providing lengthy and tedious year-by-year descriptions of acting. Nor can we hope to identify the simple linear causality of such factors as editing patterns or a closer camera.[10] Rather than considering performance in isolation or in relation to one other signifying practice, we must take into account the complex interaction of performance with the entire textual system. As Metz says, "The intrinsic consideration of a code does not tell us how it may be articulated with other codes (or with which ones), and at what level it may play a part in the general economy of a long and complex text."[11]

Notes

1 Tony Bennett and Janet Woollacott, *Bond and Beyond: The Political Career of a Popular Hero* (London: Macmillan, 1987), 65.

2 Tom Gunning also uses the term "gestural soliloquy" for this performance device in his dissertation, "D. W. Griffith and the Narrator System: Narrative Structure and Industry Organization in Biograph Films, 1908–1909" (Ph.D. diss., New York University, 1986), and his book *D. W. Griffith and the Origins of American Narrative Film* (Urbana: University of Illinois Press, 1991).

3 Gilbert B. Cross, *Next Week East Lynne* (Lewisburg, PA.: Bucknell University Press, 1977), 135.

4 On the use of props, see also James Naremore, *Acting in the Cinema* (Berkeley and Los Angeles: University of California Press, 1988), 84–97.

5 Kier Elam, *The Semiotics of Theatre and Drama* (New York: Methuen, 1980), 72–75.

6 See Gunning, "D. W. Griffith and the Narrator System," 747; David Bordwell, Janet Staiger, and Kristin Thompson, *The Classical Hollywood Cinema: Film Style and Mode of Production to 1960* (New York: Columbia University Press, 1985), 189–191; and Janet Staiger, "The Eyes Are Really the Focus: Photoplay Acting and Film Form and Style," *Wide Angle* 6:4 (1985): 18–20. Chapter 7 of this book will look at trade press discourse on the verisimilar code, which also emphasizes the extreme importance of the face and eyes.

This footnote seems a good point to enumerate my disagreements with the Staiger article. I must first dispute Staiger's assertion that "the employment of theatre workers in filmmaking provides one of the strongest explanations for the appearance of a particular acting style" (19). One cannot, when discussing this period, simply refer to the theatre. One must specify which theatre: the "first class" Broadway house; the popular-priced theatre largely given over to the melodrama; the resident stock companies; or the touring combinations sent out by the theatrical syndicates. Without further investigation, the fact that many film directors had theatrical backgrounds proves nothing. In which theatre, employing what performance style, did they work? Griffith's theatrical experience [. . .] exposed him mainly to the histrionic code, though he may, of course, have seen performances employing the verisimilar code.

Of course, Griffith's attitudes, and those of his colleagues, toward acting constitute another issue, but here again Staiger oversimplifies. In the period in question, the film industry's perceptions of the relation of film to theatrical acting underwent several shifts. In 1907–1908 some critics rejected theatrical acting as unsuitable by virtue of its "repose," presumably believing that the new style would fail to "get it across." In the next few years the film industry sought, as Staiger says, to emulate the "first class theatre," but also, as she omits to mention, to distance itself from the popular-priced theatre, where the histrionic code still reigned. By 1912 the film industry had developed a consensus as to what constituted appropriate film acting, convincing itself that it could not only outdo the popular-priced theatre but could surpass the verisimilar code as seen on the legitimate stage. It is true that "by 1912, companies were filming popular stage successes with current theatrical stars" (19), but the reaction of the trade press was far from laudatory as suggested by a review of Nat Goodwin's Fagin in *Oliver Twist*: "The well defined action of the best motion picture actor is missing throughout" ("Nat Goodwin Disappointing," *The New York Dramatic Mirror*, June 5, 1912, 27). It should teach that if players of note are to enter film production it is necessary that they study to employ the art and technique of the picture, which at its best is decidedly removed from the stage.

7 Two methodological caveats, with which I did not wish to clutter the text, may be relevant here. The fact that most gesture is analogic rather than digital under normal circumstances prevents the analyst from segmenting gestural signification. The analyst armed with a Steenbeck flat-bed editing table can stop the flow of gesture at will. Although the technology enables us to note each small gesture, the reader should realize that this segmentation is an artificial process, and that one of the essential features of the verisimilar code is its analogical nature.

Although with the Steenbeck it becomes possible to annotate movement, assigning a specific meaning to each gesture or combination of gestures is much more difficult with the verisimilar than with the histrionic code, partly, of course, because the former is not predicated on a one-to-one correspondence between gesture and meaning. In the absence of a lexicon restricted by convention, gesture and especially a combination of gestures can take on an infinity of meaning, with the narrative context alone limiting the connotations. For this reason, the analyst's personal judgment becomes a greater factor with the verisimilar than the histrionic code. Suppose that an old man enters a shot, head bowed, shoulders sagging, arms hanging limply at sides. Does this signify defeat, despair, resignation, sadness, or simply momentary weariness? The problem becomes intensified with facial expression: two people can debate the meaning of a particular close-up for hours, as in often-cited instance of Garbo's expression in the closing shot of *Queen Christina*. Even facial expression combined with posture can defeat attempts at quick and facile interpretations. Certainly no one would dare to impose a single, precise meaning on the final shot of *Vertigo* as Jimmy Stewart, having witnessed the second death of his beloved, teeters on the brink of oblivion.

8 Mae Marsh, *Screen Acting* (Los Angeles: Photostar Publishing Company, 1922), 54.

9 Throughout the Biographs, actors use deictic gestures, leading me to include them in the histrionic code. However, I have no evidence that the deictic gesture was frequently employed in the theatrical histrionic code. Because the theatrical performers could have used verbal shifters and might not have needed deictic gestures, it may be the case that the standardized and conventional use of deictic gestures originates with silent film. If so,

it would be inaccurate to label conversational gestures as either histrionic or verisimilar. However, between 1908 and 1913, while actors continued to point, their pointing movements became smaller, less emphasized, and more flowing.

10 The importance of the face and eyes to the verisimilar code may tempt one to conclude that the increasing closeness of the camera between 1908 and 1913 accounts for the transformation of performance style. The reverse could just as well be true, however: the new performance style may have brought about the closer camera.

11 Christian Metz, *Language and Cinema* (The Hague: Mouton, 1974), 103. Some data about changes in signifying practices during Griffith's Biograph years, particularly those practices most often associated with performance, editing, and camera distance, may be helpful. In "D.W. Griffith and the Narrator System," Gunning tells us that the average number of shots per thousand feet of film was 16.6 in 1908 and 87.8 in 1913 (761). As for scale, the long shot, with space above and below the characters' heads and feet, was standard in 1908. By 1910 the characters were framed at the ankle, and by 1911 characters were framed in three-quarter shot, which became the predominant scale of the classical Hollywood cinema. As Gunning points out, however, beginning in 1909 characters increasingly step forward to be framed between ankle and knee, so that camera distance does not remain a constant even in the earlier films.

Intertitles do not survive for many films. Because the earliest Biograph with intertitles at the Library of Congress is *A Change of Heart* (September 1909), there has been confusion about the presence of intertitles in the earlier Biograph, our knowledge of which derives primarily from the Paper Print Collection. Gunning has concluded that most, and probably all, of the Griffith Biographs originally had titles. We do know that dialogue titles became increasingly frequent, a factor bearing directly on the construction of character.

For further information about the film style in this period see Bordwell, Staiger, and Thompson, *The Classical Hollywood Cinema*, 155–240, and Barry Salt, "The Early Development of Film Form," in John Fell, ed., *Film Before Griffith* (Berkeley: University of California Press, 1983), 284–89.

Pictorial Styles and Film Acting 6

BEN BREWSTER AND LEA JACOBS

[. . .]

The problem [. . .] is to register when and how actors are adapting pictorial stage traditions to the cinema. Most immediately, in our case, the problem is how to recognize a pose when we see one. [. . .]

[I]n our efforts to analyse this acting style, the time of the pause could not be the sole criterion for defining a pose or attitude. Instead we have looked for the following:

1 There is a slight pause in the actor's movement when the film is viewed at the correct speed of projection (remember Humboldt's term, of a 'hesitant calm'—*zögernde Ruhe*);
2 The actor assumes a stereotyped posture;
3 The posture expresses the character's interior state or in some other way clearly and directly relates to the dramatic situation;
4 The posture is systematically iterated and varied by the actor;
5 The blocking of the actor's movement, or of the acting ensemble, clearly leads up to the pose or leads from one pose to the next.

Obviously the frame stills used in this chapter do not 'prove' the existence of an attitude, since they represent no more than one-sixteenth of a second of the actual time of the performance. Rather, they are used to facilitate the work of description.

Poses in the sense proposed above appear in a wide range of silent film. Perhaps the most systematic attempt to describe how they function is Roberta Pearson's discussion of what she calls the 'histrionic code' of film acting at Biograph in the period between 1908 and 1912. While we find Pearson's analyses of individual films compelling, we believe the theoretical terms of her argument misrepresent pictorial styles of acting on the stage and make it difficult to understand the various ways poses were adapted to film.

Pearson defines the histrionic code in opposition to the verisimilar code. The former does not aim to create psychologically complex characters, nor an effect of realism, while the latter does. The former frankly admits its theatricality—the actor palpably 'acts', striking conventionalized poses and attitudes—while the latter eschews such self-consciousness, favouring stage business and byplay with props. But we have tried to indicate the difficulties of defining pictorialism in acting simply in opposition to realism. Nineteenth-century discourses on acting appealed to concepts of realism quite frequently, and often in ways which did not preclude an emphasis on attitudes and posing, but simply served to reinforce notions of expressiveness, restraint, or decorum that were not clearly specified as such.

We find the calls for realistic or subtle acting in the film industry trade press similarly amorphous. In general, with the possible exception of Frank Woods, the trade press does not provide enough detail about what actors were doing on screen, or what they should have been doing, to provide a fruitful definition of realism.[1] Albert Goldie's 'Subtlety in Acting', for example, argues that self-conscious acting is bad, but he does not specifically mention poses or attitudes, and it is not clear if posing would necessarily be seen as self-conscious in his terms.[2] In her memoir 'Growing Up with the Movies', Florence Lawrence is somewhat more specific, criticizing an unnamed stage actor who appeared in a feature in the following terms: 'The actor I speak of would strike a pose in nearly every other scene which seemed to ask, "Now am I not the handsome lover?" or "Don't you think I'm some hero?"[3] However, it still is not obvious whether Lawrence is objecting to what she sees as the stage actor's narcissistic showing off, or if any pose, even an expressive one linked to character or situation, is in her view inappropriate for film acting. Humboldt, who tremendously admired Talma's pictorial style of acting, none the less criticized 'mannered' or 'exaggerated' poses which became obvious as such.[4] The problem is not simply how to interpret Lawrence's language here, but more generally that analysis of the film industry trade discourse in terms of an opposition between posed and realistic styles of acting is logically fraught. Because people strike poses in real life, often quite conventional ones, even an avowed advocate of 'realistic' acting might admit some poses on the grounds that they were 'lifelike'. For example, a *Moving Picture World* critic like Goldie was not likely to comment adversely on an actor playing the part of an Italian immigrant who used large, vivid, and fully extended gestures, given that the lack of 'subtlety' would be motivated by ethnic stereotypes. Stanislavsky himself was willing to admit that the actor in *Werther* could strike a pose upon his entrance to Charlotte's cottage provided there was sufficient motivation, that is, supposing he had discovered her corpse. Even a very strict commitment to realism can accommodate poses in certain narrative contexts. Moreover, there does not seem to be a principled way to determine from the reviews or commentary when an actor is being criticized for posing as such, and when the issue of posing is raised simply because a particular attitude was found inappropriate or unconvincing.

But of course we do not have only the reviews. We have at least some of the films, and this evidence suggests that there was posing throughout the years 1908–12 and beyond, even as the trade press praised realistic acting. Pearson's own analyses of films suggest that what she has defined as two distinct codes coexisted, and that well into the 1910s Biograph actors continued to use poses alongside elements such as stage business or the employment of props. For example, she notes that, in the otherwise 'verisimilar' film *His Lost Love* (1909), the actors fall into poses during the climactic scene in which the wife discovers her husband's adultery.[5] She finds a similar mixture of the two codes in Henry Walthall's performances in the films *Thou Shalt Not* (1910) and *The Avenging Conscience* (1914), and indeed throughout his career.[6]

Our examples, taken from a European context, confirm Pearson's observations that actors use attitudes more prominently in some scenes than in others. *Le Homard* (The Lobster; Léonce Perret, 1912), a part of Gaumont's Léonce series, represents typical comic acting of the period, which involves a great deal of complex pantomime, as well as attitudes and gestural asides to the camera. In the film, Suzanne (Suzanne Grandais) quarrels with Léonce (Perret) over his refusal to purchase an expensive lobster from a local fisherman. He then pretends to go out fishing for lobsters on a stormy night while in fact having made arrangements to buy them. He finally returns home and, with much mugging to the camera, pretends that he is exhausted and suffering from cold after having spent a difficult night at sea. The revelation of his deception leads to a quarrel which is only resolved by the fact that he must rescue the sea-bathing Suzanne by removing an offending crustacean from her posterior. While Perret and Grandais employ vivid and expressive gestures, these often take the form of a rapid 'dialogue', gestures expressing exasperation or reproach exchanged between man and wife during their quarrels. The only attitudes notably held in the film occur during what is for Suzanne (but not the spectator) a potentially tragic moment; during the long night that Suzanne awaits Léonce's return, Grandais poses, first at the window looking out to sea, then in her bedroom, on her knees in prayer. The contrast between the comic and the serious tone is particularly shown up later in this scene when, through a split screen composition, the film composes a triptych showing Grandais on the left, in an attitude of prayer, the sea in the middle of the frame, and Perret on the right, seated comfortably at the movies, and laughing with glee at the Gaumont comedy on the screen.

Note that Perret does not hold a pose in the triptych; this is reserved for Grandais's expression of grief and remorse. It is as if Grandais's acting in *Le Homard* falls out of the comic mode in order to convey Suzanne's state of mind. In general, it seems quite clear that genre was an important factor in determining whether or not the actors choose to adopt attitudes, and the length of time the attitudes were held. Serious drama called for a slower style than comedy, with more pronounced poses and gestures (this was true on the stage as well as film, as Coquelin's discussion of theatrical genres already cited indicates). One tends to find the longest and most marked posing in historical or costume pictures such as *L'Assassinat du Duc de Guise* (1908) or *Quatre-vingt-treize* (1914–21), or sentimental stories, especially those dealing with dignified, upper-class characters such as *Ma l'amor mio non muore!* (1913). Pearson notes a similar division in her survey of Walthall's films for Biograph, with one of his most 'histrionic' performances being a historical romance, *The Sealed Room* (1909).[7]

But even within serious films, poses become more pronounced at climactic moments, as if the actors are 'saving' them for the big scenes. That is, posing is determined by situation as well as by genre. One of the clearest examples we have seen of this tendency is the Danish film *Klovnen* (The Clown, 1917). Joe Higgins (Valdemar Psilander) is the clown in the travelling circus run by Mr and Mrs Bunding in which their daughter Daisy (Gudrun Houlberg) is the bareback rider. Joe and Daisy are in love, and when a major impresario offers Joe a big city contract, he makes it a condition of accepting that the Bundings accompany him. Two years later he is a great success and has married Daisy, but Daisy is courted by Count Henri. One day after his performance, Joe sees Henri kissing Daisy in the mirror in the green room of the theatre. He goes home in despair and finds Daisy there waiting for him. He asks her if she loves the Count; she says yes, so he tells her to go to him. The plot then takes a predictably unhappy turn. After the Count tires of her, Daisy tries to return to Joe, is rebuffed by her father, and commits suicide. Having forgiven Daisy on her deathbed, and mourning her loss, Joes goes downhill himself, and is working in a cheap circus when he meets the Count once again and kills his old rival before expiring.

The scenes of Joe's happy life—the courtship of Daisy, eating dinner with the family, the back-stage preparations for their acts in the travelling circus—are all done at normal tempo and without marked posing. However, the whole tempo and style of the acting alter after Joe sees Daisy and the Count kissing in the mirror. The shift is particularly evident in the confrontation between the two at the house which follows Daisy's departure from the theatre (the titles are translations from the Danish ones in the print):

1 A salon in Joe's palatial mansion: the anteroom brightly lit rear centre and right, with a closed glass portière at the top of a short flight of steps; a bay window left; a small table, chair, and settee front centre. Houlberg is sitting on the settee, her head on her hands on the table. Psilander enters from the rear right, opens the portière, looks at Houlberg (who does not yet look at him) and stops (Figure 1). He staggers slowly down the steps, then comes forward more quickly, pauses midground right, crosses to stand between the chair and the settee, with his right hand on the chair back. He speaks. Houlberg raises her head with a start, looks up, and leans slowly backwards as he leans forward to her. She apologizes (Figure 2). She leans forward again and looks off right. He leans down and seizes her hand. She rises. He releases her hand and steps back, briefly wringing his hands. Without looking at him, she looks down at the table as he leans back towards her, his fist on the table (Figure 3). He speaks.

2 Title: 'Daisy, do you love him?'

3 Cut-in to medium shot. Psilander is in profile left, Houlberg's head is raised. She very slowly nods assent, then wipes tears from her eyes. Psilander looks off front centre vacantly in grief. He puts his hand on his forehead (Figure 4).

4 As 1. Cut on action. Psilander with hand to forehead, Houlberg looking down left front (Figure 5). Psilander backs unsteadily to stand with his right hand on the chair back. He speaks to her. She turns to him, starts, and looks him full in the face. He comes forward and leans on the table.

5 Title: 'Then you have only one thing to do; go to him!'

6 As 1. Houlberg turns quickly to face front left and puts her left hand to her heart. She leans over to front right in agony (Figure 6). Psilander comes forward, raises his hands as if to grasp her shoulders but drops them again. He retreats round the settee, his left hand on its back. He points listlessly off left (Figure 7). She tries to face him, raises her arms halfway in appeal, drops them again, turns to face front right, then back again, and passes in front of Psilander and off left slowly. Psilander watches her go, makes a full gesture of appeal off left, raising his hands to head height (Figure 8). He leans back and puts his hands on his head. He turns to front left, pulls his hands down the sides of his face and leans slightly forward (Figure 9).

The plot is nominally advanced in these six shots. Daisy decides to part from Joe, but with regret, and Joe's agony at the loss is reaffirmed. However, much more important story events occur in the prior discovery scene in the green room, or a subsequent scene in which Bunding disowns his daughter, thus preparing for his later dismissal of her after she has repented, and her suicide. In contrast, this scene is almost entirely devoted to extending and elaborating upon the situation put in place by Joe's discovery of the betrayal. The acting does not operate to further the action, but to delay it—to maintain the situation and exploit its emotional resonances, before the next turn of events. Our sense that the pace of the acting slows down here is partly a function of the length of the shots (the six shots comprise 173 feet or 2 minutes, 53 seconds at 16 frames per second), partly one of the tempo of the action, as, for example, in Psilander's pose at the top of the stairs and the slow movement from the background to the foreground in shot 1. The gestures and poses adopted by the actors tend to be iterative expressions of grief; this also helps to provide a sense of long duration in the scene, since the succession of poses does not provide us with new information about the characters or events, but merely a variation on what we already know. After this scene, the acting never returns to the rapid and unmarked gestures of the early scenes; as the plot shifts to a serious and sentimental register, the acting style changes in accordance with it.

Because posing was keyed to genre and situation, and effectively coexisted with other, more fluid, uses of gesture, it does not make sense in our view to define it theoretically as opposed to realism, or historically as a precursor which was eventually superseded by a realistic acting style. This is not to deny, however, the observation by Pearson, Gunning, Thompson, and others that acting style changes in American films in the period from 1908 to 1912. For us, the questions are somewhat different. How did the actors in the newly forming stock companies in 1907–8—actors largely trained in the theatre—adapt pictorial traditions to film? How did their style change in relation to later developments in film technique?[8]

In this connection it is worth iterating the conditions which impinged on film acting as opposed to the stage in 1908. There was no spoken dialogue, and the whole register of diction and the voice was lost. There was no live audience whose reaction to and understanding of a scene could be gauged. The relatively great figure/camera distance which was the norm in this period meant that the actor was shown full figure but relatively small and on what was usually a small screen. The 'speed' of the one-reel film required that a complex sequence of actions be conveyed in a relatively short span of screen time as compared with any but the most brief one-act play or vaudeville playlet.[9] In response to these conditions, a theatrically trained actor moving into film at this time might well have been motivated to develop a more emphatic style than he had formerly employed on stage. Several points about acting in the 1908–9 Biographs can thus be explained not as a direct carry-over of popular stage traditions, but rather as an attempt to adapt these traditions to the specific requirements of the new medium.

For example, one aspect of acting in the 1908–9 period is what Pearson categorizes as overly emphatic uses of gesture. She argues that actors in the early Biographs often adopt poses with fully extended arms or legs, as in the discussion of Griffith's own acting in *Rescued from an Eagle's Nest* (1908).[10] In one instance, this tendency is evident even in the use of the hand and fingers. Pearson contrasts two proposal scenes in which the principal actor makes his appeal by placing a hand upon his chest, one, *The Voice of the Violin* (1909) with Arthur Johnson, the other, *A Summer Idyl* (1910) with Henry Walthall:

> Because Walthall stresses his gestures less than Johnson, the performance does not connote the same degree of theatricality. This becomes clear in comparing the way each actor places his hands on his chest. Johnson uses both hands with the palms flattened, to modern eyes parodying a lover declaring himself, as the pose absolutely reeks of theatricality. Walthall places one hand lightly on his chest, the palm slightly raised and fingers slightly cupped. Though Walthall employs a conventional gesture, the lack of emphasis reduces the deliberate self-consciousness of the histrionic code.[11]

While we would agree with Pearson that actors often use fully extended limbs during 1908–9, we would dispute her claim that this kind of posing is simply carried over from pictorial acting

Figure 1

Figure 2

Figure 3

Figure 4

Figure 5

Figure 6

Figure 7

Figure 8

Figure 9

styles in the theatre (although, of course, bad actors were everywhere). The fully outstretched hand position adopted by Arthur Johnson in this example would have been anathema to most nineteenth-century teachers of acting. What she characterizes as the 'slow and graceful' movements typical of Walthall's performance in *A Summer Idyl* are much closer to the way in which we understand the elements of pictorial style in the theatre.[12]

As we have noted, the late eighteenth-century and nineteenth-century acting manuals repeatedly stress the importance of grace and good bearing; they also specifically recommend against fully extended limbs. For example, in his lesson on hand position, Jelgerhuis argues that the fingers should always be gracefully curved, to give 'play and contrast' to their position. He cautions against either one of two extremes:

> I used to know a very good speaker on the Stage, who out of unthinking habit, always appeared with crooked fingers; what a wretched habit! I hope, that this example will be enough, to draw your attention to it, so that you will always avoid it.—Yet don't think, Dear Students! that the hand hanging down with straight fingers can wholly redress this, no, although better than with crooked fingers. . . . For the hanging arm, and the free and unforced hand, there must be play and contrast in the posture of the fingers, to make it look elegant, to give it looseness, freedom and decorum.[13]

Similarly, he characterizes a fully extended arm as 'without grace, stretch[ed] out like a pole' and cautions against movements involving both hands and arms together unless 'one adopts them purposely, in order to become ridiculous'.[14] Riccoboni also tells students to avoid having both arms equally extended, and raising them to the same height. He cites a 'well enough known rule' that the hand should not be raised above the eye, adding the caveat that 'when a violent passion carries him away, the Actor can forget all the rules; he can move with despatch, and lift his arms even above his head'.[15] Riccoboni's remarks suggest that actors could use fully extended, and thus relatively emphatic gestures, but only sparingly, and in accordance with extreme situations. Recall that Yeats makes just such an analysis of Édouard de Max's performance in *Phèdre*, in which he apparently saved his biggest gesture for the climax of the scene: 'Through one long scene De Max, who was quite as fine, never lifted his hands above his elbow, it was only when the emotion came to its climax that he raised it to his breast.' Lessing's remark already cited about wild or baroque gesture also suggests the importance of modulating such gestures in a sequence; he argued that they could be made acceptable if the actor prepared for them and finally resolved them into more harmonious poses.

The sequence already discussed from *Klovnen* provides a good example of the way in which emphatic gesture could be controlled through the modulation of poses. The actors adopt a series of attitudes expressing grief. These are 'smaller' in shot 1, with Psilander posing far in the background, or, after he has come forward, leaning on a chair or table for support, with Houlberg turning away from him. The scale changes in shot 3, a medium shot, so that facial expressions can be emphasized with very little movement on the part of the actors, as in Houlberg's small nod of her head in affirmation to the question whether or not she loves the Count. The scene returns to the long-shot framing and builds to the largest gestures in shot 6: Houlberg's attitude in which she puts her hand to her heart and leans her body away from Psilander to the right to express her grief, and Psilander's attitude, in the same shot after her exit, in which he extends his arms and raises his hands to head height, and then later, when he pulls his hands down the sides of his face (Figures 6, 8 and 9).

In sum, the extended gestures of the Biograph actors described by Pearson were not the inevitable result of stage practices, but particular applications of them—in some cases without enough care to prevent clumsy postures, and in others without the calculation and timing by which experienced stage actors built up to 'big' or pronounced poses. Aside from inexperience or incompetence, we attribute this kind of posing to difficulties already adduced in the period before 1912—particularly problems of coping with the small scale of the actor's image in the typical long-shot framings, and the effort to make a story clear in a restricted amount of time to an audience that the actor could not play to nor get reassurance from directly.

Clearly then, another constraint on actors in this early period was the demand for a swift pace. Pearson discusses this, as does the perceptive Frank Woods in a 1910 'Spectator's' column in which he asserts that 'the most marked change that has taken place in the style of picture acting in the last year or two has been in the matter of tempo' and praises Biograph acting for the 'deliberation and repose' in its recent films.[16] Again, the fast tempo Woods disapproves of does not seem to be a direct carry-over from the theatre, since all the evidence we have seen about the length of poses there suggests that they were held for much longer than they ever were in film. In the same column, Woods attributes the emphasis on speed to the novelty of the moving picture itself: 'Everything had to be on the jump. The more action that could be crowded into each foot of film the more perfect the picture was supposed to be.' The limitation of length in the one-reel film may also have contributed to the relatively swift pace of film acting. This is how we would interpret Florence Lawrence's recollection about her differences with Griffith over acting tempo:

> What seemed to annoy us 'Biographers' very much and hold us back from achieving greater artistic success was the speed and rapidity with which we had to work before the camera. Mr. Griffith always answered our complaint by stating that the exchanges and exhibitors who bought our pictures wanted action, and insisted that they get plenty of it for their money. 'The exhibitors don't want illustrated song slides,' Mr. Griffith once said to us. So we made our work quick and snappy, crowding as much story in a thousand foot picture as is now portrayed in five thousand feet of film. Several pictures which we produced in three hundred feet have since been reproduced in one thousand feet. There was no chance for slow or 'stage' acting. The moment we started to do a bit of acting in the proper tempo we would be startled by the cry of the director: 'Faster! Faster! For God's sake hurry up! We must do the scene in forty feet.'[17]

The problem then, was not simply that the exhibitors wanted 'action' in every foot, but that such a rapid pace was considered necessary if all the relevant action was to be conveyed in the requisite length.

Perhaps as actors and directors such as Griffith mastered the one-reel form, that is by the date of Woods's column in 1910, it had become possible to 'slow down' to some degree. Note, however, that six months before he praises the deliberation and repose of Biograph actors, Frank Woods criticizes the final scene of the same company's *All on Account of the Milk* (1910) with the comment: 'The last scene appears to degenerate into farce, and to be acted hastily and with too little dramatic effect, due, perhaps, to the lack of film space.'[18] In general he praises the acting in the film (by Mary Pickford, Arthur Johnson, Mack Sennett, and Blanche Sweet) and we assume that the problem of 'film space' to which he refers is that the filmmakers were forced to rush the last scene to ensure that the film was the proper length. Even if Woods is wrong in his guess about what happened at the end of this specific film, the comment suggests that he was aware of the lack of 'space' on the reel as a problem for actors. We would argue that it continued to be, and, as compared to the early feature, actors in the one-reel film were given many fewer opportunities to dwell on situations, to hold poses or develop elaborate sequences of them. A three-minute sequence of the sort described in *Klovnen*, in which almost nothing happens at the level of the plot, would be extremely difficult to accommodate within a sixteen-minute movie.

Our attempt to search out the most accomplished and technically elaborated examples of pictorial styles has thus led us to focus primarily on the early feature film. But at the same time this periodization introduces a new limitation or constraint on pictorial acting, since by this point the editing options open to filmmakers begin to interfere with the actor's performance in ways that would not have been imaginable in the theatre. As Tom Gunning has argued in relation to the example of *After Many Years* already cited, editing can potentially disrupt and reconfigure the actor's pose and gesture. Cross-cutting of the kind in *After Many Years*, and, later, the kinds of scene dissection which Gunning discusses in relation to *The Lady and the Mouse* (1913), effectively displace some of the actor's traditional functions, providing filmmakers with other means of directing the spectator's attention within a space, regulating the pace of a scene, expressing emotion, and underscoring dramatic situations.[19] This possibility is evident as well in the scene of Little Eva's death in the World version of *Uncle Tom's Cabin*, in which the various expressions of grief on the part of the actors are directed and controlled by the editing pattern which alternates between the bedroom and the various spaces outside it. In contrast, in the theatre this regulation of the spectator's attention would have been structured largely through the acting of the ensemble, through the actors taking turns, the gesture of one setting off or leading to the gesture of another in what Riccoboni compared to 'musicians who sing a piece in several parts'. Editing could thus at least partially fulfil functions which had previously been fulfilled by the actor(s) through the generation of pictorial effects. This is not to say that film editing could not coexist with posing and pictorial styles; but it is to say that a highly edited film could more easily support bad pictorial acting, or non-acting, or a more reduced, i.e. less emphatic, style.

Pearson argues the latter case. In a careful comparison of *After Many Years* (1908) with *Enoch Arden*, she shows how the later version of the same story requires fewer gestures, and less extended ones, because *Enoch Arden* can rely on more cross-cutting and glance/object editing to convey important information about story events and character states.[20] But moving away from the example of the Griffith Biographs, we would also suggest that highly edited films could help to accommodate very bad, or at least inexperienced, acting.

Indeed, while Biograph films are usually praised by reviewers in the trade press when they are discussing acting specifically, discussions of Biograph's fast-paced editing usually elicited complaints about its effect on acting style. One review of *A Girl's Stratagem* (1913) notes 'The action is held in pretty closely to its center of interest, and the scene-making searchlight snaps back and forth from one actor to another and seems to pick out the different elements of the situation almost simultaneously. This is a speedy method and makes the picture, as a whole, clear at the expense, now and then, of the acting. The scenes change so fast that the players now and then seem all arms and hands.'[21] And from a review of *The Hero of Little Italy* (1913): 'There is a good story in this picture and the producer has made it exciting. As it approaches its climax, the scenes, flashed back and forth, keep the action concrete and almost breathless. But this playing for the thrill is not the best use of the motion picture camera; for in such there is almost no individual acting—everything goes to situation, nothing to character.'[22] Epes Winthrop Sargent reports on Dr Stockton's experiment in 1912 counting the scenes in over twenty one-reel and split-reel films by various manufacturers, with most companies having what he considered high cutting rates (the one Biograph on the list is the fastest cut). Sargent quotes Stockton's opinion of this tendency: 'It looks very much as if Edison and the foreigners were the only ones not bitten by the lightning bug, with the result that his releases are, to my mind, the only ones that are really drama. The others have lots of action, but no acting and no chance for any.'[23] The point is that not only did editing *permit* the actor to do 'less' in terms of posing and gesture, but the pace of a highly edited film *required* it.

Notes

1 Frank Woods consistently complained about actors looking at the camera, and in one of his columns he specifically objects to posing in the sense of standing or speaking to the camera, and thereby acknowledging its presence. See Frank Woods, "'Spectator's' Comments," *New York Dramatic Mirror* 67, no. 1736 (27 March 1912): 24.

2 Albert Goldie, "Subtlety in Acting," *New York Dramatic Mirror* 68, no. 1769 (13 November 1912): 4; and for a confused account of whether or not film acting should be emphatic see Hanford C. Judson, "What Gets Over," *Moving Picture World* 8, no. 15 (15 April 1911): 816.

3 Florence Lawrence in collaboration with Monte M. Katterjohn, "Growing Up with the Movies," *Photoplay* 7, no. 2 (January 1915): 103.

4 William Von Humboldt, "Über die gegenwörtige Franzäsische tragische Bühne: Aus Briefen," *Propylaen* 3, no. 1 (1800): 396.

5 Roberta Pearson, *Eloquent Gestures: The Transformation of Performance Style in the Griffith Biograph Films* (Berkeley: University of California Press, 1992), 62.

6 Ibid., 110–11 and 119.

7 Ibid., 105.

8 Charles Musser, "The Changing Status of the Film Actor," in *Before Hollywood: Turn-of-the-Century American Film* (New York: Hudson Hills Press, 1987), 57–62, gives 1907–08 as the date of the formation of the stock companies, a time when the demand for story films had increased to the point that it was no longer practicable for the major producers to hire actors only on a per-day basis. Lawrence, "Growing Up," 96, refers to the formation of the stock company Biograph in 1908. Many in the Biograph stock company had stage experience; see Pearson, *Eloquent Gestures*, 83–4, on Griffith making the rounds of the theatrical agencies. The extent to which theatrically trained actors predominated in other motion-picture stock companies is indicated by the biographies of members of the Vitagraph stock company in Anthony Slide, *The Big V: A History of the Vitagraph Company*, rev. edn. (Metuchen, New Jersey: Scarecrow Press, 1987), 134–55.

9 On the latter two conditions see Kristin Thompson in David Bordwell, Kristin Thompson and Janet Staiger, *The Classical Hollywood Cinema: Film Style and Mode of Production to 1960* (London: Routledge, 1985), 189–92.

10 Pearson, *Eloquent Gestures*, 27 (on the unchecked historic code with fully extended gestures

as typical of "melodramatic" acting), and 79–81 (on Griffith's acting as an example of this style), and 2 (for another example of these sorts of fully extended gestures).

11 Ibid., 40–1.

12 Ibid., 41.

13 Johannes Jelgerhuis, *Theoretische Lessen over de Gestericulatie en Mimiek: Gegeven aan de Kweekelingen van het Fonds ter Opleiding en Onderrigting van Tooneel-Kunstenaars aan den Stads Schouwburg te Amsterdam* (Amsterdam: P.M. Warnars, 1827; repr. Uitgeverij Adopf M. Hakkert, 1970), 97–8; cit. Dene Barnett, *The Art of Gesture: The Practices and Principles of 18th Century Acting* (Heidelberg: Carl Winter, 1987), 98.

14 Ibid., 89 and 87; cit. Dene Barnett, "The Performance Practice of Acting: The Eighteenth Century, Part III: The Arms," *Theatre Research International* 5, no. 1 (1977): iii. 82–3. In *The Art of Gesture*, iii, 132, Barnett suggests that this remains a problem for performers today: "One of the worst (and most common) examples of the lack of pictorial contrasts is to have both hands raised to the same height and equally extended; this always looks gauche and lacking in grace and proportion."

15 Francois Riccoboni, L'*Art du theatre, suivi d'une lettre de* M. *Riccovini fils a* M*** *au sujet d l'art du theatre* (Paris: Simon et Giffart, 1750; repr. Geneva: Slatkine Reprints, 1971), 13–14; cit. Barnett, "Performance Practice," iii. 84. For similar comments about the possibility of extending gesture, and raising the arms above the height of the eyes in moments of passion, see Barnett, *Art of Gesture*, 107–8.

16 Pearson, *Eloquent Gestures*, 27, seems to assume that "melodramatic" acting on the stage as well as the "unchecked histrionic code" employed by Biograph actors was fast-paced; see also 80 and 87 on Griffith's preference for "fast acting." Frank Woods's remarks appear in his column " 'Spectator's' Comments," *New York Dramatic Mirror* 63, no. 1641(4 June 1910): 16; repr. in George Pratt, *Spellbound in Darkness: A History of the Silent Cinematic Writings* (Greenwich, Connecticut: New York Graphic Society, 1966), 84.

17 Lawrence and Katterjohn, "Growing Up," 107. Note that Pearson, *Eloquent Gestures*, 87, has abridged this quotation to remove the reference to the thousand-foot reel and the comparison with the feature film. She also interprets this quotation differently, assuming that Griffith's preference for "fast" acting derived from the fact that he had still not abandoned habits acquired in the theatre and his preference for the "histrionic" code. We think the full quotation amply demonstrates the specific cinematic need for speed in this period, i.e. that scenes had to be completed within the requisite number of feet given the limitation of the one-reel film.

18 Frank Woods, "Reviews of Licensed Films . . . *All on Account of the Milk*," *New York Dramatic Mirror* 63, no. 1622 (22 January 1910): 17; repr. in Anthony Slide (ed.), *Selected Film Criticism 1896–1911* (Metuchen, New Jersey: Scarecrow Press, 1982), 4–5. Woods's review of *The Merry Wives of Windsor* (Selig, 1910), 'Reviews of Licensed Films', *New York Dramatic Mirror* 64, no. 5177 (30 November 1910): 30, makes a similar point: "The part of Falstaff was adequately taken, although it suffered like all the rest from the necessity of hastening the action to make it fit into the allotted time."

19 Tom Gunning, D.W. *Griffith and the Origins of American Narrative Film: The Early Years at Biograph* (Urbana: University of Illinois Press, 1991), 113–14 and 262–70.

20 Pearson, *Eloquent Gestures*, 63–74.

21 "Comments on the Films, . . . *A Girl's Strategem*," *Moving Picture World*, 15, no. 12 (22 March 1913): 1219; repr. in Pratt, *Spellbound in Darkness*, 104.

22 "Comments on the Films . . . *The Hero of Little Italy*," *Moving Picture World* 16, no. 3 (19 April 1913): 279; repr. in Pratt, 105.

23 Epes Winthrop Sargent, "The Photoplaywright: Scenes and Leaders," *Moving Picture World* 13, no. 6 (10 August 1912): 542; repr. in Pratt, *Spellbound in Darkness*, 101–3.

Crafting Film Performances

Acting in the Hollywood Studio Era

7

CYNTHIA BARON

In the 1930s and 1940s, studio publicity focused the public's attention on stars' personalities rather than their craftsmanship. In promotional campaigns for specific pictures and behind-the-scene bios of individual stars, audiences were told that Hollywood actors were natural actors whose unique qualities were captured by the camera. That image – of Hollywood actors playing themselves – might in some circumstances be entirely accurate. Clearly there was little craftsmanship involved in cases where inexperienced actors simply memorized their lines and hit their marks, or, to portray emotional intensity, worked themselves into agitated states by remembering traumatic experiences. Similarly, it makes no sense to discuss stars' agency and expertise in cases where established, experienced actors chose not to prepare for parts, and instead relied on habit, guidance from directors, and support from fellow actors.

Cases such as these, however, need not be taken as representative. In marked contrast to the view that film performances were produced with no effort expended by actors themselves, practitioners of the period consistently argue that training, labour, and practical craft experience allowed actors and their collaborators to create performances and respond to the specific challenges of Hollywood studio productions in the 1930s and 1940s. Put most broadly, professionals working in Hollywood during this period seem to have found ways to integrate methods developed in American silent film with principles formulated by individuals working in American theatre. Hollywood workers whose focus was dramatic performance appear to have derived strategies based on their understanding of Moscow Art Theatre productions and Stanislavsky's System, or to have found similar solutions to shared problems of 'modern' performance.

Throughout the period, the disparate demands of specific characters, narratives, and genres required actors and their collaborators to use an eclectic collection of methods borrowed from dance, modelling, vaudeville, and the legit stage. Rather than there being a single method, or even style of acting, actors' methods and performance styles reflected the demands of each screenplay. For example, a Marx brothers' comedy like *A Night at the Opera* (1935) required methods of preparation and performance styles that were very different from those built into John Ford's expressionistic drama *The Informer* (1935). Similarly, the screwball comedy *Bringing Up Baby* (1938) would necessarily lead an actor like Cary Grant to acting methods and performance styles quite different from those called for by Clifford Odets' low-life melodrama *None but the Lonely Heart* (1944).

Recognizing that descriptions of methods and styles of acting cannot and need not apply to any and all film performances of the period, in the discussion that follows I shall consider points of contact that do exist in accounts that address the basic demands of film performance, for there is a remarkable consistency in acting professionals' views on relationships between stage and screen acting. I shall also examine repeated patterns in practitioners observations on methods for approaching and executing performances in character-driven narratives, for in material concerning dramatic performances or character-based comedic performances a few central points consistently emerge. Professionals of the period believed that actors' minds and bodies formed a unified, organic whole, and from that position continually argue for the value of training body and voice. Practitioners assumed that the actor (not the director) was responsible for studying the script to create a character with a complete life history, and they consistently argue that the script must serve as the blueprint for building characters. Professionals believed that only after exhaustive preparation could an actor integrate direction and accommodate the unique demands of film production, and they repeatedly discuss the need for dispassionate execution of performance. In short, rather than presenting a single method or theory of acting, practitioners describe a collection of assumptions, beliefs, strategies, and pragmatic guidelines for training the actor's instrument, developing characterizations, representing characters, and accommodating the demands of sound cinema.

Production context and the transition to sound

While methods for creating film performances became increasingly formalized and well articulated in the years following the transition to sound, the mystery or perhaps confusion about what was actually involved in producing film performances seems to have been heightened by production conventions that accompanied that transition. No longer were actors and directors rehearsing on stages next to productions in progress. No longer were directors guiding actors through performances with verbal instructions and/or the support of musical accompaniment to set the mood. As a consequence of production demands that developed in the years between 1926 and 1934, film performances were the result of ever-increasing levels of division of labour. Most pointedly, the people who developed acting talent and worked with actors during rehearsals were often not the same people who worked with actors on the set. Beginning in the 1930s, the studios hired *dialogue coaches* or *dialogue directors* to work with actors on specific parts and dialogue scenes. The studios also brought in *drama coaches* to train young contract players and prepare even experienced actors for screen tests and actual performances. In the years following the transition to sound, these acting experts became an integral – but consistently hidden – part of the process of producing film performances.

The transition to sound not only led to changes in actual production processes and the creation of new positions. Sound cinema also provided work for actors and directors who would draw on their sometimes extensive experience in theatrical stock companies and Broadway productions. Industry observers of the period saw the migration of acting talent from Broadway to Hollywood as highly significant. One finds that by 1929, articles in the *New York Times* are often discussing the central role theatre actors had played in the casts of 'audible pictures'. In an article entitled 'Acting for the Sound Film', *New York Times* critic Otis Skinner perhaps summarizes the received wisdom of the day in arguing that the 'traditional actor', the stage actor 'schooled in the method of bringing life, emotions, and humor directly to the audience' looked to be the dominant type of actor in theatre and the Hollywood sound film.[1]

The transition to sound made stage experience a valuable commodity, and opened the floodgates to scores of theatrically trained actors. It also indirectly and incrementally led to new venues and methods for actor training, for Hollywood's transition to sound not only made stage training increasingly important, it also made securing that experience increasingly difficult. In the teens and twenties, actors had learned their craft through apprenticeships in film and/or theatre, but the arrival of sound reduced actors' opportunities for on-the-job training, and in particular training in theatrical venues. Participating in a process shaped by multiple economic and industrial forces, Hollywood sound cinema contributed to the decline of vaudeville, Broadway, and theatrical stock companies by cutting into stage productions' already reduced audiences. Exemplifying the trend of all American theatre, the number of productions mounted on Broadway dropped from 300 in the 1928/1929 season to 80 productions ten years later.

As the 1930s progressed, film executives openly discussed the fact that traditional training grounds for Hollywood actors had been raided to breaking point. The steady decline in the number of stage productions forced the studios to search for other ways of developing and maintaining acting talent. They began to hire acting experts and establish actor training programmes on the lots. The first dialogue directors and drama coaches were brought into the system in 1933, when Paramount hired veteran stage producer/director Lillian Albertson as a dialogue coach, and, as head of the talent department, Phyllis Loughton, who had stage managed for Norman Bel Geddes and the Jesse Bonstelle stock company. In 1935, Florence Enright, a founding member of the prestigious Theatre Guild in New York, became a drama coach at Universal, and the next year moved to Twentieth Century Fox. In 1936, Lillian Burns, an actress who learned her craft with the Belasco Company and had been a member of the Dallas Little Theatre, was put in charge of MGM's drama department. In 1938, Warner Bros hired Sophie Rosenstein to design their actor training programme. Rosenstein came to Warner Bros with ten years of experience as a drama teacher at the University of Washington. As a child she had studied with Josephine Dillon, yet another figure who in the studio years joined the ranks of film acting teachers. In the mid to late 1930s, drama schools were established throughout Hollywood and by 1939 all of the major studios had actor training programmes.

In addition to opening drama schools on the lots, the studios developed an increasingly close relationship with established institutions such as the American Academy of Dramatic Art and the Pasadena Playhouse, as well as drama schools set up by Moscow Art Theatre expatriate Maria Ouspenskaya and theatre companies such as the Actors' Laboratory. The Academy of Dramatic Art, founded in 1884, was the oldest acting school in America, and from its inception had been guided by the philosophy that 'imitative methods' of coaching must be replaced by what Academy directors such as Charles Jehlinger believed were 'methods of scientific training'. Courses in acting were first offered by the Pasadena Playhouse in 1928. The two-year programme that emerged from those first classes provided training in what Playhouse founder Gilmor Brown and his colleagues believed were the principles of 'modern stagecraft' that guided developments at the Moscow Art Theatre and the 'little theatre' movement in America. An interest in providing scientific, modern, and systematic methods for developing acting skills and specific performances also informed the actor training programs at the other noteworthy drama schools in Hollywood. Maria Ouspenskaya's School of Dramatic Art, founded in New York in 1929 and moved to Hollywood in 1940, offered a two-year programme which, like other programmes of the period, required actors to spend the first year working almost entirely on developing the actor's instrument. The Actors' Laboratory – established in 1941 by former members of the Group Theatre such as Morris Carnovsky, Roman Bohnen, J. Edward Bromberg, and Phoebe Brand – provided actor training for a collection of contract players from RKO, Twentieth Century Fox, and Universal throughout the 1940s. The two-year programme they developed integrated courses in diction, body movement, improvisation, and life study, and was shaped by a philosophy Lab members referred to as a 'conscious approach to acting'.

The emerging importance of formal training for film actors was accompanied by increasingly systematic methods for developing skills and specific performances. Acting teachers working in Hollywood seem to have played a significant role in articulating and formalizing the period's methods of acting, for there is a collection of manuals authored by individuals who were integral to the network of actor training programmes in Hollywood. For example, *Modern Acting: A Manual* (1936), co-authored by Sophie Rosenstein, became a basic primer for Rosenstein's students in the drama school at Warner Bros, and also for contract players at Universal-International after Rosenstein became head of their talent development programme in 1949. *General Principles of Play Direction* (1936) by Gilmor Brown was a primary text for actors and directors at the Pasadena Playhouse, which for two decades served as a training ground and showcase for scores of film actors, and stage actors making the transition to film. In 1940, freelance acting teacher Josephine Dillon, who was Clark Gable's first acting teacher and later his first wife, published *Modern Acting: A Guide for Stage, Screen and Radio*. One finds Dillon's exhaustively detailed textbook consistently listed as a reference for courses offered at the Pasadena Playhouse and the Actors' Laboratory. In 1947, Lillian Albertson summarized the methods she had been presenting to contract players at Paramount and later at RKO in a manual entitled *Motion Picture Acting*, which opens with endorsements from actors Rosalind Russell and Cary Grant, journalist Adela Rogers St Johns, RKO casting director Ben Piazza, director Leo McCarey, and producer Jesse Lasky.

At this stage of research, it is not possible to determine how widely these manuals were studied. There is evidence, however, that following the transition to sound, acting experts became a recognized part of the Hollywood system. Trade papers of the period refer to the Actors' Lab as the best independent drama school in the country. Files from the Pasadena Playhouse show that a collection of film executives consistently secured casting advice from Playhouse directors, and openly admitted to using the Playhouse as a feeder school. Newspapers and archival records reveal that in 1940 Hedda Hopper asked drama coach Maria Ouspenskaya to write a guest column in which Ouspenskaya described the two-year programme offered by her drama school. A year later, the recognized role of acting experts, and of Ouspenskaya's unique contributions, is suggested in a Louella Parsons' column where Parsons describes Ouspenskaya as 'one of the finest coaches in the business'.

Stage and screen: quantitative adjustments

The transition to sound brought new acting experts to Hollywood and led to reconfigured working relations between actors and directors. It also brought with it a reassessment of stage and screen acting. In film acting manuals from the early 1920s, practitioners consistently argue that 'screen acting had become an art in itself [and that] it is not acting as we understand the word from what we see on the stage'.[2] Yet professionals working in Hollywood after the coming of sound no longer saw acting on stage as fundamentally different from acting on screen. Finding quantitative rather than qualitative distinctions in this later period, they discuss the need to adjust gestures and vocal delivery when moving from one venue to the other, and the fact that film acting required more training, experience, and concentration.

The period's changed perspective on screen acting is suggested by the fact that while practitioners in the early 1920s held conflicting views about the value of training in drama schools and theatrical productions, by the mid to late 1930s Hollywood professionals seem to have developed a definite consensus that training in dramatic schools and on the stage was not only valuable, but essential training for film actors. Training in tone production and diction were seen as important for work on both stage and screen. Training to create and maintain a body flexible enough to represent different types of characters was seen as a basic requirement of both stage and screen acting. Doing exercises to develop one's sensibilities, emotional recall ability, and skill in observation and concentration were considered part of any actor's work. The labour of building a character by analysing the script as a whole, creating a backstory for the character, and breaking down each scene to discover its purpose and the character's task, was seen as central to an actor's preparation for performances on both stage and screen.

In an article in *Theatre Arts*, American Academy of Dramatic Art graduate Hume Cronyn argues that 'the difference between acting for the screen and acting for the stage is negligible and the latter is, despite the exceptions, the best possible training for the former'.[3] He explains that the difference is negligible because in film, the actor's 'business, as in theatre, remains with the character he is to play and this will require his full powers of concentration'.[4] In another article in *Theatre Arts*, Bette Davis demystifies the stage/screen opposition by explaining that acting in theatre and film does not require actors to approach their characters differently, but that in preparation and performance certain adjustments need to be made. She writes that while 'it is axiomatic that a screen actor works in a medium that has its own, its special technical demands . . . this is not a qualitative distinction; it is merely quantitative'.[5] Davis explains the difference is merely quantitative because 'the art itself is not different . . . there does not exist one kind of acting for the stage, another for the films'.[6] Instead, stage and screen actors all 'work with the same tools. Our craft requires slight modification in them, that is all'.[7]

Practitioners of the period emphasize the fundamental bond between acting on stage and screen, and at the same time acknowledge that film practice in the studio era had its own technical demands. One finds actors consistently discussing the adjustments actors made when moving from one venue to another. They explain that 'acting in the movies [is] the same as acting anywhere [and that while they use] different projection, [they use] the same energy [because the transition is] like going from a big to a small theatre'.[8] Actors who came to film from theatre had to unlearn the practice of presenting large gestures on the stage, and discovered instead that 'shades of feeling could be made intimately visible by minute contractions of a muscle'.[9]

Many theatre actors came to enjoy working in film precisely because it allowed them to use small pieces of business to convey meaning. As Bette Davis explains, 'while the process of acting is basically the same [on stage and screen], the screen is a fantastic medium for the reality of little things'.[10] Cronyn echoes that point in saying that

> it may take a little time and some guidance for the stage actor to become accustomed to the degree of projection which will be most effective on the screen, but the technique of film acting is no unique or mystic formula.[11]

He explains that in film

> a whole new range of expression is opened to the actor. He can register with a whisper, a glance, a contraction of a muscle, in a manner that would be lost on stage. The camera will often reflect what a man thinks, without the degree of demonstration required in the theatre.[12]

These observations are repeated throughout materials from the period, for practitioners found that a film actor's new range of expression did not appear 'naturally' by virtue of being photographed, but instead had to emerge under his or her conscious control.

Working in a medium that magnified everything, actors and their collaborators clearly articulated the specific demands of acting in film. One finds acting experts explicitly stating that 'the fundamental difference between acting on the stage and the screen [was] the size of the actor from the viewpoint of the audience'.[13] Acting teacher Josephine Dillon explains that because images projected on the screen were sometimes 30 feet high, gestures and expressions would be 'huge and ridiculous if exaggerated . . . even if they [were performed only] as large as sometimes used in real life'.[14] Discussing the effect of performances being framed in close-up and projected on large screens, MGM drama coach Lillian Burns explains that actors coming to film from theatre had

> [to learn] projection from the *eyes* instead of just the voice [for] in motion pictures there is a camera, what I have termed a 'truth machine'. You cannot say 'dog' and think 'cat' because 'meow' will come out if you do.[15]

The magnification of actors' expressions and gestures led acting experts to formalize methods for creating film performances devoid of exaggerated, distracting, meaningless, and confusing movement. In her analysis of 'thought conversation', Josephine Dillon clarifies Burns's observation that the camera is a truth machine. Dillon explains that

> the expressions of the eyes . . . represent the emotions of the part played [and so] the actor should, in studying the part, improvise the probable mental conversations of the person portrayed, and memorize them as carefully as the written dialogue.[16]

Even more specifically, Dillon points out that

> the dialogue ascribed to the persons in the play conveys what the other people in the play are to believe [while] the expressions in the eyes and the body show to the audience what the character in the play is actually feeling and thinking.[17]

Dillon's advice to use internal dialogue to colour expression in actors' eyes suggests the integral points of contact between stage and screen acting in this period, for the method is in fact an extension of practices developed for performances in 'modern' theatre. As Rosenstein and her colleagues explain in *Modern Acting: A Manual*, actors should give themselves 'positive silent lines [that are] as true and absorbing as any lines' spoken on stage.[18] The authors point out that it will be easier for the actor 'to guarantee his attention in [a] particular scene if he works out a suitable thought pattern of definite reactions which he undergoes as religiously as he adheres to the written dialogue the author has given him.'[19] Rosenstein and her colleagues refer to the thought pattern developed for each and every scene as 'silent thinking'.[20]

Echoing observations about *quantitative adjustments* made for performing on camera, practitioners of the period consistently discuss shooting out of sequence, and having little or no rehearsal on the set in terms of adjustments to established (theatrical) methods. That is, even given the logistics of Hollywood film production, the transition to sound seems to have led professionals to minimize distinctions between methods for approaching stage and screen performance. With the addition of filmed 'dialogue scenes', at least some practitioners seem to have considered various methods of preparation for film performances as modifications of processes involved in theatrical rehearsals. Actor Hume Cronyn explains that when he worked in his first film 'it became obvious that in theatre terms there was to be practically no rehearsal'.[21] Understanding that, Cronyn responded like other experienced actors working in Hollywood and took the task of preparation on himself. He studied his script, chose his wardrobe, studied his character's relationship to other characters in the screenplay, developed 'some detailed ideas on [his] own character's background and his action throughout the story'.[22] He used an extension of theatre's dress rehearsal routine by choosing his character's house in the neighbourhood they were shooting, his character's place of work, and so on. He kept a notebook that gave him 'a point of reference . . . to return to, and recheck, character fundamentals'.[23] Cronyn explains that a film actor's individual preparation makes it possible to 'step before the camera with a clear and logical plan of what you would like to do and how you would like to do it'.[24]

Repeating points made by theatrically trained actors like Cronyn, MGM drama coach Lillian Burns describes the work of film professionals who came to the set fully prepared, able to incorporate directors' suggestions precisely because they had done their homework and could create characters on their own. In an interview with columnist Gladys Hall, Burns explains that little rehearsal time on the set meant more, not less, labour for film actors. Burns argues that while 'they say it's so easy [to act in film] you don't go over and over it [on the set] as you do on stage'.[25] Burns sees overcoming the problem of working without rehearsal and shooting out of sequence as one that required skill, rather than reliance on a larger-than-life personality. Noting that she gets 'angry when people say [film acting] isn't as difficult as the stage', Burns points to the example of Greer Garson, who in playing a scene in *Madame Curie* 'sat absolutely quiet, didn't talk for ten minutes, then walked to a drape and broke down and sobbed'. Burns remarks, 'to walk into that on a cold morning, that takes doing'.[26]

Coming from Burns, the insight and the compliment is worth noting, for before Burns came to MGM in 1936, there had been classes in diction, body movement, and so on, but 'working through production [helping to cast and rehearse actors] had never been done quite the way [she] did it'.[27] Burns not only worked with executives on hiring and casting, she also worked with, and sometimes around, studio directors. She would work privately with leading actors because, as MGM executive Al Trescony explains, she could 'get performances out of actors that even surprised them'.[28] Trescony notes that Burns not only prepared 'most of our stars for their specific roles . . . often she would be asked by the heads of the other studios to work with their stars'.[29] 'Respected because of her talent and feared because she leveled with everyone',[30] like other dialogue directors and drama coaches of the period, Lillian Burns played a pivotal role in the production of film performances in the 1930s and 1940s.

Building a dramatic character

For the people whose job it was to produce performances, the script served as a blueprint that was studied to ensure that actors arrived on the set prepared to deliver their performances. Bette Davis explains that 'without scripts none of us can work. It's the beginning of the work.'[31] Hume Cronyn points out that the actor's first task is to establish the facts, and he remarks, 'it's surprising how much information is contained in the text, how many questions are answered by careful re-reading.'[32] He argues that 'your own creative work should be based on the fact and suggestion supplied by the author, rather than on independent fancy.'[33]

Echoing the actors' observations, Lillian Burns explains: 'the writer – that's the seed'.[34] Working with Burns, one learned that after studying the script, actors begin to give their characters life by 'establishing a complete person, a complete life', for example, where the character went to school, what he or she liked to wear, what that character would do in a certain circumstance because of his or her relationships with parents, brothers, and sisters, and so on.[35] Janet Leigh recalls Burns taught her that

> you give that person a real entity, so that wherever you happen to start the story you are coming from somewhere; you know where this person's been, why this person reacts the way she does. Because it may not be your way of reacting, but it would be the character's.[36]

Cronyn echoes her point. He explains that an actor's own responses are immaterial, and that actors must always ask, 'If I were *this kind of person* in this situation, what would I do? How would I feel, think, behave, react, etc.?'[37]

In her 1947 acting manual, drama coach Lillian Albertson also presents the script as the starting point for the production of film performances. Albertson argues, in no uncertain terms, that '*before performance comes interpretation*. By that, I mean the strictly intellectual analysis of a role.'[38] In a strictly intellectual analysis, actors use the script to determine the character's background, asking 'what made this person feel the way he or she does, and do the things they do?'[39] Albertson points out that 'if there is not enough in the dialogue to provide you with all the motives animating them, *make up stories about them* so that they seem alive to you.'[40] For actors in the studio era, the practice of filling in characters' backgrounds was part of the process of slowly and methodically entering into the world of the characters. That process required actors to be touched by the characters emotionally. Actors' Laboratory member Morris Carnovsky explains that great parts 'give us "thoughts beyond the reaches of our souls" . . . they are great images [that actors] learn to use and to be shaken [by].'[41]

Like other professionals of the period, Albertson acknowledges that acting was not simply a matter of transcribing what one found in the script. She argues that an actor is a kind of prism through which the character is refracted, and explains that *'the author supplies the material which |actors| cut and fit to their own personalities and physical appearances'*.[42] Here Albertson is not suggesting that actors play themselves. Instead, she is articulating the era's dominant view that an actor's instrument necessarily colours a performance, and that as a consequence an actor must take conscious control of it. Echoing Albertson's point, the Actors' Laboratory teaching staff describe the art of acting as one that incorporates in *sensible* terms and by means of the actor's personal equipment an impression or image previously indicated by the author. Acting experts of the period saw the process of acting as one in which actors take in an impression of the character from the script, and in the process of representing the character necessarily colour it with their own expression. Underscoring the period's holistic or organic view of this process, Morris Carnovsky explains that acting is never a passive experience because, as he puts it, 'there's no taking in |of the character| without giving out – no reaction without action. All is in process of becoming.'[43]

Representing a dramatic character on screen

Materials from the period suggest that in the 1930s and 1940s, actors and their collaborators believed that actors should work to produce convincing performances without recourse to 'living the part'. Lillian Albertson explains that 'mental pictures', which an actor develops in the course of studying the script, make the events of the scene *'alive in |the actor's| memory'*.[44] Consequently they can be used by the actor to make his or her performance convincing, vivid, lifelike. Albertson exhorts actors to

> make all the mental pictures you can in *preparation of the scene* – and the more graphic the better . . . make your mental pictures as real as you possibly can in *studying* the part, then *play from memory – the synthetic memories you have invented*.[45]

An interview with Jessica Tandy provides a gloss on Albertson's statement. When asked how she prepared for and then enacted her portrayal in the Actors' Laboratory stage production of *Portrait of a Madonna*, Tandy explained that she worked through the process she always had, first reading and rereading the script, then looking for points of contact with her own experience she could draw on, then developing a background for the character. For the performance she explains that she never recalled an emotion, but instead that the feelings which coloured her performance were always the result of seeing the pictures she had created in her study, and that each speech led to another through a series of mental pictures.

Manuals from the period explain that actors could and should use their mental pictures once they developed their ability to concentrate on them. Albertson explains that 'through *concentration* you learn to *use* the creative acting imagination, and concentration is something that *can be developed*'.[46] She argues that actors must develop their ability to concentrate on the character during performances because it is only 'concentration |that| enables you to shut out every thought but the scene and the character you are portraying'.[47] By using concentration to connect to the mental pictures one creates in studying the character in his or her given situations, 'you develop the *mood* that must "color" every action and every word you speak'.[48] Albertson argues that it is not enough to move gracefully and naturally and to read lines intelligently. Instead, actors need to understand that 'to get every ounce of meaning out of your lines . . . your MOOD [must] be what it should be [because] *spoken words mean practically nothing unless mood colors them*.'[49]

For experienced practitioners of the period, moods that colour actions and lines of dialogue were established by actors making decisions about how a character would feel in a certain circumstance. Those decisions would become 'scripted' into a series of mental pictures, which actors would then recall during performance. Because they were 'synthetic memories' invented by actors during their study of the script, they could be activated by opening one's 'mental notebook', and let go of immediately after the scene or take was over. Albertson explains that 'as your powers of concentration increase, you will be able *to turn mood on and off* as readily and as surely as you turn on a faucet and get water, and turn it off to stop the flow!'[50]

Rosenstein's *Modern Acting: A Manual* anticipates Albertson's observations, and is especially clear that actors must learn to transfer emotions to the circumstances of the scene. Describing the role imagination plays in the process of preparing a part, Rosenstein and her colleagues explain that 'once we recall a former emotion we must sustain it long enough to transpose it to the new situation', and that while it may not be easy to dispense with recollected details, 'by constant drill . . . we can learn to drop them at will and preserve only the emotion they served to revive'.[51] In other words, for acting experts of the period, developing the ability to concentrate did not just keep actors from being distracted – it was seen as the basis of convincing performance.

For practitioners in the 1930s and 1940s, concentration, not feeling, was the key to great acting. Like other acting professionals of the period, Morris Carnovsky articulates the logic of striving to maintain emotional distance from the feelings portrayed. He explains that actors cannot get lost in emotional moments because they need to keep up with and anticipate the sequence of actions in the narrative. He writes: 'I always think of the actor as not only doing, but standing aside and watching what he is doing, so as to be able to propel himself to the next thing and the next thing and the next.'[52] Josephine Dillon also makes the point that actors need to be able to think about what they are doing, and she argues that acting in film makes emotional distance an especially high priority. Dillon explains that 'to submerge one's self into the emotion of the part being played would be to put the actor at the mercy of his emotions and make him incapable of using the skillful technique that the camera demands.'[53]

Drama coach Lillian Albertson continually contrasts the methods she describes with positions that encouraged actors to use their own feelings to generate convincing performances. Albertson notes that she had seen 'young actors in motion pictures try to lash themselves into a pathetic mood [by trying] to think of something *real* that [would] harrow their souls'.[54] She explains that in the process, actors would find themselves in an 'agonizing attempt to *feel* something' that was easily and invariably disturbed by the concrete reality of the performance and production context.[55] Albertson argues that the strategy of drawing on mood patterns and voice patterns that have been embedded into the mental pictures actors construct in their study of the part was a technique for generating lifelike performances that was 'much surer and far less wearing on the nervous system'.[56]

The ability to 'divorce outward gestures and expressions from their ordinary affective content',[57] prized by practitioners in the 1930s and 1940s, is precisely what proponents of Method acting in the 1950s would reject, for they saw that 'ability' as the source of inauthentic performance, and argued that dispassionate execution of performance, along with extensive preparation and an investment in training the actor's physical instrument, necessarily led to performances and performance styles that were 'unrealistic' and unimaginative. Yet the methods described by Albertson, Carnovsky, Davis, Cronyn, and others who articulated the views of the 1930s and 1940s are not necessarily recipes for conventional performances. Instead, they represent a definable position in a long history of debates within the acting profession.

As stated by Denis Diderot in the eighteenth century, the paradox of acting is that one cannot act without feeling, yet if one feels one cannot act. For practitioners in the 1930s and 1940s, the solution to the paradox was to use synthetic memories to fuel controlled emotional experience during performance. Like Stanislavsky, they believed that actors should welcome personal and primary experience for the insights it could offer in the process of studying a script and building a character, but that during performance, actors needed to summon feelings that they had connected to the mental pictures they themselves had crafted after close study of the script. Like Stanislavsky, they argued that training, preparation, and cool-headed acting provided the secure basis for performances and performance styles that emerged from the unique demands of each script. And prosaic as it may sound, acting professionals of the period seem to have found that Hollywood's assembly-line mode of production, with its intense division of labor, developed within it rather efficient ways for actors and their collaborators to craft performances.

Notes

1 O. Skinner, 'Acting for the Sound Film', *New York Times*, 25 January 1931.

2 I. Klump and H. Klumph, *Screen Acting*, New York, Falk Publishing, 1921, p. 104.

3 H. Cronyn, 'Notes on Film Acting', *Theatre Arts* 35, June 1949, p. 46.

4 Ibid.

5 B. Davis, 'On Acting in Films', *Theatre Arts* 25, September 1946, p. 634.

6 Ibid.

7 Ibid.

8 L. Penn, 'Stanislavski and a Ten Day Shooting', *Actors' Laboratory Newsletter*, Actors' Laboratory Collection, University of California, Los Angeles, *c.* 1946.

9 D. Powell, 'Acting for Motion Pictures', *Theatre Today*, Actors' Laboratory Collection, University of California, Los Angeles, *c.* 1947.

10 B. Davis, interview, *Filmmakers on Filmmaking: The American Film Institute Seminars on Motion Pictures and Television Vol.* 2, Los Angeles, Tarcher, 1983, p. 106.

11 Cronyn, 'Notes on Film Acting', p. 46.

12 Ibid.

13 J. Dillon, *Modern Screen, and Radio, Acting: A Guide for Stage*, New York, Prentice Hall, 1940, p. 3.

14 Ibid., p. 4.

15 L. Burns, interview, Performing Arts Oral History Collection, Southern Methodist University, 17 August 1986.

16 Dillon, *Modern Screen, and Radio, Acting*, p. 9.

17 Ibid.

18 S. Rosenstein, L. A. Haydon, and W. Sparrow, *Modern Acting: A Manual*, New York, Samuel French, 1936, p. 61.

19 Ibid., P. 62.
20 Ibid., p. 110.
21 Cronyn, 'Notes on Film Acting', p. 45.
22 Ibid.
23 Ibid., p. 46.
24 Ibid., p. 47.
25 L. Burns and G. Sidney, interview, Gladys Hall Collection, Margaret Herrick Library of the Motion Picture Academy of Arts and Sciences, *c.* 1945.
26 Ibid.
27 Burns, interview, Performing Arts Oral History Collection, 1986.
28 A. Trescony, interview, Performing Arts Oral History Collection, Southern Methodist University, 20 August 1986.
29 Ibid.
30 Ibid.
31 Davis, interview, *Filmmakers on Filmmaking*, p. 107.
32 Cronyn, 'Notes on Film Acting', p. 48.
33 Ibid.
34 Burns, interview, Performing Arts Oral History Collection, 1986.
35 J. Leigh, interview, Performing Arts Oral History Collection, Southern Methodist University, 25 July 1984.
36 Ibid.
37 Cronyn, 'Notes on Film Acting', p. 48.
38 L. Albertson, *Motion Picture Acting*, New York, Funk & Wagnalls, 1947, p. 65.
39 Ibid.
40 Ibid.
41 M. Carnovsky, 'Let's Talk', *Workshop Craftsmen*, Actors' Laboratory Collection, University of California, Los Angeles, January 1948.
42 Albertson, *Motion Picture Acting*, p. 66.
43 Carnovsky, 'Let's Talk'.
44 Albertson, *Motion Picture Acting*, p. 63.
45 Ibid.
46 Ibid., p. 55.
47 Ibid.
48 Ibid.
49 Ibid., pp. 55–56.
50 Ibid., p. 57.
51 Rosenstein, Haydon, and Sparrow, *Modern Acting: A Manual*, p. 29.
52 M. Carnovsky, 'The Actor's Eye', *Performing Arts Journal*, 1984, p. 23.
53 Dillon, *Modern Acting*, p. 7.
54 Albertson, *Motion Picture Acting*, p. 61.
55 Ibid., p. 62.
56 Ibid.
57 J. Roach, *The Player's Passion*, Ann Arbor, University of Michigan Press, 1996, p. 135.

PART THREE

STYLE AND TECHNIQUE

Introduction

The essays in the last two sections dealt with acting in general, either analyzing the status of film acting in general or broad historical trends in the creation and transformation of film acting in the early twentieth century. Essays in this section, by contrast, attend to specific performances or modes of performance, ranging from Lillian Gish's performance in *True Heart Susie* (1919) to Marlon Brando's performance in *On the Waterfront* (1954), and from 1930s American film comedies to European avant-garde and independent cinema. These essays represent a range of approaches to cinema acting. In addition to analyses of the external signs of performance, or, in other words, descriptions of what an actor or actress does on screen, these essays consider various theories of acting and actor training that lay behind individual performances, as well as general principles of performance for specific genres or modes of filmmaking. Just as the essays in the last section attested to the resiliency of seemingly outmoded styles of acting, such as the "histrionic" style, and the overlap among acting styles in different historical periods, the essays in this section suggest that at any given moment in time, and even within a single performance, there is not a simple or singular approach to acting involved, such as a Delsartean system of poses or pure Method acting. Instead there exists a host of options that will be employed by an individual actor in a single film, within a genre across a series of films, or among members of an ensemble in a film or series of films. Offering varied approaches to acting and providing close and detailed analyses of acting in four distinct styles and time periods, the essays here furnish a glimpse of the wide-range of styles and techniques employed in film acting and provide models for future research.

Following on the heels of the transitional period in silent-film acting discussed in the essays by Roberta Pearson and Ben Brewster and Lea Jacobs in the last section, it would seem that Lillian Gish's performance in *True Heart Susie* would be easy to place within the well-established "verisimilar" style. However, despite the fact that the dominant discourse around acting since at least 1914 emphasized "natural," transparent behavior, James Naremore claims that a close examination of Gish's 1919 performance shows her employing a wide variety of acting styles, and not just the dominant "natural" style. In a performance that Naremore says "ranges between innocence and experience, between stereotypical girlishness and wry, sophisticated maturity," Gish draws on techniques that range from the much-praised naturalism for which Griffith and his actors are famous to the seemingly outmoded but nonetheless effective practices of gestural "signing," pantomime, and pictorial poses. Naremore claims that Gish shows a gift for physical comedy and adopts a wide vocabulary of movement akin to emergent silent comedians such as Harold Lloyd. In addition, she utilizes small gestures and extremely subtle changes in expression—akin to the "polyphonic play of features" Balàzs describes—in close-ups where she "reduces theatrical pantomime to its most microscopic form, displaying a stream of emotions."

Rather than a single performance, Henry Jenkins's contribution examines general principles of performance in early sound comedies. Looking at five classes of comedian comedy, including revue films, showcase films, comic romances, anarchistic comedies, and affirmative comedies, Jenkins suggests that there are certain tendencies in comedian comedy of the 1930s, which will be employed to varying degrees in these varied subgenres and which differ from classical realist styles. First, he notes that, as in the musical, moments of comedic performance will be more or less integrated with the narrative, but that, in general, comedian comedies will allow moments of virtuoso comedic performance to exceed and even abandon narrative motivation. Second, unlike classical realist cinema, where the character and star will usually be well-integrated to create a neat fit, in early sound comedies, the performer's personality will often overtake the role. Related to both of the above, Jenkins finds that comedies allow a kind of "expressive anarchy" in which the comedian's gags are not coordinated with the development of a rounded character, but function independently of character. This goes against a classical realist tendency toward "expressive coherence" between actor and role. This "expressive anarchy" factors into a more presentational style of performance in which comedians frequently violate the representational convention of the fourth wall and employ direct address, reflexive gags, and muttered asides to the audience. Finally, Jenkins claims that actors in a single film will represent a heterogeneous mix of contrasting acting styles, rather than homogeneity across the cast. Thus, in a Marx Brothers movie, for instance, there may be differing codes of performance for Groucho, Harpo, and Chico, as opposed to straight comic foils like Margaret Dumont, and there may be an entirely different set of performance principles at work for the romantic leads.

Taking a different tack from both Naremore and Jenkins, Virginia Wright Wexman situates her analysis of Marlon Brando's performance in *On the Waterfront* in a discussion of Method acting and the sexual politics of 1950s America. Wexman claims that American films in the 1950s adopted the Method as a more realistic style of acting not only because of the style's emphasis on a close fit between actor and character but also because Method techniques were "peculiarly well-suited to delineate a new type of male romantic hero." Wexman traces the tenets of Method acting from its origins with Stanislavski and the Moscow Art Theatre through its incarnation at the American Group Theatre in the 1930s to Lee Strasberg's interpretation of the Method at the Actors Studio in the 1950s. She argues that the Strasberg version of the Method was especially well-suited to the Hollywood star system because Strasberg transformed a socialistic, egalitarian theory of acting into a more solipsistic, confessional approach to acting that mapped the actor's personal feelings onto those of the character. Through a close reading of Brando's Method techniques in *On the Waterfront*, Wexman finds that he "recreates romance as a drama of male neuroticism" and also invests his characterization "with an unprecedented aura of verisimilitude."

Finally, Andrew Higson offers an assessment of acting in independent European cinema that is, at the same time, proscriptive for British independent cinema. In order to characterize an acting style, Higson suggests that one can examine the *intentions* behind acting, by looking at theories of acting, such as Brecht, or actor training, such as the Method, or examine the *effects* of acting, or what happens on screen. His interest is "in the relationship between the two," to consider both the skills and forms of concentration specific to certain schools of acting and the "meaningfulness of acting signs" produced under various institutional and ideological conditions of cinema. While considering theoretical positions from Brecht, Kuleshov, Bresson, and others, as well as actual performances in films by Bresson, Deren, Kuleshov, Straub-Huillet and Eisenstein, he proposes a semiotics of the following acting signs: the facial, the gestural, the corporeal (or postural), and the vocal. He advocates descriptive parameters for acting in independent or avant-garde cinema that would include: economy of the voice; economy of the face, gesture and body; precision of movement; fragmentation of character and externalization of emotion; stylization and distanciation; and working in an ensemble across a number of films. By categorizing independent acting in this way, Higson hopes to be able to capture the unintended effects of acting, moments when intention and effect seem at odds, and to be open to the ambiguities, contradictions, and imprecision of meaning built into any acting strategy. He also aims to escape rigid assumptions about the ideological efficacy of any particular theory of acting, or false polarizations, such as the common opposition between naturalist and anti-naturalist acting.

8

Lillian Gish in *True Heart Susie* (1919)

JAMES NAREMORE

Griffith's *True Heart Susie* opens in a one-room Indiana schoolhouse, where a teacher is conducting a spelling bee. The students are standing in a row around the walls of the room, arranged according to their ages. The camera isolates two students—William and Susie (Robert Harron and Lillian Gish)—showing them facing the camera as if in a police lineup. Susie stands on the left, holding herself at attention with her arms stiffly at her sides; her head is cocked slightly, her eyes opened wide, her brows raised in an exaggeratedly cute, almost dopey, innocence. Next to her William stands more awkwardly, rocking from one foot to the other in discomfort over the teacher's impending question. Although a title card prior to the shot identifies Susie as "plain," the girl we see is quite pretty. Her tiny nose and rosebud mouth are set off against her large eyes, and her pale face is surrounded by wispy blonde hair gathered into pigtails. A simple plaid frock conceals her body, but obviously she is slender and well proportioned.

Griffith now cuts to the teacher, who quizzes the younger students and turns to glance offscreen in the direction of William and Susie. "Anonymous," she asks, and we return to a shot that appears identical to the previous one; at any rate the camera angle is the same, the clothing and the relative positions of the players are the same, and Robert Harron still looks like the same clumsy boy. Gish, however, might be a different person. One reason for the change is a subtle, unmotivated alteration in the lighting, which makes her hair seem much darker; but she also wears the hair differently, so that bangs fall over her forehead and her curls are less evident. Moreover, her posture and her facial expression suggest that she has totally revised her conception of the role. Her arms are relaxed, her hands are clasped calmly in front of her, and she glances sidelong up at William; gone is the kewpie-doll innocence, replaced by a quite mature face, less self-consciously pretty and more knowing.

Suddenly, a jump cut returns us to the first image of the couple, as if Griffith had discovered an error, partly erased it, and restored the original shot. William raises his hand for another chance at answering the question. Susie, looking rather dotty, her eyes wide with fake innocence and her head wobbling from side to side, seems to say, "I know!" She spells the word, ending her recitation with a self-satisfied smile.

When the sequence is slowed down with an analyzing projector or when a single frame is isolated from the two shots, the transformation in Gish is remarkable. During an ordinary viewing, however, the error in continuity goes by almost unnoticed. I mention it chiefly because the two images of Gish indicate a polar opposition that she keeps in balance throughout the film. Her performance ranges between innocence and experience, between stereotypical girlishness and wry, sophisticated maturity—the latter quality giving *True Heart Susie* much of its continuing interest. In other ways, too, Gish adopts a variety of expressive attitudes for the role. As the narrative develops, she exhibits distinct personae that mark the growth of the character; and within individual sequences, her performance involves multiple faces that the audience is *supposed* to notice—especially when Susie is shown masking her feelings around others. If we look at her work more closely, we can see that it also entails a variety of acting styles, creating a complex emotional tone within Griffith's otherwise simple story. Thus, although Susie may be a "true heart," her identity (much like Gish's public identity as a star) is created out of disparate, sometimes contradictory, moments, all held together by a name, a narrative, and a gift for mimicry. The minor disturbance of illusion in the sequence I have described helps call attention to the way Gish normally keeps differing elements of the characterization in harmonious relation, maintaining a sense of unity across scores of shots.

I want to emphasize Gish's variety because *True Heart Susie* requires a good deal more actorly invention than is usually recognized. Then, too, I hope to counter the misleading notion that good movie acting consists of *being* rather than *meaning*. In certain ways, of course, we hardly need to be reminded that Gish was a player who contributed artistic labor to her films; her scenarios were constructed to highlight her emotive talents, and the silent medium made her seem an artist by definition, a "poet" who suggested character through pantomime. Even so, the dominant theory of movie acting after 1914 was articulated in terms of "natural," transparent, behavior. "We are forced to develop a new technique of acting before the camera," Griffith wrote. "People who come to me from the theater use the quick broad gestures and movements which they have employed on the stage. I am trying to develop realism in pictures by teaching the value of deliberation and repose" (quoted in Gish, 88).[1] As a result, performers like Gish were frequently praised for their authenticity, a quality that transcended mere art.

The star system contributed to an increasingly antimimetic conception of acting because it made some of the links between actors and roles seem inevitable. Almost from the beginning, movie stars were regarded as aesthetic objects rather than as artists, or as personalities who had a documentary reality. Griffith and many other directors strengthened the "organic" effect by inserting details from an actor's real life into the fiction. In *True Heart Susie*, for example, when Susie carries on imaginary conversations with the photograph of her dead mother, the picture she looks at shows Lillian Gish's own mother, cradling the infant Lillian in her arms. When William later tells Susie that men flirt with "painted and powdered" women but marry the "plain and simple ones," the joke is partly on Robert Harron, who said the same thing during his offscreen courtship with Dorothy Gish. It hardly matters whether anyone in the audience recognized these details, since the deepest purpose of biographical material was to facilitate performance, helping players to merge with their parts. The emphasis on personal relevance and sincerity was further enforced by the early critical discourse on stars, which helped shape the attitudes of viewers and moviemakers alike. Thus Edward Wagenknecht, who in 1927 wrote the first extended appreciation of Gish, remarked that "she always claims the right to make her roles over to suit Lillian Gish." He praised her for expressing "her own point of view, a distinctive something which is Lillian Gish and nobody else on earth." "The part and the actress are one," he wrote. "In a very deep and very true sense, she is the profoundest kind of actress: that is to say she does not 'act' at all; she *is*" (249–50).[2]

At first glance, *True Heart Susie* lends additional support to such romantic-realist attitudes. It contains a virtual sermon on the theme of Art versus Nature, and its central character is valued precisely because she is what she seems. "Is real life interesting?" Griffith asks in the first title card, and the story, as it develops, becomes a parable about craft and deception in conflict with simple, artless goodness. Susie, the true-hearted country girl, is contrasted at every point with Bettina (Clarine Seymour), the scheming milliner from Chicago: Bettina drives around in "Sporty" Malone's flashy car, dances the Charleston, and engages in loose sex; meanwhile Susie embraces her cow, does spontaneous dances of joy, and lives in single-minded devotion to William. Bettina spends a good deal of time in front of a mirror, fashioning an image, whereas Susie is shown hoeing the fields or sitting by the hearth. Bettina "acts" in flamboyant style, deceiving men with her paint and powder, but when Susie tries to follow suit, daubing her face with cornstarch (a homelier, more "honest" substance that is all she can afford), her puritanical aunt berates her: "Do you think you can improve on the Lord's work?" The equation seems exact: if Art is as bad as Bettina, then Nature is as good as Susie—hence, by a process of association, we might argue that Gish is profound to the degree that she rejects old-fashioned theatrical mimesis, letting her moral "self" shine through the fiction.

But when we examine Griffith's parable more closely, it doesn't work out so neatly. All three major characters aspire to middle-class respectability, and this desire involves them in various degrees of "acting." *True Heart Susie* is therefore filled with performances-within-performance: Bettina is the most obviously theatricalized figure, batting her eyes seductively at William, playing a carefully contrived role that enables her to capture the town's most eligible bachelor. Prior to her entry on the scene, however, William has also developed an image for himself. When he returns from college, he no longer behaves like a rube; grandly stroking a new mustache, he parades the streets and practices a sermon, using Susie as his enraptured audience. As for Susie herself, she is in one sense as much a schemer and actor as Bettina. She decides early in the film that she will change William from a bumpkin into an educated pillar of the community ("I must marry a smart man!"). She sells her farm animals in order to pay William's college tuition, and then keeps the source of the money secret, playing the innocent companion. From the first we see that she is more clever than William; unable, because she is a woman, to become a Horatio Alger, she determines to create one and marry him. And although she is less sophisticated than Bettina, she seems no less sexually and romantically driven, ready at any moment to dress up for William. Bettina is in fact Susie's doppelgänger, as Susie inadvertently acknowledges in the scene where, overcome with pity, she holds her ailing rival in her arms. The real difference between the two is that Susie is wiser and more self-sufficient, and her craftiness is benign; William is her work of art.

It is difficult to say exactly how much Griffith wants the film to be interpreted in this ironic fashion. Like the novelist Samuel Richardson, he is too didactic to be described as a formal realist, and too realistic to be described as a "primitive" or a wish-fulfilling fantasist. Terry Eagleton's remarks on Richardson's *Pamela* could be applied with little qualification to *Susie*: "Do we laugh with Pamela at the novel's solemn moralizing of her 'baser' motives, or laugh with the novel at her . . . self-apologies? Do we have the edge over both the novel and Pamela, or does the novel have the edge over us all?" The problem confounds us because

Richardson's writing (like Griffith's direction and Gish's performance) seems compounded of two voices, neither having absolute priority. The result is what Eagleton describes as an uneasy relation between "the metalanguage of bourgeois morality" and a "still resilient popular speech" (*The Rape of Clarissa*, 32–33).

The film seems only partly aware of the discrepancy, and its plot goes through a series of improbable twists in order to achieve a happy ending. Bettina steals William from Susie, marries him, and becomes a philandering wife. One evening, she finds herself accidentally locked outdoors during a rainstorm. Her exposure to the elements gives her pneumonia, and even though Susie nurses her, she dies. Later, one of Bettina's friends tells William the truth about his dead wife's infidelity, and at nearly the same moment he learns that Susie paid for his education. Soon afterward, in an especially coy scene, we see him proposing marriage to Susie from outside her flower-bedecked window. They consummate a long-deferred kiss, and to make the ending still more rosy the film transforms Susie—now a mature woman who has suffered rejection—back into a girlish innocent: Griffith closes with a reprise of an image we saw near the opening, showing William and Susie *as children*, walking together down a country road. The soft focus shot is bathed in a nostalgic light, and a title card asks us to imagine the two "as they once were." Thus, using plot conventions of nineteenth-century melodrama, together with certain events from Dickens's *David Copperfield* and *Great Expectations*, Griffith has awkwardly smoothed over the many contradictions that sustain an ideology of the natural self.

As Thomas Elsaesser and others have pointed out, this sort of plot has a long history; where *Susie* is concerned, the ancestry of the narrative can be traced back not only to Richardson's novels but also to the eighteenth-century dramatic genre known in England as "sentimental" or "weeping comedy." Literature for the stage in the eighteenth century was designed to challenge the cynical attitudes of Restoration drama (much as Griffith denounces flappers and city slickers), showing bourgeois life in its best light. Leading characters were admired for their sincerity or "sentiment"—a term that suggested "virtuous or moral emotion"—and the chief acting style, made famous by the tragedian David Garrick, involved painterly *tableaux*, in which the players struck elaborate poses (Todd, 34). The typical plot formula combined pathetic and comic situations, resolving all conflict in the fifth act and confirming marriage and sensitive fellow-feeling as the ultimate good. Oliver Goldsmith joked about the form, noting its hypocritical tendency to forgive any fault or reprieve any character "in consideration of the goodness of their hearts." Nevertheless, sentimental comedies multiplied, directly influencing Victorian literature and, indirectly, the Hollywood narrative. The leading characters of such dramas also helped to form the style of early movie stars. Gish, for example, repeatedly played women whose emotions were "spiritualized," motivated by a simple goodness of heart. Charles Chaplin is a more complex, refined version of the same type. As David Thomson notes, "Chaplin's persona is often very close to eighteenth-century sentimentality: a beautifully mannered dreamer who has trained himself into the emotional sensibility that will sometimes shame a woman" (98).

Variants of bourgeois sentimental comedy can still be found in modern theater and films, disguised somewhat by naturalistic conventions and inflected by the Freudian "family drama." Critics nearly always treat Griffith's uses of the form with condescension, but the survival of the basic plot indicates that we have not moved far from his values—especially as they are expressed in marriage, family life, and charity toward the weak. Raymond Williams has cautioned historians not to take these values lightly:

> The wider basis of sentimental comedy, and of a main tradition in the novel, was the particular kind of humanitarian feeling, the strong if inarticulate appeal to a fundamental "goodness of heart"; the sense of every individual's closeness to vice and folly, so that pity for their exemplars is the most relevant emotion, and recovery and rehabilitation must be believed in; the sense, finally, that there are few absolute values, and that tolerance and kindness are major virtues. In rebuking the sentimental comedy, as in both its early examples and its subsequent history it seems necessary to do, we should be prepared to recognize that in point of moral assumptions, and of a whole consequent feeling about life, most of us are its blood relations. (*The Long Revolution*, 288).

Seen in Williams's terms, one of Lillian Gish's achievements was to embody a "feeling about life"—making "good heartedness" plausible, conveying sweetness and moral sentiment without making us doubt her sincerity. The somewhat Cavalier ethos of American life after World War I, when a good many important stars were beginning to resemble college boys or flappers, made this job especially difficult; Gish was able to maintain her stardom into the middle twenties (when L. B. Mayer tried to talk her into having an "affair" that the studio could publicize) only because she was a master at expressing believable contradictions within her old-fashioned characters, hinting at sensuality and sophistication even in a purely bucolic role like that of Susie.

Gish's ability both to play comic scenes and to give a relatively complex tone to pathos also suggests that she was far from being a "natural" personality whom Griffith employed in appropriate fictional contexts. True, she had physical characteristics well suited for Griffith's fantasies of delicate, idealized girls tormented by brutish males. Never an extraordinarily beautiful or striking woman, she had a china doll's complexion and an ability to look young (which she retains even today). To a degree, however, her physical appearance was the product of design. Her features seem petite and regular—the perfect incarnation of WASP beauty—but she has said that she never laughed in her early films because her mouth, which is so tiny on the screen, was oversized in relation to her eyes.[3] She is usually described as "frail," but her softness was an illusion, like Chaplin's. She was small but strong, as anyone can see from her erect carriage, which in some contexts made her look prim. She had an iron constitution, a highly conditioned and flexible body, a cheerful and attractive face, and a capacity for delicate gestures. Out of this raw material, aided by her intelligence and apparently Spartan devotion to her job, she made herself into a memorable character type and an expressive instrument with more range than is immediately apparent.

Gish specialized in child-women with a strong maternal streak—a description that already suggests some of the oppositions she was able to contain. Despite the cloyingly sweet roles she was given, she was able to seduce the audience and redeem the movie, sometimes with such skill that her art was invisible. Thus Charles Affron, who recognizes her inventiveness in other contexts, finds her merely "adorable" in *True Heart Susie*, a film he describes as a "personal" and "original" Griffith work in which Gish is "never asked to be anything more than cutesy-pie." Her performance, he claims, is "simplistic" and "shackled by sweetness" (48–47). The trouble with this conclusion is that if the film works—and virtually everyone seems to agree that it does—it must do so largely because of Gish, who contributed to its most compelling imagery and who completes what one might call the "writing out" of the plot through action. In fact Gish is asked to do a great deal in the course of the film. Not only must she convey Susie's growth from innocence to experience, charting the turns of the narrative;

she must also provide a lively charm that will countervail self-sacrificing goodness. As she herself once put it, "Virgins are the hardest roles to play. Those dear little girls—to make them interesting takes great vitality." At every moment, therefore, she suggests a duality in her character, making us feel cleverness beneath youth, strength beneath fragility, humor beneath spirituality, and sexual warmth beneath propriety. To do all this, she has to call upon a variety of skills and a number of possible "selves." In the following brief analysis, I try to point out some of them, illustrating the range of tasks she accomplishes in the course of what might seem one of her simplest performances.

Gish was influenced by the pantomime, or mimetic, form of acting she had learned in turn-of-the-century theater. But in Griffith's films, even at this relatively late period, players could swing back and forth between radically different kinds of behavior. At one extreme, especially in comic episodes, his characters used a rudimentary gestural "signing." Notice, for instance, the scene in *True Heart Susie* where Susie shares her bed with the ailing Bettina: first Gish purses her lips, squints, and doubles up her fist as if she were going to sock her rival in the jaw; then she virtually wipes away the angry expression and registers ostentatious pity, tenderly putting her arm around the sick woman. At another extreme, Griffith inherited some of the performing conventions of eighteenth-century sentimental drama. In close-ups, his actors could sometimes behave with remarkable naturalism, but they were also required to model for artfully posed moments of gestureless "restraint." The style was influenced by late Victorian portrait photography and painting, which meant that Gish had to serve not only as Griffith's Little Nell, but also as his Elizabeth Sidall and his Jane Burden. She seems to have been eager and skillful at turning herself into a pictorial representation, an object of desire; she selected her own clothes with fastidious care, she persuaded Griffith to hire Hendrick Sartov because of his ability to light her hair, and she was able to pose for virtually still, "painterly" imagery without appearing as rigid as a figure in a *tableau vivant*. *Susie* is full of these images, largely because the central character spends so much time "waiting" for her man. It is worth considering some of them to illustrate how even as a photographic model Gish appears in a variety of guises.

At one point, for example, she is Susie the rural maid, patting her cow on the neck and kissing it farewell; the dumb animal nuzzles her, its broad, hairy face in vivid contrast to her own, which is childlike, pigtailed, sad, and very pretty beneath a flat little hat. Later, preparing herself to be a "fitting mate" for her hero, she is posed like a young Lincoln, reading books by firelight, her hair gathered in a bun and a look of eager studiousness on her face. Still later, in a shot titled "Susie's Diary," we see her in her room at night, her hair down to its full Pre-Raphaelite length, as in an illustration for a pseudo-Arthurian romance. Wearing a loose dressing gown, she is seated on a stool at the right of the frame, her knees toward us and her upper body twisted slightly to the right as she leans forward on a desk to write—an unnatural position that creates a languid, graceful line and contributes to the sublimated eroticism of the image. An unmotivated keylight falls from the upper left, making her skin glow white, and backlighting halos her fine hair, which spills in ringlets down her cheeks; her lashes are lowered to the paper, her slender hand holds a pencil, and her features are relaxed and aristocratically serene. By contrast, toward the end of the film she is depicted as a "single-track heart" and is seated more naturally at the same desk, her hair gathered in a spinsterish bun and romantically backlit; two white, furry kittens are perched on her shoulders, making her look like an angelic *Venus im Peltz*.

In shots like these Gish is virtually a piece of statuary, but in the more dynamic portions of the film she employs a wide vocabulary of movement. The demands on her in this regard would have been great in any film, but Griffith's rehearsal methods gave the leading players an especially important function in the "writing" of his stories. He seldom used a script, preferring to start with a vague outline and develop the action by positioning the players on a bare stage. Sometimes he demonstrated all the parts himself, but by 1919 Gish had become so sensitive to his methods that she was allowed to create the details of her behavior and appearance. Much of her activity in *Susie* consists of variations and sudden departures from a simple graphic set of movements: she holds her head straight and high, squarely topped by a flat, narrow-brimmed hat, keeping her arms stiff at her sides, so that when she walks her upper body seems disassociated from her legs. In the first part of the film the posture and walk are comically stylized and exaggerated; in context with the rest of the action, they suggest various things about Susie: her naive innocence, her puritanism, her directness, her single-minded devotion to a man, her almost soldierly courage, her sense of duty, and her "unaffected" country truthfulness. Her movements make an amusing contrast to Bettina's swiveling hips and butterfly gestures, especially in the scene where the two women are brought together at the ice-cream social in the local church; and although Gish modulates her behavior slightly as the character grows older and gains dignity, she often duplicates the best work of the silent comedians. Her doggedness as she paces along behind her lover is much like Keaton's; her slump-shouldered movement away from Bettina's flirtations with William is pure Chaplin; and her innocent, level-headed gaze whenever she enters or exits a scene makes her resemble no one so much as Harry Langdon.

Susie's wide-eyed face and fairly rigid upper body become a character "tag" and a recurrent joke (at one point, delighted to discover that Bettina is showing interest in another man, she skips across the floor of her room and spins in a joyful circle without moving her arms and head), but they also establish a pattern that can be broken in interesting ways. Because her posture suggests the idealism, determination, and restraint bred into her by an aunt who tells her, "Deport yourself," her moments of letting go have a special force, like emotions breaking through repression. Sometimes they also reveal new aspects to the character, as if a mask had been dropped briefly.

One of the best examples of the latter effect occurs in Gish's pantomime during the comic sequence when Susie and William walk through a lovely, almost expressionist, bower of trees on their way home from school. Susie is in an adoring trance, walking about one step behind William but occasionally brushing his arm. Each time he moves, she follows. He pauses, turns, and paces toward the camera with her immediately behind him. Awkwardly pretending that his mind is on something other than the girl at his side, he turns again and walks toward the trees; she wheels and turns with him, patiently waiting for his attention but not demanding it. Griffith cuts to a closer view as they come to a stop before a tree, showing them from the waist up, looking at each other in a shared composition. Susie stares straight up at William from beneath her flat bonnet, her eyes no longer adoring nor quite so innocent; in fact, the look has a great deal of frankly knowing sexual desire behind it, so that it tempts William and flusters him at the same time. He bends slightly to her; suddenly she leans forward on tiptoe most of the way toward his face, closing her eyes in a comic gesture of passivity. At the crucial moment he hesitates, backs off, and turns his head toward the tree so that his back is to the camera. For just an instant Gish makes a gesture that almost breaks the representational surface of the fiction: she turns her own face away from William for the first time, showing it to the camera but not quite looking into the lens. She registers frustration and sad disappointment, but she also seems to comment on William, taking the audience into Susie's confidence as if she were a roguish character in a farce. Almost immediately her expression turns back into the sad look of a little girl, but not before it has told us that her character is more clever and self-aware, more of an "actor" than we had thought.

Gish also changes the basic pattern of her behavior when she expresses hysteria or inconsolable grief. Her pantomime when she receives William's first letter from college is silly (she wrote that she had a "constant argument" with Griffith because he wanted her to play little girls as if they had "St. Vitus's dance" [99]), but her moments of pain are among the most effective in the film. At one point, wearing the flat hat and a frilly, beribboned dress that makes her look as old-fashioned as ever, she prepares for an "overwhelming assault" on William. Marching to his house, she arrives only to find him embracing Bettina, and she instantly shrinks back against a door to hide herself, holding a small black fan like a shield in front of her body. As she leaves the scene, she is hunched over and hobbling slightly, shaking with ironic laughter and tears. Later in the film, her spunky, straight-backed posture gives way completely. After the wedding of William and Bettina, she waves goodbye to the married couple, backs away into the garden behind her house, walks slowly and weak-kneed toward a fence, holds it briefly for support, and then suddenly collapses to the ground, her body curling into a fetal position. It is one of many occasions in Gish's career when she is subjected to overwhelming torment; yet here there are no bullies, no ice floes, no blasts of wind or ravages of disease—only the force of the character's emotions and a sudden release of stiff muscles.

Gish's most impressive moments, however, involve her face alone. I am referring not only to the relatively crowded middle-distance shots, which she usually dominates by her position in the frame and the animation of her features, but also to the several instances when she is given large, lengthy close-ups. Here, virtually unaided by *mise-en-scène* or expressive objects, she reduces theatrical pantomime to its most microscopic form, displaying a stream of emotions, conjoining her movements so gracefully and inventively that we hardly notice how various they are.

One of the most protracted examples of the technique is the scene in which Susie, hoeing in a garden, overhears William and Bettina conversing on the other side of a hedge. The scene serves both to illustrate how much emotion Gish could gather into a single close-up and to rebut oversimplified interpretations of the Kuleshov effect. In one sense, of course, Kuleshov was correct: the various muscular arrangements of a human face (which are "coded" differently in different cultures) have little force or meaning outside a specific narrative context. We are able to "read" the lengthy succession of emotions in this scene—tension, pain, worry, grief, numbness, anger, fear, suspicion, curiosity, confusion, shame, and so forth—partly because of Griffith's repeated crosscutting between Susie and the couple on the other side of the hedge. Once a general context has been established, however, we are able to make clear distinctions between the emotions by reference to Gish's face alone.

Later in the film—in what must be one of the more complex reaction shots in the history of movies—Gish employs the same close-up pantomime without benefit of crosscutting, using only her face and her left hand to speak to the audience. After Susie accidentally discovers that William and Bettina are engaged, she backs out of William's doorway and leans against a wall. Unseen by the couple in the next room, she tries to recover from the shock and assess her new situation. In close-up, Gish makes Susie waver between shock, grief, fear, and a sense of ironic detachment that keeps her from falling into self pity. In fact, Gish elicits more emotion from the audience than she herself shows—although there are tears in her eyes at one point, she demonstrates how the close view of the camera enables the actor to use smaller and less extreme emotional gestures. At no time is she the wilting, suffering heroine who gives way to hysterics. She laughs ironically more often than she cries, creating a drama out of Susie's precarious balance between strength and pain.

[. . .] A few of the many faces she gives us during this crucial close-up [. . .] give the impression of expressive gymnastics, but in the shot itself they are linked together with such fluid transitions that Gish seems to be doing hardly anything. Turning her head away from the scene she has just witnessed, she faces the camera and looks abstractedly downward, her lids half lowered. She seems dazed or lost in thought, and her left hand rises to finger the dark choker around her neck. (This movement echoes a gesture from earlier in the film when William sits on her front porch and asks if she thinks he should get married. Trying to conceal her emotions, Susie smiles pleasantly and lifts her hand involuntarily, somewhat nervously, to stroke her neck and cheek.) There is just a hint of crazed numbness in her face, an effect that owes chiefly to the unfocused look in her eye, and to a tiny wisp of hair sticking wildly out from under her bonnet. Her fingers rise slowly from the choker, moving up her throat and cheek to pluck at her right earlobe. Her head tilts and she "thinks," a sad, faraway look in her eyes. Her half-closed lids blink, her head straightens almost imperceptibly, and the corners of her eyes turn down more; she blinks again, looks up a bit, and a wry little smile breaks over her mouth. For a moment Gish allows herself a half-suppressed laugh that seems to block her tears, her hand moving down from her ear to cradle her chin. She lowers her eyelids again and purses her lips slightly, continuing to smile. Turning her head, she glances toward the room where she has just seen William and Bettina; still holding her hand to her cheek, she smiles more openly, presumably amused by the foolishness of everyone concerned in the love triangle. (At this point she looks older than at any time in the film and evokes the same sort of saddened, tolerant, maternal amusement she uses in Laughton's *Night of the Hunter* thirty years later.) Her smile fading a bit, she turns her head back toward the camera, her eyes cast to her left, looking at nothing in particular. Her head then turns to the left, and she brings her hand from her cheek to her chin. Cradling the chin once more, she brushes her lips thoughtfully with her extended little finger. Her smile has faded almost completely, and her mouth parts while her finger moves gently, pensively, back and forth across her lower lip; maternal only a moment ago, she now looks sexual and childlike, her lips forming into a moue. Her eyes blink again and glass over, as if she were in a trance. Her little finger plucks more roughly at her lip, rubs it, and then plucks it again. She turns her head back toward the room and inserts the tip of her finger between her lips, nibbling it thoughtfully. Her other fingers, spread across her cheek, clutch slightly at her face, the nails digging into her flesh in a way that suggests a sudden painful surge of emotion. She holds this position for a moment and then relaxes, moving her hand away; a slack, heavy-lidded look passes over her, and her head bobs. She seems on the verge of fainting, but then rights herself, raising her head. Her mouth opens slightly and her eyes widen in fear, her brow furrowing. She tilts her head to the right, her hand touches the choker again, and she softly rubs her neck to dispel the fearful thought.

I have dwelled upon this shot because it shows various articulations of Gish's face and also because shots of its type occur in modified form in virtually all "women's melodrama"—a genre that *True Heart Susie* prefigures. The full close-up of a woman suffering for love is the very centerpiece of such films, the image to which they all gravitate. But the actor is seldom called upon to register suffering alone. Usually, the film wants the woman to express some delicate, "restrained" mixture of pain, renunciation, and spiritual goodness—a smiling through tears that leads up to a kind of acquiescence in suffering. Barbara Stanwyck's *Stella Dallas* is a classic example, and it is interesting to compare Gish's long close-up to one of Stanwyck. In both cases, the actor's job involves *combining* conventional expressions (anger or indignation are the only emotions the genre seems to rule out), so that the shot has a slightly ambiguous effect.

Where Gish is concerned, the close-up is especially notable on technical grounds, giving her an opportunity for straightforward, bravura pantomime, showing the remarkable range of effects she could achieve within the limits of a formula and without the aid of props, editing, or expressive photography. Her carefully modulated changes of expression also reveal something about the structure of her performances in general. She was a superb instrument for Griffith's obsessive "visions" of maidenhood crushed like a flower, and she was also good at suggesting other qualities—maternal care, sexuality, intelligence, and a prim courage and resolve that embodied elements of the pioneer ideal. In some ways, she was a more sophisticated artist than the director she always referred to in public as "Mr. Griffith"; in both the comic and pathetic episodes of this film, she gives her character an ironic self-awareness, cutting against the grain of Griffith's pastoral allegory, as if she were constantly tending toward the more plausible version of Susie that can be seen in the second image at the beginning of this chapter. Whatever her personal motives, however, her success depended on the way she collaborated with and complicated Griffith's sentimental fictions; ultimately, her different faces and gestures were organized into the illusion of a "personality," and her mime took on the power of myth.

Notes

1 Gish recalled that one of Griffith's favorite mottos was "Expression without distortion," and Mack Sennett once claimed that when he tried acting for Griffith he was congratulated by the director for simply standing in front of the camera.

2 Wagenknecht's rapturous mystification of Gish is understandable, given her charm, and is no different from countless other essays about actors. Compare, for example, George Bernard Shaw's comments in the English *Saturday Review* of the 1880s, on the stage performances of Mrs. Patrick Campbell: "Who wants her to act? Who cares twopence whether she possesses that or any other second-rate accomplishment? On the highest plane one does not act, one is. Go and see her move, stand, speak, look, kneel—go and breathe the magic atmosphere that is created by the grace of all those deeds. . . ."

Interestingly, although Hollywood promulgated similar ideas, it sometimes tried to create counterillusions that would selectively dispel them. Hence, the typical fan magazine story that showed an actor like Edward G. Robinson at home among his paintings and children, a happy bourgeois rather than a Little Caesar. Dorothy Gish once joked about how her sister was confused with her screen persona: "The popular conception of Lillian as soft and dreamy makes me think of the gag used too often in the comic strips. A hat lies upon the sidewalk; some person kicks it enthusiastically and finds to his astonishment and pain that there is hidden inside it a brick" (*The Movies, Mr. Griffith, and Me*, 96).

3 Griffith's racist imagination prompted him to turn Gish into an Aryan ideal, but he was not alone in such attitudes. Throughout the silent period, the faces of "spiritualized" characters were supposed to have small, delicate features. As late as the thirties, Humphrey Bogart was typed as a villain partly because executives at Warner Brothers thought his lips were too large to play a sympathetic leading man; ironically, as Louise Brooks has pointed out, Bogart's mouth was quite beautiful, and once he became a star, it turned into his most expressive feature: "Bogey practiced all kinds of lip gymnastics . . . Only Eric von Stroheim was his superior at liptwitching" (*Lulu in Hollywood*, 60).

References

Affron, Charles. *Star Acting: Gish, Garbo, and Davis*. New York: Dutton, 1977.

Brooks, Louise. *Lulu in Hollywood*. New York: Knopf, 1983.

Eagleton, Terry. *The Rape of Clarissa*. Minneapolis: University of Minnesota Press, 1982.

Gish, Lillian. *The Movies, Mr. Griffith, and Me*. Englewood Cliffs, N.J.: Prentice Hall, 1969.

Thomson, David. *A Biographical Dictionary of Film*, 2nd ed. New York: William Morrow, 1981.

Todd, Janet. *Sensibility: An Introduction*. New York: Methuen, 1986.

Wagenknacht, Edward. *The Movies in the Age of Innocence*. Norman: University of Oklahoma Press, 1962.

Williams, Raymond. *The Long Revolution*. Harmondsworth: Penguin, 1961.

9

"A High-Class Job of Carpentry"

Toward a Typography of Early Sound Comedy

HENRY JENKINS

[. . .] While it is beyond the scope of my current project to propose a general framework for discussing film acting across different genres, I would like to isolate a series of five fairly basic criteria that, if not exhaustively, point toward some key issues surrounding performance in the early sound comedy. These five criteria reflect the five central relationships that constitute film performance—the performer's relationship to the narrative, to the character, to the signs of his or her own performance, to the other performers in the production, and to the audience. One might, of course, add the player's relationship to the script and to the director, but those relationships are less open to textual analysis and can be resolved only through historical investigation.

Narrative integration. Performance within some genres, such as the musical or the comedian comedy, may be foregrounded in certain more or less enclosed sequences of self-conscious spectacle rather than integrated into the overall development of the narrative.[1] Patricia Mellancamp characterizes the song-and-dance numbers within Hollywood musicals as "closed units within the larger narrative, set off by a system of brackets"; the audience's attention shifts at such moments from plot development onto the materiality and atemporality of performance.[2] The interaction of certain codes of visual and aural representation (musical accompaniment, centered framing, elevated staging, internal audiences) mark these sequences as privileged moments of heightened interest. Historians of the musical trace a general movement toward the causal and thematic integration of these performance spectacles. Many comedies, as we have seen, are also characterized by a fairly sharp division between sequences of performance virtuosity and sequences of narrative development and exposition. This heightened attention to performance is partially a product of certain visual codes (frontality, flattening of narrative space, long takes and camera movements, absence of point of view cutting). Much as in the musical, these sequences may be presented as diegetic performances (as in the mangled magic act William Gaxton, Ole Olsen, and Chic Johnson perform in *50 Million Frenchmen*, Warner Brothers, 1931); they may also stand apart from narrative actions because of their qualities of excess, stylization, and exaggeration (as in Mitchell and Durant's acrobatic display in *Stand Up and Cheer* or the Marx Brothers' mirror act in *Duck Soup*). These scenes exceed their narrative motivation through their flamboyance, their refusal of narrative economy, and their prolonged duration. Some such sequences exist in almost all film comedies, though many comedies actively foreground performance as performance while others subordinate performance almost entirely to the demands of narrative and character development.

Character integration. As Richard Dyer has argued, there is almost always a problematic fit between the film character and the star's image.[3] The star's image is an extratextual construct developed through the audience's familiarity with the performer via other film appearances, promotional materials, publicity discourse, and reviews and commentary. As such, the polysemic and fully articulated star image often overpowers the character played in any given film. Some film movements, such as Soviet montage or Italian Neorealism, cast nonactors who bear no such semiotic traces to maximize the fit between performer and role. Classical cinema minimizes the gap between star image and character, typically by casting stars into roles closely corresponding to their preexisting images. Humphrey Bogart may become Rick Blaine in *Casablanca* (Warner Brothers, 1942), largely because the character is a composite of traits already associated with the Bogart persona; much of the film's dialogue further develops the character as a unique individual. Rick fought in the Spanish Civil War, once lived in Paris, was unlucky in love, owns the Café American, never drinks with his customers, etc. Steve Seidman argues, however, that comedian comedy heightens audience awareness of the central clown's extratextual status at the expense of integration into a specific character.[4] Dialogue functions less to reveal information about characters than to present gags; characters are reduced to stock roles and can be completely overpowered by the performer's own personality. In some cases, as when Groucho Marx is cast as the president of Freedonia in *Duck Soup*, the performer is asked to accept a story role so at odds with our preexisting perceptions of the star that it produces an active gap between performer and role. Groucho makes little effort to act presidential, remaining Groucho while being placed into situations where he might reasonably be expected to conform to the demands of his office—if not to the particularities of his character. This focus on the performer's personality was a central component of the vaudeville aesthetic and contrasts sharply with expectations about performance within the realist theater and the classical cinema.

Expressive coherence. Closely related to the second category, expressive coherence refers to the degree of consistency that exists within an individual performance; expressive coherence occurs when all the performance signs are coordinated into the development of a rounded character. James Naremore argues that realist performance maintains a high degree of "expressive coherence" even in sequences where characters are themselves expected to give diegetic "performances" (e.g., Humphrey Bogart's visit to the bookshop in *The Big Sleep* (Warner Brothers, 1946).[5] Comedy, on the other hand, is marked by "expressive anarchy," as largely unmotivated performance signs (physical gestures, vocal mannerism, etc.) disrupt coherent characterization. Such signs frequently become a source of interest and amusement in their own right (as when Hugh Herbert, playing a Chinese henchman in *Diplomaniacs*, suddenly slips into a Yiddish accent and inflection).

Ensemble consistency. This term refers to the homogeneity of performance styles among all the actors within a film's cast. Realist theater typically strives for an ensemble effect in which there is a high degree of stylistic consistency across the various performances, while many early sound comedies combine different acting styles (realist, melodramatic, vaudeville) within a single text. Wheeler and Woolsey, for example, adopt a much broader, more exaggerated style of performance, in contrast to the young couples in their romance plots who are more naturalistic; these contrasting acting styles emphasized the clown's eccentricity and the performer's virtuosity. This heterogeneity may occur between different syntagmatic units (as in *Stand Up and Cheer*, where the administrator reviews a succession of different would-be variety acts) or between paradigmatic clusters of characters (as in the example of the Wheeler and Woolsey comedies discussed above).

Audience consciousness. This category refers to the relationship between performer and the spectator. Theater historians frequently draw a distinction between representational and presentational styles of performance. Representational styles create an invisible "fourth wall" separating actor and audience; the actor displays no awareness of the spectators (or in film acting, of the camera). Presentational styles are directed at the spectators and are shaped by the audience's affective response. [V]audeville encouraged the maintenance of the presentational style long after it was out of fashion in the legitimate theater; variety entertainment rewarded the performer's direct engagement with spectators. While the extreme transgressions of the separation between spectator and performance space found in vaudeville (Olsen and Johnson's bombardment of the audience, the magician's call for volunteers to come onstage) were clearly impossible within the cinema, traces of that tradition may be found in the frontality of staging, direct address to the camera, muttered asides, and other reflexive gags. Certain gestures mark the comic star's awareness of the potential presence of film spectators. Robert Wolsey punctuates gags with looks into the camera, puffs on his cigar, and raises his eyebrows, sometimes accompanied with a prolonged "Whoa!" Groucho Marx suggests that the spectators might wish to go into lobby for popcorn until a particularly dull scene is completed. Ed Wynn giggles at his own gags and mutters, "Isn't that the silliest thing?" Jimmy Durante mutters, "Ev'rybody wants to get into de act." These performance signs reflect a higher degree of audience consciousness than would be generally characteristic of the classical cinema.

Each of these categories should be interpreted as a continuum of possible choices, not a set of binary oppositions. To take character integration as an example, most film performances maintain some degree of distance between the star's image and the film's character, though certain types of films (comedy, musical) focus audience attention on that gap while others (social problem films, melodramas) efface it as much as possible. The other categories offer a similar range of possibilities. John Mueller has revised traditional distinctions between integrated and nonintegrated musicals by suggesting other different relationships that might exist between a musical number and its larger narrative context.[6]

By focusing on these five categories, one may make fairly precise distinctions between the acting styles preferred by different genres and subgenres. It is possible to identify a set of five different classes of comedian-centered comedies in the early sound period based upon their utilization of distinctive performance strategies. Remember, however, that this particular taxonomy is constructed through critical analysis and does not necessarily reflect the explicit distinctions employed by the filmmakers or contemporary viewers, who typically categorized films from any of the five classes as "comedies" or "musical comedies."[7] Filmmakers, as was shown in the case study of *Hollywood Party*, did make implicit assumptions about the strategies of performance appropriate to different comic texts, and those distinctions are consistent with the classifications proposed here.

"The Melting Pot of Music": The Revue

Revue films, like *Hollywood Revue of 1929*, *Paramount on Parade*, *King of Jazz* (Universal, 1930), and *The Show of Shows*, stand at one extreme in their exclusive concentration on performance at the expense of any attempt at narrative or character development. These films preserved many conventions of the theatrical revue or the vaudeville show. Each presents a succession of totally independent performance units, acts, numbers, or sketches, marked off by such rhetorical practices as the opening and closing of curtains, the use of title cards, the dimming of lights, the crescendo of orchestral music, or the reappearance of a master of ceremony. Only minimal narration creates unity. *King of Jazz*, for example, opens with the image of a giant book announcer Charles Erwin explains is the scrapbook of Paul Whiteman and his orchestra: "Its pages are crowded with melodies and anecdotes, which we are going to bring to life for you by the magic of the camera." The initial segment—an animated cartoon by Walter Lantz—does indeed explain in a humorous fashion how Whiteman became known as the "King of Jazz." Subsequent sequences, however, are linked by the recurring image of the book or by introductions from Whiteman or Erwin. These segments, however, frequently have little or nothing to do with Whiteman and his band. They are selected not to reflect his "melodies and anecdotes" but rather to constitute a varied program. *Paramount on Parade* and *Show of Shows* make far less pretense at thematic coherence, depending upon the periodic appearances of masters of ceremony to introduce the individual "acts" and to create minimal unity between the segments. As Skeets Gallagher, Jack Oakie, and Leon Errol explain at the beginning of *Paramount on Parade*, "Anytime you grow confused or find yourself perplexed, one of us will stagger out and tell you what is next. . . . We're the masters of ceremony—keeping you people in touch with *Paramount on Parade*."

Performers make few efforts to blend into characters here. Their introductions identify them by name and focus attention on their particular skills and talents. These introductions may range from a simple announcement that "Chevalier's next" (*Paramount on Parade*) to elaborate sequences, such as Frank Fay's prolonged build-up for many of the performers in *Show of Shows*. The most lengthy introductions, in fact, are given to dramatic performers, like John Barrymore in *Show of Shows* or Ruth Chatterton in *Paramount on Parade*, who normally sought to blend more fully into their characters. Here, however, it is the performers' status as performers that is stressed, focusing attention not on the characters they are playing but rather on the skills with which they execute those roles. In *Paramount on Parade*, Skeets Gallagher appears outside Chatterton's dressing room, enters and berates her for being late to the show and keeping the other actors waiting; this scene plays with the disjunction between her slangy talk in the dressing room and the more pretentious language Chatterton employs onstage. She promises to appear in "less than five minutes," so Gallagher steps outside and introduces the sketch, which then builds toward Chatterton's entrance. Barrymore appears before the curtain in *Show of Shows* to explain the context for his soliloquy from Shakespeare's *Richard III*, before disappearing and reappearing again in character as the demented hunchback. This brief introduction also serves to highlight the gap between Barrymore's normal appearance and delivery and his assumption of a Shakespearean role.

Moreover, the revue films actively play with the celebrity status of some of their featured performers, highlighting their extratextual status. Maurice Chevalier's performance of "All I Want Is Just One Girl" in *Paramount on Parade* is immediately followed by an appearance by Mitzi Green who not only impersonates Chevalier's rendition but also shows how the same song might be performed by Moran and Mack. Green's act places attention both on Chevalier's status as a celebrity performer and on Green's impersonation skills—especially given the disjunction between her frilly dress and the male stars she mimics. *King of Jazz* plays extensively with the image of rotund bandleader Paul Whiteman. Not only does Whiteman serve as master of ceremonies but he is also impersonated by a double who does elaborate dances; he is caricatured on the book's cover, on the heads of drums, even on the face of the moon; he is transformed into a cartoon character within the Walter Lantz animated sequence. *Show of Shows* directs attention to the fact that Al Jolson was one of the few Warners stars not to appear and has Sid Silvers impersonate him while Frank Fay jokes about Jolson's characteristic gestures and vocal mannerisms.

Expressive coherence is generally maintained within individual acts, though the same performers may play multiple roles in the same film and adopt different acting styles for different appearances. The revue films, like vaudeville itself, exhibited a diversity of entertainment: everything from Shakespearean drama and poetic recitations to eccentric dancing and acrobatics, from classical music to cartoons and dog acts; these works displayed little interest in stylistic consistency between the various segments. Ensemble effects were, for the most part, reserved for the closing numbers—"Sweeping the Clouds Away" in *Paramount on Parade*, "Lady Luck" in *Show of Shows*, "The Melting Pot of Music" in *King of Jazz*, etc.—which brought the entire cast together in one musical extravaganza. Even here, the numbers were staged so that each performer was allowed one final moment in the spotlight to reprise or introduce a specialty, before blending back into the larger chorus. Such sequences involved a constant play between the ensemble and the individual, between moments of novelty and a general movement toward homogeneity.

The revue films maintain a degree of audience consciousness unprecedented in the classical Hollywood cinema. As a result, they are often dismissed as overly "theatrical." A few sequences—Ruth Chatterton's "My Marine" and Helen Kane's "Boop-Boop-A-Doo School" in *Paramount on Parade*, for example—follow later Hollywood practice of constructing an internal audience to justify the more presentational aspects of performance numbers. More often, the presenters directly address the camera and through it, make concrete references to the "ladies and gentlemen" in the movie audience. Jack Oakie, who appears as a murder victim in a mystery movie parody in *Paramount on Parade*, suddenly breaks character, bursts out laughing, and points directly into the camera; Oakie claims that the sketch was "written especially for me" rather than for its alleged stars—Warner Oland, Clive Brook, William Powell, and Eugene Pallette—each of whom had previously claimed top billing. Skeets Gallagher enters one scene and thanks the audience for an anticipated ovation, holding his ear so that he may hear the applause better; there is the sound of one pair of clapping hands on the soundtrack. An off-screen voice, presumably from the cinema audience, harasses and insults his performance, before he walks off screen, glaring at the camera. Frank Fay adopts a similarly reflexive stance throughout *Show of Shows*. During his introduction of Irene Borodoni, for example, Fay explains that if the audience does not understand the French lyrics of the chanteuse's numbers, they may speak to him after the show and he will be glad to translate. Paradoxically, such devices increase the sense of spontaneity and immediacy, allowing screen performances to substitute more fully for live stage appearances, but they also direct attention upon the temporal and special gap between the performance and its reception.

Stop the music! the showcase film

The showcase film embeds the nonintegrated units of the revue film within a frame story. Comedies, like *International House* (Paramount, 1933), *The Big Broadcast* (Paramount, 1932), and *Stand Up and Cheer*, were initially viewed as an improvement upon the earlier revues because their interest was not entirely conditional upon the entertainment value of the individual segments. Yet, as the case study of *Hollywood Party* suggested, the attempt to merge spectacle with narrative, performance with characterization, presents problems not faced by the more openly presentational revue films. First and foremost, there was the problem of how to build narrative motivation for these performance sequences. For the most part, these films solved this difficulty by adopting settings in or around the world of show business; such a context not only provides a narrative rationale for the performances but also presents opportunities for diegetic audiences with whom the performers can interact. In *Stand Up and Cheer*, the central character's job (Secretary of the Department of Amusements) requires him to audition and recruit variety entertainers. *International House* concerns the initial public demonstration of a new form of television, with the revue segments displaying the technological wonders of this novel invention. *The Big Broadcast* films are set in or around radio studios and include "broadcasts" from popular performers. *Thrill of a Lifetime* (Paramount, 1933) concerns the production of a revue at a summer resort and opens in the office of a vaudeville agent—both settings where performances may naturally occur. In *Here Comes Cookie* (Paramount, 1935), a series of miscalculated business transactions leaves Gracie Allen in charge of her father's estate; the ever daffy Gracie mistakes her father's desire that he appear penniless for instructions to spend all his money. As a result, she turns his mansion into a free boarding house for vaudeville troupers. The screen space overflows with performance, embodying the vaudevillians' disruptive presence in the characters' lives. In one shot, the camera pans across Gracie's living room, showing, in quick succession, jugglers, acrobats, trained dogs, magicians, unicycle riders, knife throwers, a jazz band, and a lasso artist, all practicing their acts simultaneously in a cramped domestic space.

In each film, a certain number of performance numbers are introduced as part of the general atmosphere of the film's show world setting and are treated as pure spectacle, while others assume a higher degree of narrative significance. In *The Big Broadcast*, the survival of Station WADX depends upon a radio appearance by Bing Crosby, although the star is so embroiled in his romantic difficulties that it seems unlikely he will reach the studio in time to make the broadcast. Station manager Stuart Erwin frantically searches all over town for a phonograph recording of Bing Crosby to air instead. Meanwhile, back at the station, a series of performers (Kate Smith, Cab Calloway, the Boswell Sisters, the Mills Brothers, and Vincent Lopez and his Orchestra, among others) delay for time. The film cuts back and forth between the narratively centered actions of Erwin and performance numbers at the studio. Bing's performance is thus doubly marked as the film's entertainment highpoint and the resolution of its plot action.

The showcase film is characterized as well by a high degree of stylistic diversification; heterogeneity is introduced not simply between different forms of entertainment within the performance segments but between the presentational style of the explicit performance units and the more representational style of the narrative segments. *International House*, in fact, involves at least four different levels of performance:

1 Performers who appear only on the radioscope or in the hotel's stage show and who appear under their own names (Rudy Vallee, Cab Calloway, Baby Rose Marie, Sterling Holloway);
2 Performers who appear under their own names but assume some narrative role (Peggy Hopkins Joyce, George Burns and Gracie Allen);
3 Performers who appear as totally fictionalized characters but are only minimally integrated into those characters (W. C. Fields as Professor Quail);
4 Performers who blend into their characters and maintain the primary narrative responsibilities within the film (Stuart Erwin as Tommy Nash, Bela Lugosi as General Petronovich, Lumsden Hare as Sir Mortimer Fortescue).

The interplay between these four levels of performance is quite complex. Each level involves its own conventions regarding character integration, audience consciousness, and expressive coherence. Sequences of pure performance are explicitly marked through the presence of a diegetic audience, the constant reinscription of the frame of the radioscope during presentations of broadcast material, and the acceptance of a fairly high degree of audience consciousness including direct address. Narratively active characters (i.e., those in categories 2–4) do not appear within the radioscope; rather, their narrative tasks involve an effort to bring the radioscope more fully under their control. Dramatic actors, like Lugosi or Hare, are frequently cast as straight men or foils for the more comically exaggerated performers. Comic stars like Burns and Allen or Fields may break the flow of the narrative to engage in more ambiguously marked performance sequences within the story space proper: Gracie Allen interrupts a narratively significant conversation to perform a magic trick that she completely muddles, thus pulling the more serious performers into her comedy; George Burns and Franklin Pangborn take turns feeding straight lines to Gracie, their movements choreographed into a near dance. Such sequences fit comfortably neither in the world of explicit performance (i.e., the radioscope broadcasts) nor in the world of the narrative (the struggle for the rights to the invention) but rather work to blur the sharp boundaries between the two.

The greatest ambiguity surrounds W. C. Fields's status. Fields, as an international explorer and inventor, is first shown in a mock documentary presented on the radioscope, a scene that strongly evokes his extrafilmic image as a heavy drinker: the ground crew loads barrels of beer and trays of mugs into an airplane, a white-gloved hand reaches down to lift a mug of beer from the tray, and the camera follows it up to show Fields sitting in the cockpit, downing the drink. If the first few images are clearly established as radioscope broadcasts, the frame of its screen soon disappears and their diegetic status becomes more ambiguous. Later, Fields appears in a photograph in a newspaper Gracie reads, again as a representation rather than a narrative participant. Finally, the misdirected explorer appears in person at the International House ("Say, this isn't Kansas City?"), though he retains a privileged relationship to the broadcast images. When Fields enters the room during one of Dr. Wong's demonstrations, the broadcast image of Rudy Vallee yells at him to stop interrupting his number; Fields shoves his cane into the machinery and blows it out, changing channels to a view of a navy ship, which Fields sinks by firing a pistol into the screen. Fields's actions not only disrupt broadcast performances and narrative developments but also destabilize the space between the two.

This fairly radical (though sometimes unstable) separation of actors according to plot-centered and performance-centered functions distinguishes the showcase film from the backstage musicals of the same vintage.[8] Typically, the plot of a backstage musical, such as *42nd Street* (Warner Brothers, 1933) or *Footlight Parade* (Warner Brothers, 1933), centers upon the process of putting on a show. The performers in the onstage sequences become characters within the frame narrative; their resulting performances are rich in narrative significance. It is not Ruby Keeler the star who steps onto the stage in the climactic moments of *42nd Street* but rather her character, the young dancer who has waited all her life for her chance at stardom. Her musical number primarily marks the young woman's triumph, rather than showcasing Ruby Keeler's virtuosity, though these two cannot be easily separated. For the most part, performances in backstage musicals display a high degree of character integration and a low degree of audience consciousness when compared to the performances in showcase films. A notable exception may be cameo appearances by famous stage stars, such as the appearance of Eddie Cantor in *Glorifying the American Girl* (Paramount, 1929), that often motivate numbers existing primarily to display these performer's talents; the onstage appearance by fictional characters decreases attention to the performer's extratextual status and more fully integrates performance into narrative.

Acting in society: the comic romance

The distinction between plot-centered and performance-centered actors breaks down further within the comic romance. While the frame story in the showcase film is merely a device for structuring the performance sequences, plot becomes the primary appeal of the comic romance. Here, comic performance is subordinated to narrative demands and appears only sporadically. *Dixiana* (RKO, 1930), for example, is first and foremost a romance concerning two young lovers (Bebe Daniels, Everett Marshall) who must overcome parental opposition and the threat of a powerful rival (Ralf Harolde). Unlike traditional romantic comedy, such romances are treated melodramatically rather than comically, with particular emphasis placed upon the pain of the lovers' separation. Dialect comic Frances Cawthorne and the bulky Jobyana Howland appear as the boy's squabbling parents, who alternate between comic scenes involving the wife's hopeless efforts to cultivate her immigrant husband and more dramatic sequences involving the couples' reservations about their son's unsuitable choice of a bride. Their performance style shifts abruptly between the exaggeration of the comic scenes and the more naturalistic tone of the dramatic scenes. As dramatic performers, Cawthorne and Howland block Dixiana's upward mobility; as comic performers, they pose questions about rigid class barriers. After all, if these two can achieve acceptance in genteel society, the more ladylike Dixiana seems assured of eventual success in her attempts to leave burlesque and join the southern gentry.

Bert Wheeler and Robert Woolsey offer a comic contrast to the romantic couple. Their own buffoonish dispute over Dorothy Lee parallels and parodies the rivalry over Dixiana. This function is particularly apparent during a broadly played duel between the two comic leads that foreshadows the film's climactic and far more serious duel between the two dramatic leads. Like Cawthorne and Howland, however, the two comics also adopt a more restrained and naturalistic acting style during scenes that have greater narrative consequences, as when they must comfort Bebe Daniels following her forceful expulsion from her lover's house. These shifts pose a threat to the expressive coherence of individual performances not present within the revue or showcase films, where individual performers retained a more fixed status. The more performance-oriented sequences must be more restrained, displaying little audience consciousness and a higher degree of character integration if the comic performers are going to be successful in making the transition to more dramatic sequences.

Most of the comic romances share a thematic concern with the problems of social assimilation, with how to "act" in proper society; such a focus helps to naturalize these disjunctions in performance style. In *Dixiana*, *Her Majesty Love* (First National, 1931), *Rain or Shine* (Columbia, 1930), *Everything's Rosie*, *Love in Bloom* (Paramount, 1935), and *Poppy* (Paramount, 1936), leading ladies escape from their show world past into high society. Their successful transition is prefigured by their conformity to a more naturalistic style of performance. The comic stars are often cast as the girl's relatives or friends. The comic stars' inability to make a similar transition into naturalistic acting, their tendency to revert back to broader styles of performance, offers not only a source of amusement for the audience but also a tangible threat to the leading lady's own assimilation. Their buffoonery often results in her expulsion from society when their "bad manners" directs attention on her disreputable background. In *Love in Bloom*, Vi (Dixie Lee) has run away from her drunken father and his rundown traveling carnival, finding a place for herself as a song plugger at a big city music shop and winning the love of a young songwriter (Joe Morrison). The father, suffering business difficulties, dispatches her brother (George Burns) and his wife (Gracie Allen) to go to the big city and bring her back with them. The film cuts between Burns and Allen's comic misadventures along the road and the progression of Lee's preparations for her wedding; the two comedians' antics provide comic relief from the more realistic romance plot as well as a vivid manifestation of the world that Lee hopes to escape. By the time they arrive in the city, just in time to make a shambles of the wedding, their disruptiveness can be reread as tragic rather than comic.

The apparent incompatibility of these two very different ways of "acting" is dramatically evoked in many of these films through the device of a disastrous social affair, such as the interrupted wedding in *Love in Bloom*. This sequence often involves an engagement dinner given in honor of the leading lady and attended by characters from both worlds. Initially, the playfulness and spontaneity of the comic stars is accepted by the other guests as a refreshing novelty. Soon, their enthusiastic reception pushes the clowns toward broader and broader performances. Joe Cook in *Rain or Shine* showers the dinner guests with spaghetti, while W. C. Fields in *Her Majesty Love* tosses pastry across the table, alarming other diners. Bert Wheeler in *Dixiana* does a ballancing and juggling act with fancy china and crystal, smashing it against the floor, while Robert Woolsey in *Everything's Rosie* engages the guests in the old shell game and takes all their money. The leading lady's embarrassment at the clown's performances, usually followed by the revelation of her disgraceful ties to show business, gives these sequences a melodramatic edge. Their consequences for the romantic couple colors our perception of what otherwise might be read as pure comic spectacle. Performance has intruded too abruptly into the narrative space, and, as a consequence, not only the comic stars but also the upwardly aspiring female lead must be expelled; expressive performance must be suppressed in favor of rigid conformity to plot demands. The irreconcilability of these two spheres allows only two possible resolutions: either the leading lady must reject the stuffiness of high society and return to show business or she must break totally with the realm of exotic performance and enter completely into the space of narrative accountability.

Comic romance serves as an interesting intermediary category between the comedian comedy and the screwball comedy traditions. While the plots of films like *Poppy* and *Her Majesty Love* follow the same story conventions as screwball comedies like *You Can't Take It with You* (Columbia, 1938) or *Bringing Up Baby* (RKO, 1938), their performance style is fundamentally different. The screwball comedy owes relatively little to the vaudeville aesthetic, representing the translation of theatrical farce into classical Hollywood narratives. While the comic romance still contains some nonintegrated performance sequences, specifically those centered around the star clowns, screwball comedy always endows impersonations or performances with narrative consequences. Clark Gable and Claudette Colbert impersonate a bickering married couple in *It Happened One Night* (Columbia, 1934); this scene, however, contributes to the plot development in a way that Wheeler and Woolsey's performances in *Dixiana* generally do not. The characters' ability to act as a married couple prefigures their own union at the film's conclusion. Stage-trained performers like Katharine Hepburn and Cary Grant melded directly into their characters, with casting designed to maximize the match between performer and assigned role. Screwball comedy, moreover, maintains a high degree of stylistic consistency between the film's performers, while comic romance is characterized primarily by the thematization of multiple styles, the radical separation between comic and dramatic performers. For the most part, the screwball comedy tries for a style of performance that is less naturalistic than the dramatic segments of the comic romance and less exaggerated than the comic sequences.

"Like a playful child": the anarchistic comedy

If the revue and showcase films display the performance skills of various entertainers, the anarchistic comedy is constructed as a vehicle for a particular comic personality; it consistently creates opportunities for a comic star or team to demonstrate the full range of their abilities. Comic director Norman McLeod has characterized the development of such a film project as "a high class job of carpentry"; the stars' repertoires of existing stage business provided raw materials that could be assembled into a flimsy narrative structure.[9] This reuse of already familiar material ensured that the comic performer remained imperfectly integrated into any particular character role. Certain sequences (Eddie Cantor's blackface numbers, Harpo's harp solos, Bert Wheeler's female impersonation, W. C. Fields's golf or pool tricks) stand apart from the rest of the film, marked as star turns inserted into the narrative with only the most transparent attempt at motivation. These moments invite comparison with previous films and thus direct attention away from their context within this particular story. In *Ali Baba Goes to Town* (Fox, 1937), Eddie Cantor resorts to blackface, jive, and jazz when his efforts to communicate with a group of Nubian slaves prove unsuccessful, while he poses as an "Ethiopian Beauty Specialist" in *Roman Scandals* (United Artists, 1933). The resulting numbers are totally anachronistic and have next to nothing to do with the plot; they do, however, showcase Cantor's trademark singing style and incorporate jazz performers and tap dancers. Audience members often expressed dissatisfaction if these specialties did not appear in a particular vehicle, expecting their repetition regardless of narrative context.[10]

Individual scenes are conceived as set pieces, opportunities for performance, with their narrative significance often added as an afterthought. Story information is compressed into tight units of intrusive exposition at the beginnings and ends of scenes; the bulk of each sequence is spent on largely unmotivated and unintegrated comic performance. Unlike the previous categories, however, anarchistic comedies do not create a fixed separation between narrative space and performance space. The comic performers act within the diegesis, entering narrative spaces so they may be transformed into an impromptu stage for their clowning. Frank Krutnik writes of these films:

> It is as if the comedian—the disruptive element in the smooth functioning of the genre—has been dropped into the fictional world by accident, and, like a playful child, proceeds to toy with its rules. The comedian refuses to act "straight"—unlike the other characters in the film—or is incapable of doing so. . . . Thus two sets of expectations come into conflict: the comedian "interferes" with the ostensible fiction, the fiction "constrains" the comedian. It is the play between the two which is responsible for much of the comedy.[11]

The Marx Brothers in *Monkey Business* are almost literally "dropped into the fictional world by accident," having stowed away on a luxury liner inside barrels of kippered herrings. By this somewhat unorthodox means, the brothers enter a world with which they would ordinarily have little contact. The captain and his men try to capture the stowaways, resulting in a series of chase scenes in which the various clowns burst into new rooms and disrupt the other passengers' ongoing activities. Running across the ship's ballroom, the brothers pause long enough to play a short musical piece and bow to their astonished audience, before darting away again. Harpo stumbles onto a children's puppet show and assumes a puppetlike persona, integrating himself into the entertainment; he draws first the ship's steward and then the captain himself into the Punch and Judy act. Harpo and Chico seize control of the barbershop, shaving away a customer's mustache in their attempts to "even it up a little," while Groucho takes command of the captain's quarters and devours his lunch. Trying to sneak past customs, each of the brothers impersonates Maurice Chevalier with varying degrees of success. Every nook and cranny on the ship poses new possibilities for comic appropriation; divorced of its usual functions, the ship becomes an ideal space for the Marx Brothers' performances and each plot action provides new opportunities for the display of their virtuosity.[12]

Moreover, the comic stars exist almost entirely outside of the restraints of stable characterization. Characters have names and social positions, serve particular narrative roles, yet they offer little competition for the stars' engaging personalities. In extreme cases, as when Wheeler and Woolsey, cigar, glasses, and all, are inserted into historical settings in *Cockeyed Cavaliers* (RKO, 1934) and *Silly Billies* (RKO, 1936), the films play upon a tension between their extratextual personae and their narrative roles. The comic stars are literally reduced to icons in the films' opening credits, where caricatures of the central performers rely upon certain familiar facial and costume details (Groucho's cigar and painted mustache; Harpo's fright wig and horn; W. C. Fields's red nose, top hat, white gloves, and cane; Robert Woolsey's glasses; Eddie Cantor's owlish eyes; Joe E. Brown's big mouth) to evoke audience's extratextual knowledge of their familiar personae. While additional character information particularizes that persona to the needs of a specific narrative, this information is minimal and may be disregarded later, if the characterization interferes with the filmmakers' desire to introduce a particularly entertaining sequence. Little in the common man characters Eddie Cantor plays in his films justifies his ability to suddenly burst into song and dance or don blackface. At such moments, established characterization simply dissolves to allow Cantor the performer to emerge. One might contrast that fluidity between characterization and performance to the complex narrative motivations surrounding Marlene Dietrich's stage appearances in films like *Morocco* (Paramount, 1930) or *Blonde Venus* (Paramount, 1932).

Anarchistic comedies places a relatively low value on expressive coherence, openly creating disjunctures between character and performer or allowing for fairly abrupt shifts in performance style. In the course of a single scene in *Monkey Business*, Groucho Marx adopts the style and rhetoric of a patriotic stump speaker, a dance instructor, a gangster, a quiz show host, a little boy, and a flirtatious woman, all while remaining one step ahead of a mobster and his seductive moll. This "expressive anarchy" creates space as well for the performer to break character and confront the audience directly, as Groucho does in almost all of his films, though the performers generally display far less consciousness of the audience than do the stars of revue or showcase films.

"Taking one's place in the social order": the affirmative comedy

Steve Seidman and Frank Krutnik have advanced a model of the comedian comedy that sees the clown's antics as signs of "identity confusion" and "behavioral disfunction," an inability to integrate into adult society.[13] The comedian comedy, they argue, depicts the comic protagonist's efforts to work through these personality difficulties and gain social acceptance.[14] The normalization of the character's conduct is mirrored by a normalization of performance; the performers are more fully assimilated into their narrative roles as the characters fit more perfectly within their social roles. Such a model of the comedian comedy implies not a contestation between performance and narrative but rather a final subordination of performance to plot demands. The comedian's virtuosity must yield to the demands of a character role; "expressive anarchy" must be transformed into "expressive coherence." Such a model seems inadequate to classes of comic films that either maintain a radical separation of performance-centered stars and plot-centered actors (as in the showcase film or to a lesser degree, the comic romance) or make the demands of character and story subservient to spectacle and showmanship (as in the anarchistic comedy). There is, however, another group of early sound comedies more closely conforming to the Seidman-Krutnik model. Perhaps best represented by the films of Joe E. Brown, the affirmative comedy contrasts sharply with the anarchistic comedy both in its thematic of social integration and in its emphasis upon plot and character over spectacle and performance.

Joe E. Brown's comedies depend less upon extended sequences of comic performance than upon small bits of character business. Even in films like *Circus Clown* (Warner Brothers, 1934) or *Six Day Bike Rider* (Warner Brothers, 1934), where Brown must perform onstage, these performances are heavily determined by their story situations and have direct consequences on future plot actions. In *Circus Clown*, Brown plays Happy Howard, the son of a famous circus performer. Happy, like his father, aspires toward stardom under the big top. Periodically, the film shows Happy rehearsing on a trampoline, allowing Brown to display his acrobatic abilities. These moments of performance are so closely bound with the protagonist's personal goals that they read as reflecting the developing abilities of Happy Howard the character, not the already well-developed talents of Brown the former circus performer. Similarly,

Happy's appearances in the circus ring later in the film enact the character's efforts to gain professional recognition and romantic acceptance; such actions are so rich in narrative interest that the audience is inclined to forget the virtuosity of the clown who performs them (even in remarkable scenes where Brown plays both Happy and his father). The opening of *Six Day Bike Rider* establishes the rivalry between Harry St. Clair, a vaudeville performer, and Wilifred (Joe E. Brown), the baggage clerk at the local railroad station. When Harry performs stunts on his bicycle during the variety show, Wilifred insults him from the audience and is challenged to come onto the stage to show whether he can do any better. Blindfolded, Wilifred performs such stunts, much to the embarrassment of his girl friend, and ends up riding his bike into the orchestra pit. Again, this performance is thoroughly integrated into the story action, serving to alienate Wilifred from his fiancée and to intensify his hostility toward the film's antagonist. This performance thus motivates his subsequent decision to enter the six-day bike race and to challenge St. Clair for the hand of the woman they both love.

Unlike other performers who played essentially similar characters in all of their films, Brown adopted various personae: fast-talking young playboys (*Broad-Minded*, First National, 1931), bespectacled buffoons (*Six Day Bike Rider*, *You Said a Mouthful*, *Local Boy Makes Good*, First National, 1931), gangling athletes (*Alibi Ike*, Warner Brothers, 1935; *Elmer the Great*, First National, 1935; *Sit Tight*, Warner Brothers, 1931), and ill-fated braggarts (*Son of a Sailor*, Warner Brothers, 1933; *Earthworm Tractors*, Warner Brothers, 1936). Brown adjusts his limited vocabulary of grimaces, gawks, and guffaws to the particular needs of each role. Brown more fully submerged his own personality to the demands of characterization than any other early sound comedian. As a result, Brown, like the classical silent clowns, can move from comedy to pathos, where such a shift would be impossible for a performer like Groucho Marx. Frequently, the films ask us to share Brown's pain at his inability to gain social acceptance and his temporarily frustrated ambitions, as in a sequence in *Circus Clown* when Brown is unjustly fired from the show. The film lingers on a close-up of Brown's tear-streaked face as the circus train pulls away into the night, leaving him alone and dejected on the open road.

Moreover, Brown's comedies develop a high degree of stylistic consistency. Brown's body movements and vocal mannerisms are certainly broader and more stylized than other cast members, making his character appear eccentric, clumsy, and ill-adjusted to his social environment, yet those gestures shed insight onto his characters. We find here none of the more radical breaks with naturalistic performance style that we associate with other film clowns. Brown remains oblivious to the presence of the camera, avoiding not only direct address but also the frontal staging so common in early sound comedy. The internal monologues in *You Said a Mouthful*, modeled after a similar device in *Strange Interlude* (MGM, 1932), are the exception that proves this rule. Here, Brown steps momentarily out of the story action, the background movement is suspended, and he strikes a thoughtful pose. The camera pulls into a tight close-up, while Brown's voice on the soundtrack reveals his character's thoughts. Groucho Marx parodies *Strange Interlude* in *Animal Crackers*, using the device to comment on the constructedness of the plot and to engage in his familiar wordplay; Brown's internal monologues, like those in *Strange Interlude* itself, reflect the character's thoughts and convey plot information; they are not a reflexive gag. As the narratives progress, Brown adjusts his acting style into closer conformity with the other characters, frequently concluding with sequences where he displays the physical prowess and social grace previously denied his characters. The normalization of Brown's performance becomes a measure of his character's social integration; earlier moments of stylization and expressive incoherence are read as signs of the comic protagonist's social immaturity rather than as moments where the performer's personality surfaces. The relative restraint and coherence of Brown's performances may be the product of the limited range of his performance skills. Whatever its origins, this style of comedy, with its high emphasis upon the integration of comic performance into character and narrative development, proved far more compatible with the norms of the classical Hollywood cinema than the other classes of comic texts described above. The comedian comedies of the late 1930s and 1940s (the vehicles of Joe Penner, Abbott and Costello, Bob Hope, Danny Kaye, and Red Skelton) follow Joe E. Brown's example rather than adopting the anarchistic comedy model. Even anarchic performers like the Marx Brothers or Wheeler and Woolsey were forced to restrain the more excessive aspects of their performances and to integrate their comic routines more fully into the plot progression. The gag sequences in *Monkey Business* thwart plot development, interrupting and derailing the gangster subplot, rendering its actions ridiculous (as when Groucho acts as a sports announcer providing running commentary on the final fist fight); similar sequences in *A Day at the Races* further narrative purposes, as when the Marx Brothers create disturbances to allow Allen Jones to sneak the horse away from its stable or to block efforts to investigate Dr. Hugo Hackenbush's credentials. What is read as performance virtuosity in the early Marx Brothers films comes in their later works to signify the characters' eccentricity, with the sudden shifts of performance registers restrained by a greater attention to character motivation.

Each subgenre described above represents a different strategy for reconciling the competing demands of the vaudeville aesthetic and classical Hollywood narrative. The revue film resolves the contradiction by abandoning narrative altogether, offering the film as a substitute for a stage presentation, as a text made of nothing but performances. The showcase film introduces a minimal degree of plot development, yet interrupts the narrative periodically to allow extended sequences of performance that have little or no direct bearing on the storyline. The comic romance transforms the problematic relationship between performance sequences and causal narrative into a dominant thematic concern, depicting the shifting styles of individual performers as a process of class assimilation and posing eruptions into pure performance as a threat to the romantic couple's happiness. The anarchistic comedy provides perhaps the most unstable balance between performance and plot, with each scene transformed into a battleground between these two competing forces. Here, stories exist to be disrupted and overwhelmed by excessive performances, while narrative destabilization is experienced as a liberation of the comic performer's creative potential. By contrast, the affirmative comedy subordinates performance almost totally to the demands of characterization, with the comic star's movement from performance excess to stylistic restraint reflecting the character's increased integration into the social order.

[. . .]

Notes

1 Richard deCordova, "Genre and Performance: An Overview," in *Film Genre Reader*, ed. Barry Keith Grant (Austin: University of Texas Press, 1986), 130.
2 Patricia Mellencamp, "Spectacle and Spectator: Looking Through the American Musical

Comedy," *Cine-Tracts* (Summer 1977), 28–35. See also Jim Collins, "Towards Defining a Matrix of the Musical Comedy: The Place of the Spectator Within the Textual Mechanisms," in *Genre: The Musical*, ed. Rick Altman (London: Routledge and Kegan Paul, 1981), 134–145; Jane Feuer, *The Hollywood Musical* (Bloomington: Indiana University Press, 1982); John Mueller, "Fred Astaire and the Integrated Musical," *Cinema Journal* 24.1 (Fall 1984): 28–40; Rick Altman, *The American Film Musical* (Bloomington: Indiana University Press, 1987), see especially 59–89.

3 Richard Dyer, *Stars* (London: BFI, 1979), 38–98.

4 Steve Seidman, *Comedian Comedy: A Tradition in the Hollywood Film* (Ann Arbor: UMI Research, 1981), 15–57.

5 James Naremore, "Expressive Coherence and the Acted Image," *Studies in Literary Imagination* (Spring 1986), 39–54.

6 Mueller, "Fred Astaire and the Integrated Musical."

7 See Altman, *The American Film Musical*, for a useful discussion of the process by which genre definitions are established. My methodology for developing these definitions closely resembled the practices he describes.

8 Altman, *The American Film Musical*, 372, lists *The Big Broadcast* as an exemplar of the show musical based on its syntactic and the semantic components, though I would argue that its performance style fits more closely with the showcase film.

9 Gerald Weales, *Canned Goods As Caviar: American Film Comedy of the 1930s* (Chicago: University of Chicago Press, 1985), 92.

10 Charles Lee Hyde, Grand Theater, Pierre, South Dakota, wrote of *Duck Soup*: "Good entertainment but lots of disappointed people. . . . The usual music furnished by the harp and the piano was missed. Another example of how dumb smart people can be. Would any exhibitor have made a picture with the Marx Brothers in it and kept the harp and piano out?" "What the Picture Did For Me," *Motion Picture Herald*, February 17, 1934, 65. Similar complaints were heard from other exhibitors.

11 Frank Krutnik, "The Clown-Prints of Comedy," *Screen* (July–October 1984), 52–53.

12 A *Motion Picture Herald* ad for the film (May 9, 1931) foregrounds the brothers' performance sequences as a key selling point for the film: "Groucho has a brand new crop of rapid-fire nonsense. Mute Harpo wangs the harp and chases the blonds. Chico, the tough guy, prowls his omnivorous way. Zeppo provides the one sane spot in the lunatic Marxian universe. The buffooning brothers are invading an unsuspecting Hollywood for this opus."

13 Krutnik, "The Clown-Prints of Comedy," 52–53; Seidman, *Comedian Comedy*, 79–141.

14 Seidman, *Comedian Comedy*, 146.

Masculinity in Crisis

10

Method Acting in Hollywood

VIRGINIA WRIGHT WEXMAN

> The imagery of libidinal revolution and bodily transfiguration once again becomes a figure for the perfected community.
>
> –Fredric Jameson

> Masculinity is not something one is born with but something one gains . . . in American life, there is a certain built-in tendency to destroy masculinity in American men.
>
> –Norman Mailer

> Marlon was a tortured man in the early days, and he was great on screen.
>
> –Sam Spiegel

In an often-repeated story, Sir Laurence Olivier, playing opposite Dustin Hoffman in the 1976 *Marathon Man*, is said to have been astonished at the American actor's lengthy and exhausting Method-inspired preparation activities. Finally, Olivier decided to offer Hoffmann some advice. "Why don't you try acting?" he suggested. This story directs us to the Method's version of itself as so realistic that the term *acting* cannot properly be applied to it. In fact, however, the Method is not different from acting; it is simply a special style of acting. Method performances in such popular films from the 1950s as *A Streetcar Named Desire* (1951) and *Baby Doll* (1956) today seem as artificial as any other historically dated performance technique. When advocates of the Method argue that this style is more "real" than "acted," they are in fact adapting a rhetoric routinely applied to all acting styles in the realist tradition. Changes in courtship conventions entail changes in the fashions of Hollywood performance styles, which can then lay claim to superior status by virtue of their putative ability to achieve greater realism than the style that preceded them. The movies' appropriation of Method acting during the 1950s was yet another strategy by which Hollywood could lay claim to a "realist effect" because of the style's emphasis on a close fit between actor and character and because Method techniques were peculiarly suited to delineate a new type of male romantic hero.

Method acting and cinema

The special quality of Stanislavskian Method acting can be most readily understood by comparing it to the British tradition, the other school of performance best known to American film- and theatergoers. Where the British school focuses on external technique, emphasizing makeup, costume, and verbal dexterity, the Method relies on understatement and what it calls "inner truth," cultivating an aura of mood and emotion derived from the actor's own persona rather than stressing the interpretation of the language in the written script. The British system encourages audiences to appreciate the actor's craft from an intellectual distance. The Method, by contrast, seeks to maximize the audience's identification with the performer.

Inspired by realist playwrights like Chekhov and Ibsen, Stanislavsky developed his own interpretation of realism at the Moscow Art Theatre. His concept focused on the psychology of the actor rather than on the social milieu of the character. This he termed "living the part." In *An Actor Prepares* he wrote, "Always and forever, when you are on the stage, you must play yourself" (167). The audience identifies with Stanislavskian actors in part because these performers ignore the audience, even going so far, at times, as turning their backs to the front of the stage.[1] Instead of interacting with the spectators, actors merge their own psyches with those of the characters they play. Through what Stanislavsky termed "affective memory" the actors recreate their roles in relation to aspects of their own personal histories.[2] By emphasizing the subtle processes associated with the performer/character's inner life, such actors position themselves as creative forces who collaborate with the playwright. As Timothy Wiles has observed, "Stanislavsky was the first to sense . . . that what is essentially 'real' about theatrical realism lies as much in the reality of the performance itself as in the true-to-life quality of the play's details" (14). In this sense Stanislavsky's method foregrounds the actor in the same way that the nineteenth-century concept of the virtuoso foregrounded the musical performer. Like virtuosos, Stanislavsky's actors emphasize the difficulty of performance. The painful struggle that such actors subject themselves to in order to reach buried feelings is often manifest in the tortured quality identified with Method style.

As some critics have observed, such a performance strategy is analogous in many ways to the experience of psychoanalysis—not least because of its emphasis on releasing the power of the unconscious. "The fundamental objective of our psycho-technique," Stanislavsky wrote, "is to put us in a creative state in which our subconscious will function naturally" (266). This approach gave Stanislavsky's system affinities to modernism as much as to realism, for, like the stream-of-consciousness prose of Virginia Woolf and James Joyce, the style of Stanislavskian actors is designed to allow glimpses of their characters' unconscious inner conflicts.

The specific techniques used in Method performance—improvisation, relaxation, the cultivation of psychologically meaningful pauses, and the use of emotionally charged objects—are designed to reveal psychic conflict. The first three of these techniques create characters who appear to be speaking as if from a psychoanalyst's couch. The use of objects is a device used in all realist performance. In his book on Hollywood cinema Gilles Deleuze comments on the significance of this technique for the creation of what he calls the action image: "[T]he emotional handling of an object, an act of emotion in relation to the object, can have more effect than a close-up in the action image. It simultaneously brings together, in a strange way, the unconscious of the actor, the personal guilt of the director, the hysteria of the image" (159). Method actors are specifically trained to use objects as a means of revealing feelings that have been repressed by the character's conscious mind. In the words of Stanislavsky, "Only your subconscious can tell you why [a] particular object [comes] into the foreground of your mind" (292).

Although Stanislavsky's theories were developed for the theater, they are readily adaptable to film performance.[3] The absence of a live audience gives an obvious advantage to actors who are specifically trained to ignore spectators. Further, Stanislavsky's preoccupation with expressing inner conflict rather than cultivating external effects is well suited to the cinema's use of close-ups. Long takes allow for the expression of subtle changes in the character's feelings. The Method actor's concentration on the emotional texture of individual scenes ("pieces" or "units") is also readily adaptable to the moviemaking process, where individual scenes are shot separately and there is always ample time to prepare each one. Finally, the Method actor's reliance on emotional freshness rather than on outward technical mastery may in some ways be better served by a recorded medium than by the theater, where a role might have to be repeated more or less verbatim every night over a period of many months. Film can preserve the best, the freshest, of a varied series of performances of a single scene.

Despite its adaptability to film, however, Stanislavsky's Method failed to influence movie performance styles significantly until it was taken up by Hollywood in the 1950s. In the USSR film directors were wedded to a cinematic formalism that stressed the primacy of the director's editing function and thus had little interest in this new acting style. "The Moscow Art Theatre is my deadly enemy," Eisenstein wrote. "It is the exact antithesis of all I am trying to do. They string their emotions together to give a continuous illusion of reality. I take photographs of reality and then cut them up so as to produce emotions" (Wollen 65).

In his classic study of cinematic performance, *Film Acting*, V. I. Pudovkin attempted without success to negotiate a rapprochement between Stanislavskian technique and the reliance on editing that stood at the center of Soviet filmmaking.[4] His earlier *Film Technique* had advocated the Eisensteinian concept of actors as physical types ("typage") and had reported on the famous "Kuleshov effect," wherein the same close-up of an actor was read by different audiences as expressing widely divergent emotions depending on whether it was followed by a shot of a child playing, a bowl of soup, or a dead woman (168).[5] Both typage and the Kuleshov effect implicitly denigrated the contributions that Method-trained performers could make to the creation of complex and individuated filmic characters.

Kuleshov himself advocated a modified version of the older Delsarte method of performance in which emotions were conveyed through broad, conventionalized gestures. Such an approach, which communicated strong, simple emotions quickly, was much more in keeping with the aesthetics of Soviet montage than was Stanislavskian acting technique. Kuleshov specifically dismisses the expressive potential of Stanislavsky's Method when he states, "One must construct the work of film actors so that it comprises the sum of organized movement, with 'reliving' held to a minimum" (100). In *Film Acting*, however, Pudovkin denies the Kuleshov experiment's implicit valorization of the power of editing over the artistry of acting. He speaks of "the pseudo-theory of the *montage* (edited) image (a theory for which no single individual is responsible). This theory deduces, from the fact that an impression of acting can be composed mechanically by sticking pieces together, the illegitimate assumption that separate pieces, not connected inwardly within the actor, will necessarily give an optimum result" (273).

Pudovkin had begun his film career as an actor and continued to perform roles in his own films and those of others throughout his life. Because of his concern with actors, his work was sometimes labeled "theatrical" by other members of the Soviet film movement (Leyda 222). By advocating a collaboration between actor and director during the editing process Pudovkin's *Film Acting* attempts to retain the Soviet aesthetic of film as montage and at the same time rehabilitate the status of the actor as a center of creative expressivity rather than a passive tool of the director. Through their participation in editing, Pudovkin argues, actors could overcome the fragmentation brought about by having their scenes cut up into pieces and recreate their performances into a larger emotional unity. Tellingly, Pudovkin's single extended example of how this larger emotional unity could be created does not involve acting at all but instead focuses on the juxtaposition of music and image in the climactic sequence of his 1933 film *Deserter*. After describing the sequence, he concludes somewhat apologetically:

> Though the example we have dealt with here does not relate directly to the actor's work, it yet is important for him, for he is one of those who must understand particularly clearly the significance of the treatment of sound and image[in the editing process], not in their primitive *naturalistic* association, but in a more profound—I should term it *realistic*—association enabling the creative worker in the cinema to portray any given event, not merely simply in direct representation, but in its deepest degree of generalization (313–14). [Emphasis added.]

Despite Pudovkin's lavish praise of Stanislavsky and his repeated protests against the misapplication of the notion of typage to describe the characteristic Soviet approach to cinematic performance, the argument put forward in *Film Acting* cannot surmount the inconsistency that is apparent in the above passage, where "realism" is opposed to "naturalism" and signifies the utopian social vision that lay at the heart of Russian formalist film theory's concept of dialectical montage editing. Stanislavskian realism, focused as it is on the inner feelings of the actor and the development of subtle emotional states made possible by long takes, represents a radically different quality. Pudovkin's fundamental commitment to editing over acting is evident when he writes, "I must confess that during my work I have admitted actors to creative collaboration only grudgingly and to a miserly extent" (354–55).[6]

Hollywood's appropriation of the method

In Hollywood, Stanislavskian theory at first exercised a similarly negligible influence. Despite the immigration of members of the Moscow Art Theatre like Alla Nazimova, Richard Boleslavsky, and Maria Ouspenskaya during the 1920s and 1930s, the Hollywood studios' story-centered view of actors as script readers precluded the intense actor involvement in the creation of character advocated by the Method.[7] The emergence of Stanislavskian techniques as a major force in film performance was not to occur until historical conditions were propitious and the theories themselves had undergone considerable revision.

For Stanislavsky's Moscow Art Theatre, as for the American Group Theatre of the 1930s which modeled itself on Stanislavsky's theories, the Method approach had political implications. Both the Moscow Art Theatre and the Group focused on contemporary social problems and used improvisation to build an ensemble performance that challenged the older, hierarchically organized "star-centered" theater. For example, a filmed rehearsal for a production of *The Three Sisters* staged by the Moscow Art Theatre includes a sequence in which Stanislavsky asks his players, "Did you try to adjust to each other, to feel each other out?" (Nash). In the American Group Theatre the ensemble ideal extended to the playwright as well; its most characteristic productions, such as *Waiting for Lefty* and *Awake and Sing*, were written by Clifford Odets, one of the Group's own members. Odets's plays for the Group were contemporary dramas of working-class frustration, conforming to Stanislavsky's ideal of an indigenous theater of social protest.

The early political and group-centered orientation of Stanislavskian practice, however, had eroded by the 1950s when Lee Strasberg promulgated his own version of the Method at the Actors Studio. As has frequently been noted, Strasberg emphasized the individuated psychoanalytic dimension of Stanislavsky's program by supplementing the Method's affective memory techniques with new exercises. The most famous of these required performers to stage reenactments of "private moments" using material from their own lives. Although these exercises enhanced the actor's ability to portray powerful emotional states, Strasberg's training techniques also encouraged his students to substitute their own feelings for those of the characters they played rather than to merge the two together as Stanislavsky had envisioned.[8]

Under Strasberg, Method acting became more confessional than communal.[9] Such an emphasis on the actor in isolation undermined the ensemble-oriented aspect of Stanislavsky's system, producing actors like James Dean, whose on-screen aura of alienation from those around him was enhanced by a solipsistic acting technique that could lead him to step on the speeches of his fellow performers with line readings of his own that were often inaudible. At the Actors Studio Stanislavsky's conception of improvisation as a way to develop a sense of community among actors was replaced by an approach to improvisation that largely celebrated the neurosis of the individual performer.[10]

Because of their tendency to substitute their personal feelings for those of the characters they were playing, Actors Studio performers were well suited to become Hollywood stars.[11] In Hollywood, star types were defined through their participation in specially tailored films ("star vehicles") and through publicity surrounding their offscreen activities. Thus, the closer the fit between the roles that actors could play and their "real" personalities, the more easily promotable they were as stars. In the case of performers from the Actors Studio, who were oriented toward submerging the characters they played into their own psyches, this fit was especially close. In short, Lee Strasberg transformed a socialistic, egalitarian theory of acting into a celebrity-making machine.

Movie stars spawned by Strasberg's Actors Studio were of a new type which is often labeled the rebel hero (Houston, Kael, Morella and Epstein, Spoto, and Zaratsky). The three actors who epitomized the new rebel type associated with the Method were Marlon Brando, James Dean, and Montgomery Clift. In fact, none of these stars was trained primarily at the Actors Studio. Clift never attended at all. Dean took only a few classes there, virtually abandoning his training after the first time that Strasberg criticized him. Brando was trained primarily by Stella Adler, a former member of the Group Theatre who had had a falling-out with Strasberg over his interpretation of Stanislavsky's ideas.[12] By contrast, other equally talented actors of the 1950s with far closer ties to the Studio, such as Julie Harris and Eli Wallach, did not fit Hollywood's image of the male rebel hero and thus never achieved an appreciable degree of Hollywood success.

In part because of the confusion generated by these popular associations of Method acting with stars not trained at the Actors Studio, the two major studies of film acting published to date, Richard Dyer's *Stars* and James Naremore's *Acting in the Cinema*, both question the distinctiveness of Method performance (Dyer 154, Naremore 197–98). However, whether directly influenced by Strasberg or not, the new male stars all to some degree or other adapted Method techniques to support their identification as rebels, transforming Stanislavsky's emphasis on relaxation into the "Method slouch," his interest in improvisation into libidinous temper tantrums, and his concept of inwardness into mumbling, tortured pauses and sloppy grooming. Although these histrionic affectations quickly assumed the status of clichés, it is important to bear in mind that they represented a clear application of Stanislavsky's theories. Such strategies decisively shaped the kinds of characters that these actors portrayed and the manner in which they portrayed them.

[. . .]

The cinematic Method text: *On the Waterfront*

In the three films of the 1950s most often cited in connection with Method performance—*On the Waterfront* (1954), *East of Eden* (1955), and *Rebel Without a Cause* (1955)—the central conflict concerns the rebel hero's difficulty defining himself in relation to a father figure. This conflict is depicted in each film by means of climactic, highly charged scenes in which a young man attempts to assert a model of virility different from that of his elder. Such scenes call forth the Method actor's ability to indulge in the kind of emotional outpouring traditionally associated with feminine behavior. James Dean's anguished cry in *Rebel Without a Cause*, "You're tearing me apart!" highlights the rebel hero's conflict over his masculine role. The most acclaimed of these films, *On the Waterfront*, is also the one that makes the most extensive use of Method techniques. Directed by Elia Kazan, a man with close ties to the Actors Studio, it features a performance by Marlon Brando that has come to be regarded as the preeminent example of Method acting in film (Hirsch 299; Kazan, Interview, 8).[13] When the film was made, Brando was not only a movie actor but also a Hollywood leading man, and his performance in Kazan's film won him not only an Academy Award but also a place on the list of the top ten Hollywood stars of 1954 and 1955, a place that he would not regain until the release of *The Godfather* in 1971 assured his rebirth as a preeminent character actor (Steinberg).

Brando's performance in *On the Waterfront* uses Method techniques to define a new type of male movie star and a new concept of romantic love. But the nature of his achievement was not consciously appreciated by those most intimately involved with creating this vehicle for him. In recalling the process of writing and selling the screenplay, both Kazan and writer Budd Schulberg have repeatedly referred to the film's romantic element as a concession to the commercialism of Hollywood. As they saw it, they had attempted to write a story of labor struggle, drawing on the experiences of Father John Corridan, the "Waterfront Priest," and on Malcolm Johnson's *New York Sun* series "Crime on the Labor Front." Terry Malloy, the film's protagonist, was based on Anthony De Vincenzo, a key witness in the New York State Crime Commission's investigation of the docks in 1952. "We had taken real characters and put them through a struggle that was still being waged," wrote Schulberg. "Was it too somber, too real for the Hollywood Dream Machine?" (145). Evidently it was, for Hollywood executives like Spiros Skouras and Daryl F. Zanuck, to whom the pair attempted to sell the screenplay, repeatedly urged them to "'make it a beautiful love story'" (147). The disdain for the boy-meets-girl formula evident in Schulberg's reminiscences has been echoed by critics, who for the most part treat *On the Waterfront* as a "social problem film" with a love story that is peripheral to its central concerns.[14] Such a conception of the film misses how essential the love story is to its articulation of the male hero. Kazan's and Schulberg's enterprise in fact takes its vocabulary from a commercial language in which the love story sets the terms by which manhood is understood and evaluated.

The hero's name, Terry, immediately presents him as a figure of ambiguous gender possibilities. These possibilities are articulated in relation to a class discourse that defines two different modes of masculinity. Terry's developing sense of himself eventually leads him to affirm his male identity in relation to a middle-class mode of social organization different from the working-class values with which he has grown up. This mode involves a companionate relation with a woman in the course of which the issues of gender confusion that he is struggling with are enacted.

Initially Terry sees himself as part of a society that the film codes as one constituted in terms of a residual discourse. This world is made up of competing constellations of male power held by localized groups of longshoremen and union officers who define their masculinity through the exclusion of women. Terry's primary loyalty is to the all-male gang of union officials led by the corrupt boss Johnny Friendly (Lee J. Cobb) and his dandified second-in-command, Terry's brother Charlie the Gent (Rod Steiger). Terry's unquestioning participation in this male-identified system begins to break down, however, when Friendly orders him to set up the murder of Joey Doyle, one of the dockers who is about to violate the accepted intergroup loyalties by giving information to a federal commission that is investigating corruption in Friendly's union. Prodded by Father Barry (Karl Malden) and by Edie Doyle (Eva Marie Saint), the sister of the man he has helped to kill, and despite Friendly's effort to dissuade him by killing his brother, Charlie, Terry cooperates with the federal investigation. He also falls in love with Edie. Terry decides to obey the impersonal law of the land rather than the tough-guy code of the docks, and he chooses the companionship of a potential marriage partner over that of his male cronies. His new roles, constituted in terms of the emerging discourses of bourgeois citizen and companionate husband require a radical change in his sense of himself as a man. Brando dramatizes this change by drawing on the classic techniques of Method performance: improvisation, pauses, the use of objects, and relaxation.

Brando's improvisations are delivered in the context of a rigid structure of oppositional languages that define self-enclosed and irreconcilable groups. The middle-class government officials speak in the most stilted manner, making statements that sound artificial and scripted, such as "You have the right to remain silent if that is what you choose to do." At the other extreme, the working-class dockers and union men speak more informally; yet, sensing their isolation from the more official forms of bourgeois utterance used to intimidate them, they have developed an ethic of silence in relation to outsiders. As Kayo Dugan (Pat Henning) says, "Down on the docks, we've always been D and D," betraying even by this locution an argot that must be translated for the benefit of those who are not initiates (Dugan must explain to Father Barry that D and D means "deaf and dumb").

If the speech of the officials conveys itself as an artificial script and that of the dockers as a muted vernacular code, the speech of the women in the film aspires to be a form of personal expression that will bridge the communication impasse. Early in the film Edie Doyle and her female neighbor make strenuous efforts to "speak the truth" about the dockers' victimization and to encourage others to do so. To the men who surround them, however, their efforts appear naive and they are summarily silenced. The men are determined to keep their women mute—even if this involves sending them away. If meaningful communication is to occur, a more potent spokesperson is needed.

This role is assumed by Terry Malloy. His special position is signaled by his manner of speaking. Brando's improvisations set his dialogue apart from that of the other characters.[15] The unrehearsed quality of his speech is conspicuous to anyone watching the film in statements such as "Never's gonna be much too much too soon for me, Shorty," an utterance impossible to imagine as scripted in the form in which Brando delivers it.[16] Similarly, Terry's exchange with Edie during the much-praised scene in which he appropriates her glove contains statements that invite the spectator to construe the character's words as beyond the scriptwriter's control. When Edie tells him she is going to a college run by the Sisters of St. Anne, he asks, "Where's that?" When she responds, "Tarrytown," he says again, "Where's that . . . uh . . . where's that?" When this question, too, is answered, he goes on, "What do you do there, just . . . what . . .? Study?" Further, when Edie drops her glove, Brando mumbles, "Wait a second," suggesting a motivation having to do more with a command from an actor who has decided to depart from the script than with anything preplanned for the character of Terry.

As these last examples suggest, Terry's moments of improvised speech set him apart not only from the other characters but from the screenplay as well. It is worth noting that Budd Schulberg's script for *On the Waterfront* contains an extraordinary number of repeated phrases (for example—Father Barry: "Don't you see that? Now don't you see that?" Edie: "No wonder people call you a bum. No wonder."). In the taxicab scene, surely one of the best known in all cinema, Terry himself speaks many of his lines twice ("Before we get to where, Charlie? Before we get to where?"; "There's a lot more to this than I thought, Charlie; I'm telling you, there's a lot more"; and, in one of the most famous lines of all, "It was you, Charlie; it was you"). Such a use of language has a quality of obsessive return that presents the characters as part of an inflexible social and psychological milieu in which they feel trapped and helpless.[17]

When Brando improvises broken utterances against such a background, his clumsy syntax suggests a freewheeling actor's intermittent attempts at revolt against a constraining structure that relies on shrilly defensive patterns of repetition to assert its authority. In place of Stanislavsky's ideal of actors as *collaborators* in the process of creating a text, merging their psyches with the script that they are performing, *On the Waterfront* uses Stanislavskian improvisation to depict an actor who often appears to be *competing* with a text that sets itself against him by its adherence to rote patterns of repetition. The rebellion of Marlon Brando the star against a traditional cinema of overly scripted performances can thus be read as an analogue to that of Terry Malloy the character against traditional patterns of masculine behavior. Both actor and character appear as isolated figures, Terry in the context of the world depicted in the film and Brando in the context of the circumstances of its production. Each seeks to define his identity in opposition to rigid, empty systems of authority.

The view that sees *On the Waterfront* as a rationalization of Kazan and Schulberg's friendly testimony before the House Un-American Activities Committee cannot account for the fact that it plays down its "great moment" of informing. Terry's explosive testimony is almost thrown away; Kazan even cuts away from it at a climactic moment to show "Mr. Upstairs" switching off his television set. The courtroom scene cannot become the site where the film's issues are resolved because it focuses only on words; but *On the Waterfront* is at least as concerned with images, which are part of a visual texture that masks their psychological significance. The bleak black-and-white photography and gritty location shooting that give the film its distinctive visual feel identify it with a tradition of documentary realism. But many of the images, especially those of Brando's face and the objects that he interacts with, also convey the inward struggle that marks the character of Terry Malloy. Like its words, the images of the films are gender identified.

Brando's performance must define masculinity against a visual background that represents the male body as diminutive and vulnerable. Boris Kaufmann's bleak black-and-white photography overpowers the film's male groups with a superhumanly scaled and menacing urban landscape: great loading docks, tall iron fences, vast desolate tracts of rubble, and buildings with endless colonnades. In the film's first shot the figures of Johnny Friendly and his group are dwarfed by the looming shape of a docked freighter, and the whistle blast from another freighter obliterates Terry's first attempt to speak what he knows to Edie. The threatening quality of this landscape is emphasized by wide-angle shots in which people and things move backwards and forwards in the frame with disconcerting rapidity: a truck chasing Terry and Edie down an alley, Johnny Friendly's henchmen scurrying out of the bar when Father Barry momentarily distracts Terry's attention. Most ominously, this world of overscaled structures and precipitous movement involves the threat of falling. We see Joey Doyle fall off the roof of his apartment building and later watch a cargo of whiskey cartons drop on Kayo Doogan, another would-be informer.

As the film's primary representative of femininity, Edie thinks only of escaping from this environment back to the country where she goes to college or to the older way of living represented in her fantasy of a farm. Terry, in turn, tries to escape through his pigeons, with which he is more than once identified. He releases one of these pigeons into the air just before Joey Doyle's fatal fall. The bird's ability to counteract the gravitational pull that ensures Joey's destruction is underscored by Friendly's bodyguard Tillio (Tami Mauriello), who compares Joey to a bird who could sing, "but he couldn't fly."

As if in response to this threatening visual context, Brando's Method techniques depict a character who is cautious and uncertain. The anguished pauses that mark his performance are dramatized by high-key lighting and by Leonard Bernstein's overwrought musical score. At such moments the film's long close-ups of the character of Terry Malloy suggest a level of experience that is verbally inexpressible. Like the silences that occur on the psychoanalyst's couch, these pauses convey inner confusion and blockage. Terry cannot articulate what is going on inside of him because he does not consciously understand it.

Brando also draws on a Method-inspired use of objects to represent his character's repressed gender-related insecurities. As I have indicated, one of Brando's most celebrated scenes in this film involves his appropriation of a woman's glove. When Terry first meets Edie, he takes up a glove that she has accidentally dropped and refuses to return it to her, playing with it and eventually putting his hand into it as he engages her in conversation. As James Naremore has noted, "Few virile male leads before him . . . would so effortlessly have slipped on a woman's glove" (*Acting in the Cinema* 194). A further motif that brings out Terry's "feminine" side involves his pigeons. In a curious scene on the roof he tenderly holds a pigeon erroneously referred to as "she" by Edie, then clearly identified as a male by Tommy, the young Golden Warrior ("She's a he. His name is Swifty"). Immediately following Tommy's statement, however, the pigeon lays an egg in Terry's hand. This hermaphroditic creature, to which Terry refers approvingly on more than one occasion, can be taken as a model for Terry's own confused identity, which effects a complicated mediation between masculinity and femininity.

In keeping with the Method's psychoanalytically oriented preoccupations, Brando also interacts with objects in such a way as to bring out psychologically coded meanings having to do with enclosure, which Freud identified with femininity, or thrusting and penetration, which he identified as male. Terry's habit of chewing gum, which involves the body's enclosing properties, has overtones of femininity. These overtones are further played upon when Terry offers gum to Edie to comfort her during the wedding scene. His gesture of exchange here contrasts to some of the film's instances of male bonding, which are marked by exchanges of cigarettes—objects with more phallic overtones. A cigarette is exchanged between Father Barry (Karl Malden) and one of the dockers as the priest is being hauled up out of the hold, for example. Women may also be included in this ritual of male bonding: the snatches of dialogue we overhear among members of the wedding party indicate that, like the men, the tough-talking bride smokes, a further sign of her accommodation to a traditional male world.

The film's major example of a male-coded object is the gun given to Terry by his older brother, Charlie. Despite the scenario implied by Charlie's decision to give him this gun, Terry cannot bring himself to use it to carry out the traditional role of the male who acts rather than speaks.[18] The gentleness with which Brando pushes this object away as Steiger begins to brandish it in front of him and the careless way that he holds it in the bar suggest the character's lack of traditional male authority. Terry soon abandons the gun and gives testimony at the hearing instead. When the hearing fails to clarify his sense of himself, Terry must find another strategy. At this point Brando engages with yet another object: Joey Doyle's jacket. The feminine associations of enclosure inherent in this jacket are called forth when Father Barry makes a show of zipping it up after Terry's beating. Yet the jacket is nonetheless clearly identified as male. It thus constitutes an appropriate image for the androgynous persona that Terry ultimately adopts. In wearing Joey's jacket, Terry affirms his commitment to a sexual identity that can encompass both masculine and feminine traits.

Terry's ambivalent gender identity increasingly centers on the representation of his body, and this representation is complicated by Brando's relaxed Method posture. In an essay entitled "Don't Look Now" Richard Dyer has explored the significance of the aura of hardness surrounding erotic representations of the male body. This aura is typically achieved by means of an emphasis on visible musculature and an association of the body with action, often through the use of an active, upright posture. By contrast, Brando's Method slouch depicts his body as limp rather than upright, and he plays the first love scenes with Eva Marie Saint in a passive position traditionally identified as feminine. At the same time, however, his broken nose and the cut eyebrow that he affects for this role announce the character's association with the prototypically male world of boxing. The body image of the character that emerges has conflicting associations with both pugnacity and weakness. If the film is to rehabilitate his image as a romantic male hero, these contradictions must be addressed. Like his pigeon Swifty, who sits on the highest perch and attacks all who try to displace him, Terry must establish his superiority to women and to other men.

The masculine side of Terry's persona begins to take precedence when he makes love to Edie. Here, in a sequence noteworthy for its eroticization of female surrender to a forced sexual encounter, Terry asserts the traditional male right to dominate women.[19] Brando's rendering of this scene, however, differs from the performance strategy followed by prior male stars in that he exhibits an explosive rage that is perceived as passionate rather than merely controlling; it is the antithesis of the repressed state earlier expressed in his tortured pauses. The character appears to have "unblocked" himself through a brutally physical assertion of masculine privilege vis-à-vis women. Only after this dramatic assertion of male dominance is Terry willing to carry out the femininizing role of speaking out at the hearing.

Even though Terry's violent encounter with Edie has satisfied him regarding the superior capabilities of his body in relation to those of a woman, Friendly's attempt to assault him at the hearing serves as a reminder that he must assert this superiority in relation to the male world as well. Throughout the film his physique is contrasted with that of Friendly. Whereas Cobb's body is massive and his gestures aggressive, Brando's body is flaccid and his gestures indecisive. Although Terry's movements are identifiably those of a former boxer, he demurs when Friendly tries to involve him in a playful sparring match near the beginning of the film. Although he no longer identifies himself as part of an individualistic world of competitive male groups that define their dominance in terms of pure muscle, Terry must prove his masculinity by means of a test of physical prowess. He approaches this test as a bourgeois man who is ruled by the law. His new masculinity is purely symbolic, exemplified by his ability to stand up after being beaten and to thrust himself through the door of the leading dock. This action calls forth associations with a sexual act in which Terry's whole body is deployed as a phallus, and it incorporates him into the visual environment that has previously posed such a threat to the dominance of the male figure. His walk into the loading dock contrasts his body to Friendly's for the last time as the former union boss is dunked in the harbor by Pop Doyle (John Hamilton) in a comic inversion of Friendly's original crime of throwing Doyle's son Joey off the roof.[20]

Terry's stoic assertion of bodily supremacy speaks more eloquently to the dockers than any words; but it does move them to words. Here the pattern of repeated utterances that has heretofore prevailed is appropriated in the service of a new commitment to intergroup communication. Now the repetitions are combined with variations that emphasize the relationship between Terry and the other dockers. "If *Terry* don't work, *we* don't work . . . If *he* walks in, *we* walk in with him." This new sense of community, fragile and tentative, constitutes the film's ultimate resolution, a resolution centered on the battered but still identifiably male body of Terry Malloy.

This choric solidarity is made possible, both thematically and dramatically, by the strong vulnerability of the protagonist. Thematically, the resolution is classic and archetypal; the scapegoat purges and renews the society. But dramatically it is innovative, made possible by the particular ideological potency of the new man that Brando enacts. Brando's performance elaborates a model of male gender insecurity that recreates romance as a drama of male neuroticism. The Stanislavskian techniques that he employs not only lend themselves to the expression of this motif but also invest his characterization with an unprecedented aura of verisimilitude. Brando's acting in *On the Waterfront* is thus designed to persuade movie fans of the 1950s that Hollywood's newest love stories were not only pleasurable but also "realistic."

In recent years the influence of the Method on the creation of male star personas has been to some extent reformulated. In place of the anxiety-fraught romantic relationships suggested by the neurotic male Method stars of the fifties, newer Method stars like Robert de Niro, Dustin Hoffman, and Al Pacino typically project a cold narcissism that suggests that they are beyond romance. These actors represent the self-absorption that Lee Strasberg brought to Method performance not by revealing an anguished inner torment as the stars of the fifties were inclined to do but rather by projecting a truculent incommunicativeness that pointedly excludes the audience.

Many of the most successful films made by these actors, such as *Raging Bull* (1980), *The Godfather* (1972 and 1974), and *Kramer vs. Kramer* (1979), treat the failure of romantic coupling. By contrast, attempts to feature these stars in traditional romantic plots in films like *Bobby Deerfield* (1977), *John and Mary* (1969), and *Falling in Love* (1984) have for the most part been notably unsuccessful. For these performers the drama of identity does not necessarily involve a relationship with a woman. De Niro, for instance, is at his best playing psychotic characters like Travis Bickle in *Taxi Driver* (1976) or Johnny Boy in *Mean Streets* (1973). Pacino has been successful at portraying homosexuals in films like *Dog Day Afternoon* (1975) and *Hustling* (1980). Hoffman plays at transvestitism in *Tootsie* (1982) and autism in *Rain Man* (1988). The identity issues raised by such roles and by these stars' offscreen personas as difficult loners suggest that a pre-Oedipal scenario may have replaced the Oedipally related crises of gender roles acted out by the Method stars of the 1950s. How this shift relates to the changing conventions of romance and marriage is as yet unclear. In the world of commercialized artistry that is Hollywood cinema, however, such changes are always meaningful.

Notes

1 In keeping with Stanislavsky's commitment to exploring the limits of realist representation, this manner of playing represented the furthest extension of the "fourth wall" convention first espoused by Diderot as a means of increasing drama's capacity for illusionism. For a discussion of Diderot's influence on the development of theatrical realism, see Arnold Hauser's essay "The Origins of Domestic Drama."

2 For an attack on the efficacy of the technique of affective memory, see Bentley.

3 Stanislavsky himself was not hospitable toward the idea of Method acting in film. As Jay Leyda reports, "Stanislavsky's personal feeling about cinema began in contempt, warmed into antagonism, and never went beyond tolerance in later years" (76).

4 In the films he made as a director, however, Pudovkin's primary identification is with the Soviet tradition. Jay Leyda reports that *Deserter*, for instance, contained 3,000 shots as compared to the average sound film's 800 to 1,000 (297). In such films character is delineated through editing much more than through acting. Pudovkin freely resorted to other nonperformance techniques to portray character as well. In *Mother*, for instance, high-angle shots of the mother designated in the title suggest her helplessness, and the father's self-indulgence is revealed by a close-up of his hand scratching his stomach. In both *Film Technique* and *Film Acting* Pudovkin also proudly recounted his ability to elicit desired reactions from nonperformers. In his 1928 *Storm Over Asia*, for example, he was able to draw an awed and fascinated response from a crowd of Mongolian peasants by presenting them with a show put on by a Chinese conjurer out of range of the camera (170). And in *The Story of a Simple Case* (1932) he evoked a smile from a young boy for a scene in the film through similarly deceptive means (339–41). In such a creative context the

controlled and integrated acting techniques cultivated by Method performers are ill served.

5 It is doubtful that the Kuleshov experiment ever actually took place; if it did, it is unclear what form it took. However, the status it is accorded in the writings of various Soviet theorists attests to the significance that they attached to the concept of character depiction through editing rather than acting. For a recent discussion of the problematic status of this well-known experiment see Holland and Kepley.

6 Pudovkin equates realism with the theory of montage even more emphatically later in *Film Acting* when he writes,

> Naturalism, idealism and realism in art stand in the same relation to one another as do mechanism, idealism, and dialectical materialism in philosophy.
>
> Those of the naturalist school, in copying a phenomenon of actuality and not generalizing it, create a mere cold mechanism, without the inner links that exist in actuality within the phenomenon, and without the outer links that bind it to other phenomena as a part to the whole (330).

In a later essay, "Stanislavsky's System in the Cinema," Pudovkin avoided this inconsistency in his discussion of cinematic realism and called upon the director to create unity in the actor's performance. Even here, however, the paradox of how the actor could develop inward feeling in the context of a filmic practice that gave primacy to editing remained unanswered.

7 Hollywood's orientation toward well-crafted stories did not necessarily reflect a valorization of writers over actors. Scripts were often tailored to the talents of specific actors, and important stars could have scripts rewritten to suit their preferences. But the highly polished surfaces of most studio-made films of the period precluded the ragged effect of too much creative participation by actors on the set.

Richard Blum argues that *Theodora Goes Wild*, directed by Boleslavsky in 1936, shows the effects of Method-style improvisation (29). Yet the film plays far more like a polished 1930s comedy than it does like the emotion-charged realistic dramas most associated with the Method school.

8 Useful accounts of this process can be found in Blum, Hirsch, Garfield, Lewis, and Strasberg.

9 Jean Benedetti's recent biography of Stanislavsky blames Richard Boleslavsky for this shift. Boleslavsky was the person primarily responsible for introducing Americans to the principles of Method acting, and he emphasized affective memory. Meanwhile, Stanislavsky himself was developing his theories in another direction which stressed physical action (259).

10 The lack of commitment that Marlon Brando had to the communal ideals of Stanislavskian performance has been attested to by Rod Steiger, who has complained bitterly about Brando's predilection for leaving the set during the production of *On the Waterfront* after his speeches had been filmed so that Steiger was forced to deliver his own lines to an assistant director in scenes such as the famous taxicab tête-à-tête. (Kazan's autobiography excuses Brando's discourtesy by explaining that the star had to leave the set to attend his psychoanalytic sessions [525].)

Published accounts of the group improvisations that Brando participated in at the Actors Studio reveal him as having been competitive and hostile toward his fellow performers, often expressing these feelings through the use of obscenities and physical violence. In part this behavior can be seen as a function of Strasberg's design of the exercises themselves, one of which was labeled "ineluctable force versus immovable object." An example of Brando's interpretation of this exercise is offered by David Garfield:

> Brando was supposed to be returning to his apartment where he had hidden some drugs. Eli Wallach was told he was an FBI agent who had been assigned to find the narcotics in Brando's apartment. He said to Brando, "Give me a minute to walk around the room, then you walk in." When Brando entered he looked at Wallach and said, "Who the fuck are you?" Wallach, shocked at the language—not usual on the stage at that time—said, "What?" Brando repeated the question. Wallach sputtered something about the super having let him in to look at the apartment, which he was interested in renting. Brando's language got cruder and cruder. Wallach said, "Just a minute." Brando pushed him and said, "Just get out." Wallach said, "Don't push, don't push." Brando continued the stream of threat and invective and kept pushing him. Wallach resisted and Brando picked him up and threw him out of the room, slamming the door behind him. Wallach opened the door to get back in; he was furious and really ready to kill Brando. But Marlon was laughing. So was the class—uncontrollably. In the post-scene discussion Wallach was criticized for not finding the narcotics (61–62).

Needless to say, such an approach has little to do with Stanislavsky's ideal of collaboration and ensemble playing.

11 The compatibility of the Method with the Hollywood star system has also been noted by Robert Brustein (*Culture Watch*) and Gordon Gow (*Hollywood in the Fifties*).

12 For Adler's interpretation of the Method, see her book *The Technique of Acting*, which has a foreword by Brando. In it she argues that Stanislavskian actors should attend to matters of style and craft—to the outer as well as the inner aspects of performance. Even in his early career, Brando followed this practice, taking on roles that emphasized accents, costume, and makeup in films like *Viva Zapata* (1952), *Julius Caesar* (1953), and *Teahouse of the August Moon* (1956). Nonetheless, Hollywood typed him as a rebel along with Clift and Dean.

Brando's ease with the techniques of self-exposure that the Method represents was later attested to by Bernardo Bertolucci, who commented on the star's bravura turn in *Last Tango in Paris* (1972). "Instead of entering the character, I asked him to superimpose himself on it," Bertolucci has recalled. "I didn't ask him to become anything but himself. It wasn't like doing a film. It was a kind of psychoanalytic adventure" (Morella and Epstein 139).

13 Kazan's reputation has suffered because of his identification as an actor's director. (See, for example, Robin Wood's essay "The Kazan Problem.") My own analysis of *On the Waterfront*, by contrast, implies that the integration of a strong performance style into a cinematic text is in itself a considerable directorial achievement.

14 See, for example, Biskind, Christiansen, Hey, Mellen, Murray, Neve, Roffman and Purdy, and Sayre. Most of these discussions see the film as a glorification of the act of informing, and thus as an apologia for Kazan's and Schulberg's friendly testimony before the House Un-American Activities Committee. The fullest statement of this argument can be found in Navasky.

Although persuasive on its own terms, this line of argument has tended to obscure elements of the film that distinguish what happens to its hero from what happened to its authors. The federal investigation in *On the Waterfront* is in no way corrupt or ill advised; it is based on the Kefauver hearings of corruption on the docks, not on HUAC. Thus, Terry's decision to inform is of a different order from the decision made by the filmmakers regarding HUAC. Although this shift may be thought of as placing the actions of Kazan and the others in a more favorable light, its relationship to the central concerns of the film is quite another matter. (I am indebted to Robert Savage for bringing this point to my attention.)

Other readings of the film have argued that its complications are focused on an isolated individual divorced from society as well as from romance. See, for example, Michaels, Kitses ("Elia Kazan"), and Higson. An exhaustive history of the making of the film and the backgrounds of its various collaborators can be found in Hey.

15 In an analysis of performance in *East of Eden* Joanne LaRue and Carole Zucker have pointed out the way in which James Dean's Method style also functions to set his character apart from the others. However, LaRue and Zucker assert that this strategy is wholly attributable to Elia Kazan's direction rather than Dean's acting, claiming that the star's Method-derived style does not contribute to a sense of the character's alienation. My own discussion of Brando in *On the Waterfront* makes a case against such a view by emphasizing the way in which any performer's extensive use of Method techniques associated with inwardness will tend to produce a characterization in which alienation is a central feature.

16 The final shooting script, which was later published, gives this line as, "Never will be much too soon" (26). Almost all Brando's dialogue departs from the published script in a similar manner, although the speeches of the other characters tend to follow Schulberg's written dialogue quite closely.

17 The strategy of repeating lines was to become a central feature of Sanford Meisner's version of the Method. Meisner contends that this technique "is emotional and impulsive, and *gradually*, when the actors I train improvise, what they say—like what the composer writes—comes not from the head but truthfully from the impulses" (36–37). Meisner's very different view of the effect of repeated lines speaks to the usefulness of this strategy in training, not in actual performance.

18 Terry's decision not to stage a climactic shoot-out calls into question Robert Ray's characterization of *On the Waterfront* as a "disguised Western" (145).

19 Here, as in many Hollywood films, the woman's resistance is seen as a function of her misunderstanding of the situation, which the film's authors have constructed to validate the male point of view, and of her own emotions. It is only by subjecting woman to physical force that the man compels her to acknowledge her "true" feelings. Thus the film's rhetoric works to undermine the integrity of the female will and to sanction the use of force in heterosexual relations. For discussions of the conventions governing the cinematic representation of forced sexual encounters, see my *Roman Polanski*.

In an essay on *American Gigolo* Peter Lehman has argued that representations of male passivity during erotic interplay lead to "hysterical" overcompensations in other parts of the narrative. My own reading of *On the Waterfront* supports this view by reading the scene of sexual assault as a compensation for the male's earlier passivity.

20 In an influential article Lindsay Anderson argued that this scene reflects a fascistic world view, for the men who follow Terry behave like "leaderless sheep in search of a new master"

(130). By contrast, Michel Ciment and Kenneth Hey see the scene as a crucifixion, with Brando as a Messiah who suffers in order to lead the men into a better world (Ciment 112, Hey 690). But because neither of these positions considers the role played by sexuality in the film, they are unable to account for the scene's extreme emphasis on physicality and its relationship to Brando's distinctive performance style.

References

Adler, Stella. *The Technique of Acting*. New York: Bantam, 1988.

Anderson, Lindsay. *About John Ford*. London: Plexius, 1981.

Benedetti, Jean. *Stanislavsky*. New York: Routledge, 1988.

Bentley, Eric. "Emotional Memory." In *Theory of the Modern Stage: An Introduction to Modern Theatre and Drama*, edited by Eric Bentley, 275–282. New York: Bantam, 1976.

Biskind, Peter. "The Politics of Power in *On the Waterfront*." *Film Quarterly* 29.1 (1975): 25–38. Reprinted in *Seeing is Believing: How Hollywood Taught Us to Stop Worrying and Love the Fifties*, 169–182. New York: Pantheon, 1977.

Blum, Richard. *American Film Acting: The Stanislavsky Heritage*. Ann Arbor: University of Michigan Press, 1984.

Brustein, Robert. *Culture Watch: Essays on Theatre and Society*, 1969–1974. New York: Knopf, 1975.

Christiansen, Terry. *Reel Politics*. New York: Basil Blackwell, 1987.

Ciment, Michael. *Kazan on Kazan*. London: British Film Institute, 1973.

Deleuze, Gilles. *Cinema I*. Minneapolis: University of Minnesota Press, 1986.

Dyer, Richard. *Stars*. London: British Film Institute, 1979.

—— "Don't Look Now." *Screen* 23, no. 4 (1982): 61–73.

Garfield, David. *A Player's Place: The Story of the Actor's Studio*. New York: Macmillan, 1981.

Gow, Gordon. *Hollywood in the Fifties*. New York: A. S. Barnes, 1971.

Hauser, Arnold. "The Origins of Domestic Drama." In *Theory of the Modern Stage: An Introduction to Modern Theatre and Drama*, edited by Eric Bentley, 403–424. New York: Bantam, 1976.

Hey, Kenneth. "Ambivalence as a Theme in *On the Waterfront*. An Interdisciplinary Approach to Film Studies." *American Quarterly* 31, no. 5 (1979): 667–696. Reprinted in *Hollywood As Historian: American Film in a Cultural Context*, edited by Peter C. Rollins, 159–189. Lexington: University Press of Kentucky, 1983.

Higson, Andrew. "Acting Taped – An Interview with Mark Nash and James Swinson." *Screen* 26.5 (Sept.–Oct. 1985): 2–25.

Hirsch, Foster. *A Method to Their Madness: The History of the Actors Studio*. New York: Da Capo, 1984.

Holland, Norman. "Film Response from Eye to I: The Kuleshov Experiment." *South Atlantic Quarterly* 88, no. 2 (1989): 415–442.

Houston, Penelope. "Rebels Without Cause." *Sight and Sound* 25.4 (1956): 178–181.

Kael, Pauline. "Marlon Brando and James Dean." In *The Movie Star*, edited by Elisabeth Weis. New York: Anchor, 1989.

Kazan, Elia. "Interview." *Movie* 19 (1971–72): 8.

—— *A Life*. New York: Anchor Books, 1989.

Kepley, Vance Jr. "The Kuleshov Workshop." *Iris* 4, no. 1 (1986): 5–24.

Kitses, Jim. "Elia Kazan: A Structural Analysis." *Cinema* 7, no. 3 (n.d.): 26–35.

Kuleshov, Lev. *Kuleshov on Film: Writings by Lev Kuleshov*. Translated and edited by Ronald Levaco. Berkeley: University of California Press, 1974.

LaRue, Joanne and Carole Zucker. "James Dean: The Pose of Reality: *East of Eden* and the Method Performance." In *Making the Invisible: An Anthology of Original Essays on Film Acting*, edited by Carole Zucker, 295–324. Metuchen, N.J.: Scarecrow Press, 1990.

Lehman, Peter. "*American Gigolo*. The Male Body Makes an Appearance of Sorts." In *Gender: Literary and Cinematic Representations*, edited by Jeanne Ruppert, 1–9. Tallahassee: Florida State University Press, 1989.

Lewis, Robert. *Slings and Arrows: Theater in My Life*. New York: Stein and Day, 1984.

Leyda, Jay. *Kino: A History of the Russian and Soviet Film*. Princeton: Princeton University Press, 1983.

Meisner, Sanford and Dennis Longwell. *Sanford Meisner on Acting*. New York: Vintage, 1987.

Mellen, Joan. *Big Bad Wolves: Masculinity in the American Film*. New York: Pantheon, 1977.

Michaels, Lloyd. "Critical Survey." In *Elia Kazan: A Guide to References and Resources*, 19–34. Boston: G. K. Hall, 1985.

Morella, Joe and Edward Z. Epstein. *Brando: The Unauthorized Biography*. London: Thomas Nelson, 1973.

Murray, Edward. "*On the Waterfront*." In *Ten Film Classics: A Re-Viewing*, 86–101. New York: Ungar, 1978.

Naremore, James. *Acting in the Cinema*. Berkeley: University of California Press, 1988.

Nash, Mark *et al*. *The Acting Tapes*. Produced for Channel 4, Great Britain, 1985.

Navasky, Victor. *Naming Names*. New York: Viking, 1980.

Neve, Brian. "The 1950s: The Case of Elia Kazan and *On the Waterfront*." In *Cinema, Politics and Society in America*, edited by Philip Davies and Brian Neve, 97–118. Manchester: Manchester University Press, 1981.

Pudovkin, V. I. "Stanislavsky's System in the Cinema." Translated by T. Shebunina. *Sight and Sound* 22, no. 3 (1953): 115ff. Reprinted in *Pudovkin's Film and Film Theory*, edited by Peter Dart, 186–206. New York: Arno, 1974.

—— *Film Technique and Film Acting*. Translated and edited by Ivor Montague. New York: Grove Press, 1976.

Ray, Robert. *A Certain Tendency in the Hollywood Cinema*. Princeton: Princeton University Press, 1985.

Roffman, Peter and Jim Purdy. *The Hollywood Social Problem Film*. Bloomington: Indiana University Press, 1981.

Sayre, Nora. "Behind the Waterfront." In *Running Time: Films of the Fifties*, 151–172. New York: Dial, 1982.

Schulberg, Budd. *On the Waterfront*. Carbondale: Southern Illinois University Press, 1980.

Spoto, Donald. *Camarado*. New York: New American Library, 1978.

Stanislavsky, Constantin. *An Actor Prepares*. Translated by Elizabeth Reynolds Hapgood. New York: Theatre Art Books, 1948.

Steiger, Rod. Interview in *Filmmakers Speak*, edited by Jay Leyda, 440–441. New York: Da Capo, 1984.

Steinberg, Cobbitt. *Reel Facts: The Movie Book of Records*. New York: Vintage, 1978.

Strasberg, Lee. *A Dream of Passion: The Development of the Method*. Edited by Evangeline Morphos. Boston: Little, Brown, 1987.

Wexman, Virginia Wright. *Roman Polanski*. Boston: Twayne, 1984.

Wiles, Timothy. *The Theater Event: Theories of Modern Performance*. Chicago: University of Chicago Press, 1980.

Wollen, Peter. *Signs and Meaning in the Cinema*. Bloomington: Indiana University Press, 1969.

Wood, Robin. "The Kazan Problem." *Movie* 19 (1971–72): 29–31.

Zaratsky, William. "Epitaph for a Rebel." *Rolling Stone* 16 (October 1980): 50ff.

Film Acting and Independent Cinema 11

ANDREW HIGSON

In September 1985, *Screen* published a special issue on acting and cinema, an issue which included my interview with Mark Nash and James Swinson, co-directors of Channel 4's *Acting Tapes*. The tapes and the special issue of *Screen* together seek ways of discussing the question of film acting within the theoretical frameworks developed over the last few years and in relationship to debates about independent cinema in Britain. More recently, the tapes were shown as part of a short season focusing on film acting on Channel 4's *Eleventh Hour* slot, and as part of a much longer season on the same topic at the National Film Theatre (NFT) in London. In addition, there have been various events organised around the tapes, including a *Screen* day school at the NFT, and a weekend of discussions, screenings and video/acting workshops at Phoenix Arts, Leicester. What follows is an attempt to develop in a relatively systematic way some of the ideas thrown up in these various contexts, and to relate them both to the writings of Meyerhold and Kuleshov, Bresson and Brecht, and to the context of British independent cinema in general.[1]

At the NFT event, John Caughie argued that it is important to distinguish between two ways of thinking about acting,[2] which we might loosely summarise as the difference between the *intentions* of specific traditions of acting, and the *effects* of acting in terms of the production meaning. My interest here is in the relationship between the two, and particularly the implications of such an approach for the development of appropriate acting strategies for independent cinema.

On the one hand, different traditions of acting involve specific forms of training, the development of particular skills and forms of concentration, and specific assumptions about the relationship between interiority/exteriority, and/or between the individual subject/social relations. This can perhaps be most easily characterised in terms of an example developed in the *Acting Tapes*. For Stanislavsky, we might have the following structure –

> I saw a bear (stimulus)
> I was frightened (emotion)
> so I ran (response).

Here the actor's training must concentrate upon developing the skill and concentration necessary to *emote fear*. But in Meyerhold's biomechanical schema, we have the following structure –

I saw a bear (stimulus)
I ran (response)
because I was frightened (implication).

(In Bresson's exhortation, 'Let the cause follow the effect, not accompany it or precede it.')[3] Meyerhold's actor must concentrate upon developing a visually expressive physical dynamism, which in terms of cinema acting still seems useful, despite the behaviourist undertones of the training.

The *Acting Tapes* deal specifically with the two acting traditions as distinguished here – the naturalist tradition of Stanislavsky, the Group Theatre, the Actors' Studio and the Method; and the anti-naturalist tradition of Meyerhold and Kuleshov, Brecht and Bresson. This means that the tapes are more concerned with institutions, forms of training and performance conventions, than with acting as a sign-system capable of producing specific meanings in specific contexts.

The second way of thinking about film acting is, however, directly concerned with the semiotics of acting: the meaningfulness of acting signs produced in various systems of difference and identity, under the particular conditions of the institution of cinema.[4] As soon as one starts considering acting in these terms, it becomes clear that acting signs are caught up in a polysemic production of meaning and pleasure, crucially dependent upon the moment of viewing. As such, the intentions of a particular acting strategy (in the context of the (inter)textuality of a film) do not have any necessary relationship to any particular predetermined effect. As John Caughie argued at the NFT event, it would be wrong to operate upon a rigid distinction between the ideological efficacy of naturalist and anti-naturalist acting, where naturalism automatically means empathetic identification = bad, and anti-naturalism automatically means distantiation = good. Formal devices (and in this respect acting functions as a set of formal devices) cannot be assumed to have a fixed ideological effect in all circumstances. Thus Brecht, in his essay 'Against George Lukacs', agrees with those who 'did not believe in such things as "the" method. They knew that many methods were necessary to attain their goal.' Later in the same essay, Brecht writes:

> We must not derive realism as such from particular existing works, but we shall use every means, old and new, tried and untried, derived from art and derived from other sources, to render reality to men – in a form they can understand.[5]

As an example of the way in which an acting style may produce quite unintended effects, Caughie pointed to the way in which the Method school of naturalist film acting may in fact drift into self-reflexivity, signifying a power of presence and an inner truth which may actually *exceed* the requirements of narrative. Thus, the gestures of Marlon Brando in *The Godfather* tend to exceed narrative motivation – to exceed that which is narratively required of character. *Intended* as a display of descriptive, realistic detail (ethnicity, authority, etc), it may actually be read as a display of the actor as such. In such cases, the dialectic of control/egotistic self-expression tends to draw attention to the actor's mastery (of actorly skills, of self-control . . .), the ability to generate beguiling but superfluous gestures, and to string out narratively redundant actions – so that to watch Method acting is to be fascinated by the obsessive nature of the performance, rather than by the signified or the represented of the action. Further, this spectacle of mastery too easily articulates a masculinity which is hardly appropriate to all roles. The other side of this dialectic is the tendency to draw attention away from the exigencies of character or role and towards the actor's persona in terms of a mysterious inner truth. In other words, the attempt to 'portray reality' is blocked by the imprecision, irrelevancy and distraction of naturalism's trivial verisimilitude.[6] On the other hand, it should be recognised that there will always be a certain ambiguity, coincidence and redundancy of meaning built into any acting strategy.

These considerations suggest that at the level of a semiotics of acting, the distinction between naturalism and anti-naturalism, or between 'the natural' and 'the stylised' is actually not very useful. More useful is the distinction made by Barry King at the NFT event[7] between four levels or categories of acting performance, thus specifying the material site of production of acting signs:

the facial
the gestural
the corporeal (or postural) and
the vocal.

However the actor may think about these different categories, for the spectator they function as signs, which are themselves caught up in two distinct meaning systems.

First, we can note that the four categories are all, including the vocal, physical categories; consequently, the meaningfulness of each category, the extent to which they register, is, in part, dependent upon physical type (e.g., long face, large body, high-pitched voice . . .) calling up specific cultural connotations. John O Thompson has argued that such types are at one level *givens*, or *positivities*: their meaningfulness is relatively autonomous of any system of difference.[8] But at another level these types are further pitched into the play of meaning through the system of physical differences scattered across a film. Thus the meaning of a physical type is constituted partly in terms of positive *identity*, and partly in terms of its *difference* from other types.

Secondly, there is a differential system of movement/stasis of the face, the gesture, the body and the vocal chords. Again, there is an external (or extra-textual) and an internal (textual) level of meaning produced here. 'Externally', there is both a highly conventionalised cultural coding of movement (as in Delsarte's codification of melodramatic gestures, or the gestures of Peking opera) and a much more ambiguous though still readable cultural codification of 'everyday' gestures signifying different emotions or states of mind (e.g., raised eyebrows as a sign of surprise). 'Internally', further meaningful differentiations can be produced, between minimal and frenetic movement, between precise control and looseness or ambiguity of movement, between economy and superfluity.

The exact range of these various intersecting fields of meaning in any particular film will depend on several other factors: casting decisions; the skill of the actor; the persona of the actor; the nature of character and role;[9] make-up and dress; *mise-en-scène*, camerawork and montage.

I now want to consider, in a relatively programmatic way, the practice of film acting in relation to independent cinema, under six headings:

1 the economy of the voice;
2 the economy of face/gesture/body – 'doing nothing';

3 precision of movement in relation to the camera's field of vision;
4 fragmenting character and externalising emotion – identity and identification;
5 stylisation and distantiation in the cinema;
6 continuity and systematisation of work with actors – the ensemble.

There is, however, a major problem in attempting to address independent cinema as if it were a unified sector, or a unified practice. In what follows, I have not attempted to deal with the current problems of funding facing independent film and video workers, or with the different sites of 'independent' film and video practice, and how these affect the aesthetics, politics and ideologies of oppositional and interventionist work. What follows is a polemical call for a more imaginative cinema of ideas, which embraces both fictional and documentary forms – and crucially a cinematic practice which thinks seriously about the acting strategies it mobilises.

The economy of the voice

Cinema is too often characterised as simply a *visual* medium, which is clearly inadequate. On the other hand, British theatre is too often characterised as simply an oratorical medium, which is not only in itself inadequate but has also produced a particular style of theatrical voice-training inappropriate for film-work in most cases. The stylisation and class-specificity of that training allows for only a very limited range of uses of the voice in British cinema, where it has been used primarily 'to enunciate and project text or dialogue'.[10] As has often been noted, this has resulted in overly theatrical scripting of films, with the burden of 'intended meaning' (the 'message' of the film) loaded on to dialogue, at the expense of a visually complex cinematic form. Obviously this is crudely put, but it does signal the need for a different approach to script-writing, *mise-en-scène* – and the vocal level of acting. Useful though they may be in certain circumstances, it is important not to fall back on conventional English theatrical speech patterns when different vocal work may be more meaningful. Brecht's practice of using the voice in a gestic manner[11] suggests that it is important to work on different speech patterns, speeds of delivery and rhythms, on different tones and accents, and on the varying possibilities of conversational speech, song, reading, oratory, etc. In part, this is a question of developing a precise and economic use of the voice in relation to the microphone rather than the acoustics of the theatre.

Various cinematic references offer examples in which the voice has a quite different signifying practice to that demanded of the English theatrical actor: the meaningfulness of Method acting's vocal strategy is as much dependent upon a *redundancy* of linguistic units as it is upon the clear articulation of a verbal message; Bresson consistently uses a distantiating flat vocal tone, a voice without conventional intonation or emphasis; certain British independent films have also adopted unconventional vocal strategies (e.g., *In the Forest*, *A History and the City*, *At the Fountainhead*). Developing a strategy which requires a 'complex listening' on the part of the spectator does not necessarily mean resisting theatrical conventions completely. *Darkest England*, for instance, in part depends upon the class connotations of different English theatrical voices: it is near-parodic in its use of these representational conventions.

Before leaving the category of the vocal, it is important to consider the voice in documentary, another key aesthetic and ideological practice within British cinema, including the independent sector. Thirties documentaries such as *Housing Problems* (1935) established the generic convention of the voice-over; but it was a convention with specific relations of power built into it. *Housing Problems* has a key voice, which introduces the film and each of the various other speakers of the film to the audience; in that sense it is the voice of authority – and of course it is the voice of a white male upper-middle-class Southerner.

During World War II documentarists cast different voice-types for the voice-overs of their films, seeking more 'populist' voices (e.g. in Humphrey Jennings' wartime films or *Desert Victory*).[12] Authority was now blended with trustworthiness and familiarity, and these three categories have been crucial to the development of the documentary genre on television, where similar vocal strategies have been used for voices-over, with a similar relationship between the voice of authority (e.g., the newscaster) and other voices of the programme, mediating their more 'partial', since less authoritative, 'information' to the viewer at home. Recent documentary programmes produced in the independent sector have attempted to use the voice in different ways. Two recent *Eleventh Hour* films from Newcastle's Trade workshop, whose vocal strategies are reminiscent of Rotha's films of the mid-'40s, have been particularly interesting in this respect. Both *Farewell to the Welfare State* and *Mothers Don't Forget* resist the use of any single voice of authority, having instead a montage of voices, some of which are identified as the voices of people interviewed in the course of the programmes, but others of which split the function of *Housing Problems'* single voice of authority, presenting 'impartial' information across a number of voices. More specifically, differently gendered voices are used, as well as voices specifying different regional, racial and class accents. In addition, *Farewell to the Welfare State* uses a very specific modulation of the voice – consistently deep (women as well as men) and consistently quiet (as opposed to strident). It is this sort of attention to the voice, both in relation to its cultural connotations and the formal relations of different voices, that the independent sector as a whole must develop.

The economy of face/gesture/body – 'doing nothing'

> The things one can express with the hand, with the head, with the shoulders! . . . How many useless and encumbering words then disappear! What economy![13]

If British actor-training is voice-specific, it is also inadequate in its attention to facial, gestural and corporeal movement (and non-movement), particularly in relation to the requirements of cinema. From Kuleshov on, film directors and film actors have felt that the gestural requirements of cinema are different to those of theatre, calling for a different training. In part, this reflects a belief that it is cinema's 'natural' propensity to be a photographically realistic medium, a belief in the 'essential' (ontological) realism of cinema, and a desire to have as naturalistic a performance as possible, stripped of all theatrical mannerisms and stylisations, which are believed to look wrong on the screen. Yet consider, on the other hand, the highly stylised performances of Kuleshov's actors in *The Extraordinary Adventures of Mr. West in the Land of the Bolsheviks*; the expressionistic acting used by Eisenstein in his films, but particularly *Ivan the Terrible*; and the use of music-hall performers such as George Formby and Tommy Trinder in certain British popular films. Clearly, in certain circumstances, stylised and mannered performance is useful – and just as clearly there is not a perfect fit between Kuleshov's theory and practice.[14] He writes 'stylization in the cinema simply does not work'[15]

– but it does not work because he makes a distinction between 'theatrical fake' and 'real material'. Where an ambiguity of reality and illusion is to be played upon in the film, stylisation may well work.

At the same time, even within a stylised acting practice, physical movement must still be economic, and regulatable. Kuleshov again:

> In order to give maximum expressiveness to the symbol, one must exploit the given plane of the screen with optimal economy – in other words, there must not be one piece of superfluous space on the screen, and if you show something which cannot occupy the whole surface, then all excess must be eliminated.[16]

This applies as much to acting as to any other aspect of *mise-en-scène* (and indeed is developed by Brecht as a key facet of his 'epic' acting strategy for the theatre), and involves stripping away all that is not required within the scene or image. Whether in a stylised acting practice, or in a naturalist acting practice (although of course naturalism is just as much a style as any other acting practice), there are moments when one or more actors are required to *'do nothing'*, thus calling for a minimalist style of acting (although still calling for work and concentration): shots involving characters waiting, or watching, or thinking, or day-dreaming, where the key to the success of the scene is the absence of movement or expression (which is expressive in itself; of course). It's interesting to note that it is precisely this minimalism that English theatrically trained actors find most difficult about acting for the camera. Indeed, as Barry King has pointed out, within the ideology of the acting profession, such requirements seem like an abuse of or failure to appreciate the talents of the actor – in King's term, it seems like a process of de-skilling.[17]

Bresson is perhaps the director who has most rigorously developed the skill of getting his 'models' (as he prefers to call his non-professionally trained actors) to do nothing:

> It is not a matter of acting 'simple', or of acting 'inward', but of not acting at all.

For Bresson, this is bound up in a metaphysics of the subject (the actor/character as subject); a search for an inner truth:

> Unusual approach to bodies. On the watch for the most imperceptible, the most *inward* movements.[18]

But once again, we may note a slippage between intention and effect. While we may agree with Bresson that 'it is the flattest and dullest parts that in the end have the most life',[19] from a materialist point of view it is not a revelation of some 'inner truth' which is remarkable, but the extent to which this 'minimalist naturalism' becomes *strange*, in the Brechtian sense, drawing attention to the actor-character's performance of everyday events, perhaps de-familiarising the everyday. This is certainly one of the effects of the use of a similar acting style in the films of Straub-Huillet. Further, as Nick Burton suggested at the Phoenix Arts workshop, from the point of view of directing actors, it may be useful to think in terms of stripping an action of all extraneous details, but then continuing to re-work the action (rehearse it) until it becomes deliberately, but almost imperceptibly, strange. This is perhaps comparable to Eisenstein's approach which, at one point, he describes precisely in terms of 'the elimination of all that is accidental' but then adds that he wants to elevate those elements that remain 'to the highest level of expressiveness'.[20] As in Kuleshov's films, the economy of the acting is produced in the relation between the removal of unwanted gestures, and the exaggeration and intensification of those that remain. Thus in *Ivan the Terrible*, Eisenstein 'makes the acting strange' by strongly stylising facial, gestural, corporeal and vocal movement. Whether Bresson or Eisenstein, the principal remains the same: a regulation, an economy of movement/non-movement (control/excess). For Bresson and Kuleshov, the achievement of economic acting is crucially dependent upon the actor/model's *automatic* and *mechanical* performance of actions. For Bresson, this task of 'recovering the automatism of real life' is a question of good directing: working with models in such as way that they do not think about what they are saying or doing: 'Radically suppress *intentions* in your models'.[21] (Again, this is open to both a materialist and a metaphysical reading.) For Kuleshov, automatic performance of acquired skills is a question of rigorous and systematic training, and he compares the good actor to the good driver:

> The whole secret to driving a car lies in its being driven automatically; that is, one does not consciously think about when it is necessary to change gears, as all of this is done mechanically and instinctively. . . . The qualified film actor, whose entire technique is calculated to give an efficient reading of his screen performance, is the result of precisely this same sort of training.[22]

But it is worth bearing in mind a warning from Brecht:

> We get empty, superficial, formalist, mechanical acting if in our technical training we forget for a moment that it is the actor's duty to portray living people.[23]

Brecht, in his later writings, continually stresses the need to not simply make strange, to distance the spectator, and refuse empathy, but to create a tension between pleasure and instruction, between empathy and critical distance, between the strangely revealing and the natural. . . .

The theatrical training of actors in Britain is particularly unsuited to the development of minimal, economic facial, gestural and corporeal aspects of acting. If the voice is dominant, there is another strong element in the discourse of British theatrical acting which sees good, professional acting in terms of work with props, 'business' – that is, quite the opposite of doing nothing. British theatrically trained actors thus tend to 'overact', to project voice and gesture within the theatre space. That professionalism comes to constitute 'actorliness'.[24] For the cinema (or TV) it thus becomes necessary to develop ways of concentrating on underacting, on minimal vocal and gestural movement, and the ability to appreciate, professionally, silence, stillness and duration. Within the Stanislavskian tradition, a form of concentration has been developed around the use of objects: in training and in rehearsal/performance the actor works with objects (the *Acting Tapes* focus on the example of Brando's work with Eva Marie Saint's glove, in a scene from *On the Waterfront*) in order to take his/her mind off the fact of acting, to forget the presence of the audience, to erect the fantasy of the fourth wall of the stage space. (An American critic, quoted in the *Acting Tapes*, writes of the Moscow Arts Theatre, 'The acting is so good we are convinced it is not acting.')[25]

Aside from the fact that we may want the actors to be self-critical of their performance *as a performance* rather than completely engrossed in their character, we might also note that this work with objects may bring in to the visual space (on to the screen) objects which are there for the benefit of the actor, and not the benefit of the spectator. This potential excess of 'added' actions and objects may well be a useful way of breaking the illusionary effect of naturalism (quite to the contrary of Stanislavsky's intentions) and drawing attention to performance, to actorliness; it may contribute to the redundancy of detail productive of a realistic effect;[26] it may have a symbolic effect within the space of the fiction, where the object or gesture functions as an exterior sign of the interiority of the character (as in the case of Brando and the glove). But where this use of props either suspends the narrative in a pandaemonium of detail, or foregrounds the relationship of actor/subject and prop/object, this would be a very weak means of drawing attention to the relationship between the characters in a space (if what we are after, for instance, is the relationship between character A silently watching character B eating at another table in a restaurant). In other words, to do nothing effectively, and economically, may require a quite different form of concentration on the part of the actor. This suggests that it is more important to concentrate in this case on what you *are doing* (silently watching . . .) in the scene/shot, rather than using an object to escape the scene as a moment of acting, by concentrating on some superfluous action.

Precision of movement in relation to the camera's field of vision

One might suggest that in acting for the cinema (or TV), the problem is not trying to forget that there is an audience present observing your every move, but in trying to establish who or what is to be addressed at the moment of delivery, in the absence of an audience. The key here is obviously to articulate the performance in relation to the camera, or, to be more precise, the camera's field of vision. Crucially, what determine the scope of the actor's facial, gestural and corporeal register are the details of framing, angle and distance of shot and focus within the overall framework of the montage. Again, Kuleshov provides the starting-point. Ron Levaco has described his concern for the

> relationship of actor movement to cutting and composition. He strove to make his actors aware of duration as movement – a first principle of the cinema that is still valid, namely that screen action always has to conform to the imperatives of cutting, to the montage of a particular sequence as conceived by the director. . . .[27]

In order to achieve as precise movements as possible in the relationship between actors and camera, Kuleshov developed a series of exercises for his actors, enabling them to develop an ascetic codification of body and gesture, a semiotically complex choreography. But crucially that choreographic training is developed in relation to a three-dimensional conceptualisation of the camera's field of vision. Kuleshov refers to this as a spatial grid, or a spatial metric web. In effect it is a pyramid turned on its side, where the apex corresponds to the lens of the camera – although it would make more sense to use the analogy of a *cone*, rather than a pyramid. While Kuleshov's writings on how the spatial web is to be used make interesting reading, it is probably more useful as a conceptual device than as a model for actual exercises, a way of thinking the camera's field of vision three-dimensionally.

On the other hand, it should be recognised that the spatial grid metaphor takes for granted the place and function of the camera-eye, and Kuleshov's system depends upon and reproduces a centring of the subject perspectivally. This corresponds to classical cinema, which is founded upon spectator identification with the look of the camera. As Ben Brewster has put it, in commenting on Brecht's distrust of the cinematic institution: 'acting is, as it were, directed at that ubiquitous place, there is no oblique view.'[28] If a sense of distantiation is to be achieved, it may be necessary to refuse that system which centres the subject, and to somehow prise open, rather than close down, the apparently natural conjunction of camera-identification and character-identification. As Brewster puts it,

> in the theatre there are always as many points of view as there are seats, and some of these points of view can be quite oblique, so the play is not directed at each spectator in the same way. . . . In the theatre my viewpoint remains my own from a particular place in the auditorium, looking at a performance as well as at a fiction. It is this identification with the camera that . . . makes it difficult to separate the objects being shown from the process by which they are being shown, that is, the particular performance.[29]

One possibility which might be developed as a means of wresting apart camera-identification (film performance) and character-identification (acting performance) is the strategy of *abusing* Kuleshov's metaphor of the spatial grid: refusing the desire to perform actions centrally for the eye of the camera (central to the camera/spectator's field of vision), deliberately producing oblique views of action, stressing the position and process of the look at the actor. (Certain dance films might serve as a model here, and perhaps some of the work of Maya Deren – though certainly, the films of Bresson, Straub-Huillet and Kuleshov at moments work in this way.) In effect, this is a question of exploiting off-screen space, at the margins of the camera's field of vision. (Of course, the same sorts of effects might be achieved in the montage – that is, in the mapping together of different looks, different points of view at the same action.)

Fragmenting character and externalising emotion: identity and identification

For the actor, there is, additionally, the problem of how to prepare her/his part, given the extreme fragmentation of the film-making process (scenes shot out of sequence, etc), and the necessity to respond to events, views and people where they are not actually in the field of vision of the actor (reacting to the camera, in the place of the absent co-respondent is a shot-reverse shot structure, for instance). There are various strategies by which a sense of continuity and coherence might be achieved. Rehearsals and shooting schedules could, of course, be reorganised; alternatively, one might consider the script as the site of coherence, the framework which holds together the various fragments of the film-making process, and within which character is constructed. But in each case, there is a tension between the attempt on the part of the actor to hang on to character as a coherent sense of identity and the need in shooting to actually develop only a minimal aspect of character, a discrete fragment. Within a 'Brechtian' practice, such a tension could be worked on as immensely fruitful and productive, but within the naturalist tradition it is inevitably constructed as a problem: from Stanislavsky on, the centre of coherence and identity has been the acting subject, or rather the role into which the actor attempts to transform her/himself. But immediately this tradition is developed within the cinema, a further tension arises – because the centre of coherence and identity for cinema is not so much the acting subject, or the inner truth of the character, but the eye of the camera.

What is important for a radical film practice is to acknowledge these tensions between fragmentation and coherence, separation and identity, and between the camera-I and the acting-subject – rather than attempting to develop for the actor a psychologically rounded identity prior to constructing character and action for the camera. What is important, in the final analysis, is not the inner feelings of the actor, but how the image of actor-as-character and the performed gestures look on the screen; the important question to ask is 'does the visible action demonstrate the necessary points?' (A question which, incidentally, cannot be answered by recourse to the script alone as the site of coherence.)

Thus, rather than adopting as the starting-point an assumption of psychological unity and coherence, and acting as the embodiment of character, it may be more useful to start from a training which sees acting as the production of visual and aural signs – that is, which sees the body, its physical characteristics and its economy of movement, as a field of discourse. This suggests that the anti-naturalist training of actors – and especially the strategy of externalising emotions – may be more appropriate to *all* forms of cinema acting: the conditions of cinema demand that emotion be read *visually* from facial, gestural and corporeal signs, and *aurally* from vocal signs both diegetic (lip-synch, etc) and extra-diegetic (voice-over as a means of signifying character interiority, etc). Brecht, for instance, writes:

> Everything to do with the emotions has to be externalised; ie it must be developed into a gesture. The actor has to find a sensibly perceptible outward expression for his character's emotions, preferably some action that gives away what is going on inside him.[30]

Acting, in this framework, becomes not the enactment of a coherent, psychologically complex character, but a montage of gestures (or 'gests'), each one refined for the requirements of the shot (the eye of the camera), rather than the supposed inner consistency of the character. This is precisely the implication of Kuleshov's montage experiments, but also of Bresson's reference to actors as models for the montage, and Hitchcock's statement (reputedly) that 'actors are like cattle'. Brecht, again:

> The coherence of the character is in fact shown by the way in which its individual qualities contradict each other. . . .
>
> Splitting such material into one gest after another, the actor masters his character by first mastering the 'story'. It is only after walking round the entire episode that he can, as it were by a single leap, seize and fix his character, complete with all its individual features. . . .[31]

Brecht's gestic technique is comparable to Kuleshov's semiotic range of facial expressions, gestures and choreographies of the body. What Kuleshov can add, because he is talking about the cinema, is that 'people performing organised efficient work appear best on the screen.'[32]

Stylisation and distantiation in the cinema

> The actor: 'It's not me you are seeing and hearing, it's *the other man*'. But being unable to be wholly *the other*, he is not that other.[33]

Brecht's strategy of distantiation is a means of establishing a critical distance between the performance of an action and the reading of that action, the process of making sense of it. It is a means of foregrounding the ideas, or the ideological processes at stake in the action, rather than encouraging the audience to become inextricably bound up in the psychological predicament or emotional state of the character performing the action. It is a means of linking the individual to the social as well as, or rather than, to the 'inner self', and the discrete action to its historical context. This distance is achieved in part through the stylisation of speech, movement, posture. The intention is to perform actions in such a way that the actions themselves, and the issues at stake, are open to question, open to criticism. Thus, compare Brecht commenting on Stanislavsky's theatre:

> What he cared about was naturalness, and as a result, everything in his theatre seems far too natural for anyone to pause and go into it thoroughly. You don't normally examine your own home, or your own feeding habits, do you?
>
> There is a complete fusion of the actor with his role which leads to his making the character seem so natural, so impossible to conceive in any other way that the audience has simply to accept it as it stands.[34]

The actor must demonstrate an action as if it were an ideological statement, in such a way that the audience feels obliged to form an opinion, to take sides in relation to the action. For Brecht, good acting is that which makes familiar characters and actions strange and astonishing again: not the reassurance of conventional documentary's recognition effect, but the *shock* of recognition. As Brecht puts it, 'everyday things are thereby raised above the level of the obvious and the automatic.' Or Bresson: 'an old thing becomes new if you detach it from what usually surrounds it.'[35] In general, Brecht suggests, there are two conditions necessary for the achievement of these sorts of effects. The first requires that the actor should resist complete identification with the role and attempt to develop a form of demonstrative acting. Secondly, as Ben Brewster has argued, it is crucial for Brecht that in theatre there is a *co-presence* of audience and actors, in order that

> a distinction be maintained throughout the performance between the actors and the parts that they are fictionally playing. . . . One can identify with the actor, which implies a separation from the role, and then identify with the role and that implies a separation from the actor.[36]

Brecht's epic theatre exploits these conditions, producing a constant oscillation between identification and non-identification, an oscillation which is central to his view of acting:

> The contradiction between acting (demonstration) and experience (empathy) often leads the uninstructed to suppose that only one or the other can be manifest in the work of the actor. . . . In reality, it is a matter of two mutually hostile processes which fuse in the

> actor's work; his performance is not just composed of a bit of one and a bit of the other. His particular effectiveness comes from the tussle and tension of the two opposites, and also from their depth. . . .[37]

In cinema, however, no such co-presence of actor and audience is achieved. On the contrary, much of the fascination of narrative cinema is derived from the *present-absence* to the spectator of the actor/persona/character.[38] Hence distantiation cannot be achieved by the same means in theatre and in cinema. Classical cinema, as Brewster notes, has produced a style of acting, or more specifically an institution of star-making, which uses the cultivation of persona as a means of achieving an almost seamless coincidence of actor/persona and character (or narrative role), that is, between star-image and narrative image. But it is only an apparent seamlessness: there is a tension at the heart of the process, since 'naturalistic presentation is consistently broken within the commercial system in the interests of the star-system.'[39] Ostensibly, Hollywood depends upon a form of screen acting 'where the performer is just supposed to "be", his or her technique invisible',[40] but the institution of the star-system means that Hollywood constantly runs the risk of foregrounding the actor's persona, potentially against the grain of the narrative. There is always a certain disarticulation at stake, the identity of character is never entirely present or coherent.

It is at the site of this tension that it seems useful to think through the possibilities of distantiation *in the cinema*, despite – or rather, *because* of – the state of presence *and* absence. Within the cinema, the actor is present only as *image*; this image can be stylised to such an extent that it falls out of the flow of the narrative, halting that flow and resisting the struggle to contain it *as* character, *in* role: momentarily, it functions precisely as an image. A radical cinema performance might usefully exploit the split in identification between the image (the actor as persona), and the narrativisation of the role. In addition, it is still possible in cinema to separate out narrative role (the signified) from the performance of narrative actions (the signifier). King, for instance, defines naturalism as in part a system in which particular movements by the actor of face, gesture and body are to be read as natural to the narrative character, as his or her own movements (and not, therefore, the movements of an actor).[41] Therefore a distantiating acting strategy might also attempt to execute such movements in such a way that they do *not* seem to be the natural movements of the character, producing a 'strange' lack of fit. I now want to detail various means by which these separations, these distances, these split identifications might be achieved.

First, there is the possibility of playing on the casting of actors according to or against 'type'. I would suggest that casting decisions involve a combination of relating the professional skills of the actor to the style of performance required, and relating the actor as a 'type' to the conception of narrative role. Casting on the basis of 'type' is itself at least a twofold concept. First, there is the question of the physical look of the actor, in terms of facial and corporeal characteristics as more or less culturally coded signs (and to this we may add the vocal sound of the actor). Secondly, although clearly the first feeds into the second, then the question of *persona*, which brings into play such ambiguous concepts as charisma, personality, presence, aura, etc. In these senses, recognition of type involves a signification of the actor as always already an ideological construction: 'look' and 'persona' function as signs of both interiority and social status, establishing the actor as a relatively complex social and psychological type, a complexity which is brought into play in the narrative development of the film. The extent to which this has any impact on the way in which the film and the performance are read will depend on the extent to which the audience 'knows' the actor from other roles, or other extra-filmic discourses, the range of facial, gestural, corporeal and vocal movements brought into play, the details of make-up and costume, and narrative determinations of character.

It is worth noting that different types of film draw on these implications of type-casting in different ways – but also that, as John O Thompson has argued, there is a certain typicality in all acting: 'individuality', the fully rounded character, always involves a sense of typicality, or what Thompson calls category-meaning.[42] The conventional British documentary tends to foreground type in terms of physical look (and vocal sound) while the naturalist narrative film tends to foreground type in terms of persona. Both extremes involve a sense of the actor as 'document', but the former is assumed to be a more 'objective' form of document, while the latter implies a more 'subjective' documentation of the 'inner self'. It is also worth noting that *all* actors 'possess' a persona, and not just Hollywood stars.

One means of using 'type' to create the desired distance, the desired oscillation between identification and separation, is, as Simon Watney pointed out at the NFT event, to exploit the effects of *mis*casting (or casting against type). Watney's starting point was a quotation from Andrew Britton:

> The very concept of 'mis-casting' may well serve to naturalise the explicit appearance of ideological contradition rather than its successful elision, just as the sense that an actor is 'ideally cast' may indicate that the critic is underwriting the projects of the film.[43]

On the other hand, as Watney pointed out, the sense of an actor being 'mis-cast' does point to an ideological tension in the film, between the meanings brought into play by the actor as 'type', and the meanings brought into play in the narrativisation of role and character. Clearly it would be possible to exploit this tension as ideologically productive. (It is worth comparing this to a comment in parenthesis by Brecht: 'It often helped the educational effect to have bad actors instead of good ones.')[44]

Another means of using 'type' is the possibility of developing the line of 'stereotyping', or what Eisenstein called 'typage'. That is, casting *according to* 'type', but on the basis of a sort of intensification of the category of the type in question. In part this is the strategy discussed earlier of using exterior signs as signs of both interiority and social status, a strategy which draws on a usually implicit and fairly crude semiotics of the body ('as if all cooks were fat, all peasants phlegmatic, all statesmen stately',[45] or as in the case of Eisenstein's films of the '20s, as if all capitalists were grotesquely bloated). The usefulness of this strategy (and it contributes to a radical reading of, for instance, *Coronation Street*) is the extent to which it reveals character to be *constructed*, as opposed to natural: character can thus be recognised as an ideological category, separate from (but tied into) the body of the actor or the details of the narrative and role. The type thus functions as a gestic summation of ideological traits; the strategy insists that character be read precisely as *image*, and not as 'real' (indeed it seems *un*real and yet still functions adequately as actant within the narrative). Caught up in the paradox of present absence, the actor/persona/character has been pushed more and more into the realm of the image, it has become more ideal, less tangible – and yet at the same time it is so heavily coded that it has become almost leaden, almost concretely tangible ('the characters are no more than cardboard cut-outs . . .'). What seems useful here is the tension between real person and image, between the tangible and the intangible. The possibilities of such an approach can be seen in Eisenstein's films of the '20s, of course, but also in the casting and acting of contemporary British independent film-maker Richard Woolley's *Telling Tales* and *Brothers and Sisters*. Think also of the effects of casting Bernard Miles and Brenda de Banzie opposite James Stewart and Doris Day in Hitchcock's 1956 version of *The Man Who Knew Too Much*.

A second way of playing on the disjunction of identification with the actor/persona, identification with narrative role, and identification of the performance of the actions, is in terms of developing that eminently post-modern strategy of parody. Mark Nash pointed to the usefulness of parody at the NFT event, but perhaps the most pertinent description of the potentialities of parody in general is provided by Peter Wollen:

> First, parody has an emancipatory aspect. It is always doubly coded. It is read alongside, through and apart from its 'target'. It depends on a complicated interplay of identity and difference, accepting the authority and priority of the 'target' text, converging with it, yet at the same time, separating itself from it, diverting, detracting, rebelling and subverting. Imitation, influence and allusion blend in, but parody constantly veers towards the hybrid; towards the *graft*, both compatible and incompatible with its apparent model. The model itself is subject to a kind of *dehiscence*, a peeling apart (to steal another favourite term from Derrida) which leaves it entire yet divided, releasing it for a new form of understanding, of re-inscription.[46]

It is this process of double coding that is important for our purposes: identity *and* difference, convergence *and* separation, compatibility *and* incompatibility, entire *yet* divided. Each set of terms seems to make sense in relation to Brecht's theory of distantiation, and the possibility of developing it as a practice for the different conditions of the cinema – and, of course, Brecht is famous for his radical plagiarism, in itself a form of parody. Note also the way in which the new inscription of the 'original' provides a new form of understanding of it, a changed meaning: a new political space is opened up (in film acting terms, between image, role and performance of actions). The impact of parodic acting can be seen in a stunning moment in *Pumping Iron II: The Women*, when Bev Francis parodies the posing routines of other body-builders.

What lay behind Nash's interest in parody was an argument that if British independent cinema is to progress, then it must draw on the most useful aspects of film, TV and stage acting as already developed in Britain. In fact, one might suggest that all well-executed British theatrical acting as it has been taken up in TV and film works as parody, particularly of assumptions about class. King suggests that repertory acting in general involves a form of behavioural imitation,[47] and we might suggest that, by a process of inadvertent parody, the British theatrical tradition as taken up in film and TV work underlines or acknowledges that sense of *imitation* (specifying, in gestic manner, the specificities of the British class system at the level of representation). Nash's own example was to see the acting in Ealing comedy as a form of parody. Consider, for instance, that of Alec Guinness in *The Lavender Hill Mob*. Guinness' character is a petty-minded, ineffectual, asexual bank clerk. That is, a stereotype of the bank clerk mentality. Guinness' performance of the actions of the role, however, both ties in with this stereotype, converges with it, identifies (with) it, but at the same time *exceeds* what is necessary to represent it. Each sign of the bank clerk is exaggerated, but in an almost imperceptible way (hence, perhaps, its success as a comic performance). Each facial expression (the *subtly* knowing smile in the opening sequence in a South American bar) each gesture (twee and hesitant but highly controlled hand movements) and posture (tight, diminishing, highly repressed, but methodical) becomes a sign in itself, escaping the narrative body, foregrounding the performance, but also the stereotype, as such.

A third strategy for achieving distantiation in the cinema is that adopted by Straub-Huillet in their films. Moving away from the exigencies of typage, and the various ways of (ab)using or parodying it, but still clearly dependent on questions of casting and direction, their films seem to *refuse* the presence of either actor or character, thus unbalancing the sense of present-absence: performance is consistently de-stylised, producing a radical non-presence of the actor. This process can be seen, for instance, in the de-dramatised, non-charismatic (i.e., non-theatrical) acting in their film *Class Relations*. Here the actors refuse the conventions of emphatic gesture and voice; they operate mechanically, such that identification with character in an empathetic sense is almost impossible, and we can relate to them only as figures formed in the ideological conditions of the society which the film establishes.

A fourth strategy is found regularly in at least those films of the melodrama genre described as 'Brechtian' (e.g., the films of Losey, Sirk and Minnelli in the 1950s). The performances of certain male actors stand out as exemplary in these films – notably Stanley Baker (in Losey's *The Criminal*, though also in his work for other directors – in *Helldrivers* and *Violent Playground*), Kirk Douglas (in *Two Weeks in Another Town*) and Robert Stack (in *Written on the Wind*). The productivity of such acting depends not only on the stylisation of movement, but also on the economy of the performance: the tension created between periods of minimal, apparently expression-less and emotion-less acting (the static, as it were), and sudden explosive bursts of facial, gestural and postural movement. Highly controlled acting here functions as the signs of repression, the body not just restrained, but visibly *strained* (the same would be true of the voice); the outbursts function as the return of the repressed, the out of control. For the spectator, this style of acting may have the effect of producing a double, and contradictory, presence of the performance, a performance which may become self-reflexive. The strategy is comparable to Barthes' comments on 'the grain of the voice' – for our purposes, the voice which, over and above any articulation of linguistic utterances, signifies its own materiality, its own performance (the voice, for instance, of Alpha 60 in Godard's *Alphaville*).

In one way or another, each of these strategies involves a form of vocal or choreographic stylisation (or de-stylisation, which amounts to the same thing), playing on the paradox of present-absence as a means of achieving a distancing effect. This seems close to Brecht's theory of the *gest* (gestus), the attempt to 'get to the gist of things' by pin-pointing with a gesture, in a physical dynamism of ideas. Although it would be wrong to collapse the idea of a gest solely into a gesture (in the sense of a physical movement of an actor, as I am using the term here), clearly some gestures will work gestically. In order for the physical gesture of an actor to work gestically, it must both make sense within the narrative text, as the 'natural' action of a character, and point *outside* the text, to make some point about the social context and meaning of the action. It must work as a moment of summation, not just of narrative development, but also of the ideological conditions pertaining at that moment. Thus the suicide of a young unemployed man in *Kuhle Wampe* is not just the death of the 'heroine's' brother, not just another episode in the unfolding of the plot – but, at the same time, a comment on the conditions of unemployment in Germany in 1931. It is a gesture which exceeds narrative meaning.

In his discussion of Brecht's epic theatre, Walter Benjamin suggests that one of its most significant achievements is 'making gestures quotable'.

> Quoting a text implies interrupting its context. It will readily be understood, therefore, that epic theatre, which depends on interruption, is quotable in a very specific sense. That its texts are quotable would be nothing very special. But the gestures used in the process of acting are another matter.[48]

All acting is made up of gestures, but while Brecht talks about breaking acting down into its component parts, naturalism attempts to hold gestures in place, to mould them into a coherent whole – the unity of character. Brecht's theatre thus draws attention to the way in which a character/actor may use a gesture *here*, but may lift it out of that context, and use it also *there*. To quote a gesture in this way will tend to make the gesture as such stand out – acting is revealed as a montage of gestures; but, further, the process by which meanings congeal to the gesture will be 'revealed'. Quoted outside its initial context, the gesture takes on a different meaning; out of context, the gesture may be recognised as precisely a gesture, and no longer the natural action of a real living character. To quote a gesture in this way establishes it as sign, and constitutes an interruption at the level of language; it also, of course, impresses upon us the connotations of the gesture.

But gestures are constantly quoted by spectators of 'naturalist' films also. Certain gestures stand out in classic Hollywood films: the form cannot contain them, the narrative cannot exhaust their meaning. They become eminently quotable *as gestures*. For instance, part of the pleasure of the Western is the extent to which each successive film quotes the familiar gestures and posture of the cowboy drawing his gun to shoot down the hero/villain. But the gesture is also quoted outside the cinema by many spectators (not just in children's games, and perhaps even by those who have never even seen a Western!). Does such quoting reconstruct the gesture as *gestic*? Perhaps, insofar as we thereby wrest it from its narrative place, it becomes recognisable as a *sign*, and not just a narrative action: it thus draws attention to the construction of meaning, and the conventionality of the representation. Perhaps it is also gestic insofar as the quoting of the gesture is rarely to specify a precise moment of narrative action in the film in which the gesture was last seen (though it must in part involve that meaning), but tends to establish a particular image or construct of heroic masculinity – in other words, to stand as a summation of a particular aspect of patriarchal ideology.

A style of acting which deliberately draws attention to the *skilful* execution of actions will consistently tend to produce gestures which exceed the narrative demands of a performance. As John Caughie pointed out at the NFT event, this was exactly the aim of Brecht's theatre practice. Brecht called upon his actors to deliberately break the power of the naturalist illusion by perfecting the performance of a gesture in itself, so that the audience could come to appreciate, in a critical way, the skill of the actor *as an actor*. Thus, in addition to becoming involved in the story and the predicaments of the characters, and in the ins and outs of the ideological problematic of the play, the audience also become connoisseurs of acting skills, in a mood of 'relaxed' appreciation. In this respect, it is interesting to read Lee Strasberg's reaction to the acting skills of the Berliner Ensemble: he is *astonished* by the realism of their performance, and full of admiration for the skill with which the actors perform the most basic tasks, the way in which they just do things (to perfection): he experiences no sense of 'actorliness', and at the same time he is fascinated by particular gestures, or, strictly, *gests* (the peeling of potatoes, the plucking of a real chicken) which are extended beyond their particular plot significance so that they come to have a 'higher' meaning which *encapsulates* the ideological moment of the action.[49]

As a comparison, Caughie also discussed the acting of Buster Keaton,[50] in whose films, he argued, gestures are presented in such a way that the audience again appreciates them as marvellous acting skills, over and above any narrative function they may have. And in citing the use of gestures in Method acting, Caughie noted that, while the intention may be different (attempting to achieve a completely naturalist performance), the effect may be the same: drawing attention to the skills of the actor, a certain actorliness, a bravura performance. In other words, naturalism may itself have an anti-naturalist effect!

The gesture which exceeds could clearly be accommodated in the framework of most of the 'distancing' strategies outlined above, and certainly the potential contradiction between the desire for a naturalist effect and the desire for skilfully executed actions can be exploited as a useful means of making strange. There is also clearly a potential contradiction between the call above for *both* the gesture which exceeds *and* an economy of movement in front of the camera: this is intentional. The means of finding a space for these contradictions within the film text is to construct the text as montage rather than as organic unity, allowing for a heterogeneity of possibilities, of effects. Perhaps the most productive work is that which produces a tension between 'the natural' and 'the strange', an acting strategy which is capable of constantly drawing the spectator into the story but repeatedly pushing the spectator away to a position of critical appreciation.

Thus, where 'classical naturalism' demands a coherent text, seamless, without contradictions, resolvable within its own terms, the strategy of montage can precisely play on the productive contradictoriness of the text. Montage can also be a means of drawing attention to the complexity, the contradictoriness, the ideological constructedness of character, made up of fragments, of separate gestures. In such a text it may be appropriate to draw on and develop a variety of 'incompatible' acting styles and approaches to casting and characterisation. *At the Fountainhead*, for instance, uses three different actors to play the same character: an English actor, an actor from the Berliner Ensemble (i.e., Brechtian trained), and the 'non-actor' on whom the character was based. More recently, and perhaps more surprisingly, there is the case of *Revolution*, which Pam Cook and Richard Combs have described as a form of epic cinema. Two strategies in relation to acting are important here: firstly, the use of two quite distinct acting styles (British theatrical acting/Method naturalism) to set up the opposition between oppressors and rebels (and between the past and the present); and secondly, a refusal to organise the plot around the development of character. Character is not established as psychologically rounded and developing with the narrative; rather, it is established only in terms of what is necessary for each specific event. Event thus displaces personality as the focus of attention.[51]

Continuity and systematisation of work with actors – the ensemble

Stanislavsky, Kuleshov, the Group Theatre, Brecht's Berliner Ensemble, Fassbinder and Oshima (and *Coronation Street*?) all developed their work in the context of ensembles. British independent cinema, on the other hand, has in the main been marked by an extreme instability and discontinuity of work, making it difficult to build up a close working relationship with actors, or to develop appropriate, systematic and rigorous forms of training. Even if directors wanted to follow a Bressonian line – preferring *not* to work with the same actor-models more than once, in order to achieve the required effects of automaticity and non-actorliness (non-theatricality) – continuity of work would be important in order to gain experience of *directing* actors. A Kuleshovian style of acting would clearly be almost impossible to achieve without a period of intense physical training and long rehearsal periods. But it is not just a matter of physical training that is important: there is also the world-view of the actor, and her/his attitude towards each project. In part, ensemble work is a means by which actors can retain some control over their work – without becoming Bresson's unthinking models, or Hitchcock's cattle. Further, Brecht noted that his epic style of acting 'demands a considerable knowledge of humanity and worldy wisdom and a keen eye for what is socially important'. And Benjamin notes that this orientation towards knowledge 'in turn determines not only the content, but also the *tempi*, pauses and stresses of (the actor's) whole performance.'[52] How then to establish the conditions for ensemble work? Perhaps by arguing for adequate funding of longer rehearsal periods; perhaps, as Adam Ganz suggested at the NFT event, by employing actors, as well as film-makers and administrators as members of film and video workshops. . . .

Notes

1 In addition to those acknowledgements made in the text, I would like to thank all those involved in the Phoenix Arts and NFT events, and especially Val Baxter, Nick Burton, James Swinson and Mark Nash.

2 See also John O Thompson, 'Beyond Commutation – a Re-Consideration of Screen Acting', *Screen*, Sept–Oct 1985, vol 26 no 5, p 75.

3 Robert Bresson, *Notes on Cinematography*, New York, Urizen Books, 1977, p 51.

4 See Lev Kuleshov, 'Art of the Cinema', in Ron Levaco (ed.), *Kuleshov on Film: Writings of Lev Kuleshov*, University of California Press, 1974; Barry King, 'Articulating Stardom', *Screen*, Sept–Oct 1985, vol 26 no 5; John O Thompson, op cit; John Ellis, *Visible Fictions*, London, Routledge and Kegan Paul, 1982, pp 91–108; Richard Dyer, *Stars*, London, BFI, 1979; and Stephen Heath, 'Film and System: Terms of Analysis, part II', *Screen*, Summer 1975, vol 16 no 2, pp 101–107.

5 Bertolt Brecht, 'Against Georg Luckacs', published as 'Popularity and Realism', in Francis Frascina and Charles Harrisson (eds), *Modern Art and Modernism*, New York, Harper and Row, 1982, pp 231 and 228.

6 See Michael Patterson's account of Peter Stein's work with actors, in Patterson, *Peter Stein – Germany's Leading Theatre Director* (Directors in Perspective), Cambridge University Press, 1981.

7 See also Barry King, op cit, p 29.

8 John O Thompson, op cit, p 65.

9 For a discussion of the terms 'actor', 'character', 'actant', 'persona', and 'role', see Barry King, op cit, pp 38–41; and Stephen Heath, op cit, pp 101–107.

10 Mark Nash and James Swinson, 'Acting Tapes', *Framework*, no 29, 1985, p 82.

11 See e.g. his article 'The Question of Criteria for Judging Acting', in John Willett (ed), *Brecht on Theatre*, London, Methuen, 1978, pp 53–56.
12 See John Ellis, 'Victory of the Voice', *Screen*, vol 22 no 2, 1981.
13 Robert Bresson, op cit, p 64.
14 See Ron Levaco, 'Introduction', in Levaco, op cit, p 11.
15 Lev Kuleshov, op cit, p 61.
16 Ibid, p 63.
17 Barry King, op cit, p 33.
18 Robert Bresson, op cit, pp 49 and 19 (my emphasis).
19 Ibid, p 35.
20 Sergei Eisenstein, 'Montage in 1938', *Notes of a Film Director*, London, Lawrence and Wishart, 1959, p 81.
21 Robert Bresson, op cit, pp 32, 8.
22 Lev Kuleshov, op cit, p 67.
23 Bertolt Brecht, in Willett (ed), op cit, p 234.
24 See Barry King, op cit.
25 Quoted in Constantin Stanislavski, *Stanislavski's Legacy*, (trans E. R. Hapgood), Theatre Arts, 1968.
26 See Roland Barthes, 'The Realistic Effect', in *Film Reader* no 3, February, 1978.
27 Ron Levaco, op cit, p 10.
28 Ben Brewster, 'The Fundamental Reproach (Brecht)', in *Cine-Tracts*, Summer 1977, vol I no 2, p 48.
29 ibid. Compare Lev Kuleshov, op cit, p 79.
30 Bertolt Brecht, in Willett (ed), op cit, p 139.
31 Ibid, pp 196 and 200.
32 Lev Kuleshov, op cit, p 99. See also Richard Combs' discussion of the Donald Sutherland character in *Revolution*, in 'Landscape after Battle, or Revolution's History Lessons', *Monthly Film Bulletin*, March 1986, vol 53 no 626, p 69.
33 Robert Bresson, op cit, p 24.
34 Bertolt Brecht, in Willett (ed), op cit, pp 237 and 235.
35 Ibid, p 92; and Robert Bresson, op cit, p 26.
36 Ben Brewster, op cit, pp 46–47.
37 Bertolt Brecht, in Willett (ed), op cit, pp 277–278.
38 See John Ellis, op cit.
39 Ben Brewster, op cit, p 49.
40 Richard Combs, op cit, p 69.
41 Barry King, op cit, p 29.
42 See John O Thompson, op cit, p 67.
43 Quoted in Simon Watney, 'Katherine Hepburn and Cinema of Chastisement', *Screen*, Sept–Oct 1985, vol 26 no 5, p 53; see also Watney's discussion of these issues, ibid, pp 53–56.
44 Bertolt Brecht, in Willett (ed), op cit, p 132.
45 Ibid, p 242.
46 Peter Wollen, *Komar and Melamid*, exhibition catalogue, Edinburgh Fruitmarket Gallery, 1985, p 39.
47 Barry King, op cit, p 30.

48 Walter Benjamin, *Understanding Brecht*, London, Verso, 1983, p 19.

49 See Robert H Hethmon (ed), *Strasberg at the Actor's Studio* (tape-recorded sessions), London, Jonathan Cape, 1966, pp 383–395.

50 See also Bertolt Brecht, in Willett (ed), op cit, p 56: 'The actor Chaplin, incidentally, would in many ways come closer to the epic than to the dramatic theatre's requirements.'

51 See Pam Cook, review of *Revolution*, *Monthly Film Bulletin*, March 1986, vol 53 no 626, pp 67–68, and Richard Combs, op cit, pp 68–70.

52 Bertolt Brecht, in Willett (ed), op cit, p 95; and Walter Benjamin, op cit, p 11.

PART FOUR

CHARACTER AND TYPE

Introduction

Film actors have decried typecasting almost since the beginning of filmmaking. For instance, silent-film actress Louise Brooks viewed typecasting as a measure of Hollywood success but also as a limitation of the system: "I just didn't fit into the Hollywood scheme at all. I was never, neither a fluffy heroine, nor a wicked vamp, nor a woman of the world. I just didn't fit into any category . . . You see, I didn't interest them because I couldn't be typed" (Kobal 1986, 46). Where Brooks described type in terms of roles, classical British actor Eric Portman linked typing to stardom and the actor's personality. He wrote, "So, personality can make you a film star. Whether you are a film actor or not, will depend on your histrionic talent . . . Still, if you have only a little talent, and a lot of personality, you may succeed—as a type. This means you will always be cast for the same parts. Your film life will, then, not be a long one" (Cardullo *et al.* 1998, 97). Bringing home Portman's threat, silent-film star Mary Pickford, explaining why she left the screen, suggested the dangers of being successfully typecast:

> "I didn't want what happened to Chaplin to happen to me. When he discarded the little tramp, the little tramp turned around and killed him. The little girl made me. I wasn't waiting for the little girl to kill me. I'd already been pigeon-holed . . . I could have done more dramatic performances . . . but I was already typed."
>
> (Brownlow 1989, 135)

For these actors—and I could cite many more—typecasting represents commercial, mass-production instincts that are opposed to artistry and disenfranchise the actor who wishes to perform more complex roles.

However, while the assumption seems to be that typecasting is a sign of an actor's limitation, a concession to commercialism, and the antithesis of art and originality, we also expect actors to stick to type and often reject actors' efforts to play against type. As with typecasting, critics and audiences will frequently view an actor's efforts to play against type as evidence of the actor's lack of talent—because the actor is unconvincing in the new role—or as gross commercialism—insofar as the role is assigned to a money-making star rather than a better-suited but lesser-known actor. In line with this view, in the book *Starring John Wayne as Genghis Khan! Hollywood's*

All-time Worst Casting Blunders, author Damien Bona chastises Hollywood studios for casting actors against type and seems to view actors' desire to play against type as the worst kind of *hubris*. Bona's categories of miscasting include "ethnic impersonators," such as Marlon Brando in *The Teahouse of the August Moon* (1956), because they show a disregard for verisimilitude in favor of star power; "generation gap," including actors who refuse to age gracefully on screen or, alternately, are in too much of a hurry to grow old (think of an aged Mae West in *Sextette* (1978) or a youthful Barbra Streisand in *Hello, Dolly!* [1969]); "performers whose personas and modern sensibilities were completely out of place when they traveled to the past" (famous examples include John Wayne as Genghis Khan in *The Conqueror* [1956] and Tony Curtis in *Spartacus* [1960]); and, finally, a category called "out of their league," for "movie stars whose attempts at roles different from those they usually played were stymied" by a "too strongly established screen persona" (Bona 1996).

As these tangled and somewhat contradictory responses to typecasting suggest, typecasting in film is, to a large degree, inescapable. Insofar as film acting is part of the business of film, typecasting will be crucial to the institution, enabling brand-naming and marketing of star commodities. But it is not the case that typecasting is simply imposed on actors from above by studio publicity departments; rather, typecasting occurs at the level of performance, through casting, and through audience demand. Typecasting contributes to narrative economy, allowing audiences to quickly and easily recognize a character by associating him or her with an actor's previous roles. Further, types and typing play into our everyday notions about people and identities, and our tendency to read people in terms of their age, sex, race, gender, region, nationality, class, or other categories, whether insidiously in racial profiling or in less sinister but no less stereotypical ways of assessing persons. Types in film do not, however, simply duplicate social stereotypes, but may create new types, or even the seeming contradiction of a unique type; they may mirror stock types from literature or advance new stereotypes. Rather than something static, types change according to changing notions of identity, changing politics, changing conceptions of realism, and changing aesthetics.

Given all these complications, the essays in this section consider types, typecasting, and stereotypes from a variety of perspectives, considering typecasting as institutional practice, in relation to stereotyping and identity politics, and at the level of stardom as well as among character actors. They share in common a concern with the ideologies of identity embodied in notions of type and character and each, in different ways, proposes that the hierarchical institution of cinema should be modified to more realistically represent the lived experience of humanity.

In "Typecasting," Pamela Robertson Wojcik explores competing notions of type, especially as they relate to discourses of realism, and discusses typecasting in its most literal sense as a labor issue and as institutional practice in Hollywood: that is, in terms of historical casting practices. Wojcik argues that the discourse of realism in most twentieth-century theories of acting deals with *performance style*, whereas typecasting reflects a complex web of *institutional practices*. She claims that, in Hollywood, acting style and institutional practice, and in particular casting practices, represent a case of uneven development, with acting style shifting increasingly to the dominant naturalist model while casting maintains a residual outmoded theatrical model that predates Stanislavskian realism. In particular, she links casting practices in Hollywood to the eighteenth-century lines-of-business tradition, which assigned an actor to a certain kind of role across his career. Ironically, Wojcik suggests that despite today's discourse of diversity, contemporary casting practices may be more rigid in their conception of identity than the earlier theatrical traditions, as casting directors, operating under shifting conceptions of realism, increasingly delimit the actor's roles by tying them to her physical appearance, race, age, gender, and sex.

Donald Bogle's contribution examines three major African-American stars of the 1950s and asserts that these stars represented a shift in black representation from "mythic types" and stereotypes of earlier decades to "the emergence of distinct black personalities who, through their own idiosyncrasies" came to be true stars. Bogle focuses on Ethel Waters, Dorothy Dandridge and Sidney Poitier, characterizing each star in relation to his or her roles and public reception in the 1950s. In each case, Bogle finds traces of a more "mythic" type, but is interested in the way each star personalized that type within a contemporary context. For Bogle, Waters represents an Earth Mother figure, but one who no longer fits into an alienated society. He describes her as signifying "some noble part of our heritage that was quickly becoming extinct . . . the individualist foolish enough to assert herself yet strong enough to pay for the consequences." Dandridge portrays the classic tragic mulatto, though she was marketed as a more contemporary and daring figure. A socially significant figure—the first black actress ever to appear in the arms of a white actor on screen—Dandridge was also a tragic figure who seemed doomed to live out the sad plotline of her films. If Waters and Dandridge represented the revivification of classic black stereotypes, and ultimately suffered for it, Poitier seems to have created an original hero, perfectly in tune with his times. Bogle calls him a "hero for an integrationist age" and argues that he appealed to white liberals and middle-class African-Americans because he embodied middle-class ideals of education and refinement, and was the antithesis of the black buffoons of earlier decades. Despite his claim that Poitier was a throwback to the Uncle Toms and servants of the 1930s, Bogle still suggests that Poitier's integrationist message was a "beautiful dream," which is "what great movies and careers are all about."

Rather than stars, the remaining essays in this section examine the often overlooked role of character actors. Rudolf Arnheim and David Thomson each offer an ontological view of the character actor. For Arnheim, writing in 1931, the character actor can be differentiated from the lead actor because he represents a specific type, close to reality, whereas the lead actor represents a more general, idealized type. Arnheim recognizes a difference in modes of performance for character actors and leads and suggests that the character actor's ability to individualize a role, and especially to bring out its grittier qualities, needs to penetrate into the hero's territory. Thomson similarly suggests that character actors represent us, the unnamed throng, as opposed to idealized heroes. He queries whether character acting should only be viewed as "support," and argues that the "panorama of small lives" in ensemble acting may be closer to the experience of reality in which we all consider ourselves stars and not support.

Taking a different view of the character actor's role as "support," Patricia White asks "What is it that supporting characters are meant to 'support' if not the imbricated ideologies of heterosexual romance and white American hegemony permeating Hollywood cinema?" Examining the career of Agnes Moorehead, White suggests that it is no accident that character actors like Moorehead—or, we might add, Edward Everett Horton or Eric Blore—embody stereotypes of sexual difference, such as the lesbian, spinster, old maid (or, in the case of Horton or Blore, the pansy). Rather, she argues that Hollywood needs them, to define and uphold the conventional ideals represented by the lead actors. Thus, while it might be more realistic to bring the traits of character actors into the center, as Arnheim and Thomson suggest, White underlines how the center and the margin are ideologically defined and represent presumptions about norms and differences that are still difficult to overcome.

Typecasting

12

PAMELA ROBERTSON WOJCIK

In January 2000, the National Association for the Advancement of Colored People (NAACP) protested the lack of representation of people of color in American TV shows and demanded more diversity in casting, to provide more opportunities for actors of color and to more accurately reflect the multi-racial diversity of America. Shortly thereafter, the NAACP signed diversity agreements with all the major networks—NBC, CBS, ABC, and Fox. The networks agreed to increase opportunities for people of color, both behind the scenes and on-screen, but with most public attention and scrutiny focused on the promise for better casting practices and image portrayal.

This recent protest strongly echoes a World War II protest in which—frustrated with Hollywood's perpetuation of stereotypes that Donald Bogle famously encapsulates as "Toms, Coons, Mulattoes, Mammies, and Bucks" (Bogle 1973)—the NAACP demanded better representation of African Americans in Hollywood films, claiming it would be hypocritical to denounce Nazism without addressing racial issues at home. The issues of concern to the NAACP in both protests have also been of concern to the Screen Actors Guild (SAG) (est. 1933), which began issuing Casting Reports in 1977 to keep data on film and TV roles, numerically cataloguing them by gender, age, race, and ethnicity; and which resolved in 1990, following the debacle of *Miss Saigon* casting, that performers of color should receive preferential consideration for ethnic roles. A related movement is Non-Traditional Casting, which works to advance the open casting of actors of color, female actors, and actors with disabilities.[1] These movements, like the NAACP protest, endeavor to ensure that casting practices are representative and fair. They seek diversity both in the kinds of roles performed and among the actors who perform them.

Defining diversity another way, SAG staged a somewhat different protest over casting practices in March 1950. The *Los Angeles Times* reported that SAG was waging a campaign to get motion picture studios to stop typecasting. Angry that an actor would be consistently cast in, say, bartender parts, SAG spokespeople were quoted in the *Los Angeles Times* (27 March 1950) as saying "Typecasting should not prevent an actor who is established in the public mind as the portrayer of one particular role from being given the opportunity to display his acting talents in other types of roles." Rather than racial diversity, SAG's 1950 protest aimed to open up casting practices to allow individual actors the right to portray a diversity of roles, rather than be typed in one kind of role. At stake is the actors' desire to show their versatility and also to escape being typecast in bit parts, thus failing to climb the Hollywood ladder to leading roles and stardom.

Interestingly, almost a hundred years earlier, theater actors had protested *against* versatility requirements and *demanded* a form of typecasting. In 1864, the American Theatrical Protective Association formed. In its first set of resolves the union asked for 1) "a fixed minimum salary for each distinct line of business, from leading to utility" and 2) "a return to the old system of engaging members of the profession for definite lines of characters, thus obviating all professional misunderstanding and preventing any artists from undertaking any more than his or her legitimate business, and by such means keeping another professional out of an engagement" (McConachie 1992, 248). This protest differs markedly from the 1950 SAG protest in that it aims to protect an actor's right to perform a single type of role, or "line," consistently across his or her career rather than be forced to play multiple and diverse roles. Here, the stakes are job security and the right to maintain one's earned place in the "lines-of-business" hierarchy of roles (which I will discuss in detail shortly).

Each of these protests, spanning three separate entertainment forms, and crossing three centuries, protest unfair casting practices. None of them succeeded in their goals. I begin with them because they seem to me to provide useful touch-points for thinking about the relationship between acting and identity, and particularly changing notions of type. Each of them makes clear that typecasting is political practice, not only as a labor issue but also as a touchstone for ideologies of identity. The shift between the 1860s Theatrical Protective Association resolution and the 1950 SAG campaign, especially, reflect a sea change in the discourse around acting, and especially shifting notions of what constitutes realism in acting. The 1990s NAACP protest represents the culmination of that changing discourse, which leads to an increasing demand for a homology between actor and role, and which, ironically, enforces typecasting in the service of diversity.

Typecasting may be, as one critic put it, "one of the theatre's deadly sins" and the "sublimation of the unprofessional in acting" (Isaacs 1933, 132) but, as these somewhat contradictory responses to typecasting suggest, typecasting in film is, to a large degree, inescapable. Insofar as the business of film acting, and especially the star system, relies on recognizability, marketability, and the necessity for known commodities, typecasting will be part and parcel of the institution. Further, insofar as the actor represents human characters, film acting relates to changing conceptions of identity and identity politics, and thus the actor will inevitably negotiate stereotypes and represent identities inflected by race, gender, ethnicity, class, and national differences. Rather than something imposed on actors and audiences from without, or simply an effect of casting or performance style, typecasting occurs at many varied levels, and is equally something spectators and fans enact or impose on actors. As Patricia White succinctly explains: "Casting and performance are already a reading of type; the audience performs a reading on another level, informed by cultural and subcultural codes, spectatorial experience of the star in other roles, and subsidiary discourses" (White 1999, 149).

Rather than critique or defend typecasting, this essay explores competing notions of type, especially as they relate to discourses of realism, and discusses typecasting in its most literal sense as a labor issue and as institutional practice in Hollywood: that is, in terms of historical casting practices.

Types and realist discourse

Borrowing from Richard Dyer, I am defining type as "any simple, vivid, memorable, easily-grasped and widely recognized characterization in which a few traits are foregrounded and change or 'development' is kept to a minimum"(Dyer 1980, 28). Type can be opposed to the novelistic character, "defined by a multiplicity of traits that are only gradually revealed to us through the course of the narrative, a narrative which is hinged on the growth or development of the character and is thus centered upon the latter in his or her unique individuality, rather than pointing outwards to a world" (Dyer 1993, 13). Put simply, type is relatively simple, shallow, and unchanging, whereas character is complex, deep, and developing.

In terms of acting, type refers most broadly to an actor's ability to embody something typical or representative of the human condition. Bruce Wilshire captures this broad sense of type in his characterization of theater as "the theory of acting and identity—or what we must suppose about persons if we would understand how it is possible for them to be convincingly projected and enacted on the stage" (Wilshire 1991, 91). According to his formulation,

> The actor cannot stand on stage without standing in for a type of humanity. This characterization will occur even though there is no script and his character is given no name and he says nothing. We recognize him as a type in the family of man, and the fact that we abide in his presence and recognize him as such authorizes him as such; and since we stand in with the character only through his standing in, he authorizes us (Wilshire 1991, 6).

In its exemplary form, this general human type will exemplify moral or metaphysical principles, as an archetype or allegorical type. In its most insidious form, typing is exclusionary, as in the stereotype. A narrower definition of type relates to the actor herself, who functions as a unique type, characterized by her appearance, distinct performance style and type of role (often tied to certain genres) across a body of work. In between, we can locate social types such as the doctor, the politician, or the teacher; stock characters such as the heavy, the ingenue, and the clown; genre-specific types such as the *zanni* (zany) of *commedia dell'arte*;[2] and national or regional types, such as Australia's larrikin,[3] or the Yankee of American theater and film. In any given situation, these different and often overlapping functions of type are likely to be at play.

As I've said, in most modern discourses on acting, the notion of the actor as type is viewed as a sign of an actor's lack of talent, a limitation imposed on the actor by a brutal and unimaginative studio system, a sop to audiences' inartistic tastes, or a combination of all three. Stanislavski's opinion has been particularly influential in this regard. Stanislavski's views on type reflect his larger project in developing a new naturalistic approach to acting, and are typical of realists such as Ibsen who seek to replace stock types from earlier theatrical traditions with individuated, complex characters. Stanislavski says, "To my way of thinking there can be only one type of actor—the character actor" (Stanislavski 1968, 18). But he acknowledges that theaters are filled with types, not characters. Stanislavksi claims that typecasting stems from the conditions of work in 19th-century repertory theaters. In particular, he links typecasting to the "lines-of-business" tradition which dominated 18th- and 19th-century theater and was indigenous to the stock system, appearing in virtually all professional theaters of Europe from the Renaissance forward.

As James C. Burge explains, "lines-of-business" refers to the notion that, within a stock company, there is a "tacit and implicit agreement between actors and managers concerning the casting of that actor through a season or series of seasons" to allow an actor to maintain a particular line, or type of role (Burge 1986, 5, 277; see also McArthur 1984). The lines are hierarchical and based on the idea that an actor can ascend through the ranks (see Figure 1). Thus, an actor may begin as a supernumerary or extra, then gain general utility roles, until he ascends to roles in a line such as the heavy or juvenile, and possibly lead comedian or tragedian.

Men
Supernumeraries (extras)
Dancers, singers, musicians
General Utility (minor parts—filled by lower members of company and those whose lines aren't represented)
Respectable Utility (slightly bigger or more complex minor parts)
1st and 2nd Walking Gentleman (variety of small parts)
1st and 2nd Old Man
1st and 2nd Heavy Business ("heavies")
1st and 2nd Low Comedy
Juvenile Business
Light Comedy and Eccentric Business (later developed into distinct lines: Irishman, Scotsman, Jew, Yankee, Mose the Fireboy)
Leading Business (Tragedian or Comedian)

Women
Walking Gentlewoman
1st and 2nd Old Women (one usually low comedy)
Chambermaid (sometimes "singing," soubrette)
Juvenile Lady
Leading Lady

Figure 1 Lines of business

Rather than view each character as a psychologically defined individual—as realist modes of performance and dramaturgy would do—the lines-of-business tradition sorts characters into recognizable and repeatable roles. Therefore, the lines-of-business tradition emphasizes the *similarity* between plays and assumes that in each play there will be roles suited to most of the various lines. In virtually any given play performed by the company, there would be need for one or more musicians or dancers, some supernumeraries or extras, various non-speaking parts for those actors assigned to general utility roles, one or two small speaking parts for those actors slotted to play the walking gentlemen or old man, a role that could be categorized as a chambermaid role, another for an old woman, some quirky or comedic character requiring a bit of eccentric business (a catch-all for ethnic impersonation, and heavily accented roles reliant on peculiar make-up and costuming), perhaps some villainous role appropriate for a heavy, young and romantic roles for juveniles and ingénues, and two leading roles, whether tragic or comic.

Despite the promise of mobility and versatility, in the lines-of-business tradition, an actor's movement is limited and determined by the actor's seniority, rules of succession, precedence in performance, and "possession of parts." "Possession" refers to "the assumption by an actor of the privilege to play every part in which he appeared with success before the public in any and all subsequent revivals of the play until he resigned the part, retired, or died" (Burge 1986, 3). In the lines-of-business tradition, "possession" is literal. Since actors are not given whole scripts, but only the "sides," or sheets with just their lines, if an actor owns the sides, he owns the part. Thus, the actor may, through possession, stay in a line that another actor could perform better and for which he or she is no longer well suited—and there seem to be numerous cases of juveniles being played by actors with seniority who are well past their prime.

Most often, an actor in the lines-of-business tradition will settle into a line and perform all roles in the repertoire that apply to that line, occasionally picking up general utility roles when a play does not contain his or her line. As is the case with Hollywood's division between character actors and stars, actors in the lines-of-business tradition are unlikely to shift between leading roles, such as Hamlet or Tartuffe, to mid-level character roles, such as heavies or eccentric business. Rather, an actor will develop a specialty within a line, perhaps serving only as a lead tragedian, never doing comedy, or narrowing his eccentric business to specialize in Irish or Jewish roles. Furthermore, the interpretation of the role in the lines-of-business tradition is, to a large degree, fixed. Historically, the interpretation of a role was taught to an actor by the playwright, and then handed down from one actor to another, along with sides and costumes—and the interpretative mode tended toward frontal displays, declamation, and codified poses.

As the 1860s American Theatrical Protective Association protest suggests, lines-of-business and possession of parts were the actors' preferred mode of operation. In the stock system, actors worked in a number of different plays, in high rotation, with virtually no rehearsal, and they supplied their own costumes. Thus, it was in their interests to be identified with a particular line or set of roles and typecasting was a very practical response to the material circumstances of theater production.

From Stanislavski's perspective, the stock system necessarily produces bad mass-produced acting and leads actors to create types rather than characters. Citing the large number of plays performed and the general lack of rehearsal for them, he asks, "Is it astounding then that these unfortunate and hard-pressed actors have recourse first to craft and then to mass production methods in their parts? What happens is a division of labor with each actor having his own specialized field of endeavor"(Stanislavski 1968, 16). He claims that the division of labor, in turn, attracts people who cannot act but who can be a type: "The most ardent partisans of the custom of type-casting are the poorly endowed actors, whose range is not broad but rather one-sided. Such gifts as they have are somehow made to do for narrowly circumscribed types, but they are unlikely to be sufficient to meet any wider demands" (Stanislavski 1968, 16).

In an interesting twist on the Stanislavskian critique of typecasting, avant-gardists such as Brecht have viewed the anti-realist aspect of typecasting as offering a crucial alternative to mainstream commercial practice and have embraced the use of types linked to *commedia dell'arte* and other anti-realist traditions, like vaudeville, as a means of achieving alienation effects that de-naturalize the assumed fit between actor and role. By contrast, some avant-garde theorists and practitioners have regarded typecasting as a means of ensuring *greater* realism. In Soviet cinema, for instance, a form of typecasting, called "typage," calls for the use of non-actors, selected solely on the basis of appearance, to create a realist effect.

The principles of typage were articulated by Lev Kuleshov in his 1929 *Art of the Cinema*. Arguing that "real things in real surroundings constitute cinematographic material," Kuleshov states that "imitating, pretending, playing are unprofitable, since this comes out poorly on screen" (Kuleshov 1974, 56, 63). For example, he relates, "If you need a tall, stout man, but your actor is thin, and you pad your thin actor with cushions, and the like . . . the results on screen will be obviously false, theatrical, a prop, a game." Therefore, he claims:

> Because film needs real material and not a pretense of reality—owing to this, it is not theater actors but "types" who should act in film—that is people who, in themselves, as they were born, constitute some kind of interest for cinematic treatment. That is, a person with an exterior of character, with a definite, brightly expressive appearance could be such a cinematic "type" (Kuleshov 1974, 63–64).

For Kuleshov and his followers, including Eisenstein, and, later, Italian neo-realists like De Sica, the use on non-actors lends films a documentary touch. The non-actor not only fulfills realist criteria for physical appearance, but also is taken to reflect and be typical of the reality represented. As Siegfried Kracauer puts it, "It is precisely the task of portraying wide areas of actual reality, social or otherwise, which calls for 'typage'—the recourse to people who are part and parcel of that reality and can be considered typical of it" (Kracauer 1960, 99).

In its emphasis on the exterior appearance of the non-actor, and its recognition of real persons as types, typage differs from those versions of typecasting that refer to stock character types, such as the juvenile, or the heavy. Ironically, however, as Kracauer points out, the non-actor in typage clearly resembles a different concept of type in Hollywood—the star:

> The typical Hollywood star resembles the non-actor in that he acts out a standing character identical with his own or at least developed from it, frequently with the aid of make-up and publicity experts. As with any real-life figure on the screen, his presence in a film points beyond the film. He affects the audience not just because of his fitness for this or that role but for being, or seeming to be, a particular kind of person . . . The Hollywood star imposes the screen image of his physique, the real or stylized one, and all that this physique implies and connotes on every role he creates (Kracauer 1960, 99).

Both the non-actor in typage and the Hollywood star create a role homologous with themselves, a "character identical with his own or at least developed from it" that is, as Kuleshov says, defined in large part by "exterior of character" and "expressive appearance."

One term used to describe Hollywood casting that would also apply to Soviet typage is "face casting," or casting based on external appearance (Yoakem 1958). This mode of casting—in which a pretty girl and not an aged male, plays the ingénue, and the man with the broken nose and cauliflower ears will be cast as a boxer, not a banker—tends to be taken for granted. However, it is worth noting that other modes of performance and casting do not place the same emphasis upon the actor's individual appearance. For instance, certain kinds of non-realist theater—*commedia dell'arte* and kabuki among them—rely on masks and ritualized modes of performance in which the actor's face and external appearance are irrelevant. In a different vein, because of its emphasis upon song, Hindi cinema has long relied upon the use of playback singers to dub actors' voices, and in the 1940s attempted "voice casting, or the use of a singing voice that matched both the speaking voice and personality of the actor" (Majumdar 2001, 167). Later, and continuing to the present day, Hindi cinema dropped the practice of voice casting and created a new model of stardom in which both the on-screen actor and the playback singer achieve stardom with a split between visual and aural stardom. While the on-screen star may be cast according to principles like those of Soviet or Hollywood cinema, the playback singer, cast as only a voice, and equal to or greater in stardom than the onscreen actor, challenges the primacy of the face. Rather than assumed as the norm, then, face casting should be seen as merely one possible response to certain conceptions of realism.

While both Soviet cinema and Hollywood emphasize face casting, however, the non-actor in typage differs markedly from the Hollywood star because the two models of type are based on competing notions of identity and the role of the individual. In typage, the non-actor represents a social type, characterized by social class and social role—a Bolshevik, a sailor, a member of the aristocracy, etc. The individual serves as a stand-in for a class or caste and is meaningless in himself.[4] Rather than individual psychology, typage relates the character's individual personality and problems to larger social forces, such as poverty, and uses non-actors to represent "ideas, elements in an intellectual argument" (Heath 1981, 183). Thus, a person may be cast as something he is not, since the role is based on physical appearance (he *looks* like a czar) and is not meant to reflect his real identity. In fact, the role might run counter to the non-actor's ideology, personality, and class. For instance, according to Eisenstein, when he cast non-actors, they often resisted playing characters different from themselves when the role was viewed as negative, because they did not want their friends to take their screen persona as reflecting their real self. Thus, he would have to "resort to tricks." He says that when filming *Ten Days*, "Everyone wanted to play the Bolsheviks and no one wanted to play the Mensheviks . . . [so] we gave the actors the text of an inflammatory speech and they spoke it with great fervor. After this we added titles that said the exact opposite" (Eisenstein 1988, 198).

In contrast to the Soviet model, Hollywood characters are generally defined in psychological and not social terms. Social situations, such as a war or the Depression, may establish action, but then the narrative will focus on how individuals respond. Thus, Hollywood adopts a classically realist model of narration and character: narrative action springs from individual characters who function as causal agents with psychological motivation, goals, and desires. Not surprisingly, then, the Hollywood star is not generally seen as representing a member of a class or caste. Instead, she is considered a unique individual. Stanley Cavell usefully explains the distinction:

> The creation of a (screen) performer is also the creation of a character—not the kind of character an author creates, but the kind that certain real people are: a type . . . Does this mean that movies can never create individuals, only types? What it means is that this is the movies' way of creating individuals: they create *individualities*. For what makes someone a type is not his similarity with other members of that type but his striking separateness from other people (Cavell 1979, 29, 33).

This notion of type, then, emphasizes not only the actor's unique physiognomy but also his personality and performance style, and these are viewed as distinguishing him from the masses.

An additional difference between the actor in typage and the actor in Hollywood has to do with issues of recognizability and repetition. The actor or non-actor cast according to the rules of typage can appear and fulfill his role as a type in a single appearance on film. By contrast, if viewed only in a single appearance, the star might be viewed as performing a role as a realist character, in the Stanislavskian sense. Typification—and, indeed, stardom—occurs through the actor's recurrence across a number of films in different roles. Recognition of the actor in a series of films creates a double identification in which we see not only the character but also the star. This recognition is crucial both to the star's function in the text and his or her extratextual success. On the one hand, as Murray Smith notes, recognition is the most basic level on which viewers grasp and construct characters. We know a character in a film and perceive her as a continuous agent because we recognize the body that coheres around her and "the star system provides an especially well-developed set of character models" to enable recognition (Smith 1995, 119). On the other hand, repeated recognition enables the commodification of the star. As Gaylyn Studlar suggests, "acting stars who disappear into their roles are never stars for very long":

> The Hollywood system appears too dependent on the extratextual as well as textual overvaluation of star faces and bodies as recognizable commodities . . . While it is not unknown for stars to transform themselves physically in the process of creating codes of character (such as Robert De Niro's weight gain for *Raging Bull*), it is generally acknowledged that making your star unrecognizable is dangerous. This is because the value of stardom is most frequently measured in audience anticipation at seeing—and recognizing—their favorite box-office attraction (Studlar 1996, 237–238).

Whereas typage requires only the recognition of the social type through external clues, recognition in Hollywood entails a complicated relationship between audience recognition of the star and the character.

In Hollywood, the star image is used in the construction of character and the characters that a star plays are seen to reflect aspects of the star's "real" self. To borrow a phrase from Erving Goffman, the star achieves a form of "expressive coherence" between his social front—his outward performance and appearance—and his "true" inner self (Goffman 1959, 56).[5] There may be instances when the star and role seem at odds but these are generally viewed as exceptions to the rule: failures. Understood in this way, not only stars but also character actors are types. As Cavell says, "Not to remember the name of a traditional Hollywood bit player is possible, if hardly excusable; not to remember their faces and temperaments is unthinkable" (Cavell 1979, 76).

Of course, the individual actor type may *also* represent a social type, stock character, or stereotype. Smith notes that particularity, even in the realist novel, will also be in the service of types. For instance, proper names individuate agents but also perform a typifying function insofar as proper names bear connotations of class, region, nationality, gender and race (Smith 1995, 30 and *passim*). For Cavell, there is a distinction between the actor as a type, individuated through his eccentricity, or striking separateness from others, and the caste-system of social types and stereotypes. He says, "Until recently, types of black human beings were not created in film: black people were stereotypes . . . We were not given, and were not in a position to be given, individualities that projected particular *ways* of inhabiting a social roles; we recognized only the role" (Cavell 1979, 33). To be a type is to individuate the social type, stock character, or stereotype. Thus, according to this notion, Marilyn Monroe may be the quintessential dumb blonde, representative of a class; Thelma Ritter may never rise above the rank of low comedy eccentric; and Butterfly McQueen may be stuck in racist maid roles; but, as a type, each is unique in the way she inhabits the role.

Ironically, then, it is Hollywood's adherence to realist principles of individual character psychology which allow the realist character—who exists in a single film—to be transformed into a recurrent type, the star or character actor. This suggests that, despite the anti-type discourse of realism, the break between pre-Stanislavski acting and post-Stanislavski acting isn't as strong as it might seem. And, in fact, in his essay on type, Stanislavski's litany of types includes not only traditional stock roles, such as "farce comedians" and "dandies," but also realist types such as "Ibsen types" and "neurasthenic Hauptman roles," thus emphasizing his point that typecasting occurs due to the way theaters are organized, and cannot be simply altered by performing different kinds of texts (Stanislavksi 1968, 13). The seeming conflict between a realist aesthetic and typecasting in Hollywood, then, can be explained by acknowledging the fact that the discourse of realism in most 20th-century theories of acting deals with *performance style*, whereas typecasting reflects a complex web of *institutional practices*. It is not the case that acting style and institutional practice are unrelated. Stanislavski, after all, recognized that in order to transform acting one had to transform the institution of theater by enhancing the role of the director, adding rehearsal time, cutting the number of plays performed, creating new realist set designs, etc. However, in Hollywood, acting style and institutional practice, and in particular casting practices, represent a case of uneven development, with acting style shifting increasingly to the dominant naturalist model while casting maintains a residual outmoded theatrical model.

Typecasting and acting in early cinema

As many critics and film historians have argued, because technological limitations encouraged the use of a frontal, presentational style of acting and the lack of dialogue seemed well-suited to pantomime, early cinema adopted the performance style and character conception of 19th-century melodrama rather than Stanislavskian or novelistic modes of realism. Most accounts of early Hollywood acting thus recount a tale of the new film form having to overcome outmoded theatrical traditions as part of a progressive march toward a more naturalistic and more cinematic acting style. For instance, in her analysis of acting in the films of D. W. Griffith, Roberta Pearson argues that there is a shift from a "histrionic" or theatrical, melodramatic pantomime style of acting influenced by theories of pantomime, such as Delsarte's system of poses, to a "verisimilar" style, which is more realist, and involves by-play and small gestures; and she links this stylistic change to cinema's transition from its status as cheap amusement to respectable mainstream mass media (Pearson 1992). With a different emphasis, Ben Brewster and Lea Jacobs argue that more naturalistic styles developed as film developed faster editing, which left actors little time for posing and insisted instead on fragmenting the performance into parts (Brewster and Jacobs 1997, 109). Similarly, James Naremore traces the shift from melodramatic styles to more naturalistic or "invisible" approaches. Acknowledging that pantomime exists residually in classical Hollywood, Naremore also argues that cinema realizes a Stanislavskian ideal through such technical innovations as close-ups, directional microphones, and shot-reverse shot editing, that enable a transparent, gestureless, un-ostentatious acting style (Naremore 1988, esp. 9–98).

Without denying the importance of melodramatic styles and theories of pantomime, or technical limitations, for understanding acting in early cinema, I would suggest that we can supplement these accounts of early film acting by considering early Hollywood's institutional structure, which increasingly models itself on the outmoded stock system and lines-of-business tradition at the same time that it moves toward progressively more naturalistic acting styles.

By most accounts, the lines-of-business tradition and theatrical stock companies largely expired in America in the 1860s and 70s.[6] First, as I have been suggesting, the turn to realist modes of theater challenged the precepts of lines. More importantly, realist theater displaced the manager in favor of the director, and placed casting in the director's hands, not the actors'. In addition, the rise of the star system threatened stock. The rise of the star can be traced back to 18th-century Licensing Acts in England, which limited the number of new plays performed and stabilized the repertory so that companies tended to rotate a stable group of plays, thus highlighting the work of a few actors, like David Garrick, in roles that could be repeated time and again. The star system developed further in America in the 19th century through the development of long-runs and combination systems. Motivated by economic rationalization, the long-run allowed a performer to play a single role for a longer period of time than repertory theater, and thus highlighted the role of the virtuoso. Combination systems created traveling companies that would tour a single play throughout the country, rather than perform a repertory in a single theater. Consisting of a star and supporting players, combinations meant that actors were hired for single parts, instead of lines.

However, while touring companies and headliners displaced one version of stock, 19th-century melodrama created another. According to David Grimsted, melodrama arose in large part as a way of competing with the burgeoning star system. Whereas stars were associated with sure-fire old plays and revivals, especially Shakespeare, stock companies offered new plays, and especially melodrama, in order to compete (Grimsted 1968, 92–93). Due to its reliance on stock characters such as the virtuous heroine, the villain, the old man father, and low comedy men and women, melodrama was well suited to the lines-of-business tradition.

In addition, the lines-of-business tradition was still an undercurrent in casting practice outside the stock system. As Benjamin McArthur explains, the combination system created new casting needs (McArthur 1984, 17). While the star headliner might tour with the show, smaller parts were often cast city-by-city. No longer an in-house process, casting became rationalized in the 1860s and dramatic agencies were created. Much as they do today, dramatic agents served as brokers for actors and managers. Actors registered at agencies and filled out questionnaires, describing the parts they had played, their physical characteristics, and their wardrobe. When managers contacted agencies, they tended to request actors using terminology from lines-of-business, calling, for example, for a soubrette or a heavy, rather than describing the particulars of the role.

So, lines-of-business typecasting existed residually in 19th-century melodrama and casting practices. In addition, the realist theater created a new kind of type. The new realist style, as popularized in America by William Archer, advocated "a reliance on personality. By this was simply meant that the actor infused his personality into the role he played—openly and without apology" (McArthur 1984, 183). This was intended to help the actor break free from typification and toward creating individuated and psychologically defined characters, but "critics charged that modern actors . . . played every role in a similar fashion, making the author's character merely a vehicle for their individual personality" and decried "an era of typecasting, with outward appearance valued more highly than proven acting skill" (McArthur 1984, 183). This new type, defined by the actor's appearance and personality, is akin to, and often overlaps with, the star.

Thus the 19th century establishes new trends toward typecasting despite anti-type discourse and changes in theatrical institutions. Lines-of-business and typecasting by role exist residually in melodrama and the rise of dramatic agencies; and star systems and realist acting create an emergent new type, hinged on the individual actor. All these tendencies and trends will be reproduced in early cinema.

In terms of performance style, early cinema adopted many of the features of 19th-century melodrama, including not only its presentational style and use of pantomime, but also its mode of characterization and reliance on stock types (Musser 1990, 3–5). More importantly, and with more long-lasting institutional effects, early cinema modeled itself on the stock system. Initially, as Charles Musser points out, when films were first made, there was not yet a category of the film actor. Early cinema has been famously described by Tom Gunning as a "cinema of attractions" linked to novelties, amusements, and modes of display and spectacle, rather than narrative. Early film included actors from theater and vaudeville, entertainers from the circus, boxers, dancers, and non-actors caught in actualities or put on screen for staged events (Musser 1987, 57–62; Musser 1990, 3; Gunning 1990). Rather than acting, their activity on film was understood as a form of modeling, or posing (DeCordova 1990, 34f). As the "cinema of attractions" gave way to story films, the notion of film acting began to be developed. The rise in story films coincided with the nickelodeon boom in 1907 which created a demand for more films and, therefore, greater rationalization (Musser 1987, 58; DeCordova 1990, 27). To handle the greater demand, film companies could no longer rely on the casual and intermittent use of actors for individual films and so created permanent stock companies of actors.

These stock companies initially emphasized versatility. An actor in a Griffith film, for instance, might, according to Roberta Pearson, "play the lead in one film and appear as an extra at a garden party the next" (Pearson 1992, 88). And, as late as 1909, there are claims that actors in stock companies receive equal pay, five dollars a day (DeCordova 1990, 79). In addition, indicating how far removed film acting still is from theater, actors were uncredited and anonymous. Despite these differences, film production was similar to the mode of production in theatrical repertory theaters. Until about 1912, film production was still not concerned with the whole script. Leads might be given a script beforehand, but minor players wouldn't know anything about the film until they were called for rehearsal and they still wouldn't know the whole (Pearson 1992, 85–86).

Over time, rather than diverge further from theatrical models, the stock system became increasingly similar to repertory stock. According to a 1913 actor's manual by Frances Agnew, would-be film actors would register with dramatic agencies to gain entry to the studio system and both agents and studios typed actors by lines. She writes:

> The number of players carried in the stock organization differ with the various film companies. Some have as many as thirty or more on the regular list, both at the principal

> studio and in the western headquarters. Such a company includes five or six emotional and ingénue leads (actresses); about the same number of leading actors; three or four "heavies" (both actors and actresses) (this type is sometimes called the villain of the play); three or four character artists; two children for juveniles and half a dozen or more minor players who serve for general business, playing various parts and requiring some versatility (Agnew 1913, 51, 53).

As in repertory theater, actors were required to supply their own costumes, and do their own make-up (Agnew 1913, 75–78). Under the stock system, the director initially controlled casting, selecting leads from his stock company and extras from anyone who appeared at studio "bull-pens" (Bordwell, Thompson and Staiger 1985, 149). As in the lines-of-business, actors in the studio stock system could ascend through the ranks, from extra to lead (Agnew 1913, 44, 65).

As actor Charles Graham makes clear, early film casting adopts terminology and practices from the lines-of-business tradition. He describes how he was picked out of a bullpen to begin acting in 1912:

> We joined a crowd of people . . . We had said not a word to a soul, and no one had questioned us, when a man in shirt sleeves and with a green shade over his eyes came into the room and scrutinized first one and then another. He picked out one or two, then came to Arundel and myself. "I can use you," said he, and handed each of us a card. My card bore a number and the mystic words "Walking Gent Card Scene." Arundel's card bore the same number and the same words. We learned that the film would be known by this number till its name was revealed to a waiting public, that we were the "walking gents" in a card playing scene which was to be shot that morning and that we were to take the card to the wardrobe room.

Told to wear their own clothes, but with straw hats, Graham and Arundel are made up and sent to the studio. For about three hours, "we smiled the same smiles, we frowned the same frowns, we played the same cards and at last the big lights went on and we did it all again while the cameras shot the scene." Graham, limited in knowledge to his activities, has no idea of the whole film: "Mr. Young . . . was the producer, and if he knew what he was producing I certainly did not" (Graham 1998, 19–20).

As film production expands, and director units are overseen by producers, the assistant director takes over casting and major players hire agents. Then, in 1915, the first casting director is hired.[7] As Janet Staiger explains:

> The phrase "type-casting" has literal implications within this mode of production. In order to set up such a system, the casting director, an expert who replaced the more casual approach which the firm had employed, needed some method to classify the potential players for his system . . . the selected classification became somewhat permanent as it went down on a card with other statistics and into the casting director's indexed and cross-indexed files (Bordwell, Thompson and Staiger 1985, 149).

Increased rationalization of the stock system thus leads to more codified systems of casting and increased typecasting.

At the same time, the studio stock system, like theatrical stock, finds that it cannot maintain its policy of anonymity and versatility. The stock system of repetition leads film fans to recognize leading players and to nickname them according to which studio's stock company they belonged. For instance, Florence Turner becomes known as The Vitagraph Girl, and first Florence Lawrence and then Mary Pickford are recognized as Biograph Girls. Recognition creates a star system. Competitive bidding for leading players begins in 1909 when Carl Laemmle hires Florence Lawrence away from Biograph to become the Independent Moving Picture Company Girl, or IMP Girl (Musser 1987, 58–59). Then, publicity for individual actors is generated, producing what Richard DeCordova has called the "picture personality," an intermediate identity for film actors before a full-fledged star system develops.

Fan recognition begins with the actor's image—her physical appearance. The picture personality indicates fan interest in "the personality of the player as represented on film." According to DeCordova:

> Personality existed as an effect of the representation of character in a film—or, more accurately, as the effect of the representation of character across a number of films. It functioned primarily to ascribe a unity to the actor's various appearances in film. However . . . the illusion that it had its basis outside the film was constantly maintained (DeCordova 1990, 86).

Film discourse around personalities asserts a connection between the actor's identity and the characters she plays on screen. This in turn requires that the personality portray consistent character types, if not literally the same character from film to film. As DeCordova points out, serial films show an especially insistent version of this homology in that the serial character's identity is often conflated with the actor through naming, so that King Baggot plays a character named King in the IMP detective series, and Kathlyn Williams stars in *The Adventures of Kathlyn* (DeCordova 1990, 89). However, despite claims that the actor's real identity was an extension of her screen image, the picture personality was a "professional existence—a history of appearances in films and plays and a personality gleaned from those appearances," but did not reveal very much about the actor's private life (DeCordova 1990, 92).

The picture personality establishes the screen actor as a type defined by physical appearance and role. In the teens, "the private lives of players were constituted as a site of knowledge and truth," thus leading to the development of the star proper (DeCordova 1990, 98). As fan discourse shifts to the star's personal life—her marital status, homes, leisure, consumption, political views, etc.—the homology between actor and character is deepened. At the same time, the development of the star system alters the nature of studio stock companies so that they are more hierarchical. Rather than a company of versatiles that can be called upon to play any role, the star system creates a hierarchical system. In it, stars are cast as leads; and smaller parts are filled by a range of non-star types. The character actor develops in this period as a mid-level player, recognizable and associated with a particular line of business, but not "known" as a real or private person. In addition, there are bit players and extras, who may or may not ascend through the ranks to become stars or character actors. While stars and character actors are permanent members of stock companies, extras are freelance and hired through the Central Casting Corporation, formed in 1925.

Based on this hierarchical and ascending system of roles, the studio system therefore mirrors the earlier stock system, on the one hand; but, on the other hand, with the clear hierarchy between stars and character actors, and the tendency for studios to loan headliners out for particular projects, Hollywood re-invents the combination system. Throughout the classical system, Hollywood studios have stock companies. In addition, certain directors and producers, like Preston Sturges, John Ford, and David Selznick, maintain their own stable of players within the studio. When actors become free agents in the 1960s, the official stock system breaks down, but continues in *de facto* stock companies such as the stable of players linked to Martin Scorsese, John Cassavetes, Spike Lee, the Coen Brothers, and Paul Thomas Anderson.

Emphasizing practical considerations, many actors' manuals recommend that the actor must be willing to be typecast in order to be more easily classified with agencies. For instance, one manual acknowledges, "There are stars, of course, who are remarkably versatile. But for a beginner it is wise to work out one especial type of thing, one sort of characterization, which will be particularly good, even though he should try to learn to play every sort of role. Then there is no difficulty in making classifications when one registers with a casting director or agent" (Klumph 1922, 72–74).[8] An essay entitled "The Value of Specialization" suggests that an actor should not just adopt a broad specialization in comedy or drama, but should carve out a niche in small roles. The list of possible specialties includes butlers, smart city men, bookmakers, doctors, flunkeys, and judges for male actors; and cooks, maids, half-castes, aunts, nurses, and typists for actresses (Pickford, 6–12). This highly stratified division of labor is aimed at keeping the actor employed in a regular line of business when being a lead may not be a reality. Stuart Hemward puts it bluntly in his actor's manual:

> The average feature picture usually has two "leads" which call for a good looking young girl and boy . . . but there is also the surrounding cast . . . older men and women, heavies, comedians, singers, dancers. Therefore in point of *quantity* there is a greater demand for the *homelier, standard types* than for the ingénue and leading man . . . Your face may be your fortune, but not exactly in the way you think. There are many types of comediennes who are not known as beauties, but who, nevertheless, have been successful . . . Therefore, first of all, type yourself (Hemward 1937, 9).

Interestingly, and in contrast to Stanislavski, early cinema discourse views typecasting not only as a practical strategy but also as key to naturalistic acting. Arguing against versatility in a how-to acting book, producer Kenelm Foss argues:

> Acting, in the sense of impersonating a character foreign to the player's personality, does not exist. All actors deny this: all actors can play anything, given the chance, according to their own account . . . If an actor is not himself the part, or if his personality does not approximate to that of the part, he's not the man to play it . . . Types! That is what casting comes to, first and last—the selection of proper types (Pickford, 25–26).

Similarly, Hemward emphasizes that typing will produce more realistic performances: "You must know your type and then develop naturalness of acting within the characteristics of the personalities you desire to portray" (Hemward 1937, 13). In addition, typecasting is viewed as the result of the camera's "accuracy" which demands a particular kind of realism akin to typage. Frances Agnew writes:

> Oh, that word "type!" In days of yore, an artist was always an artist. By the aid of make-up and artistic temperament a young man or woman played a character many years his senior, or an older player was likewise considered capable of giving an artistic youthful characterization . . . To-day the cry of managers is for types; a child must be played by a child, sweet sixteen must be sweet sixteen, not only in years, but in appearance "offstage" as well as on; the stage mother, aunt, old maid, etc. must be played by actresses possessing the appearance in private life; the handsome hero, the gallant old gentleman—each must look the part to a certain extent when engaged (Agnew 1913, 59).

While the idea of typing oneself goes against the grain of most theories of naturalism, in Hollywood, typing oneself quickly became and continues to be a practical necessity, and has been institutionalized and formalized in casting practice through the production and distribution of casting directories and casting services.

Casting directories and services

Almost as soon as casting becomes rationalized through the development of dramatic agencies and in-house casting directors, casting directories that promote and categorize actors are published and circulated. These directories feature photographs of actors and actresses, sometimes listing their credits and/or studio affiliations, in alphabetical order and within certain categories. The earliest casting directories categorize actors using terminology that closely resembles the lines-of-business tradition.[9] For instance, the undated *Directory of Artists Under Exclusive Management of the Edward Small Company*—which we can assume to be from the "picture personality" era, due to its epigraph, "Personality is a Commodity"—categorizes actors in descending order as either leading men, juveniles (including leads, characters and heavies), males (including second leads and heavies), or character men. Women are similarly categorized as leading women, ingénues, females (including second leads and heavies), and character women. In 1924, *The Screen Artist* breaks down its listings into feature men, feature comedians, leading men, juveniles, heavy men, and character men, with virtually the same groupings for women and a separate category for children. Reflecting the need for increased specialization, *The Standard Directory of Motion Picture Talent* from 1922 lists principals according to compressed lines-of-business—feature men, leading men, juveniles, character men, feature comedians—but also adds a section for "supporting cast," comprising those minor roles that would have been filled by the lower ranks in the lines-of-business tradition. This "supporting cast" includes an amazing array of specializations, defined by appearance or role, and including male roles as acrobats, bits and parts, character men (old) and character men (young), Chinamen, doctors, female impersonators, Jewish (old and young), Russian types, twins, underworld types, and well-dressed men (old and young). For women, supporting parts include not only character women and ingénues, but also cooks, dancers, grande dames, nuns, small town (old and young), tall women (old and young), and witch types.

Eventually, these specializations will disappear from primary casting directories and will be relegated to casting services dedicated to extras. For instance, in 1946 the classified groupings for the Central Casting Corporation include the following: American Indians; Arabians, able to handle camels; beards—dress and character; butlers; Chinese; cigarette girls; clowns; cops; girls—sweet looking; Hindus, able to handle elephants; midgets; rough characters; strong men; and short men. These specializations also exist residually in studio files on contract players such as those of casting director William "Billy" Gordon. Gordon was casting director at MGM Studios from the 1930s to1947, and then at 20th Century-Fox until 1960, and he became head of talent at Columbia for the 1960s and 1970s. Gordon's files on actors from his tenure at MGM consist of typed lists of actors placed in folders with headings such as the following for male actors: Anglo Saxons, Arab, bald, bartender, beards, character, collegiate, colored/Negro, cripples/midgets/freaks, fat, fencers, juveniles, nances, rubes, and underworld. For actresses, Gordon's files include: beautiful, blonde, characters (young), colored/Negro, exotic, fat, heavies, hookers, maids, old, old maids, prison matrons, showgirls, and singers.

As general utility and supernumerary specialties fall increasingly under the category of extras and bit parts, most casting directories are then focused on actors who can fill principal parts; and typical directories list lines-of-business and include information about whether an actor is under contract. There is some overlap among categories. For instance, in 1924's *The Screen Artist*, Francis X. Bushman is listed as both a leading man and a feature man, indicating a distinction between starring roles and other major roles. Similarly, in *The Players Inc. Screen Casting Directory* of 1928, Skeets Noyes is listed as both a heavy and a character. There is some mobility among the lines—an actor can ascend from juvenile or ingénue to lead—but the distinction between starring roles and roles as characters or comedians seems firm.

At this time, the actors listed are almost all white but race and ethnicity figure heavily in the category of "character," which seems to refer back to the categories of light comedy and eccentric business in traditional lines and generally includes actors who play distinct ethnic types, roles in uniform or other elaborate costumes, and roles in heavy make-up.[10] For instance, in a June 1928 issue of *The Players, Inc.*, character actor William Vox Mong lists his specialities: "Chinamen, Frenchmen, Russians and Americans and am learning English, Roman and Eskimo."

By the 1930s, race becomes its own category as *The Academy of Motion Picture Arts and Sciences: Players Directory Bulletin* (generally referred to as *The Academy Players Directory*) includes separate sections labeled "Colored" and "Oriental," which list all African American and Asian actors and actresses, adults and children, together while it classifies white men (without identifying them as such) as leading men, younger leading men, characters and comedians; white women as leading women, ingénues, characters and comediennes; and white children as boys and girls. While African American and Asian actors and actresses exist outside the lines, as it were, with no indication of whether they are, for instance, characters or ingénues, white actors such as Bela Lugosi and Peter Lorre who play ethnic types are still listed in the main male categories as "characters." By 1945, possibly in response to NAACP calls for better representation in Hollywood, actors of color are included among the regular categories but are *indexed* separately. Initially, there seems to be an unwritten rule that an African American or Asian actor cannot be a lead. Lena Horne, for instance, is listed as a "character and comedienne" in the 1945 *Academy Players Directory*, despite her groundbreaking star contract. While actors of color were eventually included among leads, they were still indexed separately as, first, Colored, then Negro, and eventually as Black. Today, this practice continues with increasing attention to multiculturalism and political correctness, as actors and actresses are cross-indexed as not only Black Artists, but also as Artists with Disabilities (including the specific nature of their disability, such as quadriplegic, amputee, etc.), Deaf and Hard of Hearing Artists, Little People, Asian Pacific Artists, Hispanic Artists, Native American Artists, and, oddly, Twins.[11]

Ultimately, through the combined forces of increasing rationalization and the star system, Hollywood develops a complex and hierarchical ladder of types—some defined by lines, some by appearance, some by personality, some associated with certain stereotypes, and some with social types, some operating as stars and some as character actors. Over the years, the categories into which these types can be sorted changes according to changing tastes and mores. And, as the assumed homology between actor and role, and role and appearance gets increasingly rigid and increasingly politicized, types are diversified and increase exponentially but are still recognizable as types. For instance, a recent survey of casting calls in Breakdown Services, the leading print and web source in Hollywood for casting, found roles described largely in terms of types. These types ranged from stock characters such as "high school sweetheart" and "mother type" to racial categories and corresponding stereotypes ("African American, 20–35. Dance . . . Basketball skills required") to types defined by pre-existing actors and characters ("a young Jodie Foster or Queen Latifah, or Peppermint Patty from *Peanuts*" in a call for "real" and diverse girls).[12]

Thus, in a certain sense, the older lines-of-business practice was less traditional in its conception of casting—insofar as what enabled an actor to play a line was not strictly speaking his physical appearance but rather his costume and make-up, whereas in today's seeming diversity, the actor is defined increasingly by physical appearance, race, body type, age, gender, and sex. In the interests of upholding shifting conceptions of realism, Hollywood has proliferated rather than blurred the lines.[13]

Conclusion

To conclude, I would suggest that a consideration of casting helps deepen and expand our understanding of film acting. First, casting needs to be seen as an interpretive process. A consideration of casting could complicate current models of authorship and of stardom. Examining casting helps acknowledge not only the way roles are characterized but also the ideologies about identity they embody. In addition, a consideration of casting helps show changes in performance styles as only one part of what constitutes acting on screen. We need to more consciously relate performance styles to casting practices and take into account political, cultural, and labor issues at the time of performance. On a related note, just as the meaning of the word "type" has evolved, notions of "realism" have undergone a metamorphosis to reflect changing ideas about acting and identity; and, therefore, the discourse of realism which has dominated studies of classical cinema needs to be more specifically informed by an understanding of institutional practice and historical context. Finally, while recognizing the influence of embedded 18th-century theatrical traditions on contemporary casting may lead us to view typecasting as inevitable, it should also open a door to change. If, as Stanislavski suggests, performance style and institutional practice go hand in hand, then we need now to envision ways to break free from residual and perhaps outmoded casting traditions, to denaturalize naturalism and break free from modes of realism that simply reproduce our own everyday tendencies to typecast.

Acknowledgments

Portions of this essay were presented at the Chicago Film Seminar, at the University of Notre Dame, and at the Society for Cinema and Media Studies and a slightly longer version of the essay appeared in a special issue of *Criticism*. Special thanks to James Naremore, Tom Gunning, Donald Crafton, Lesley Brill, and readers at *Criticism* for their comments. Casting directors Jane Alderman and Debra Zane generously shared their thoughts with me; Gary Marsh at Breakdown Services provided sample breakdowns; and Barbara Hall at the Margaret Herrick Library of the Academy of Motion Picture Arts and Sciences helped me to find archival casting materials.

Notes

1 For more on Non-Traditional Casting, see Gibbons 1991; Schechner 1989; and the website for the Non-Traditional Casting Project, www.ntcp.org
2 The *zanni* is the clownish underling or servant, an acrobatic mimic, a Harlequin.
3 The Australian larrikin is a young street rowdy, a delinquent. Though the term refers to minor criminals, it can also be used to name valued Australian characteristics such as irreverence, non-conformism, and impudence.
4 Typage tends toward representations of what Richard Dyer calls "member types." Member types "are linked to historically and culturally specific and determined social groups or classes and their praxes, which are almost bound to be outside the present cultural hegemony (in so far as it has so much invested in the notion of individuality)." Dyer values member types because they hold out the promise of collective identity, and therefore, political action, as opposed to social types and stereotypes which operate on an exclusionary basis. See Dyer 1980, 37.
5 On "expressive coherence" and theories of acting in Hollywood, see Naremore 1988, 68–82 and *passim*.
6 On the demise of the lines-of-business tradition, see Burge 1986, 212–213; McConachie 1992, 248–256; and McArthur 1984, 7–8.
7 See "Casting Efficiency," *Motion Picture World* 26, no. 11 (11 December 1915): 1985.
8 Similarly, in contrast to her own discomfort with typecasting, Mary Pickford advises actors to know their strengths and weaknesses and find types or roles they can play. She writes: "The producer will probably help you in your selection of the part. If he knows his work, as most producers do, he has divided humanity in sections—young men, old men, comedians, tragedians—and within a few minutes of your first appearance before him he will have allotted you to one of those sections, and more often than not his judgment will be the right one." Pickford, 29.
9 All casting directories listed here are available at the Margaret Herrick Library of the Academy of Motion Picture Arts and Sciences, Los Angeles.
10 This sense of the category of "character" parallels the use of the term "character" in dance, where, the "character dance" is invariably ethnic in nature and principally from the Russian or Slavic traditions, although there are Mediterranean character dances such as the Tarantella; and "character dancer" refers to those dancers who portray older or comical characters such as Dr. Coppelias in *Coppelia*, or the step mother in *Cinderella* (usually played by a male dancer.) I am indebted to Kevin Dreyer for his explanation of this terminology.

11 According to a February 2001 telephone interview with Keith Gonzalez, the current editor of the *Academy Players Directory*, actors and/or their agents decide whether to list themselves as leads, younger leads or ingénues, or characters and comedians, and they also decide whether or not to be cross-indexed. Gonzalez, like casting directors I interviewed, feels that actors are poor judges of their type and often mis-categorize themselves.

12 Breakdown Services, Ltd. Provides "breakdowns" or capsule descriptions of all roles needing to be cast for most Hollywood productions, including feature films, TV shows, commercials, student films, and industrials. The breakdowns are written by casting directors and/or in-house writers and breakdowns are sent to agents, managers, and other subscribers daily. See www.breakdownservices.com

13 An anecdote will indicate how traditional "non-traditional" casting can be. When I was doing research for this article, I had a conversation with a Chicago-based casting director who told me that if a director asked to fill a role for a Polish female bank teller (which she assumed would be played by a Polish female actress), she might suggest the role be played as black, gay, and male instead; but her conception of who could play black, gay, and male was limited to actors who were themselves black, gay, and male. Thus, her conception of "non-traditional" casting consisted of swapping one type for another and her conception of type was tied to the actor's individual "real" identity. I had similar conversations with casting directors in Los Angeles.

References

Agnew, Frances. *Motion Picture Acting: How to Prepare for Photoplaying, What Qualifications are Necessary, How to Secure an Engagement, Salaries Paid to Photoplayers*. New York: Reliance Newspaper Syndicate, 1913.

Bogle, Donald. *Toms, Coons, Mulattoes, Mammies, and Bucks: An Interpretive History of Blacks in American Films*. 1973. Reprint, New York: Continuum, 2001.

Bordwell, David, Kristin Thompson, and Janet Staiger. *The Classical Hollywood Cinema, Film Style and Mode of Production to 1960*. New York: Columbia University Press, 1985.

Brewster, Ben and Lea Jacobs. *Theatre to Cinema: Stage Pictorialism and the Early Feature Film*. Oxford: Oxford University Press, 1997.

Burge, James C. *Lines of Business: Casting Practice and Policy in the American Theatre, 1752–1899*. New York: Peter Lang, 1986.

Cavell, Stanley. *The World Viewed: Reflections on the Ontology of Film*. Enlarged edition. Cambridge, MA: Harvard University Press, 1979.

DeCordova, Richard. *Picture Personalities: The Emergence of the Star System in America*. Chicago: University of Illinois Press, 1990.

Dyer, Richard. "Stereotyping." In *Gays and Film*, edited by Richard Dyer, 27–39. London: British Film Institute, 1980.

—— "The Role of Stereotypes." In *The Matter of Images: Essays on Representations*. New York: Routledge, 1993.

Eisenstein, S. M. "The Principles of the New Russian Cinema." In *Selected Works, Volume I: Writings, 1922–1934*, edited and translated by Richard Taylor. Bloomington: Indiana University Press, 1988.

Gibbons, John J. *The American Theatre's Attempt to Achieve Multiculturalism on Stage Through Non-Traditional Casting*. Ph.D. diss., Northwestern University, 1991.

Goffman, Erving. *The Presentation of Self in Everyday Life*. New York: Anchor Books, 1959.

Graham, Charles. "Acting for the Films in 1912." In *Playing to the Camera: Film Actors Discuss their Craft*, edited by Bert Cardullo, Harry Geduld, Ronald Gottesman, and Leigh Woods, 19–21. New Haven: Yale University Press, 1998.

Grimsted, David. *Melodrama Unveiled: American Theater and Culture, 1800–1850*. Chicago: University of Chicago Press, 1968.

Gunning, Tom. "The Cinema of Attractions: Early Film, Its Spectator and the Avant-Garde." In *Early Cinema: Space/Frame/Narrative*, edited by Thomas Elsaesser, 56–62. London: British Film Institute, 1990.

Heath, Stephen. "Body, Voice." In *Questions of Cinema*. Bloomington: Indiana University Press, 1981.

Hemward, Stuart J. *How to Get in Motion Pictures*. Hollywood: The Hemwood Publishing Company, 1937.

Isaacs, Edith J. R. "Type-Casting: The Eighth Deadly Sin," *Theatre Arts* 17 (1933): 131–138.

Klumph, Inez and Helen. *Screen Acting: Its Requirements and Rewards*. New York: Falk Publishing, 1922.

Kracauer, Siegfried. "Remarks on the Actor." In *Theory of Film: The Redemption of Physical Reality*. 1960. Reprint, Princeton: Princeton University Press, 1997.

Kuleshov, Lev. *Kuleshov on Film*, translated and edited by Ronald Levaco. Berkeley: University of California Press, 1974.

Majumdar, Neepa. "The Embodied Voice: Song Sequences and Stardom in Popular Hindi Cinema." In *Soundtrack Available: Essays on Film and Popular Music*, edited by Pamela Robertson Wojcik and Arthur Knight, 161–184. Durham: Duke University Press, 2001.

McArthur, Benjamin. *Actors and American Culture, 1880–1920*. Philadelphia: Temple University Press, 1984.

McConachie, Bruce A. *Melodramatic Formations: American Theatre and Society, 1820–1870*. Iowa City: University of Iowa Press, 1992.

Musser, Charles. "The Changing Status of the Actor." In *Before Hollywood: Turn-of-the-Century American Film*, 57–62. New York: Hudson Hills Press in Association with the American Federation of Arts, 1987.

—— *The Emergence of Cinema: The American Screen to 1907. History of the American Cinema*, vol. 1. Berkeley: University of California Press, 1990.

Naremore, James. *Acting in the Cinema*. Berkeley: University of California Press, 1988.

Pearson, Roberta E. *Eloquent Gestures: The Transformation of Performance Style in the Griffith Biograph Films*. Berkeley: University of California Press, 1992.

Pickford, Mary *et al*. *Cinema: Practical Courses in Cinema Acting in Ten Complete Lessons*. London: The Standard Art Book Company, n.d.

Schechner, Richard. "Race Free, Gender Free, Body-Type Free, Age Free Casting." TDR (*The Drama Review*) *Comment* 33, no. 1 (Spring 1989): 4–12.

Smith, Murray. *Engaging Characters: Fiction, Emotion and the Cinema*. Oxford: Clarendon Press, 1995.

Stanislavski, Constantin. "Types of Actors." In *Stanislavski's Legacy: A Collection of Comments on a Variety of Aspects of an Actor's Art and Life*, edited and translated by Elizabeth Reynolds Hapgood, 13–19. 1968. Reprint, New York: Routledge, 1999.

Studlar, Gaylyn. *This Mad Masquerade: Stardom and Masculinity in the Jazz Age*. New York: Columbia University Press, 1996.

White, Patricia. *UnInvited: Classical Hollywood Cinema and Lesbian Representability*. Bloomington: Indiana University Press, 1999.
Wilshire, Bruce. *Role Playing and Identity: The Limits of Theatre as Metaphor*. Bloomington: Indiana University Press, 1991.
Yoakem, Lola G. "Casting in Contemporary Theatrical Motion Pictures and Filmed Television Programming." *Film Quarterly* 12, no. 2 (Winter 1958): 36–42.

The 1950s 13

Black Stars

DONALD BOGLE

> Ethel Waters sways her massive shoulders as she sings "His Eye Is on the Sparrow," and suddenly, becomes—for a new generation—its great earth-mother figure. . . . Dorothy Dandridge, first as Carmen, then as Margot, later as Bess, acts her heart out, wins her Oscar nomination, and emerges on screen and off as the living embodiment of the tragic mulatto. . . . Sidney Poitier enters the era shyly as a young unknown in *No Way Out*, only to close the decade as one of the most important leading men—black or white—in the movies. . . . Writer Richard Wright, baseball player Jackie Robinson, boxer Jersey Joe Walcott, tennis champ Althea Gibson, football player Woody Strode, trumpeter Louis Armstrong, crooner Nat "King" Cole, songstress Eartha Kitt, comedienne Pearl Bailey, jazz stylist Ella Fitzgerald, and calypso artist Harry Belafonte invade the movies and go "dramatic." . . . And problem pictures continue, alternately engaging and alienating their audiences.

It was the 1950s, an era to be remembered as apathetic and sleepy-eyed, vulgar and hypocritical, grandiose, spectacular, and tasteless. Yet the Eisenhower age was one of change and turbulence, a decade that encompassed an array of incongruities: McCarthy in the Senate, troops in Korea, a Nobel Peace Prize for Ralph Bunche in Sweden, the National Guard in Cicero and Chicago, the Supreme Court Decision of 1954, Marian Anderson at the Met, Emmett Till lynched in Mississippi, bus boycotts (later bombings) in Montgomery, the rise of Martin Luther King, sit-ins in Oklahoma, federal troops in Arkansas.

The 1950s' social-political whirl penetrated the motion-picture industry, which like the rest of the country, had to undergo change. Already the industry had lost some of its best talents because of blacklisting. Slowly, too, the look of the American feature film was altered, no longer stamped with the big-studio gloss but marked now by the individual signature of the independent director or producer. Television sets had come into homes across the nation and when box-office attendance, after its great boom in the war years, tapered off drastically the film industry offered the giant wide screens—Cinerama, CinemaScope, VistaVision, 3-D—as a desperate means of holding the audience. Likewise the industry picked up bold themes in part to lure the television audience away from home and in part as a realistic reflection of the growing chaos in the streets of America and in the psyches of its citizens. Gone almost entirely was the magical, romantic, bigger-than-life daydream quality of the old movies as independent filmmakers brought to the public not only more problem pictures but "message" pictures, "serious" pictures, "thoughtful" pictures, "studious" pictures, and "controversial" pictures, all interchangeable but carrying different labels.

For black actors this era of silent change was important. The great gains of the late 1940s were continued in the 1950s with the emergence of distinct black personalities who, through their own idiosyncrasies, invigorated the Negro Lead Character and the Negro Theme. Almost immediately three diverse black personalities stood out prominently, and they were to remain so throughout the decade, making the greatest breakthrough for the black actor in American motion pictures. Sidney Poitier, Dorothy Dandridge, and Ethel Waters transformed the history of blacks in films from a study of pictures or parts or personalities to one of star dimensions.

As already seen, in the early days of moviemaking black actors were rigidly consigned to mythic types. Through the push and power of their personalities, some actors had created great pop figures. Everything in Hollywood was a game, they knew, and they did not expect to be taken very seriously. Movie audiences loved and laughed at these great comic strip characters. They left theaters having enjoyed themselves but with little reason to think twice about what they had seen. No one ever cared what Bill Robinson was really thinking as he danced up the staircases with Shirley Temple. Nor did anyone give a second thought to how Hattie McDaniel must have felt as she ripped the bandana from her head after a particularly humiliating scene.

Occasionally, with black actors such as Stepin Fetchit or Lena Horne or Paul Robeson, because their off-screen exploits paralleled their on-screen images and because they were publicized by their studios, audiences felt they had some insight into the person on celluloid. But still unlike the important white stars—such as Garbo and Gable—the old black actors were not monolithic figures. They did not symbolize disparate elements of their audience's personalities. They were not able to affect lives dramatically or touch on the mass imagination. Indeed, the moviegoing public was not yet prepared to be swept off its feet by the intrigues of a colored personality.

But in the 1950s Poitier, Dandridge, and Waters reached out and affected the imagination of the mass audience. Patrons believed in them. Often because of their private lives or because of a strongly rooted image, the trio overpowered the films in which they appeared. Moreover, in this strange psychoanalytic age when audiences started dissecting not only their own inner selves but those of their movies and movie stars as well, when patrons went to see black performers not for mere entertainment but for a comment on the black experience, these three performers became popular because of what they represented to moviegoers. Like all great stars, they were aesthetic beings in themselves. To contemplate Waters' humanity or Dandridge's beauty or Poitier's code of decency was worth the price of admission, and the three made a slight dent at the place Hollywood has traditionally cherished most: the box office.

Ethel Waters: earth mother for an alienated age

Ethel Waters was the first of the three to win mass audience approval. She had been around for a long time, and her life and career were a tale of disorder and much early sorrow. Growing up in Chester, Pennsylvania, she had stolen food to eat, run errands for whores, been a lookout for pimps and underworld figures. At thirteen she was married. At fourteen she was separated. At fifteen she was a chambermaid and laundress at a Philadelphia hotel where she earned $4.75 a week. Then almost miraculously she rose from poverty to international acclaim, first in the cellars and cafés where she was billed as "Sweet Mama Stringbean" and later on the stage in such successful productions as *Africana*, *Blackbirds of 1930*, *Rhapsody in Black*, *As Thousands Cheer*, *At Home Abroad*, *Mamba's Daughters*, and *Cabin in the Sky*.

Ethel Waters later reached a whole new audience with her impressive film work. But suddenly her spiraling career fell flat in the mid-1940s. Overwork, exhaustion, exploitation, and personal unhappiness had made her "difficult" and chronically suspicious of everyone. Her outbursts on the set of *Cabin in the Sky* remain a part of Hollywood legend. Subsequently there was a six-year period of unemployment in the film capital, and by 1948, when Darryl Zanuck asked her to test for Granny in *Pinky*, Ethel Waters was almost at the point of begging for a role. Her Granny was an old typed vehicle but she got mileage out of it, and her career swung back into full gear. Today, because of her appearances in such films as *Cairo* (1942), *Tales of Manhattan*, *Cabin in the Sky*, *Stage Door Canteen* (1943), and *Pinky*, many still think of Ethel Waters as an exclusively 1940s figure. It was during this period that, singlehanded, she brought a new style and substance to the time-worn mammy. But as significant a figure as she was in the 1940s, it was in the Eisenhower era, in the film version of Carson McCullers' play *The Member of the Wedding*, that she scored her greatest screen triumph and an overwhelming personal victory.

The Member of the Wedding was more than simply a movie. It was in two very important respects a motion-picture event. Foremost, it marked the first time a black actress was used to carry a major-studio white production. Secondly, the movie was another comeback for Ethel Waters. Her autobiography *His Eye Is on the Sparrow* had recently been published and was a best seller. In it, she told all the lurid details of her life—the fights, the lovers, the marriages, the career troubles. Curiously, instead of alienating her audience, the turbulent events in the autobiography convinced patrons that Ethel Waters, who had always portrayed long-suffering women, was indeed the characters she played. Moreover, audiences knew Ethel Waters had truly suffered. Now patrons rooted for her to succeed—to triumph. When *The Member of the Wedding* finally opened, audiences got just that.

The Stanley Kramer–Fred Zinnemann feature was a serious, oddly structured film for 1952 American moviegoers. It starred the original Broadway cast. It had little plot, and focused instead on the interactions of three outcasts: Frankie Adams (played by Julie Harris), a twelve-year-old motherless girl entering adolescence and wanting desperately to belong; John-Henry (Brandon de Wilde), Frankie's six-year-old sickly cousin-playmate; and the weathered and beaten family cook, Berenice. In the course of the film, Berenice is revealed as the guiding spirit in the children's solitary lives. She is cook, housekeeper, protectress, reprimander, adviser, and confidante. "Come on. Let us play a three-hand game of bridge," says Berenice as she and the children sit in the kitchen. "Play the King, John-Henry," she tells the boy when he is about to cheat at their bridge game. "You know you got to play the rules of the game." In these quiet or sometimes turbulent moments among the three, author Carson McCullers' great lyricism was apparent as much as her theme of human loneliness and alienation. "We go round trying one thing. Then another. Yet we're still caught," Berenice tells young Frankie. At another time, in her most moving monologue, she explains to the two children the fragmented blind alleys of her life. "He was the first man I ever loved. Therefore I had to go and copy myself forever after and what I did was to marry off little pieces of Ludi whenever

I run across them. It was my misfortune that they all turned out to be the wrong pieces." She comforts the two and helps them grow from her experiences. She sings to them "His Eye Is on the Sparrow." The film is resolved with Frankie grown and over that aching period of adolescence. Berenice stands alone in the kitchen of the house. She is leaving to work elsewhere, and we understand that her talents as an earth mother, to nourish and comprehend, are needed in a new household.

The Member of the Wedding was a critical success, but reports of its strange plotlessness and unconventional characters scared off many viewers. Others found them baffling. But Ethel Waters, the actress and the human being, was praised by everyone, even by those who did not like the film. Berenice was a perfect role for her, and there were obvious parallels between the seamy, confused tragic life of the movie's heroine and the legends about the entertainer. In the film version of *The Member of the Wedding*, the role was so well written and the character so well etched that Waters at long last had the material for a bravura performance. In her hands, every line, even a seemingly unadorned statement, was delivered with a warmth and irony that went beyond the script. "Can't bid," she said during the card game. "Never have a hand these days." "All my life I been wanting things I ain't been getting," she uttered plaintively. Ultimately, because *The Member of the Wedding*, with its skinny tomboy heroine and its pint-sized bespectacled leading man, was so unlike the typical Saturday evening movie fare, audiences tended to accept Ethel Waters and her life rather than the lives portrayed in the film. She emerged now as more than just a representative of the long-suffering, strong black woman. She was a great "serious" popular myth come true. For black audiences, Ethel Waters was the personification of the black spirit they believed had prevailed during the hard times of slavery, and they felt she brought dignity and wisdom to the race. For the mass white audience, Ethel Waters spoke to an inner spirit of a paranoid and emotionally paralyzed generation that longed for some sign of heroism. Movie stardom itself has often been based on a thin line between actress and myth, and with this performance Ethel Waters became a genuine movie star. Her personality, rather than her character or her movie, had grasped the public imagination, and thus the history of the Negro in American films gained a new perspective.

But if Ethel Waters altered black film history, she was perhaps the last to know about it. For in spite of her impressive performance, she curiously became in the mid-1950s a victim of audience indifference. From *The Member of the Wedding* she went on to important Broadway appearances. There was also the successful television series "Beulah." Then new troubles arose: income-tax evasion and other debts. Finally, her debts and problems mounted so high that she was forced to make an excruciatingly painful appearance on the television quiz show "Break the $250,000 Bank." The great actress stood before millions in their homes trying to win money to pay her taxes. Surprisingly, audiences took her plight in stride. There was neither outrage nor great sadness. In a frightening way, Ethel Waters' public sorrow and humiliation were considered fitting for the tough endurable mythic figure who had always shown America that she could prevail, even under the most trying situations. When her next film, *The Sound and the Fury* (1959), was released, Twentieth Century-Fox's publicity department announced that "everybody's favorite," indeed "America's favorite," Ethel Waters, was back. As Dilsey, the "indomitable skeleton," the part Faulkner himself might have written for her, Waters again acted the strong black woman in grand style. The movie at first looked promising, with a cast that included Yul Brynner, Joanne Woodward, and Margaret Leighton. But the actors floundered in one mess of a script, and Waters fought to stay afloat. It was her last film of the decade.

The 1950s ended with Ethel Waters having appeared in but two motion pictures. But for this anemic, insecure age, one scared of its own shadow and terrified of taking risks, she was an echo of the past. Ethel Waters seemed to be some noble part of our heritage that was quickly becoming extinct. In a period of mass uniformity, she was the individualist foolish enough to assert herself yet strong enough to pay for the consequences. In the end, her image—the myth she lived out—loomed larger than life over the decade. Through the 1950s into the early 1970s, Waters made occasional television appearances on such programs as "Route 66," "The Great Adventure," and "Owen Marshall," again playing the strong matriarchal heroine. In her later years, she appeared with Billy Graham's Crusades. In 1977, Waters died at age 80.

Dorothy Dandridge: apotheosis of the mulatto

Dorothy Dandridge was the second of the black stars. Before the apathetic Eisenhower age ended, she had infused it with her great intensity and risen as its most successful black leading lady. For a period that prided itself on appearances, hers was a startling presence. She was a great beauty. Her eyes were dark and vibrant, her hair long and silky, her features sharply defined. And she had the rich golden skin tone that had always fascinated movie audiences, black and white. Moreover, she was a distinctive personality, schizophrenic, maddening, euphoric, and self-destructive. Before her Nina Mae McKinney had displayed uncontrolled raunchiness. Fredi Washington had symbolized intellectualized despair, and Lena Horne had acquired a large following through her reserve and middle-class aloofness. On occasion, Dorothy Dandridge exhibited all the characteristics of her screen predecessors, but most important to her appeal was her fragility and her desperate determination to survive. In a way never before demonstrated by a black personality, she used her own incongruities and self-contradictions to capture and extend the mass imagination. Her life and career were vigorously reported on by the white and black press. At times she seemed to bask in her own publicity, and it was obvious that she took pains to create an image, to package it, and then to market it for mass consumption.

The irony that overshadowed Dorothy Dandridge's career was that although the image she marketed appeared to be contemporary and daring, at heart it was based on an old and classic type, the tragic mulatto. In her important films Dorothy Dandridge portrayed doomed, unfulfilled women. Nervous and vulnerable, they always battled with the duality of their personalities. As such, they answered the demands of their times. Dorothy Dandridge's characters brought to a dispirited nuclear age a razor-sharp sense of desperation that cut through the bleak monotony of the day. Eventually—and here lay the final irony—she may have been forced to live out a screen image that destroyed her.

Dorothy Dandridge came to films after a lengthy and arduous career as a stage entertainer. The daughter of a Cleveland minister and a comedienne-actress named Ruby, she performed as a child with her older sister Vivian in a vaudeville act billed as "The Wonder Kids." At fifteen she and Vivian along with another black girl appeared as the Dandridge Sisters, touring the country with the Jimmy Lunceford band. At sixteen, Dorothy Dandridge performed at the Cotton Club, where she met Harold Nicholas of the dancing Nicholas Brothers. She married him and bore him a daughter. Later the pair divorced. Throughout the 1940s, she worked in nightclubs as well as in a string of films such as *Lady from Louisiana* (1941), *Bahama Passage* (1942), *Drums of the Congo* (1942), *Ebony Parade*, and *The Hit Parade of* 1943.

In the early 1950s, a trio of low-budget movies in which she played "good girl" roles served as springboards for Dorothy Dandridge's rise. The first, *Tarzan's Peril* (1951), was typical jungle fare with one twist. In a crucial episode, Dandridge, as a kidnaped African princess, was tied to the stakes by a warlike tribal leader. As she lay with legs sprawled apart, heaving and turning to break loose, it was apparent that never before had the black woman been so erotically and obviously used as a sex object. From the way Lex Barker's Tarzan eyed the sumptuous Dandridge, it was obvious, too, that for once Tarzan's mind was not on Jane or Boy or Cheetah!

In Columbia's *The Harlem Globetrotters* (1951), Dandridge was cast as a sympathetic young wife trying to keep a decent husband from going bad. She had little more to do than look lovely. MGM's 1953 all-black *Bright Road*, followed, giving Dorothy Dandridge her first starring role. As a grade-school teacher working to reach an unhappy wayward student, she was cast opposite child actor Philip Hepburn and a shy newcomer named Harry Belafonte. Here she revealed a soft, radiant, melancholic quality. "Her work in MGM's *See How They Run* [the title was changed upon release] projects sultry Dorothy Dandridge into the enviable role of Hollywood's No. 1 female star," wrote *Ebony*. *Life* magazine also ran a special article on the film, spotlighting its leading lady. Thus by 1953, the momentum for Dandridge's career was well under way. Had she continued playing such nice-girl roles, her career might have been entirely lackluster. But Dorothy Dandridge learned early that there were better things ahead on the other side of virtue.

Carmen Jones was the celebrated movie that established her as the definitive tragic mulatto. It also contains the definitive Dandridge mulatto performance. The legend of how director Otto Preminger first decided to cast Dandridge for the lead in his film reads like a press agent's dream tale, but it appears to be true. Initially, Preminger had thought her too sleek and sophisticated for the role of a whore. But he underestimated the talent and determination of the actress. When it appeared as if she had lost the role altogether, Dorothy Dandridge completely redid her appearance and style. She taught herself a Southern dialect. She mastered wildly uninhibited body movements. She shrewdly exploited her own nervous tension. With her new image perfected, she tossed her hair about her head, made up her eyes darkly, dressed herself in a sheer low-cut blouse and a long, tight skirt, and then audaciously strutted into Preminger's office. Vivacious, sportive, alluring yet somehow haunted and vulnerable, Dorothy Dandridge was the living embodiment of the director's Carmen. The role was given to her.

Carmen Jones, released in 1954, was the 1950s' most lavish, most publicized, and most successful all-black spectacle. If audiences truly yearned for relief from the tedium and routine of their lives, surely this was perfect pop entertainment. Based on Bizet's comic-strip opera *Carmen*, it cleverly transformed the opera's colorful Spanish cigarette girl into Carmen Jones, a sexy black factory worker in the South. Her foil is a Good Colored Boy, Joe, portrayed by Harry Belafonte. Carmen lures him into deserting the army, goes with him to a sleazy Chicago hotel where they evade the law, then deserts him for a prize fighter, and finally is strangled by him for her unfaithfulness.

The plot and the characters of *Carmen Jones* were pop creations, and the film relied on the stock situations: hair-pulling fights between black females, the inevitable barroom brawl, the exaggerated dialects, the animalistic passions and furies of the leads. Old-style *kitsch*, it was made impressive nonetheless by its director's exuberant style and its cast's great élan. Everyone seemed to be there to have a good time. Diahann Carroll had a small decorative role as one of Carmen's good-time girl friends. Olga James portrayed the submissive Cindy Lou. Brock Peters snarled gloriously as the villainous Sergeant Brown. Joe Adams as prize fighter Husky Miller was such an overtly sexual performer that audiences could understand why he never went far in films. White audiences still found sexually assertive black males hard to accept. Pearl Bailey was an open delight as she belted out a rousing "Beat Out That Rhythm on a Drum." But Dandridge's Carmen dominated the production. On the one hand, cool, calculating, and perfectly confident, on the other, reckless and insecure, she is animalistic and elemental. When pursued by Belafonte, she kicks, she screams, she claws, she bites, and at one point, she crawls on all fours. Belafonte must tie her hands and feet to prevent her from escaping. Here again Dorothy Dandridge was the jungle queen tied to the stakes. But her performance was curiously detached. Certainly, audiences knew that here was a woman who was acting. But the sheer theatricality, the relish she poured into her role, made audiences forget the incongruities of the plot and instead delight in Preminger's black fairy tale and this extravagant, high-strung bumblebee. "Looka here, baby," she seemed to say, "it ain't real, but I am!"

"The range between the two parts [*Carmen Jones* and *Bright Road*] suggests that she is one of the outstanding dramatic actresses of the screen," wrote *Newsweek*. "Of all the divas of grand opera—from Emma Calvé of the 90s to Risë Stevens—who have decorated the title role of *Carmen* and have in turn been made famous by it, none was ever so decorative or will reach nationwide fame so quickly as the sultry young lady . . . on *Life*'s cover this week," wrote the editors of *Life* when Dorothy Dandridge became the first black ever to grace its cover.

Carmen Jones made Dandridge a star. Her performance earned her an Oscar nomination as best actress of the year. Although she lost the award to Grace Kelly, no black performer had ever before been nominated for a leading actor award. (Hattie McDaniel's award and Ethel Waters' nomination were for best supporting actress.) Afterward the first rushing whirl of publicity closed in on her. *Paris-Match* and *Ebony* ran cover stories on her. A score of other publications, from *Time* to *Confidential*, carried feature articles about her. Dorothy Dandridge was reported on, probed, studied, dissected, discussed, scrutinized, and surveyed. There were incredible rumors and stories about her that yet live on in Hollywood, tales about her retarded daughter, her "hidden" son, her white father, and, in keeping with the image gradually growing about her, of her white lovers. She was said to be involved with everyone in Hollywood from Tyrone Power to Otto Preminger to Peter Lawford to Michael Rennie to Abby Mann to Arthur Loew, Jr. What with the publicity and gossip, Dorothy Dandridge now seemed a star of the first magnitude.

But despite the great fanfare and recognition after her triumph in 1954, Dorothy Dandridge sadly discovered there was no place for her to go. Bigotry and bias still had their place in Hollywood. Very few film offers came her way. Those that did were little more than variations on Carmen. Always she was to be cast as exotic, self-destructive women.

Just such a character was Dandridge's Margot in Robert Rossen's *Island in the Sun* (1957). Here she was cast in the first of her interracial-love roles. Today some might think it totally unimportant that Dorothy Dandridge was the first black woman ever to be held in the arms of a white man in an American movie. Yet, because she was permitted to bring integrated love to the mass audience in an age about to erupt in chaos over the issue of integration, she remains a socially significant figure in this film. It was a testament to her importance as a star that Twentieth Century-Fox risked featuring her opposite white actor John Justin. But, significant as the move was, *Island in the Sun* was marred by compromises. Even its producer,

Darryl F. Zanuck, has admitted not liking the finished film because of them. Because of its theme of miscegenation, *Island in the Sun* was controversial even during the shooting. Before its release, some theater owners (mostly Southern) threatened to boycott it. The South Carolina legislature even considered passing a bill to fine any movie house that showed the film $5000. That bill was never passed, but the threats had their effect. Cautious steps were taken to avoid too much controversy. In the movie, Dandridge and Justin held hands and danced together, but little else happened. "The one scene I objected to seriously was the one in the summerhouse where John confesses his love for me," Dandridge later said. "We had to fight to say the word *love*." In the summerhouse scene, Dandridge's Margot seemed tense when asked about her background. Audiences associated that nervousness with the character rather than the actress. As patrons watched Dandridge and Justin dance together, surely they thought how lovely the pair looked and how happy they could have been if only the jittery beauty weren't *colored*. She had everything else going for her! Surprisingly as controversial as some thought the miscegenation theme to be, it attracted movie audiences. *Island in the Sun* was made for $2,250,000 and grossed $8 million.

That same audience reaction, however—pity for the poor racially "tainted" beauty on screen—seemed built into the subsequent Dandridge films *The Decks Ran Red* (1958), *Tamango* (1957), and *Malaga* (1960). The latter two were filmed abroad.

Like Paul Robeson, Dorothy Dandridge fled this country, hoping to find in Europe an opportunity to play diversified, untyped characters. But she too encountered only disillusionment and repeated compromises.

Tamango cast her a mulatto slave loved by a white ship captain (Curt Jurgens). Two versions, one French, the other English, of all the love scenes were filmed. Then because of the interracial love theme no major American company would distribute the picture, and it failed. *The Decks Ran Red* fared a little better. In this tempestuous tale of a ship mutiny, Dandridge was surrounded by a trio of handsome white actors, James Mason, Stuart Whitman, and Broderick Crawford. As all three furtively undressed her with their eyes, it was apparent that had she not been black she would have ended up in the arms of one or the other before the picture's conclusion. In *Malaga*, Edmund Purdom and Trevor Howard were her leading men. As a woman torn between two loves, Dandridge was peculiarly remote and melancholy. So immersed was she in despondency that her performance at times seemed separate from the rest of the movie. Here Dandridge was fully stripped of the fire and passion that dominated her Carmen. Instead she appeared at her most vulnerable. What weighed her down was not so much her character's dejection as her own. "No one knew what her nationality was to be in the picture," her manager, Earl Mills, later reported. "The problem as to whether Trevor Howard should kiss her on the screen was called ridiculous. This was Dorothy's most frustrating acting experience by far."

Curiously, the important aspect of these three European movies (as well as *Island in the Sun*) was that Dandridge was bringing her own personal disappointments and frustrations to her characters. Audiences responded to the sadness on screen as an outside force. Perhaps they told themselves that the reason Dorothy Dandridge—this exquisite black love goddess—was unfulfilled was because of that drop of Negro blood. It was wrecking her chances for fulfillment. And indeed, for Dorothy Dandridge, on screen and off, in the mass imagination, the tragic flaw was her color.

Dandridge's last important American film was *Porgy and Bess* in 1959. As Catfish Row's torrid Bess, she put her star qualities on brilliant display. Designer Irene Sharaff's long tight skirt and dark wide-brim hat made Dandridge a stunning creation. As she walked through the theatrical sets of the film, she was Dorothy Dandridge. Even star performers Pearl Bailey and Sammy Davis, Jr., failed to take the screen from her. Costar Sidney Poitier was literally dwarfed. Again Dandridge portrayed the woman at odds with society, again the Bad Black Girl trying to go right, again the tragic heroine who ends up leaving the good Porgy to wander up No'th to Harlem with Sportin' Life. Dandridge gave a highly unusual interpretation of Bess, a less obviously sexual woman (she refuses to play Bess as a whore), a far more haunting one. The performance won her a Foreign Press Golden Globe Award nomination as best actress in a musical.

The rest of Dorothy Dandridge's career was a sad story. She appeared in but two more pictures. Producers and directors seemed unable to think of her in any terms but that of the exotic, doomed mulatto, and already by the late 1950s and early 1960s the mulatto figure was dated. There was talk of starring her in *Cleopatra*, but the plans fell through. Off-screen she was beset by a number of personal conflicts. In many respects, she epitomized the confused, unsatisfied movie star dominated by the publicity and life style that informed her screen image. She was openly seen with white actors. And the stories circulated that she was attracted to white men only. On the set of one film in which she worked opposite a very dark black actor, she underwent a minor trauma, it was said, because she did not want his black hands to touch her. In the late 1950s her marriage to the silver-haired white restaurateur Jack Denison seemed to confirm suspicions that Dorothy Dandridge had fallen victim to acting out her screen life in private. In 1962 her troubles were heightened when after her divorce from Denison she found herself bankrupt. There were no movie jobs, few club offers, and only occasional television appearances. Dorothy Dandridge found herself a has-been, an anachronism unwanted in a new Hollywood. Slowly, it was rumored, she drifted into alcohol, pills, and self-destructive love affairs. Then in 1965, at the age of forty-two, Dorothy Dandridge was found dead, the victim of an overdose of anti-depression pills. In the end, Dorothy Dandridge lived out and apotheosized the role she was always best at, the doomed tragic mulatto, trapped, so the film industry believed, because of her color.

Sidney Poitier: hero for an integrationist age

Sidney Poitier was the 1950s' third black star. His career proved more substantial, professionally and personally, than those of his predecessors. Poitier came to the movies almost accidently. Born in Nassau in 1927, the youngest of eight children, he had lived in Miami before coming to New York in the 1940s. With no thought of a film career, he worked in New York at odd jobs as a dockhand, dishwasher, chicken plucker, and bus boy. One day while thumbing through the *The New York Times*, he stumbled on an ad for actors at the American Negro Theater. He auditioned—with disastrous results. But soon he became determined to be a successful actor. After minor stage roles and some road tours, Sidney Poitier came to films and just about took over.

Poitier's ascension to stardom in the mid-1950s was no accident. There were three important reasons why he succeeded and won an audience at a time when other black actors such as Hernandez and Edwards were losing out. Foremost was the fact that in this integrationist age Poitier was the model integrationist hero. In all his films he was educated and intelligent. He spoke proper English, dressed conservatively, and had the best of table manners. For the mass white audience, Sidney Poitier was a black man who had met their standards. His characters were tame; never did they act impulsively, nor were they threats to the system. They were amenable and pliant. And finally they were non-funky, almost sexless and sterile. In short, they were the perfect dream for white liberals anxious to have a colored man in for lunch or dinner.

Poitier was also acceptable for black audiences. He was the paragon of black middle-class values and virtues. American Negroes were still migrating north and were gradually increasing their political power. The rising middle classes and the power (limited as it might have seemed) of their money supported Poitier. Black America was still trying to meet white standards and ape white manners, and he became a hero for their cause. He was neither crude nor loud, and, most important, he did not carry any ghetto cultural baggage with him. No dialect. No shuffling. No African cultural past. And he was almost totally devoid of rhythm. In short, he was the complete antithesis of all the black buffoons who had appeared before in American movies. This was one smart and refined young Negro, and middle-class America, both black and white, treasured him.

But the second reason for Poitier's ascension was that in many respects his characters were still the old type that America had always cherished. They were mild-mannered toms, throwbacks to the humanized Christian servants of the 1930s. When insulted or badgered, the Poitier character stood by and took it. He knew the white world meant him no real harm. He differed from the old servants only in that he was governed by a code of decency, duty, and moral intelligence. There were times in his films when he screamed out in rage at the injustices of a racist white society. But reason always dictated his actions, along with love for his fellow man. Most important, he did not use his goodness only as a means of saving a position. Past good Negroes in the movies, notably Bill Robinson, were usually concerned about pleasing the master in order not to be booted out of the Big House. But Poitier did not care about the Big House. Nor did his goodness issue from some blind spot of Christian faith (as with his screen "mother" Louise Beavers.) He acted as he did because an overriding intelligence demanded that his characters be humane.

Finally, Poitier became a star because of his talent. He may have played the old tom dressed up with modern intelligence and reason, but he dignified the figure. Always on display was the actor's sensitivity and strength. One can trace in all the Poitier features of the 1950s the qualities that made him a national favorite. Interestingly, the evolution of the Poitier screen personality was swift. In his first film, *No Way Out* (1950), audiences saw all the qualities that would make Poitier characters so "laudable" for the rest of the decade.

Joseph Mankiewicz's *No Way Out* launched not only Poitier's career but the cycle of problem pictures in the 1950s. Literate and sophisticated, the movie spotlighted the race riots that had broken out after World War II, at the same time presenting a sensitive portrait of the educated Negro. The plot centers on a young Negro doctor, Luther Brooks, at a large metropolitan hospital. When two white hoodlums are wounded during an attempted robbery, Brooks tends the pair. One of the men dies. The other then accuses Brooks of murder. Thereafter the young doctor is embroiled in controversy, and he fights to prove his innocence. When the remaining white hoodlum organizes a group of racist friends to attack the ghetto area, the city verges on a major race riot. By a lucky stroke of Hollywood imagination, Brooks proves his innocence through an autopsy, and equilibrium returns to the city.

With its crisp and quick-witted dialogue, *No Way Out* to some degree captured the mood of postwar America and summed up its repressed racial hostilities. Likewise its Negro characters were walking exponents of the postwar black doctrines of racial integration and *overprove*. "You got 'em. All A's," the doctor's wife tells him. "No wonder you're tired. Even I'm a little tired. Cleaning up after parties. Eating leftovers. One day off a week to be with my husband. To be a woman. . . . We've been a long time getting here. We're tired, but we're here, honey. We can be happy. We've got a right to be."

No Way Out garnered critical praise. *The New York Times* called it "a harsh, outspoken picture with implications that will keep you thinking about it long after leaving the theater." But strong, original, and honestly stated as the movie was, it failed to win a large audience. The public was already weary of the Negro-struggle film, perhaps because the struggles of previous cinematic Negroes such as the mulattoes Pinky and Carter had been so hokey and superficial. From its advertising campaign, *No Way Out* must have seemed only one more in the lot.

What distinguished the picture was Sidney Poitier. As Brooks, he had the archetypal modern integrationist tom role. He was a brilliant young doctor whose achievements—the all A's, the correct diagnosis—summed up the equal-by-being-superior philosophy. He was handsome. He stood straight, spoke well, and never trod on anybody's toes. He was a man who could be reasoned with. He and his wife represented the average middle-class black aspirants trying to make it. But he never made a move against the dominant white culture. Instead he nourished it. In one scene, after having been shot by the white hoodlum, Poitier struggles to save that man's life. In a purely Christian way, he forgives his opponent, saying: "Don't you think I'd like to put the rest of these bullets through his head? I can't . . . because I've got to live too. . . . He's sick. . . . He's crazy . . . but I can't kill a man just because he hates me." What red-blooded all-American white audiences in this Eisenhower age of normalcy could not have liked this self-sacrificing, all-giving black man? What integrationist-aspiring black audience would not be proud of this model of black respectability? Poitier was clearly a man for all races.

When one thinks of how much of Luther Brooks was to remain with actor Poitier, he is tempted to ask if scriptwriters Mankiewicz and Lesser Samuels should not be credited with creating the most important black actor in the history of American motion pictures. Obviously, what they did create was the character, the screen persona that Poitier was to popularize and capitalize on. In the early days, Poitier no more molded his image than did Stepin Fetchit; he lived out Hollywood's fantasies of the American black man.

The actor's second film was Zoltan Korda's 1952 adaptation of Alan Paton's South African drama, *Cry, the Beloved Country*. The feature starred Canada Lee as an old village priest journeying to Johannesburg in search of a son gone astray. In the city, where he is saddened by the poverty and filth and bewildered by the racism, he is aided in his search by a young priest played by Poitier. The movie made an ultimate plea for racial harmony and conciliation. Canada Lee had the finest role of his career. Poitier was a supporting player, but he brought good humor and a relaxed gregariousness to his priest. Moreover, the young Poitier was there to help a battered old man no one else in Johannesburg had the time for, and the humanity of his character (in keeping with his heroic code) merely added to the momentum of his career.

His next two films, *Red Ball Express* (1952) with Jeff Chandler and *Go, Man, Go* (1953) with the Harlem Globetrotters, cast Poitier in conventional bland supporting roles. *Red Ball Express*, a military adventure tale, did provide audiences with glimpses of one of Poitier's great prerogatives as a postwar freed black man, the emotional explosion. "Look, *boy*, where I come from you don't give orders. You take 'em," a racist soldier shouts when Poitier asks for a cup of coffee. But Poitier jumps upon him with passion and regains any lost dignity. Young black audiences loved him for it. Here at long last was a sane black man, free and strong enough to shout back to whitey.

Shouting back was very much a part of *The Blackboard Jungle* (1955). In this harrowing exposé of American high schools Poitier was costarred with Glenn Ford, Anne Francis, and Vic Morrow. He portrays Gregory Miller, an intelligent, complex student who fears that in the outside world there will be no place for a second-class citizen to take the lead. He hounds and torments white teacher Ford, who represents the oppressive system. He snarls, acts tough, and displays his virility more effectively than in any other film. "Come on! Go ahead! Hit me!" he yells to Ford. Here the disaffiliated young of the 1950s saw a man with a choice. He didn't have to take anything. Even before it was fashionable, he was bucking the corroding system. Yet at the same time, Poitier's Miller was an easily hurt, sensitive young man forced to live outside society. He was the classic loner of the 1950s, much like Marlon Brando and James Dean. And young audiences understood his loneliness, his confusion, and his entrapment because it was a comment on their own in the Eisenhower age. At *The Blackboard Jungle*'s conclusion, when he aids teacher Ford against a student with a switchblade, some of his earlier impact is diminished, but his code of decency is reaffirmed, and Poitier's Miller becomes a hero for young and old.

During the next four years Sidney Poitier worked in six motion pictures. In *Something of Value* (1957), with Rock Hudson, *Band of Angels* (1957), with Clark Gable and Yvonne De Carlo, and *The Mark of the Hawk* (1958) with Eartha Kitt and Juano Hernandez, he was an unlikely amalgam of *The Blackboard Jungle*'s Gregory Miller and *No Way Out*'s Luther Brooks. Sullen, angry, quick-tempered, and headstrong, he rebelled in many of these films, occasionally playing a modernized version of the black brute. (In the movies, most black men politically militant or merely politically motivated are simplified by the scenarists into the unreasonable, animalistic brutes of old.) But always, as if to save Poitier's image and the scriptwriter's white supremacist neck, the features concluded with Poitier's goodness and humanity reasserted, and once more audiences discovered him to be on the side of the angels. In this four-year period, the archetypal Poitier roles—the two that remain among the finest in his gallery of characters—were as Tommy Tyler in *Edge of the City* (1957) and as Noah Cullen in *The Defiant Ones* (1958).

The David Susskind–Martin Ritt production *Edge of the City* was an adaptation by Robert Alan Aurthur of his own television drama "A Man Is Ten Feet Tall," in which Poitier had already appeared. The story is about two men, a white and a black. In a true gesture of integrationist harmony, railroad worker Tommy Tyler befriends a wayward and confused army deserter (John Cassavetes). The story has a twist because for once it was the black man extending his hand to the white. Poitier helps the white man find a job, and then as his greatest manifestation of friendship invites him home to meet his wife (Ruby Dee) and have dinner. A Christlike figure, he stands for conscience and humaneness. But he is destroyed by his kindness and loyalty. During an argument with a fellow white worker in which Poitier defends Cassavetes, a fight breaks out. Poitier is winning. But he begs his white opponent to quit. When he turns to walk away, the white man stabs him in the back. Poitier dies in Cassavetes' arms.

Poitier's role won him great favor with the critics. *The New York Herald Tribune* called his black man one of deceptive simplicity. "With his quick smile and exhilarating talk," wrote the reviewer, "he can cajole the boy out of deep gloom. With a joke he can stop an ugly fight before it begins. But underneath he is a man of serious faith and deep strength, and when it's time for him to listen sympathetically or to say something important, he is the finest kind of friend." After *Edge of the City*, no moviegoer in America had any doubts about Poitier's talents. Nor did any fail to see what he represented. He was fast becoming a national symbol of brotherly love.

Oddly, when viewed today, the incongruities and disparities ignored by the audience of 1957 are blatantly apparent. Poitier's character falls into the tradition of the dying slave content that he has well served the massa. His loyalty to the white Cassavetes destroys him just as much as the old slave's steadfastness kept him in shackles. In this case, writer Aurthur smooths over the black man's death by having the white Cassavetes hunt down the killer.

Curiously, *Edge of the City* also revealed Sidney Poitier as a colorless black. So immersed is he in white standards that there is little ethnic juice in his blood. The dinner scene between Poitier, his wife, and their white friends is not an interracial summit meeting because there are no cultural gaps. Nor are there any cultural bridges to cross. All four are decent American citizens. Poitier also seems sexless in this movie. In previous features, scriptwriters were sure to keep Poitier's sexuality well hidden. He seldom had a serious movie romance. In those films in which he was married, it was generally to a sweet homebody type who seemed devoid of sexual passion. Mildred Jones Smith played this part in *No Way Out*. In *Edge of the City* it was Ruby Dee. She now remains the model movie mate for Poitier. (They have appeared in five films together.) An intense and talented actress, Ruby Dee is known for deft performances as unfulfilled, timid, troubled women. Certainly in *Edge of the City*, as she smiles sweetly at Poitier or proves how understanding and sensitive she is, audiences must have found the two a well-scrubbed sexless pair. One can understand why later militant patrons would view them both as sterile products of a decadent, materialistic Western culture. It should be noted that in one of their next films together, *A Raisin in the Sun* (1961), they effectively portrayed a couple with bedroom blues. Poitier's romantic apathy just about drives Dee up the wall in this film, and it is one reason why she wants to abort their expected child.

In the 1960s, Sidney Poitier's sexual neutralization became embarrassingly apparent, particularly when Hollywood provided romantic interest for him, albeit in a compromised manner. In *The Long Ships* (1964), when as a villainous Moor he kidnaps a beautiful white woman, he has been made to take a year's vow of celibacy. Therefore Poitier's sexual impulses remain safely suppressed. In *A Patch of Blue* (1965) he has a brief screen kiss with a blind white girl (Elizabeth Hartman). Everyone knows there is a romance developing between the two, but at the movie's end, rather than assert himself and bed the girl, he dutifully ships her off to a school for the blind. And in the notorious *Guess Who's Coming to Dinner* (1967) he wins the hand of a white girl in marriage, but they are a peculiarly unromantic couple who are seen kissing but once in the film, and the audience views this passionate event through a cabdriver's rear-view mirror. Later, in *They Call Me MISTER Tibbs* (1970), Poitier was finally cast opposite a vibrant, overtly sexual black woman, Barbara McNair. But audiences were openly baffled at seeing this beauty made up (with hair neatly groomed and clothes nicely dull and "tasteful") to look like Ruby Dee! Poitier's sexuality was still a problem for Hollywood moviemakers, and the attempts to keep him cool were so obvious that he seemed ludicrous. In the 1950s, however, audiences accepted the neutrality and rather respected him for it.

The Defiant Ones was Sidney Poitier's most important film of the decade. In it he played Noah Cullen, a black convict handcuffed to a white (Tony Curtis) as the two escape the law. Neither man likes the other. But before the picture ends, something akin to love has developed. For, once they have been unchained, the good Poitier comes to the rescue of Curtis, not out of necessity but out of brotherly love. Again he sacrifices himself, this time not with his death but his freedom, all for the sake of his white friend. In this film, one of his biggest hits, Poitier alienated a certain segment of the audience. When he saved his honky brother, he was jeered at in ghetto theaters. Black audiences were consciously aware for the first time of the great tomism inherent in the Poitier character, indeed in the Poitier image. Stanley Kramer's drama had glossed over the real issues and bleached out its black hero. Yet to Poitier's credit, his power as an actor demanded that the role and the film be taken seriously, and the jeers were somewhat muffled when he received an Oscar nomination for best actor of the year.

Porgy and Bess was Poitier's last film of the 1950s. The movie portrayed blacks as the singing, dancing, clowning darkies of old. Poitier accepted the role of Porgy only after much pressuring, and, although his performance was engaging, he seemed out of place. Here it was 1959. There was Martin Luther King. There were sit-ins, demonstrations, and boycotts. And what was America's black idol doing? There he stood singing, "I got plenty of nothin', and nothin's plenty for me."

In retrospect, it can be said that all the Poitier films of the 1950s were important and significant. Because they were all made to please a mass white audience at a time when the main topic of conversation was school desegregation, today their messages may seem rigged or naïve. But they retain a certain raw-edged bite and vigor. Audiences still respond to the actor's sophistication and charm, to his range and distinctly heroic quality. In the 1960s, Hollywood belittled and dehumanized Poitier's great human spirit by making it vulgarly superhuman. He became SuperSidney the Superstar, and he was depicted as too faithful a servant, the famous Poitier code then a mask for bourgeois complacency and sterility. But in the 1950s his work shone brightly. For black and white Americans he was a marvelous reason for going to the movies. And whether an integrationist or a separatist age likes it or not, Sidney Poitier's movie characters in the 1950s singlehandedly made audiences believe things would work out, that they were worth working out. It was still just a beautiful dream, but often that's what great movies and careers are all about.

In Praise of Character Actors

14

RUDOLF ARNHEIM

The players in our films can be divided at first glance into two categories, as we would say in a German school composition: leading actors and character actors. The character actors' acting surrounds that of the heroes like a baroque frame surrounds a renaissance painting. The fat uncle with a monkey and travelling blanket, the skinny piano teacher with a bun and pince-nez, the decrepit mayor, the hunchbacked inventor, the Galician profiteer, the bloated ship's cook—these are the character actors. They lend spice to the film. Sweetness and beauty, though, we get from people of a different type and a higher pay scale: neatly combed and freshly washed, the lovers romp around the inner circle of the plot.

"Character," according to *Meyer's Universal Encyclopedia* is to be understood as an exaggerated and caricaturized element of art. On the contrary, we would like to propose that the character actor shows man as he is; the heroic actor shows man as he would like to be. The character actor is a special type, the heroic actor a general type. The character wears the individual aura of the genuine, and this starts with his clothing. From the iron cravat to the laced boots, from the coiled coiffure to the tooth on the watch fob, the character actor's costume offers up a complete, highly disparate collection of the curiosities of human apparel. The leading actor's garb presents us with schematic standard types: tuxedo and evening dress, bathing suit and pyjamas—flawless models that dare not bear the physiognomical imprint of their wearer's uniqueness. One spot on the vest, a lost button on the trousers—highly recognized means of distinguishing the character actor—would cause the hero to give the studio hairdresser a tongue-lashing and provoke the public to unseemly laughter. The character actor is by request unshaven, freckled, cross-eyed, has wrinkles on his neck, dirty fingernails, and missing teeth. Hero and heroine, on the other hand, are bathed in lily's milk, and a pimple on the chin can destroy entire days of shooting.

The acting displays the same differences as the make-up. The character actor swallows the wrong way or swallows his words, he scratches his head, he slips, he licks a stamp, he kisses someone on both cheeks with a smack. The lead actors fall into each other's arms like dancers, they glide up and down stairways, they turn their heads graciously from the *en face* view to the clear profile, they lift their shapely hands, they spread their arms, and their facial expressions show a charming symmetry even in intense pain.

Both stylize; otherwise, they wouldn't be actors. But the character actor's models exist in reality, the hero's only in the pictorial advertisements of the cosmetic industry. The hero is the "man without qualities." Of necessity he possesses a sex and an age, but this exhausts his personal traits. One can confuse lead actors, never character actors. Whether a female lead role is played by Lilian Harvey, Marianne Winkelstern, Renate Mueller, Kaethe von Nagy, Mady Christians, Maria Paudler, or Liane Haid, whether the lover is played by Froehlich, Brausewetter, Liedtke, Stuewe, Verebes, Lederer, or Trevor, only the slightest nuances and the contracts which have been coincidentally drawn up differentiate them. How, though, could we ever confuse Gerron with Junkermann, Sandrock with Wangel, Bressart with Rasp, Puffy with Arno? This is not to belittle the acting talents of the leading players, but only the way in which they are used. The character actor's individuality is often emphasized to the point of unbearability, so that he bears more resemblance to a prehistoric amphibian than a respectable contemporary man with a right to vote and a five-room apartment—the leading player's uniqueness is filed down so forcibly that such different and unique actresses as Harvey and Sten cannot be told apart under the same ship officer's cap and after the same application of makeup.

Even average directors have the most charming notions so long as they're working with character actors. They cleverly use original props and work on the most effective mannerisms of facial expression, speech, and gesture. The leading player they mold into a mannequin, forbid him everything impulsive, everything new, everything mundane. His sorrow and his pain must submit to the conventional gymnastics, and, just as in court, nothing may be added and nothing withheld.

What must be demanded of practical directorial work is the penetration of the character actor's methods into the hero's territory. The great success of Hans Albers is due in significant part to the fact that he works in this manner. He plays the hero, the lover, but at the same time he acts like a normal person, like a character actor. He yawns, he makes faces, he doesn't behave himself. Not that we're recommending bad behavior for bon vivants here. But how much liveliness, how much direct contact to the public would be gained if we got away from the childish prejudice that lovers must be on their high horses just because their enlargements appear in the advertisements. The actors would breathe sighs of relief, they would be more interested in what they're doing, and they would have more opportunity to demonstrate their individuality. We should allow ourselves to let the lead player act, without pressure being put on him regarding his costume, make-up and acting—just as individually, just as mundanely, and inflicted with just as many tragic flaws as the character actors. We should let ourselves be convinced that wrinkled trousers are thoroughly reconcilable with a love scene, and that a young hero can blow his nose upon learning of his mother's death over the telephone. If we dare it, it will immediately be apparent what a wealth of untapped possibilities lie hidden here, and what charming warmth and naturalness remain to be drawn out of the simplest plot motif.

Let us dethrone the studios' values and take a look around outside, and we will be astonished to see that in this, our real world, there aren't any leading men to be seen, only characters!

The Lives of Supporting Players

15

DAVID THOMSON

Let us wonder for a moment whether we have a shared understanding of what a character actor is. A character actor plays someone who is not at the heart of a film, or, if at the center, not someone whose decisions are the crux of the drama? Thus, Walter Brennan is a character actor in *Red River*, the narrator (either on the page or on the sound track), its observer, but not a protagonist. Walter Brennan's Groot does very little in *Red River* except toss knives or feed lines into the plot when required. He is a fond witness, a model for us. Moreover, he lets the film make fun of his false teeth: stars are edgy about such scenes.

But a character actor is not obliged to appear all through a film. He or she may need only a few moments; perhaps one drop-dead scene will do. There is not a lot of Lee Strasberg's Hyman Roth in *The Godfather, Part* II, just a weary, fragile man watching the football game on TV in Miami, and the old fellow surprised and briefly delighted by being met at the airport.

When Oscar time comes round, these people are known as "supporting players." The edifice of a picture has stars for spires, and such as Walter Brennan, Thelma Ritter, M. Emmet Walsh and Stockard Channing are their loyal, sturdy and obedient buttresses. Aren't they? Except who ever met a supporting actor who didn't serve in the belief and expectation that they could and would, and also should, be a star? Every Harry Dean Stanton has his *Paris, Texas*, or deserves it. Just by virtue of their color, eccentricity, vivacity *and* fidelity, don't our most beloved character actors suggest a logic, or a passion, in which their characters are at least as important as any others on view?

May I ask a question? How many of you readers are, in life, merely the subsidiary/supports for others? How many of you, on the other hand, are the centers of your known world? You don't have to be as assertive as Buddy Love in *The Nutty Professor*. Tactful preeminence is in order. Still, aren't *we* the subject? And in those cases where, as yet, owing entirely to unruly circumstances, our centrality has not yet been fully acknowledged, how great is the need, the hurt, the anger and the energy that build because of obscurity?

Put it another way: in the horizon of life that surrounds *The Maltese Falcon*, does Sydney Greenstreet's Casper Gutman really believe that the morose, blunt Sam Spade is at the center of things? Doesn't Sam go back to bitter sleep when the story is over? Whereas Gutman has a mission, a calling, a veritable El Dorado—Oh yes, sir! you can hear him hiss. Despite his bulk he is a driven soul, burning with quest for the falcon, and exercising that unspent, coiled rapture in droll, serpentine conversation. As John Huston found, it was very hard to put

Gutman in a composition and not have him take the eye. He is, you see, the shining idealist in the film. He is full of hope, love, need and desire—and desire is always beautiful in the movies, for it reminds us of ourselves.

So, where are we in our definition? Character actors play roles of considerable importance in pictures, yet not the biggest. And just because the action seems to employ them in the service of the gods, they may sometimes thrive, flower and linger in our memories more than the stars. Is it just because they have character? But if they have the character, then what is left for those weightier actors, the alleged stars? What could there be beyond character, except some inane, ghostly glamour that we have come to worship? What does it say about our films, and ourselves, if we put anything so mysterious, so phantom, ahead of character?

There are many practical, professional differences between characters and stars that may help us appreciate the mixture of nature and myth in our movies. The matter of composition is no small matter. Stars live through close-ups; it is there that they exist, radiate and preside. Character actors do sometimes get close-ups, but only so that their characters may explain, lie, listen, threaten, make jokes, go mad or be the kind of small, vain fusspot not worthy to 'rule over films.' Stars sometimes just wait, reflect and dwell in themselves in close-ups. Character actors never get that time: they have to be busy; that engine once known as story has to earn their time and intimacy. (We may love character actors because their scenes tend to tell the story—as opposed to suffering from it.)

It follows that character actors do not get the same kind of light. They do not have stand-ins, and so their lighting is arranged quickly; it is done so that they may be visible, not emotional or atmospheric. More or less, for 50 years, character actors had the same lighting: it was on. Thus, they do not look as good as stars—but, the system says, they never did; that's why they are character actors, not stars, with fat, scars, lines and quirks to prove it. They are the system's conciliatory gesture to the unlovely masses; they are meant to be like us. So we should defend them and urge them to keep the faith with flaw and defect. Sydney Greenstreet would have been ill-advised to lose 150 pounds. Wasn't it dieting that killed Laird Cregar? If Thelma Ritter had woken up one morning looking like Gene Tierney she'd have been lost. For no one could ever have endured a Tierney who could think and talk, and who wasn't endlessly pliant to male dreams and wishes. (That still goes on: Rhea Perlman's Carla in *Cheers* utters the wisecracks of romantic dis-abuse.)

Character actors don't get script or direction in the way stars do. (I know I am begging the question whether either of these commodities is really current. But bear with me, entertain the fancy that they help a picture.) Character actors are hired to *be* Warren Oates or Spring Byington, Elisha Cook or Eve Arden. Casting is thought to settle an identity and remove further problems. Such tried-and-true players can turn up and deliver to order. If they only see a script a few days or hours before shooting, never mind, for they know what they do, and they know that's why you've hired them. They are automatic, axiomatic. So the director can give all his time to pry the star out of his trailer and out of a bad mood/bad high/bad omen cul-de-sac long enough to be glorious. Sometimes if there isn't any script, a character actor may be looked to as the person who knows best how Ben Johnson or Marie Windsor talks. So character actors are movie buffs.

They have to love the medium, for they are not paid on anything like the scale stars enjoy. Nor do character actors come in for residuals if their pictures turn into hits or classics. This helps them, they are told; for, without security, they have to keep on working—and doesn't everyone know that an actor's craft needs to be honed every day, just the way Kirby Puckett likes four at-bats every day? It's only the stars who can get away with taking a year off. They're secure. From a tax point of view they may need to rest for the next ten months. And at $6 million a picture, who wants to work just for the sake of it and risk a dog that could drag their stock down? They don't have to hit, they only need to be the designated hitter.

Character actors must feel unusually isolated. They do not have an entourage, and their followings must be taken on trust. Even among the readers of a movie magazine, how many people today could put the right name to the face if the pictures were of John Mahoney, Dan Seymour, Richard Bright, Mercedes Ruehl, Tom Noonan, Charles Napier, Barbara Baxley, Verna Bloom, Margaret Wycherley, James Villiers? Just because they all set out hoping to be leads, they live with disappointment, draining struggle, and the lie that they are happy the way things worked out. Television is their best chance of fulfillment, for that is where natural character actors—from Ed Asner to Betty White, from Michael Tucker to Blair Brown—may get series, prominence, work and residuals. TV is certainly the arena in which the most interesting ensemble acting is to be seen in America. It is also the medium in which pressures of budget and schedule fight the last battle against the prevaricating whim and neurotic hesitation of stars.

Nor is there any evidence that America is suffering in its supply of character actors, *Hill Street Blues* and *L.A. Law* have been rich proving grounds, even if many of the Blues seem to have died with the series. In the selection that follows, there is ample evidence of quality and daring. Moreover, we still have a few so-called star actors who honor the attitudes embodied in character acting—I am thinking of Gene Hackman, Alec Guinness, Robert Duvall, Meryl Streep, Vanessa Redgrave, Susan Sarandon.

But the most important point that an introductory essay like this can make is to remind us of how often America's movie-making has excelled when it has been founded in something like a stock company, a group of actors for whom human and social character has seemed more interesting than clout.

Consider the work of Griffith, Lubitsch, Welles, Preston Sturges, Hawks, Ford, Coppola and Altman. Not that any of them have proved helpless or intransigent with stars and starry shows—so long as one remembers Welles' insinuating and Gutmanesque need to be that star himself, and Altman's preoccupied but casual urge to knock the shine off big-name actors. Griffith helped define stardom as a narrative device; Lubitsch cherished the vanity of all actors, especially the pomp of small men; Hawks made so rare an icon of Lauren Bacall that no other director could ever rediscover it. John Ford is largely responsible for what we think of as John Wayne; and Coppola has drawn extraordinary, dominating performances from Al Pacino, Gene Hackman and Marlon Brando.

But those starry triumphs cannot be detached from the aura of the group that pervades *The Godfather*, *Only Angels Have Wings*, *The Shop Around the Corner*, *The Magnificent Ambersons* or *Nashville*. In some of those cases, it may be argued that the community of actors has produced a sentimentality that hinders the action or the meaning of a film; there is a false clubbiness possible in such films. In John Ford, the rhetoric of team spirit can serve as a blithe cover for military obedience. There is so much more dispute, contradiction and everyone-talking-and-thinking-at-once in the groups of Howard Hawks. Further, in *The Godfather*, it is the very intensity of family feeling that leaves the behavior of the Corléones so ambiguous. We have such a good time watching the feeding interplay of Pacino, Duvall, James Caan, Richard

Castellano, Abe Vigoda and John Cazale, that we sometimes forget what it is the team does. The process of the movie reveals the beguiling Don in Coppola—yet there are those in his real extended family who have beheld not just a patriarch, but a loner, a user and a prince of darkness to match Michael Corleone. From Capra to Coppola, there are films that rhapsodize over community yet plot dictatorship.

There is a more challenging ideal in movie-making, which is to show us the group as a natural, helpless arrangement, not so much a unified team as the inevitable gathering together of lonely, suspicious, unhappy individuals who will occasionally rise to states of love, rapport and association, before slipping away from one another. This is a view of life that respects both solitariness and responsibility, and which sees how private lives and actions cannot help but affect public experience. It leads to a kind of film that spreads beyond the frame or a set storyline; it invokes a continuity and a crowded context that go on, seemingly, forever. Needless to say, it understands how far the common state of experience is that flux of farce and tragedy in which we would all like to be at the center of the wheel. But cannot be. Any objective observer sees a wheel, but subjectivity insists there are as many wheels as there are spokes. This is a way of seeing that confronts a factory of wheels; it is the cinema of Renoir and Mizoguchi—it is not entirely American.

For example, such a view does not fit well with tidy, conclusive and uplifting endings, or with any notion of some roles or lives being grander than others. The panorama of many small lives—of character actors—produces doubt, dismay and caution. Whereas so many American films want us to feel good.

Let me process three films which do pass this test with honors: *The Shop Around the Corner*; *The Magnificent Ambersons* and *Nashville*. In the Lubitsch picture, the title signals how far the place is the subject, even if it is a Culver City Budapest: James Stewart and Margaret Sullavan are stars, and the discovered love between their characters is the destination of the story. Yet it is a movie about misunderstanding and off-setting context, of many different things going on at once, of chance revelation and unexpected benefit. And it is in the company of Frank Morgan, Joseph Schildkraut, Felix Bressart. Sara Haden and William Tracy that we see a collection of stories and a climate of confusion such that Stewart and Sullavan pass as equal characters, noble fools living in the same light as everyone else. In *Ambersons*, love and happiness cannot be achieved anywhere without some corresponding loss elsewhere: a kind of emotional bookkeeping is at work, and no accumulation of assets or sentimental credit is proof against failure. It is that rare American film in which every character fails—no wonder the system lacked the heart to finish it. *Nashville* is the apotheosis of this way of looking: it is a film about the crowd, maybe the first American film about us, the audience, that throng of unnamed character actors.

16

Supporting Character

The Queer Career of Agnes Moorehead

PATRICIA WHITE

The main character of Robert Aldrich's *The Killing of Sister George* is a role-playing lesbian in more than one sense. In "real life" June Buckridge (Beryl Reid) is "George," a bawdy, domineering) cigar-smoking butch, whose younger lover Childie keeps house and collects dolls. As the country nurse "Sister George" on a television soap opera, she is a character actress beloved by the public. Produced in 1968, on the verge of Stonewall and just in time to receive an X under the ratings system that finally replaced the Production Code, *The Killing of Sister George* is one of the first Hollywood films to represent lesbianism openly. But, in making its main character a character actress, the film suggests that lesbians may always have been present in popular culture, accepted and loved by audiences in genres that never admitted of the existence of homosexuality.

The film thematizes the continuity between the off-screen "masculine," tweed-suited dyke type and the on-screen "asexual," tweed-suited nurse type—thus George is able to appropriate her lesbian moniker from her television character—and demonstrates that the very construction of the "asexual" is, of course, a heterosexist one. At one point the drunken George makes a pass at a group of nuns in a taxicab—a scene that at once demonstrates her butch sexual courage and visibility and wittily restates the theme of covert and overt types. George ought to be able to recognize a sister when she sees one. In the film's lesbian bar scene, filmed on location and thus with extraordinary subcultural verisimilitude at London's Gateways Club—George and Childie dress up as Laurel and Hardy. This additional level of role-playing makes reference to a practice of comic typing that conceals homoerotic logic within a wildly popular mass cultural form.

When chic BBC executive Mercy Croft takes a fancy to Childie and has the Sister George character killed off the soap, following a familiar script of homophobic narrative exigency, the question of the actress's visibility as a lesbian is preempted. The supporting actress is offered instead the leading role in her very own series—as Clarabell the Cow. In Frank Marcus's play from which the film was adapted, Sister George was a character on a radio soap opera; the movie parallels the demotion from human to animal with the step down from on-camera ham to voice-over cow. Yet the role, however demeaning and misogynist, affords a certain finesse of George's disguise. At the end of the film, George, who had at first scornfully turned down the role of Clarabell, begins to practice her "moos." But even in her humiliation lies a certain triumph—her "unrepresentable" butch persona will still enter the homes of countless television viewers, her voice recognizable to her fans.

Agnes Moorehead was a familiar and popular television personality in the role of Endora on "Bewitched" when in one of the last of some sixty film roles she provided the voice of the goose in the animated feature *Charlotte's Web*. It was not a degrading part, as Clarabell Cow was meant to be—she co-starred with her "beloved friend" Debbie Reynolds, and Paul Lynde contributed to the barnyard fun. The role drew on her roots in radio—what one reviewer described as her trademark "crackling, snapping, sinister, paranoic, paralyzing voice."[1] And, before her stardom as television's preeminent witch, Moorehead reigned as one of the most widely recognized and highly regarded supporting actresses in Hollywood cinema. Like George, she played "types"; she was the silver screen's definitive spinster aunt. In accounting for the adaptability of her persona across a range of popular media, I believe that another element of Moorehead's star image must be considered. In an interview with Boze Hadleigh, "A Hollywood Square Comes Out," Lynde, a special guest star on "Bewitched" who played an "uncle" as aptly and as memorably as Moorehead played an "aunt," remarks, "Well, the whole world knows Agnes was a lesbian—I mean classy as hell, but one of the all-time Hollywood dykes."[2]

Regardless of whether the lady really was a lesbian, the characterization complements her persona. It represents a gendered node within what Eve Sedgwick has described as the modern Western "epistemology of the closet."[3] If the "whole world" knows about Agnes, the so-called general audience may exercise what Sedgwick calls "the privilege of unknowing"—after all, it's only entertainment. I would like to argue that it is no mere queer coincidence that Agnes Moorehead can be dubbed both one of the all-time Hollywood supporting actresses and one of the all-time Hollywood dykes. Moorehead is a prime candidate for gay hagiography. Her best known incarnation, Endora, is a camp icon; she passes even the cinephile test, having been featured in films by auteurs such as Welles, Sirk, Ray, and Aldrich. But, more important, Moorehead's ubiquity and longevity as a character actress are such that she can be identified with the very media in which she triumphed, with the regime of popular entertainment itself, and with the continuities and ruptures in gender and sexual ideology that can be read off from it. At once essential to classical realism and marginal to its narrative goals, the supporting character is a site for the encoding of the threat and the promise of female deviance. As New York lesbian performance artist Lisa Kron writes in a biographical note, reflecting on the animal and grandmother roles she was asked to play in college, "It begins to dawn on her that 'character actress' is really a code word for lesbian."[4] The negative valence of many of Moorehead's roles is marked—Endora herself is the butt of a constant barrage of mother-in-law jokes. Her persona is less "heartwarming" than many a golden age supporting actress—from Anne Revere to Mary Wickes to Marjorie Main. Although the ideological stake in subordinating female difference is apparent, this negativity may also be Moorehead's most subversive edge.

My discussion of Moorehead takes up three overlapping areas of inquiry: the narrative function of supporting characters in the heterosexual Hollywood regime (as well as the ideological weight that they carry in television's world of family values); the importance of typification in these roles and in lesbian recognizability more generally; and the understanding of star images as complex, contradictory signs, as exemplified in the work of gay film theorist Richard Dyer as well as in the reception practices of gay culture.

What is it that supporting characters are meant to "support" if not the imbricated ideologies of heterosexual romance and white American hegemony permeating Hollywood cinema? They prop up a very particular representational order. As Stephen Heath describes the operation of narrativity, "The film picks up . . . the notable elements (to be noted in and for the progress of the narrative which in return defines their notability) without for all that giving up what is thus left aside and which it seeks to retain—something of an available reserve of insignificant material—in order precisely to ring 'true,' true to *reality*." Retained to speak a social "truth," the supporting character represents "an available reserve of insignificant," if "realistic," types of women—workers, older women, nonwhite women. Lacking a love interest—Hollywood deems only one type of love of interest—she doesn't get "picked up" by the story: in the most basic narratological terms, she is the witch, not the princess. By film's end she has literally been left aside, just as she is compositionally marginal in the frame. For, as Heath economically puts it, "Narrative contains a film's multiple articulations as a single articulation, its images as a single image (the 'narrative image,' which is a film's presence, how it can be talked about, what it can be sold and bought on—in the production stills displayed outside a cinema, for example)."[5] Supporting characters are sacrificed to the narrative image of heterosexual closure; their names rarely appear in the television-guide blurbs about old movies, nor are their photographs included on the videotape box that delivers a "picture" to a potential viewer.

Yet attention to the function of certain types of female characters can throw into relief the single-mindedness with which the Hollywood system re-presents heterosexuality. For example, the discourse of lesbian desire introduced by housekeeper Mrs. Danvers (Judith Anderson) in Hitchcock's *Rebecca* significantly undercuts the film's conventional romantic "resolution." And, while melodramatic pathos depends on Jane Wyman's long separation from Rock Hudson in Sirk's *Magnificent Obsession*, an alternative reading—or a different focus of spectatorial regard—might note that she spends this off-screen time in the company of her devoted nurse/companion, played by Agnes Moorehead, who offered Wyman support in four films besides. A film may be dismissive of a minor player, portray her fate as gratuitous, but it may take less time and care to assimilate her to its ideological project than it would in the case of the female protagonist. In Hedda Hopper's column "Bit Player Outshines the Stars," Moorehead remarks, "I sort of look at myself sideways on the screen."[6] While this comment indicates a failure of narcissistic identification, even, perhaps, a cringing at the conservatism to which her image is often harnessed, it also suggests an astute reading of her liminal, and at times disruptive, narrative function. It replicates, too, the oblique sightline traced on Hollywood cinema by many queer spectators.

Nurses, secretaries, career women, nuns, companions, and housekeepers connote, not lesbian identity, but a deviation from heterosexualized femininity. Gay male critics often register an affinity with such characters. Inasmuch as character actresses are enjoyed, admired, or pressed into camp service by a queer mode of reading, it is apparently character itself that is supported. Thelma Ritter, a great ironic interpreter of this type of role, was a particular favorite of gay film historian Vito Russo, for example. In his book on the gay sensibility, Michael Bronski singles out the woman friend that "many top female stars were paired off with . . . before they ended up getting the leading man" as a cinematic type with particular appeal. Portrayed by the likes of Joan Blondell and Eve Arden, "the sidekick's role was generally to act as a confidante and to give the audience a pungent analysis of the plot. Sidekicks were sarcastic, unromantic, and sensible. They were cleverly self-deprecating . . . but could also turn the wit on men. Too smart ever to get the man, sidekicks had to settle for being funnier than everybody else. For gay men who would never walk off into the sunset with a leading man, the sidekick was a dose of real life." Bronski attributes a sort of metacritical role to confidante characters and a self-conscious reading practice to their fans, but he reads these images in relation only to male characters and spectators. He goes on to cite Russo's work on sissy roles and the actors who specialized in their portrayal in Hollywood films of the thirties and forties. Bronski asserts, "Woman sidekicks were never played as lesbians, just 'old maids,' but the non-romantic male was always implicitly gay."[7]

Given the virtual conceptual blank that is lesbianism in the culture at large, it is no accident that the social types standing in for lesbians in Hollywood cinema are misogynistically coded as "asexual." They are trivialized and rendered comical rather than threatening. Although sex and ideology certainly mark the stereotypes of sissy and old maid differently, in particular in relation to tropes of gender inversion, Bronski's statement limits the operation of the connotative in the female images and thus compounds the invisibility to which lesbians are already consigned.

In contrast, one lesbian writer confidently attributes sexuality to a much later incarnation of the "old maid" type. In a cover article for *Lesbian News* entitled "The Truth about Miss Hathaway," Marion Garbo Todd defends the spinster secretary character played by Nancy Kulp on the sixties American sitcom "The Beverly Hillbillies" from the following assessment in the fan magazine *Television Collector*: "Miss Jane Hathaway could have been the prototype for the term 'Plain Jane.' Tall and lanky, with an asexual manner, the epitome of a spinster." Todd retorts, "Where does this 'plain Jane' stuff come from? How can the word plain be used to describe the handsome Miss Hathaway? 'Tall and lanky' is not the right phrase for her body; 'long and sensuous' is much more accurate. Her long neck, aquiline nose, wavy hair, and large bright eyes made her very beautiful. She had smile lines to swoon over, and her voice was a delight. . . . In her tasteful skirt suit, short hairdo, and horn-rimmed glasses, she could have been the lead character in any lesbian pulp novel."[8]

Visual codes are recognized, enumerated, and deployed to cast Kulp in a leading role in a different genre. In her groundbreaking work on studio-era lesbian director Dorothy Arzner, Judith Mayne notes that, in her films, secondary women characters can be seen sporting the dapper dress and masculine manner that Arzner herself affected. Lesbianism is made visible within the text through ironic inflection of an "asexual" type.[9]

As Richard Dyer writes, in an essay on "typical" lesbian and gay representations, "A major fact about being gay is that it doesn't show. . . . There are signs of gayness, a repertoire of gestures, expressions, stances, clothing, and even environments that bespeak gayness, but these are cultural forms designed to show what the person's person alone does not show: that he or she is gay. Such a repertoire of signs, making visible the invisible, is the basis of any representation of gay people involving visual recognition, the requirement of recognizability in turn entailing that of typicality."[10] Thus, historically and culturally specific codes in lesbian and gay communities function similarly to the codes of recognition in popular cultural forms. In this light, the often-heard demand for nonstereotypical, "well-rounded" gay and lesbian characters in film may go against the very conditions of our visibility. Dyer detects the prevalence of the sexological discourse of "in-betweenism"—the notion that homosexuals betray characteristics of the opposite gender—in a range of typical visual representations, including self-representations, of effeminate men and mannish women. Citing *The Killing of Sister George*, he sees both George's tweeds and her rival Mercy Croft's chic and tailored predatory look as variations on this "dyke" type.[11] The vexed question of lesbian stereotyping can be related to the potentially subversive implications of more general practices of visual typing in female supporting characters.

The widespread apprehension of the Sister Georges or Miss Jane Hathaways as asexual or, worse, man starved—precisely invisible as lesbian—has to do, perhaps paradoxically, with the visual overdetermination of "woman" as sexual in film. The supporting character necessarily diverges from this ideal—not incidentally, a white one—of woman in film. The cinematic system of the look constructs the singular female star as image and guarantee of masculine desire and spectatorial fascination. As images of a different version of femininity than that of female stars, supporting characters may not ultimately be so supportive of the status quo, for they can inflect with female desire the image of woman embodied in the leading lady, with whom they are narratively paired and iconographically contrasted, often within the same frame.

One of the most consequential operations of Hollywood's containment and social enforcement of difference is the near-exclusive restriction of nonwhite and visually and audibly recognizable ethnic types precisely to supporting roles. Mary Ann Doane remarks that the "woman's film" genre is really the "white woman's film": "When black women are present, they are the ground rather than the figure; often they are made to merge with the diegesis. They inhabit the textual sidelines, primarily as servants."[12] The complexity, code crossing, and incoherence of racialized sexual and gender ideology is performed by the on-screen conjunction of, and contrast between, black and white women. The mammy stereotype, often denounced as "asexual," may be inflected as "lesbian" in its close articulation with the presentation of the white heroine's desire. Such a character, or a known performer such as Ethel Waters in a mammy role, might not merge altogether with the diegesis for African American, lesbian, and gay viewers.

A process of erotic doubling between a woman of color and the white star may also serve to figure lesbianism—for example, between Anna May Wong and Marlene Dietrich as traveling companions in *Shanghai Express*, in which the signifier *prostitution* sexualizes the contiguity of the two women. Or the racist projection of sexuality onto the "other woman" may indicate erotic tension between the stereotyped woman of color and the "repressed" and only presumptively heterosexual white heroine. Bette Davis's character performs two passionate acts in *The Letter*—she kills her lover in the opening sequence and goes into the night to meet her death at the hands of his Asian widow at the end. While the man in the triangle is never shown, the "other" woman's body is insistently present, bizarrely underscored by the excessive makeup and costuming used to transform white supporting actress Gale Sondergaard. This common casting practice foregrounds the way in which the representation of racial difference turns on the attributes of whiteness in the classical Hollywood cinema. In *Beyond the Forest*, the Davis character's long, center-parted black hair is uncannily mirrored in the background by that of her mocking Latina maid, played by Mexican actress Dona Drake. At a crucial point in the story, the heroine disguises herself in the jeans and flannel shirt worn by her servant. That the masquerade involves an element of gender transgression ironically makes visible the irreducible difference between women—race, class, and power—that appears to give such doubling its frisson.

Judith Mayne goes on to discuss how images of Dorothy Arzner—often twoshots of her looking at a conventionally feminine actress—have been used to illustrate feminist critical texts that emphatically do not mention her lesbianism. When these lesbian looks, these exchanges of the gaze between contrasting female types—generally between supporting and lead actresses—are echoed in Arzner's films, Mayne argues, they can be read as her authorial signature. In a two-shot from Raoul Walsh's *The Revolt of Mamie Stover*, the look of Agnes

Moorehead in her bathrobe prevents Jane Russell's sexuality from being perceived as intended for the male spectator alone. Yet the early feminist analysis of this film, too, ignored its lesbian visual economy. In another two-shot, Agnes Moorehead and Debbie Reynolds embody the visual relation between a supporting actress "type" and a bona fide female star. On-screen and off, the couple conforms to the stereotype of older, sapphic sophisticate who preys on innocent younger woman; in this case the singing nun.

While great Hollywood supporting actresses such as Thelma Ritter or Mercedes McCambridge could perhaps be read as working-class butch or fifties inbetweenist types, Agnes Moorehead's persona fits a more upper-class sapphic stereotype.[13] As a promotional item describes her, "Rated as one of the best dressed stars of screen and radio, her preference runs to tailored suits"—to recall Lynde's words, she was "classy as hell". On-screen, the spinster type refuses both the masculine signifiers that make lesbianism visible in heterosexual terms and the hyperbolization of the feminine that is the very definition of *womanliness*. The type is a product of a misogynist and heterosexist imagination—yet within it the spinster can at once "pass" as straight and be recognizable as lesbian.

It is impossible to unpack the ambivalent character of the narrative category of *support* and the negotiable aspects of visual typification apart from a consideration of the performer as text. Donald Bogle, in *Toms, Coons, Mulattoe, Mammies, and Bucks*, his influential book on African American stereotypes, presents the most sustained argument for how particular performers become visible in these roles and transform types. As he states in an interview, "There was another life and point of view that was being suggested to me by Hattie McDaniel's rather hostile edge."[14] It is Ritter's nurses, Arden's sidekicks, Franklin Pangborn's sissies, and McDaniel's maids that capture the imagination. The more roles an actress appears in, the more unforeseen the effects that are introduced in a particular text by her casting. Star texts are ongoing, modified by shifting ideological imperatives, shaped by audience response. On series television, the weekly appearance of the performer works like typecasting in studio films. It is in this sense that I want to speak of Moorehead's *queer career*.

In his work on stars, Dyer argues that, in narrative films, novelistic conceptions of character are articulated with stars as already signifying images—which essentially function within the same bourgeois ideology of the self-consistent individual. How might this approach apply to Moorehead, who, as a character actress, however familiar, is not strictly a "star"? As Dyer notes, "Type characters are acknowledged to have a place . . . but only to enable the proper elaboration of the central, individuated character(s). In this respect, no star could be just a type, since all stars play central characters."[15] Moorehead does not have a fully individuated star image (at least not before "Bewitched"), yet neither can her on-screen type be considered merely an extension of her off-screen "self" (which would reintroduce the category of the individual in another way). She has a subversive edge that does not get "rounded off." What was distinct was the fact of her acting, which allowed her to represent and to "quote" a type at the same time.

Agnes Moorehead's long career encompassed a gallery of types connoting female difference. Her early success was achieved on radio as, among other things, a stooge to male comics. After she went to Hollywood with Orson Welles and the Mercury Theater, she continued her radio work as an all-purpose female voice, impersonating Eleanor Roosevelt and scores of other women on the "March of Time." Outside the Hollywood regime of the gaze, it seems that a deviant version of femininity could represent the norm. On-screen, she never portrayed a central character, receiving top billing only in the posthumously released horror flick *Dear Dead Delilah*. Instead, she played second fiddle, variations on the unmarried woman: nurses (*Magnificent Obsession*), nuns (*The Singing Nun*, *Scandal at Scourie*), governesses (*The Youngest Profession*, *The Untamed*), ladies' companions (*Mrs. Parkington*, *Her Highness and the Bellboy*), busybodies (*Since You Went Away*, *All That Heaven Allows*), hypochondriacs (*Pollyanna*), maids (*Hush, Hush, Sweet Charlotte*), and, of course, aunts.

In *The Magnificent Ambersons*, Jack Amberson rebukes his nephew for tormenting the Moorehead character: "You know George, just being an aunt isn't really the great career it may sometimes seem to be." But this, her second film, launched the actress on a trajectory that proved otherwise. Despite her fifth billing, she was named best actress by the New York Film Critics and went on to play aunts again in *Jane Eyre*, *Tomorrow the World*, *The Lost Moment*, *Summer Holiday*, *Johnny Belinda*, and *The Story of Three Loves*, and on Broadway in *Gigi* just before her death. For variety, she portrayed women in professions that lesbians might suitably pursue: a WAC commander (*Keep Your Powder Dry*), a prison superintendent (*Caged*), a literary agent (*From Main Street to Broadway*), a drama teacher (*Jeanne Eagels*), a mystery writer (*The Bat*), a judge (*Bachelor in Paradise*), and, in a blond wig, a "sort of school marm and madam rolled into one," offering firm support to Jane Russell's Mamie Stover.[16] When she played married women, she was generally a nagging wife, most notably in the radio play *Sorry, Wrong Number*, written expressly for her talents. Critics note the "waspish and neurotic," "mean-spirited, shrewish," "possessive, puritanical, and vitriolic," "bitter, nasty, frustrated," and "meddlesome" traits of her "old crones," "harridans, spinsters and bitches," "termagants and passionate viragos." Her many mother parts did not always evince maternal qualities. Besides Samantha, her screen offspring included Citizen Kane, Jesse James, and Genghis Khan. Her role in *The Story of Mankind* was a brief appearance as Queen Elizabeth I; she commissioned a portrait of herself costumed as the red-haired virgin queen.

The Agnes Moorehead of the "Bewitched" era (the show ran on ABC from 1964 to 1972) can aptly be described with the title of her one-woman show, in which she toured extensively in the fifties—"The Fabulous Redhead." On "Bewitched," she was a flippant, vividly costumed, outrageously madeup, impeccably coiffed, castrating witch with a mortal hatred for her daughter's husband, whose name she somehow could not recall. This is the Moorehead-as-"character" association that the contemporary viewer brings to her earlier film roles. Moorehead turned her Actress-with-a-capital-A stage image—regal bearing, exaggerated gestures and enunciation, and taste for high fashion—to high camp effect in her interpretation of Endora, flagrantly foregrounding "performance." Offscreen, she was nicknamed "Madame Mauve" because of her inordinate fondness for lavender, which she insisted on having everything "done" in—from her luggage and Thunderbird to her dressing room lightbulbs and maids' uniforms.[17]

Before the fifties stage and sixties television brought color to her roles, Agnes Moorehead was considered an actress of "character." Her Victorian-sounding name (her father was a minister), aristocratic profile, penchant for accents and other vocal trademarks, her manners, even manneredness, contributed to the public perception of Moorehead as a "serious" actress. As one critic notes, she is associated with "heavy dramatics on the grand scale. For many, Agnes's performances represent the near epitome of screen theatrics."[18] Although she was "typecast," versatility was regarded as part of her artistry.[19] A studio publicity item raved, "The accomplished character actress of stage, screen and radio is given here one of her rare opportunities to bid for romantic interest. The result is a revelation of a new facet of the versatile actress's many-sided repertory, strikingly effective."[20] The implication is that her ability to portray a heterosexual is a true sign of talent.

Moorehead was distinguished by four Academy Award nominations for best actress in a supporting role, although she never won the Oscar. As six-time loser Thelma Ritter cracked, "Always the bridesmaid and never the bride."[21] A profile in a nostalgia magazine muses about the fact that Moorehead never snagged the award: "It is an interesting speculation that one of the reasons she always lost was that she played neurotic aunts, stepmothers, spinsters who reflected the dark side of the human condition."[22] That the old maid should evoke such a grandiose conception as the dark side of the human condition attests to Moorehead's considerable achievement—she makes the spinster positively sinister. In an essay on the functions of feminist criticism, Tania Modleski chastises a male literary critic who, "casting about for an example of the trivial, strikes irresistibly upon the image of the spinster." "From a feminist point of view," Modleski argues, "nothing could be *more* 'historically and ideologically significant' than the existence of the single woman in patriarchy, her (frequently caricatured) representation in patriarchal art, and the relationship between the reality and the representation."[23] Moorehead's image captured some of this, perhaps lesbian, significance, if only in the mirror image of anxiety. The profile goes on to suggest how closely the spinster image was identified with the actress: "Never married, she, nevertheless, had an adopted son; a close friendship with Debbie Reynolds, with whom she co-starred in several of her last pictures; and a religious faith as a Methodist." This "nevertheless" means to blur over a logical relation between spinster and lesbian that the syntax sets up: "Never married, she had a close friendship with Debbie Reynolds." The statement is interesting for another reason: its blatant, symptomatic contradiction of fact, for Agnes Moorehead was married at least twice (Reynolds mentions three unions). I presume that the actress's much-vaunted privacy and cultivated "mystery" were not intended to conceal this facet of her "many-side repertory."

Moorehead's image reconciles the serious with the trivial—having "character" with being "a character"—and thus occupies the domain of camp. As Susan Sontag notes, "Camp is the glorification of 'character.' . . . Character is understood as a state of continual incandescence —a person being one, very intense thing. . . . Wherever there is development of character, Camp is reduced."[24] Camp is a crucial and far from trivial dimension of Moorehead's reception, but, with its emphasis on style, it is an insufficient analytic category for a feminist consideration of what is at stake in the "content" of her image. Looking at how that image was articulated in and utilized by certain of her films can illuminate the contradiction that she embodies, as a figure simultaneously necessary to the Hollywood system and suppressed by it. She is taken seriously, featured in so many films as to seem ubiquitous. At the same time, her parts are marginal ones, the characters she portrays trivialized or vilified. If her roles as written often smack of misogyny, as performed they suggest a different negativity—a negativity that cannot be represented within the terms of classical cinema and that shares the semiotic field of lesbianism.

Fanny Minnafer in Orson Welles's *The Magnificent Ambersons* is the role that established at once Moorehead's reviled spinster image *and* the difficulty of reconciling that image with the Hollywood plot. Lacking economic independence, Aunt Fanny lives with the fading Amberson clan as an observer rather than as a participant. *The Magnificent Ambersons* is a self-conscious film, and her restlessness and discontent contribute greatly to its mood. She accuses her nephew George, "You wouldn't treat anybody in the world like this, except old Fanny. 'Old Fanny,' you say, 'it's nobody but old Fanny so I'll kick her. Nobody'll resent it, I'll kick her all I want to.'" But the film inscribes Fanny's position on the periphery—lurking in the shadows to whisper her suspicions to George, looking on from the edge of the frame or the background of the composition—as a vantage point for the spectator. She actually prevents the formation of two heterosexual couples by her interference. In material excised from the film's release version, Fanny is shown at the end among a veritable colony of spinsters at the boarding house. Her discourse pervades the film, even if she triumphs only as the representative of its themes of frustration and barrenness.

One commentator characterizes the challenge for Moorehead as an actress, "to channel her tremendous energy so that it would emerge in accord with the film rather than as an intriguing distraction."[25] Elements of her tour-de-force characterization of Aunt Fanny erupt as fascinating "distractions" in such later roles as Mrs. Reed in *Jane Eyre* and Countess Fosco in *The Woman in White*. The question of Moorehead's discordant difference and of her relation to the fulfillment of the romance plot is marked in another literary film, *The Lost Moment* (1947). In this adaptation of Henry James's *The Aspern Papers*, Moorehead plays the elderly aunt who in her youth was the recipient of love letters from a famous poet. A mere octogenarian in the novella becomes a hideously madeup 105-year-old in the film. It is as if the plausibility of Moorehead's participation in such a romance even in the past demands extremes of disguise.

Moorehead thoroughly embraced that inexplicable quality of her characters that prompted others to react with dislike, even phobia. In *Since You Went Away* (directed by John Cromwell, 1944), David O. Selznick's sentimental story of women on the homefront during World War II, Agnes portrays a local busybody, a character who embodies a displaced anxiety about the unheroic activities in which women might become involved while the menfolk are away at war. Joseph Cotten's character repeatedly insults her, joking that the sound of her voice grates on him even when he's far away from her. The penetrating, persecuting female voice signifies here not only as a quality of Moorehead's character, Emily Hawkins, but as Moorehead as an actress, who often worked with Cotten. Ultimately, the disparate desires of the women in the film are rallied into patriotic solidarity when they castigate the Moorehead character for petty war profiteering. The film scapegoats her to consolidate both nationalist and gender ideology, a project that could be seen as operating across the forties, the period in which Moorehead's image was established.

In *Good Dames*, his book on five female "character stars" (supporting actresses rarely receive individual biographies), James Robert Parish comments on Moorehead's performance in this film:

> The role itself was a variation of the cinema type portrayed throughout the 1940s by the very adept Eve Arden. The difference in these two actresses' approach to such a part is that whenever Agnes is required to make a flip remark on the screen, it comes across in total seriousness as a reflection of her character's basic, unregenerate meanness. Her piercing eyes and overall body movements provide the viewer with no other interpretation. In contrast, Arden can toss off the most devastating remark, and it emerges as a pert observation, juicy and smart, but essentially nonvicious.[26]

Although Moorehead did play essentially nonvicious roles, she was more convincing—and less recuperable—in her moments of unregenerate meanness. The subversiveness of the best character stars, such as Arden and Ritter, can be neutralized by their being enthusiastically adopted as cuddly curmudgeons. Moorehead's unlikableness, on the razor-thin edge of misogynist dismissal, contravenes this tendency. It is hard to embrace Moorehead without being spattered with acid.

Madge Rapf in the Bogart/Bacall vehicle *Dark Passage* (1947), directed by Delmar Daves, is a curious sort of femme fatale, whose fate is a telling example of the retribution that the Moorehead character could bring down. Moorehead's being cast against character in a "sexual" role is in part responsible for the film's surreal effects.[27] As Dana Polan comments in an important analysis, "The narrative of *Dark Passage* is one in which dramatic coincidences occur so often as to break down any question of plausibility."[28] When Madge happens to knock at the door of the apartment where, through an unlikely chain of circumstances, escaped convict Vincent Parry (Bogart) is hiding, he instantly recognizes the voice of his nemesis. Madge had testified against him at his murder trial. As he observes, "She's the type that comes back, and back again." This not only indicates how she functions in the film as the return of the repressed but is a fitting comment on Moorehead's career.

Madge's character is attributed with the evil, inconsistency, and unintelligibility of motive of an ordinary femme fatale, without the movie conceding that sexuality is her tool for leading men to destruction. Instead, her fatal quality seems to be the simple fact of her existence, rendered as "interference" through Moorehead's "nagging" connotations. As Vincent describes her, "Madge knows everybody, pesters everybody." Her ex-fiancé, Bob, snaps at her, "You're not satisfied unless you're bothering people. I'm annoyed whenever I see you." Responding to her concern that Parry will try to kill her, Bob remarks, with an extraordinary mixture of outright malignance and contemptuous dismissal, "You're the last person he wants to see, let alone kill. . . . You're not the type that makes people hate." Her insignificance is thus marked in rather significant terms. It is as if the other characters recognize the difficulty of integrating her in the plot. Vincent muses, "Maybe she'll get run over or something." And his wish is granted.

In this profoundly illogical film, the logic of misogyny works with classic simplicity; it can be placated only by Madge's abjection, by the spectacle of her death. When Vincent comes to her apartment to accuse *her* of murdering his wife, she defies him to prove it. At her crowning moment of Moorehead histrionics, she "accidently" and quite improbably falls through a picture window, with a flounce of floor-length drapes. The camera dwells on her body's descent, a markedly excessive cinematic flourish. Polan has commented on the ambiguity and threat embodied in domestic space in forties films: "Significantly, in several films, murder, suicide, and accidental death through windows blur (and not only for the characters but also for the spectator), thereby suggesting the ambivalence of sense." He captures something of the spectator's bewilderment in this instance: "In *Dark Passage*, for example, it is never clear (even with motion analyzing equipment and freeze-framing) how Madge manages to fall through her apartment window to her death."[29]

Dark Passage plays out the film noir's generic fear of feminine difference. The hero is vindicated, and woman is both criminal and victim. However, here it is not the alluring but the annoying woman who is punished, an extreme case of the anxiety that the Moorehead character could provoke. Madge, as a "bad," superfluous woman, is marked for death from the beginning. But for all that it is an almost mundane exigency of plot, her killing seems to require a supernatural force, thereby foregrounding the ideology that demands it. And Madge's fall doesn't immediately benefit the hero; it has something of the quality of a self-willed disappearance. Madge threatens, "You will never be able to prove anything because I won't be there."

Here, I would like to quote the late, legendary underground gay filmmaker and Hollywood camp tastemaker Jack Smith:

> I'm being haunted now by a performance in a movie. It was in *Dark Passage*. Agnes Moorehead plays this pest. . . . In a huge close-up you see the twitch of her little purse of a mouth. [Movies] can reveal a certain personality type—a certain kind of pest or what have you—and then you have something to remember when you see a person in life. . . . That happened to me just recently. This raging pest from the Gay Men's Health Crisis just called and said she'd be right over. . . . The poor creature, her life was so empty that she had to join the Gay movement to pester AIDS victims in order to have a social life. Right away I looked at her and thought of Madge in *Dark Passage*."[30]

Smith relates the star and the practice of cinematic typification to real life and to a gay context, using her quality of "intensity" to make sense of some aspect of the tragically implausible but all too real and very dark passage that is living with AIDS.

John Cromwell's *Caged* (1950) features Moorehead as Mrs. Benton, the efficient and smartly tailored head of a woman's prison, but here her philanthropic impulse is benevolent and welcome. In such an environment, among female deviates, Moorehead's persona is not pitted against other women but appears at its most benign. This is also the most overtly lesbian of her films—it establishes a genuine genre—and Moorehead receives second billing. Like *The Killing of Sister George* or the lesbian classic *Maedchen in Uniform* with its conflict between stern headmistress and compassionate teacher, this feminist drama opposes two "dyke" types in a struggle for control over the young heroine (Eleanor Parker). The sympathetic, reform-minded prison superintendent tries to protect innocent Marie Allen from the corruptions of life inside. "You'll find all kinds of women in here, just as you would outside," Benton promises. Hope Emerson portrays Evelyn Harper, the sadistic matron in uniform who provides small comforts for her girls in exchange for payment. Of this remarkable six-foot, two-inch, 230-pound character actress (who, incidentally, provided the voice of Elsie the Borden cow), gay porn editor and film critic Boyd MacDonald writes, "Perhaps only members of a sexual elite—that is, outlaws—can instinctively appreciate the grandeur of an Emerson."[31] In one scene, Harper, grotesquely dressed up for her night off, describes in detail her upcoming "date" in order to taunt the imprisoned women. This attribution of heterosexuality, like the photograph of a "husband" displayed on Moorehead's desk, can easily be read as an out-and-out charade.

When Benton attempts to fire Harper, the latter leaks a scandalous tale to the press: "Matron charges immorality," headlines blare. "Blames superintendent." The article is accompanied by a singularly apt sketch of Benton/Moorehead's face encircled by a huge question mark. The unspoken questions dogging Moorehead's persona are here explicitly tied to a story full of "filthy lies" that euphemistically signify lesbianism.

In this classic struggle between good and evil, Harper is finally stabbed by a prisoner. But, in the meantime, Marie has gone bad—the beginning of her defiance marked when her kitten is crushed in a riot provoked by Harper's attempt to snatch Fluff away from her. Marie finally accepts the attentions of the vice queen Kitty, who arranges for her parole. Forced to relinquish her wedding ring when she went to prison, Marie tosses it away when it is returned on her release. Benton tells her devoted secretary to keep Marie's file active: "She'll be back." Ultimately, different tropes of lesbian seduction—nurturance and dominance—represented by different types of character actresses, Moorehead and Emerson, work in consort to keep the female community intact. In *Caged*, Moorehead's character can represent the film's moral center because here she presides over a homosocial world and, fittingly, over an extraordinarily talented female supporting cast.

While the pleasures of reading Moorehead's ornery forties persona are obviously augmented by her syndication canonization in "Bewitched," both her situation and its comedy on that show are made possible by the character of her prior Hollywood career. Writing on the popularization of camp taste in the sixties and on *Whatever Happened to Baby Jane?* in particular, Andrew Ross claims, "The camp effect . . . is created . . . when the products (stars, in this case) of a much earlier mode of production, which has lost its power to dominate cultural meanings, become available . . . for redefinition to contemporary codes of taste."[32] Of Robert Aldrich's follow-up to *Baby Jane*, *Hush, Hush Sweet Charlotte*, produced the year "Bewitched" debuted, Bosley Crowther ranted, "Agnes Moorehead as [Bette Davis's] weird and crone like servant is allowed to get away with some of the broadest mugging and snarling ever done by a respectable actress on the screen. If she gets an Academy Award for this performance . . . the Academy should close up shop!"[33] The slatternly Velma Cruther significantly reverses an important element of Moorehead's image—her fastidiousness. In a cycle in which the biggest female stars travestied their former images, it is appropriate for one of the great supporting actresses to play a classic supporting role, the loyal servant, in a spectacularly unsupportive manner—to indulge in upstaging and scenery chewing that puts Davis herself to shame. Velma may be killed off for her snooping by a fall nearly as dramatic as that in *Dark Passage*, but icons never die.

One of Moorehead's last films, scripted by Henry Farrell, who wrote *Baby Jane*, continues this self-conscious exploitation of her image. Set in the thirties, *What's the Matter with Helen?* (directed by Curtis Harrington, 1971) features Debbie Reynolds and Shelley Winters as the mothers of two convicted thrill killers in the Leopold and Loeb mode, who move to Hollywood to escape their past. Reynolds, intrigued by the story, which was originally titled *Best of Friends*, persuaded her friend Agnes Moorehead to play powerful radio evangelist Sister Alma. The "matter" with Helen concerns not only her psychopathic murderous tendencies but her fanatical devotion to the evangelist's message and, surprise, her lesbian love for her best friend. The role and the project thus summed up a number of strong components of the Moorehead persona: radio, religion, the famous personality, lesbianism, the relationship with Reynolds.

Endora represents the culmination of Moorehead meddlesomeness. In the premiere episode of "Bewitched," she repeatedly evicts Samantha's husband from the honeymoon suite, and she literally casts a dark shadow over heterosexual relations each week when her credit "and Agnes Moorehead as Endora" appears on a black cloud of smoke blotting out "Derwood" and Samantha's embrace. What's-his-name's anxiety about his wife's powers are well founded: she belongs to a matriarchal order of superior beings. "Bewitched" supported a veritable gay subculture among its "funny" witch and warlock character actors. A recent "Bewitched"-kitsch revival attests to the show's influence on the queer nation generation. In a recent interview with the Los Angeles lesbian and gay newsweekly the *Advocate*, star Elizabeth Montgomery even agreed that the show's premise was "the ultimate closet story."[34]

If Moorehead's earlier characters were outside the central action, Endora is transcendently ex-centric. As Pat Mellencamp writes, in the situation comedy, "expectation of pleasurable performance . . . rather than narrative suspense [is the] currency of audience exchange."[35]

Endora has an enunciative role in the series. Casting spells on small-minded mortals, she disrupts the couple's petty suburban lives and generates the weekly plot. She appears and disappears with a flutter of the wrist—her ability to materialize when least expected or to drop out of the picture altogether is almost a commentary on the disappearing act that "incidental" characters performed in countless Hollywood films.

From stern spinster to fabulous redhead to silly goose, Agnes Moorehead's queer career attests to the ideological, narratological, and iconographic congruence among old maid, witch, and lesbian. Her star image also appeals to lesbian and gay audiences because it connotes acting itself—artifice, impersonation, and exaggeration. I do not wish to suggest that the characters that Moorehead portrayed "really were" lesbians, nor to imply that lesbians can simply recover our presence in Hollywood cinema by identifying actresses who really were lesbians, although gossip in its many forms is a legitimate text to be read. Rather, the peculiarities of Moorehead's image and the enthusiasms that it has generated illustrate how supporting characters were essential but also potentially disruptive to the construction of sexual difference in classical cinema. They were the types who were meant to remain invisible so that the codes of Hollywood's heterosexual contract would also remain invisible. By resituating such performers in patriarchal domesticity, American television often ended up broadcasting forms of queer performativity. Gay criticism and culture have been alert to the pleasures and resistances embodied in star signs. Feminist film theory has explicated the patriarchal construction of woman *as* image—and demonstrated the difficulty of articulating female desire and difference in relation to that construction. An exploration of the paradoxical conditions of lesbian representability in popular culture might fruitfully draw on both approaches. Whether playing it straight or camping it up, Agnes Moorehead is quite a character, "the type that comes back, and back again," as an insistent reminder of the price of heterosexual presumption.

Postscript

The television "personality" remains a privileged locus of lesbian and gay iconic signification, as a recent, metatextual example shows. On the top-rated ABC sitcom "Roseanne," Nancy, a supporting character played by Sandra Bernhard—a notorious real-life, role-playing queer—declared that she is a lesbian. Yet, in puffing forward an overt lesbian characterization, in this age of outing and the representational politics of acting up, the show draws on a covert one. At first surprised by her friend's announcement, Roseanne then recalls a code in which the coming-out message is intelligible: "Nancy always did like that Miss Jane Hathaway on 'The Beverly Hillbillies.' That about says it all."

Notes

For Montana Silkwood. Thanks to Lisa Cohen and Cynthia Schneider for their helpful comments.

1 Quoted in Warren Sherk, *Agnes Moorehead: A Very Private Person* (Philadelphia: Dorrance, 1976), 73.

2 While filming *How Sweet It Is* on an ocean liner, Lynde recounts, "At night, we'd sit around and dish. [Director] Jerry [Paris] told me those rumors that everybody's heard about Debbie [Reynolds] and her *close friend* Agnes Moorehead. . . . I'd heard those rumors, but Jerry filled in some details that. . . . Oh, I'd better not, I'm not even sure if the story's really true" (*Outlook* 6 [Fall 1989]: 26). Hadleigh claims that Reynolds threatened to sue Eddie Fisher if he included the story in his autobiography.

Reynolds herself reports the "innuendo" that she and Moorehead were lovers without explicitly denying it (see Debbie Reynolds with David Patrick Columbia, *My Life* [New York: Pocket, 1988], 388). Moorehead repeatedly discussed "why I adore Debbie Reynolds" (interview with Sidney Skolsky, *New York Post*, 2 August 1964), avowing, "It's really the loneliest sort of life. . . . I did become good friends with Debbie Reynolds" (*New York Post*, 11 January 1969). The friendship is generally considered a salient fact about Moorehead. The two women "became close friends, in a mother–daughter type relationship" Games Robert Parish, *Good Dames* [New Brunswick, N.J.: Barnes, 1974], 122).

As corroboration goes, there is no more than ample documentation of the *rumor* in the gay press: "Hollywood knew her as its reigning lesbian, queen of Sapphic love. ('Who was Carrie Fisher's mother?' the old joke went. 'Debbie Reynolds. Who was her father? Agnes Moorehead')" (NYQ, 22 December 1991, 41). Dick Sargent, the second actor to play Samantha's mortal husband on "Bewitched," who recently came out in *People* and on "Entertainment Tonight" as well as in the gay press, was unable to confirm the tales about Moorehead's lesbianism. The knowledge that Darrin, the show's representative of put-upon normalcy, was played by a gay actor literalizes what the *Advocate* calls the "gay allegory" of "Bewitched" (30 July 1992, 69). In a gracious interview with the lesbian and gay news weekly on the occasion of her serving with Sargent as grand marshall of the Los Angeles lesbian and gay pride parade, star Elizabeth Montgomery notes, "Don't think that didn't enter our minds at the time. We talked about it on the set . . . that this was about people not being allowed to be what they really are . . . and all the frustration and trouble it can cause. It was a neat message to get across" (ibid., 69). Asked about Moorehead's lesbianism, Montgomery replies, "I've heard the rumors, but I never talked with her about them. . . . It was never anything she felt free enough to talk to me about. I wish . . . that Agnes felt she could trust me. . . . We were very fond of one another, but it never got personal." In characteristically grande dame fashion, Moorehead herself wrote, "I have played so many authoritative and strong characters that some people are nervous at the prospect of meeting me. . . . There is a certain amount of aloofness on my part at times, because an actor can so easily be hurt by unfair criticism. I think an artist should be kept separated to maintain glamour and a kind of mystery. . . . I don't believe in the girl-nextdoor image. What the actor has to sell to the public is fantasy, a magic kind of ingredient that should not be analyzed" (quoted in the *New York Times* obituary, 1 May 1974, 48).

Outside of gay publications, what often appears in place of any remarks about Moorehead's sexuality is an emphasis on her religious beliefs (see Herbie J. Pilato, *The Bewitched Book* [New York: Delta, 1992], 24–26). That Moorehead was devout is not in question. But religion seems to appear as a defense against a homosexual reading, as the very emblem and safeguard of spinsterishness. Ann B. Davis, who played Alice, the housekeeper who resembled a physical education teacher, on "The Brady Bunch" (and before portrayed Schultzy on "The Bob Cummings Show"), has also enjoyed a surge in appreciation. In a recent update, she is reported as having shared a home since 1976 with an Episcopal bishop and his wife. "The three are dedicated to prayer and Bible study." She "never married" and admits, "I basically don't do that well with children, although my sister [identical twin Harriet] says I'm a great aunt" (*People*, 1 June 1992, 86).

Material on Moorehead cited throughout this essay was found in clippings files at the New York Public Library for the Performing Arts and the Museum of Modern Art Film Study Center.

3 Eve Kosofsky Sedgwick, *Epistemology of the Closet* (Berkeley: University of California Press, 1990).

4 Lisa Kron, *Program*, "101 Humiliating Stories," performed at P.S. 122, New York City, January 7–31, 1993.

5 Stephen Heath, *Questions of Cinema* (Bloomington: Indiana University Press, 1981), 135, 321.

6 Agnes Moorehead clippings file, New York Public Library for the Performing Arts.

7 Michael Bronski, *Culture Clash: The Making of Gay Sensibility* (Boston: South End, 1984), 102. See also chapter 1, "Who's a Sissy?" of Vito Russo, *The Celluloid Closet* (New York: Harper & Row, 1981).

8 Marion Garbo Todd, "The Truth about Miss Hathaway: The Fascination of Television's Perennial Spinster," *Lesbian News* 16, no. 10 (May 1991): 40.

9 See Sarah Halprin, "Writing in the Margins" (review of E. Ann Kaplan, *Women and Film: Both Sides of the Camera*), *Jump Cut* 29 (February 1984): 32, cited in Judith Mayne, "Lesbian Looks: Dorothy Arzner and Female Authorship," in *How Do I Look?* ed. Bad Object Choices (Seattle: Bay, 1991), 115. Mayne's argument about Arzner also appears in chapter 3, "Female Authorship Reconsidered," of her book *Woman at the Keyhole* (Bloomington: Indiana University Press, 1990).

10 Richard Dyer, "Seen to Be Believed: Some Problems in the Representation of Gay People as Typical," *Visual Communication* 9, no. 2 (Spring 1983): 2. See also his "Stereotyping" in *Gays in Film*, ed. Richard Dyer (London: BFI, 1978; rev., 1984), 27–39; and T. E. Perkins, "Rethinking Stereotypes," in *Ideology and Cultural Production*, ed. Michèle Barrett et al. (New York: St. Martin's, 1979), 135–59.

11 Dyer, "Seen to Be Believed," 8.

12 Mary Ann Doane, "Dark Continents: Epistemologies of Racial and Sexual Difference in Psychoanalysis and the Cinema," in *Femmes Fatales: Feminism, Film Theory, Psychoanalysis* (New York: Routledge, 1991), 233.

13 Ritter was a member of the early lesbian community on Fire Island documented in Esther Newton's study *Cherry Grove, Fire Island: Sixty Years in America's First Gay and Lesbian Town* (Boston: Beacon, 1993). McCambridge's career encompasses a series of telling roles: the unforgettable Emma Small in *Johnny Guitar*, an uncredited bit in Welles's *Touch of Evil* as a leather-jacketed onlooker at Janet Leigh's rape, a guest spot as mom to an effeminate warlock on "Bewitched," another as the woman who wanted to marry Dr. Smith on "Lost in Space," and the voice of the devil in *The Exorcist*.

That Ritter and McCambridge were radio performers like Moorehead suggests an interesting dialectic between lesbian representability and literal visibility.

14 Lisa Jones, "The Defiant Ones: A Talk with Film Historian Donald Bogle," *Village Voice* (June 1991): 69. See Donald Bogle, *Toms, Coons, Mulattoes, Mammies, and Bucks: An Interpretive History of Blacks in American Films* (1973; New York: Continuum, 1992).

15 Richard Dyer, *Stars* (London: BFI, 1979), 117; see also 109–10.

16 The comment that character actors are a "brassiere for the star, literally holding him or her up," is difficult to resist quoting in this case (Hortense Powdermaker, *Hollywood: The Dream Factory* [New York: Little, Brown, 1950], 206, quoted in Barry King, "Articulating Stardom," in *Stardom: Industry of Desire*, ed. Christine Gledhill [New York: Routledge, 1991], 179).

17 See Sherk, *Agnes Moorehead*, 70. In Charles Laughton's bio of Moorehead for *Don Juan in Hell*, in which they toured extensively in the early fifties, he writes about her days as a drama student in New York: "She was kind of mad around this time, not because she had to pull in her belt notches, but because she hadn't enough money to buy mauve lace, and mauve taffeta and mauve velvet and mauve feathers and geegaws which are a necessity to Agnes Moorehead's breathing."

18 James Robert Parish, *Good Dames*, 78.

19 The Agnes Moorehead fan club's publication was originally entitled "Versatility," as noted in an issue of "Moorehead Memos," a later incarnation of the club's newsletter.

20 Unidentified clipping, Agnes Moorehead Clipping File, Museum of Modern Art Film Study Center, n.p.

21 Quoted in Mason Wiley and Damien Bona, *Inside Oscar* (New York: Ballantine, 1986), 241.

22 *Classic Images* 136 (October 1986): 18.

23 Tania Modleski, *Feminism without Women* (New York: Routledge, 1991), 50.

24 Susan Sontag, "Notes on Camp," in *Against Interpretation* (New York: Farrar, Straus, Giroux, 1975), 283.

25 James Robert Parish, *Good Dames*, 84.

26 James Robert Parish, *Good Dames*, 90.

27 In another revealing comparison, Parish notes that *Dark Passage* gave Moorehead an "opportunity to portray . . . a woman close to her own age without disguising costumes, makeup or foreign accents. . . . Here was a jealous, sex-starved characterization that the electric Dame Judith Anderson would have been proud to play in her heyday" (ibid., 94). Charles Higham and Joel Greenberg acknowledge that "Agnes Moorehead's prying, vicious Madge Rapf is a definitive portrait of bitchery" (*Hollywood in the Forties* [New York: Barnes, 1968], 39).

28 Dana Polan, *Power and Paranoia: History, Narrative, and the American Cinema*, 1940–1950 (New York: Columbia University Press, 1986), 195.

29 Ibid., 274.

30 Jack Smith, "Remarks on Art and the Theatre," in *Jack Smith*, ed. Ira Cohen, Historical Treasures no. 33 (New York: Haumann, 1993), 133–35.

31 Boyd MacDonald, *Cruising the Movies: A Sexual Guide to Oldies on TV* (New York: Gay Press, 1988), 21.

32 Andrew Ross, *No Respect: Intellectuals and Popular Culture* (New York: Routledge, 1989), 139.

33 Bosley Crowther, *The New York Times*, 4 March 1965, section 1, 36.

34 *Advocate*, no. 608 (30 July 1990): 69.

35 Patricia Mellencamp, "Situation Comedy, Feminism, and Freud: Discourses of Gracie and Lucy," in *Studies in Entertainment*, ed. Tania Modleski (Bloomington: Indiana University Press, 1986), 91.

Select Bibliography

Adler, Stella. *The Technique of Acting*. New York: Bantam, 1988.

Affron, Charles. *Star Acting: Gish, Garbo and Davis*. New York: E. P. Dutton, 1977.

Agnew, Frances. *Motion Picture Acting: How to Prepare for Photoplaying, What Qualifications are Necessary, How to Secure an Engagement, Salaries Paid to Photoplayers*. New York: Reliance Newspaper Syndicate, 1913.

Altman, Rick. *Film/Genre*. London: British Film Institute, 1999.

Arnheim, Rudolf. *Film*, translated by L. M. Sieveking. London: Faber and Faber, 1933.

Austin, Thomas and Martin Barker, eds. *Contemporary Stardom*. London: Arnold, forthcoming.

Balàzs, Béla. *Theory of the Film: Character and Growth of a New Art*, translated by Edith Bone. New York: Dover, 1952.

Baron, Cynthia, Diane Carson and Frank Tomasulo, eds. *More than a Method: Trends and Traditions in Contemporary Film Performance*. Detroit: Wayne State University Press, forthcoming.

Basinger, Jeanine. *Silent Stars*. Hanover, NH: Wesleyan University Press, 1999.

Battcock, Gregory and Roberts Nickas, eds. *The Art of Performance: A Critical Anthology*. New York, Dutton, 1984.

Benjamin, Walter. "The Work of Art in the Age of Mechanical Reproduction." In *Illuminations*, edited by Hannah Arendt, 217–252. New York: Schocken Books, 1969.

Bentley, Eric, ed. *Theory of the Modern Stage: An Introduction to Modern Theatre and Drama*. New York: Bantam, 1976.

Bignell, Jonathan. "Method Westerns: The Left-Handed Gun and One-Eyed Jacks." In *The Book of Westerns*, edited by Ian Cameron and Douglas Pye, 99–110. New York: Continuum Press, 1996.

Blum, Richard. *American Film Acting: The Stanislavsky Heritage*. Ann Arbor: UMI, 1984.

Bogle, Donald. *Toms, Coons, Mulattoes, Mammies, and Bucks: An Interpretive History of Blacks in American Films*. 1973. Reprint, New York: Continuum, 2001.

Bona, Damien. *Starring John Wayne as Genghis Khan! Hollywood's All-Time Worst Casting Blunders*. Secaucus, NJ: Citadel Press, 1996.

Bordwell, David and Kristin Thompson. *Film Art: An Introduction*, 6th edition. New York: McGraw Hill, 2000.

Bowers, Ronald. *The Selznick Players*. New York: A. S. Barnes and Company, 1976.

Braudy, Leo. "Acting: Stage vs. Screen." In *The World in a Frame*. New York: Doubleday, 1976. Reprinted in *Film Theory and Criticism: Introductory Readings, Fifth Edition*, edited by Leo Braudy and Marshall Cohen, 419–425. New York: Oxford University Press, 1999.

Braudy, Leo and Marshall Cohen. *Film Theory and Criticism: Introductory Readings*, 5th edition. New York: Oxford University Press, 1999.

Brecht, Bertolt. *Brecht on Theatre*. Edited and translated by John Willett. New York: Hill and Wang, 1964.

Brewster, Ben and Lea Jacobs. *Theatre to Cinema: Stage Pictorialism and the Early Feature Film*. Oxford: Oxford University Press, 1997.

Brownlow, Kevin. *The Parade's Gone By* . . . London: Columbus Books, 1989.

Butler, Jeremy, ed. *Star Texts: Image and Performance in Film and Television*. Detroit: Wayne State University Press, 1991.

Cardullo, Bert, Harry Geduld, Ronald Gottesman, and Leigh Woods, eds. *Playing to the Camera: Film Actors Discuss their Craft*. New Haven: Yale University Press, 1998.

Clark, Danae. *Negotiating Hollywood: The Cultural Politics of Actors' Labor*. Minneapolis: University of Minnesota Press, 1995.

Cohan, Steven. *Masked Men: Masculinity and Movies in the Fifties*. Bloomington: Indiana University Press, 1997.

Cole, Toby and Helen Krich Chinoy, eds. *Actors on Acting: The Theories, Techniques, and Practices of the World's Greatest Actors, Told in Their Own Words*. New York: Crown Publishers, 1970.

Conroy, Marianne. "Acting Out: Method Acting, the National Culture, and the Middlebrow Disposition in Cold War America." *Criticism* 35, no. 2 (Spring 1993): 239–263.

Cook, Pam and Mieke Bernink, eds. *The Cinema Book*, 2nd edition. London: British Film Institute Publishing, 1999.

Creekmur, Corey. "Acting Like a Man: Masculine Performance in *My Darling Clementine*." In *Out in Culture: Gay, Lesbian and Queer Essays on Popular Culture*, edited by Corey Creekmur and Alexander Doty, 167–182. Durham, NC: Duke University Press, 1995.

Curry, Ramona. *Too Much of a Good Thing: Mae West as Cultural Icon*. Minneapolis: University of Minnesota Press, 1996.

DeCordova, Richard. *Picture Personalities: The Emergence of the Star System in America*. Chicago: University of Illinois Press, 1990.

—— "Genre and Performance: An Overview." In *Film Genre Reader* II, edited by Barry Keith Grant, 129–139. Austin: University of Texas Press, 1995.

Dyer, Richard. *Stars*. London: British Film Institute, 1979.

—— *Heavenly Bodies: Film Stars and Society*. New York: St. Martin's Press, 1986.

Eisenstein, S. M. "The Principles of the New Russian Cinema." In *Selected Works, Volume* I: *Writings*, 1922–1934, edited and translated by Richard Taylor. Bloomington: Indiana University Press, 1988.

Garfield, John. "Lecture on Film Acting." *The Drama Review* 28, no. 4 (Winter 1984): 73–78.

Geraghty, Christine. "Re-examining Stardom: Questions of Texts, Bodies and Performance." In *Reinventing Film Studies*, edited by Christine Gledhill and Linda Williams, 183–202. New York: Oxford University Press, 2000.

George, Nelson. *Blackface: Reflections on African Americans and the Movies*. New York: HarperCollins, 1994.

Gledhill, Christine, ed. *Stardom: Industry of Desire*. New York: Routledge, 1991.

Goffman, Erving. *The Presentation of Self in Everyday Life*. New York: Anchor Books, 1959.

Golden, Eve. *Golden Images: 41 Essays on Silent Film Stars*. New York: McFarland and Company, 2001.

Gray, Frances. "Certain Liberties Have Been Taken With Cleopatra: Female Performance in the *Carry On* Films." In *Because I Tell a Joke or Two: Comedy, Politics and Social Difference*, edited by Stephen Wagg, 94–110. London: Routledge, 1999.

Grieveson, Lee. "Stars and Audiences in Early Cinema." *Screening the Past*: online under "classics" at www.latrobe.edu.au. Initially published as "Nascita del divisimo. Stars e pubblico del cinema die primordi." In *Storia del Cinema Mondiale*, edited by Gian Piero Brunetta, 339–370. Turin, 2000.

Grimsted, David. *Melodrama Unveiled: American Theater and Culture, 1800–1850*. Chicago: University of Chicago Press, 1968.

Gunning, Tom. "The Cinema of Attractions: Early Film, Its Spectator and the Avant-Garde." In *Early Cinema: Space/Frame/Narrative*, edited by Thomas Elsaesser, 56–62. London: British Film Institute, 1990.

Hamilton, Mary Beth. *When I'm Bad I'm Better: Mae West, Sex and American Entertainment*. New York: HarperCollins, 1995.

Hansen, Miriam Bratu. "Introduction." In Siegfried Kracauer, *Theory of Film: The Redemption of Physical Reality*, vii–xlv. Princeton: Princeton University Press, 1997.

Harvey, James. *Romantic Comedy in Hollywood: From Lubitsch to Sturges*. New York: Alfred A. Knopf, 1987.

Heath, Stephen. "Body, Voice." In *Questions of Cinema*, 176–193. Bloomington: Indiana University Press, 1981.

Hirsch, Foster. *A Method to Their Madness: The History of the Actor's Studio*. New York: Da Capo Press, 1984.

Hodge, Alison, ed. *Twentieth Century Actor Training*. New York: Routledge, 2000.

Holland, Norman. "Film Response from Eye to I: The Kuleshov Experiment." *South Atlantic Quarterly* 88.2 (1989): 415–42.

Jenkins, Henry. *What Made Pistachio Nuts? Early Sound Comedy and the Vaudeville Aesthetic*. New York: Columbia University Press, 1992.

Jenkins, Henry and Kristine Brunovska Karnick. "Acting Funny." In *Classical Hollywood Comedy*, edited by Kristine Brunovska Karnick and Henry Jenkins, 149–167. New York: Routledge, 1995.

Jones, Ken D., Arthur F. McClure, and Alfred E. Twomey. *Character People*. Secaucus, NJ: The Citadel Press, 1976.

Kaufman, J.B. "Fascinating Youth: The Story of the Paramount Pictures School." *Film History* 4 (1990): 131–151.

Kepley, Vance, Jr. "The Kuleshov Workshop." *Iris* 4.1 (1986): 5–24.

Klumph, Inez and Helen. *Screen Acting: Its Requirements and Rewards*. New York: Falk Publishing, 1922.

Knight, Arthur. "Star Dances: African American Constructions of Stardom, 1925–1960." In *Classic Hollywood, Classic Whiteness*, edited by Daniel Bernardi, 386–414. Minneapolis: University of Minnesota Press, 2001.

—— *Disintegrating the Musical: Black Performance and American Musical Film*. Durham: Duke University Press, 2002.

Kobal, John. *People Will Talk*. New York: Aurum Press/A. Knopf, 1986.

Kolker, Robert. *Film, Form, and Culture*, 2nd edition. New York: McGraw Hill, 2002.

Kuleshov, Lev. *Kuleshov on Film*, translated and edited by Ronald Levaco. Berkeley: University of California Press, 1974.

Leider, Emily Worth. *Becoming Mae West*. New York: DaCapo Press, 2000.

Loukides, Paul and Linda K. Fuller, eds. *Beyond the Stars: Stock Characters in American Popular Film*. Bowling Green: Bowling Green State University Popular Press, 1990.

Lovell, Alan and Peter Krämer, ed. *Screen Acting*. New York: Routledge, 1999.

Lowry, Stephen. "Star Images: Questions for Semiotic Analysis." In *Semiotics of the Media: State of the Art, Projects, and Perspectives*, edited by Winfried North. Hawthorne, NY: Mouton de Gruyter, 1997.

MacCann, Richard Dyer, ed. *The Stars Appear*. Metuchen, NJ: Scarecrow Press, 1992.

Mamet, David. *True and False: Heresy and Common Sense for the Actor*. 1997. Reprint, New York: Vintage Books, 1999.

McArthur, Benjamin. *Actors and American Culture, 1880–1920*. Philadelphia: Temple University Press, 1984.

—— "Star Studies." In *Approaches to Popular Film*, edited by Joanne Hollows and Mark Jancovich, 79–97. Manchester: Manchester University Press, 1995.

—— "Film Acting and Gender: Method Acting and the Male Tantrum." In *Semiotics of the Media: State of the Art, Projects, and Perspectives*, edited by Winfried North, 321–335. Hawthorne, NY: Mouton de Gruyter, 1997.

—— "Film Acting." In *The Oxford Guide to Film Studies*, edited by John Hill and Pamela Church-Gibson, 30–35. Oxford: Oxford University Press, 1998.

—— "Reconceptualising Stardom." Supplementary chapter in 2nd edition of Richard Dyer's *Stars*, 175–211. London: British Film Institute, 1998.

McDonald, Paul. *The Star System: Hollywood's Production of Popular Identities*. London: Wallflower Press, 2000.

Metz, Christian. *The Imaginary Signifier: Psychoanalysis and the Cinema*, translated by Celia Britton *et al*. Bloomington: Indiana University Press, 1977.

Mulvey, Laura. "Visual Pleasure and Narrative Cinema." 1974. Reprinted in *Visual and Other Pleasures*, 14–28. Bloomington: Indiana University Press, 1989.

Münsterberg, Hugo. *The Film: A Psychological Study, The Silent Photoplay in 1916*. New York: Dover, 1970.

Musser, Charles. "The Changing Status of the Actor." In *Before Hollywood: Turn-of-the-Century American Film*, 57–62. New York: Hudson Hills Press in Association with the American Federation of Arts, 1987.

—— *The Emergence of Cinema: The American Screen to 1907, History of the American Cinema*, vol. 1. Berkeley: University of California Press, 1990.

Naremore, James. *Acting in the Cinema*. Berkeley: University of California Press, 1988.

Pearson, Roberta E. *Eloquent Gestures: The Transformation of Performance Style in the Griffith Biograph Films*. Berkeley: University of California Press, 1992.

Pickford, Mary, *et al*. *Cinema: Practical Courses in Cinema Acting in Ten Complete Lessons*. London: The Standard Art Book Company, n.d.

Pudovkin, V.I. "Stanislavsky's System in the Cinema," translated by T. Shebunina. In *Pudovkin's Film and Film Theory*, edited by Peter Dart, 186–206. New York: Arno, 1974.

—— *Film Technique and Film Acting*, translated and edited by Ivor Montagu. New York: Grove Press, 1976.

Riblet, Doug. "The Keystone Film Company and the Historiography of Early Slapstick." In *Classical Hollywood Comedy*, edited by Kristine Brunovska Karnick and Henry Jenkins, 168–189. New York: Routledge, 1995.

Roach, Joseph. *The Player's Passion: Studies in the Science of Acting*. Newark: University of Delaware Press, 1985.

Sammond, Nicholas and Chandra Mukerji. "'What You Are . . . I Wouldn't Eat': Ethnicity, Whiteness, and Performing 'the Jew' in Hollywood's Golden Age." In *Classic Hollywood, Classic Whiteness*, edited by Daniel Bernardi, 3–30. Minneapolis: University of Minnesota Press, 2001.

Savoy, Eric. "That Ain't *All* She Ain't: Doris Day and Queer Performativity." In *Out Takes: Essays on Queer Theory and Film*, edited by Ellis Hanson, 151–182. Durham: Duke University Press, 1999.

Smith, Murray. *Engaging Characters: Fiction, Emotion and the Cinema*. Oxford: Clarendon Press, 1995.

Stacey, Jackie. *Star Gazing: Hollywood Cinema and Female Spectatorship*. New York: Routledge, 1994.

Staiger, Janet. "Seeing Stars." *Velvet Light Trap* 20 (1983): 10–14.

—— "The Eyes Are Really the Focus: Photoplay Acting and Film Form and Style." *Wide Angle* 6.4 (1985): 18–20.

Stanislavski, Constantin. *Creating a Role*, translated by Elizabeth Reynolds Hapgood and edited by Hermine I. Popper, 1961. Reprint, New York: Routledge, 1989.

—— *Stanislavski's Legacy: A Collection of Comments on a Variety of Aspects of an Actor's Art and Life*, edited and translated by Elizabeth Reynolds Hapgood, 1968. Reprint, New York: Routledge, 1999.

Stern, Lesley. "Acting Out of Character: The Performance of Femininity." In *Grafts: Feminist Cultural Criticism*, edited by Susan Sheridan, 25–34. New York: Verso, 1988.

Stern, Lesley and George Kouvaros, eds. *Falling for You: Essays on Cinema and Performance*. Sydney: Power Publications, 1999.

Street, Sarah. "Acting and Stars." *British National Cinema*, 114–146. London: Routledge, 1997.

Strasberg, Lee. *A Dream of Passion: The Development of the Method*, edited by Evangeline Morphos. Boston: Little Brown, 1987.

Studlar, Gaylyn. *This Mad Masquerade: Stardom and Masculinity in the Jazz Age*. New York: Columbia University Press, 1996.

Thomas, Deborah. "John Wayne's Body." In *The Book of Westerns*, edited by Ian Cameron and Douglas Pye, 75–87. New York: Continuum, 1996.

Thomson, David. "The Look on an Actor's Face." *Sight and Sound* (Autumn 1977).

—— *Warren Beatty and Desert Eyes*. New York: Doubleday, 1987.

Turner, Victor. *The Anthropology of Performance*. New York: PAJ Publications, 1988.

Twomey, Alfred E. and Arthur F. McClure. *The Versatiles: A Study of Supporting Character Actors and Actresses in the American Motion Picture, 1930–1955*. New York: Castle Books, 1969.

Vineberg, Steve. *Method Actors: Three Generations of an American Acting Style*. New York: Schirmer Books, 1991.

Walker, Alexander. *Stardom: The Hollywood Phenomenon*. New York: Stein and Day, 1970.

Wexman, Virginia. ed. "Special Issue on Film Acting." *Cinema Journal* 20, no. 1 (Fall 1980).

—— *Creating the Couple: Love, Marriage and Hollywood Performance*. Princeton: Princeton University Press, 1993.

White, Patricia. *UnInvited: Classical Hollywood Cinema and Lesbian Representability*. Bloomington: Indiana University Press, 1999.

Wilshire, Bruce. *Role Playing and Identity: The Limits of Theatre as Metaphor*. Bloomington: Indiana University Press, 1991.

Wojcik, Pamela Robertson. "A Star is Born Again, or How Streisand Recycles Garland." In *Falling for You: Essays on Cinema and Performance*, edited by Lesley Stern and George Kouvaros, 177–208. Sydney: Power Publications, 1999.

—— "Impromptu Entertainment: Performance Modes in Cassavetes' Films." *Senses of Cinema* 9 (Sept.–Oct., 2000): online at www.sensesofcinema.com.

—— "Mae West's Maids: Race, 'Authenticity,' and the Discourse of Camp." 1999. Reprint, *Hop on Pop: The Politics and Pleasures of Popular Culture*, ed. Henry Jenkins, Tara McPherson, and Jane Shattuc, 287–299. Durham: Duke University Press, 2002.

[Wojcik], Pamela Robertson. *Guilty Pleasures: Feminist Camp from Mae West to Madonna*. Durham: Duke University Press, 1996.

Wollen, Peter. *Signs and Meaning in the Cinema*. Bloomington: Indiana University Press, 1969.

Zucker, Carole. *Making Visible the Invisible: An Anthology of Original Essays on Film Acting*. Metuchen, NJ: Scarecrow Press, 1990.

—— ed. "Special Issue: Film Acting." *Post Script: Essays in Film and the Humanities* 12, no. 2 (Winter 1993).

—— *Conversations with Actors on Film, Television, and Stage Performance*. Portsmouth, NH: Heinemann, 2002.

Index

eBooks – at www.eBookstore.tandf.co.uk

A library at your fingertips!

eBooks are electronic versions of printed books. You can store them on your PC/laptop or browse them online.

They have advantages for anyone needing rapid access to a wide variety of published, copyright information.

eBooks can help your research by enabling you to bookmark chapters, annotate text and use instant searches to find specific words or phrases. Several eBook files would fit on even a small laptop or PDA.

NEW: Save money by eSubscribing: cheap, online access to any eBook for as long as you need it.

Annual subscription packages

We now offer special low-cost bulk subscriptions to packages of eBooks in certain subject areas. These are available to libraries or to individuals.

For more information please contact webmaster.ebooks@tandf.co.uk

We're continually developing the eBook concept, so keep up to date by visiting the website.

www.eBookstore.tandf.co.uk

Related titles from Routledge

Shakespeare, The Movie II

Popularizing the Plays on Film, TV, Video and DVD

2nd Edition

Edited by: Richard Burt, University of Florida, USA and
Lynda E. Boose, Dartmouth College, USA

Following on from Shakespeare, The Movie, this volume brings together an invaluable new collection of essays on cinematic Shakespeares in the 1990s and beyond. Shakespeare, The Movie, II covers:

- the impact of post-colonialism, globalization and digital film on recent adaptations of Shakespeare
- adaptations of Shakespeare in Europe and in the Asian diaspora, as well as American and British films
- film, television, video and DVD adaptations, including Almereyda's Hamlet, animated tales, Baz Luhrmann, Kenneth Branagh and 1990s' Macbeths.

It also offers fresh insight into issues such as the interplay between originals and adaptations, appropriations of popular culture, the question of spectatorship and the impact of popularization on the canonical status of "the Bard".

Shakespeare, The Movie II combines twelve exciting new essays from leading scholars with key essays from the earlier collection. It is quite simply a must-read for any student of Shakespeare, film, media or cultural studies.

Hb: 0-415-28298-5: £55.00

Pb: 0-415-28299-3: £15.99

eB: 0-203-42618-5: £15.99

Available at all good bookshops
For ordering and further information please visit:
www.routledge.com

Related titles from Routledge

Routledge Performance Practitioners

Series editor: Franc Chamberlain, University of Northampton

Routledge Performance Practitioners is an innovative series of introductory handbooks on key figures in twentieth-century performance practice. Each volume focuses on a theatre-maker whose practical and theoretical work has in some way transformed the way we understand theatre and performance. The books are carefully structured to enable the reader to gain a good grasp of the fundamental elements underpinning each practitioner's work. They will provide an inspiring springboard for future study, unpacking and explaining what can initially seem daunting.

Each book covers:

- personal biography
- explanation of key writings
- description of significant productions
- reproduction of practical exercises.

Volumes currently available in the series are:

Michael Chekhov by Franc Chamberlain

Hb: 0-415-25877-4: £40.00
Pb: 0-415-25878-2: £9.99

Jacques Lecoq by Simon Murray

Hb: 0-415-25881-2: £40.00
Pb: 0-415-25882-0: £9.99

Vsevolod Meyerhold by Jonathan Pitches

Hb: 0-415-25883-9: £40.00
Pb: 0-415-25884-7: £9.99

Konstantin Stanislavsky by Bella Merlin

Hb: 0-415-25885-5: £40.00
Pb: 0-415-25886-3: £9.99

Available at all good bookshops
For ordering and further information please visit:
www.routledge.com

LIBRARY
ST. LOUIS COMMUNITY COLLEGE
AT FLORISSANT VALLEY